THE YEAR
THAT DEFINED
AMERICAN JOURNALISM

THE YEAR
THAT DEFINED
AMERICAN JOURNALISM

1897 and the Clash of Paradigms

W. Joseph Campbell

Routledge
Taylor & Francis Group
New York   London

Routledge is an imprint of the
Taylor & Francis Group, an informa business

Routledge
Taylor & Francis Group
270 Madison Avenue
New York, NY 10016

Routledge
Taylor & Francis Group
2 Park Square
Milton Park, Abingdon
Oxon OX14 4RN

Printed in the United States of America on acid-free paper
10 9 8 7 6 5 4 3 2 1

International Standard Book Number-10: 0-415-97703-7 (Softcover) 0-415-97702-9 (Hardcover)
International Standard Book Number-13: 978-0-415-97703-6 (Softcover) 978-0-415-97702-9 (Hardcover)
Library of Congress Card Number 2005036057

Library of Congress Cataloging-in-Publication Data

Campbell, W. Joseph, Ph. D.
    The year that defined American journalism / by W. Joseph Campbell.
    p. cm.
    Includes bibliographical references and index.
    ISBN 0-415-97702-9 (hbk. : alk. paper) -- ISBN 0-415-97703-7 (pbk. : alk. paper)
    1. Journalism--United States--History--19th century. I. Title.

PN4864.C36 2006
071'.309034--dc22   2005036057

Visit the Taylor & Francis Web site at
http://www.taylorandfrancis.com

and the Routledge Web site at
http://www.routledge-ny.com

To my mother,

and the memory of my father.

1897 has been a year that the future historian ... cannot ignore and I fancy that he will be able to fill several interesting pages with the things that have happened during the past twelve months.

—Chauncey M. Depew,
New York railroad executive and politician,
in a retrospective of 1897

CONTENTS

ABOUT THE AUTHOR

W. Joseph Campbell is an associate professor in American University's School of Communication. He joined the university's faculty in 1997, after more than 20 years as a newspaper and wire service journalist. His career in professional journalism took him across North America to Africa, Asia, and Europe. He reported for the Cleveland (Ohio) *Plain Dealer*, the Hartford (Connecticut) *Courant*, and the Associated Press.

In 1995, he was chosen as an inaugural Freedom Forum Ph.D. fellow at the University of North Carolina at Chapel Hill, and completed an intensive doctoral degree program in 27 months.

Campbell has published three other books, including *Yellow Journalism: Puncturing the Myths, Defining the Legacies* (2000), which challenges prominent myths and misunderstandings about the yellow press period in the United States at the end of the nineteenth century. Campbell has written articles for *Journalism and Mass Communication Quarterly, American Journalism, Journalism History, Editor & Publisher, Presstime, and American Journalism Review*. He has given lectures at the National Press Club, the Library of Congress, and the Freedom Forum.

His research about the yellow press period has won awards from the Association for Education in Journalism and Mass Communication and the American Journalism Historians Association.

ACKNOWLEDGMENTS

This single-year study was four years in the making. Many people during that time extended their courtesy, insight, energy, and suggestions, for which I am deeply grateful. Throughout this project, I was helped enormously by a succession of graduate research assistants at American University. I am indebted to them all—Namrata Savoor, Rozalia Hristova, Ruxandra Giura, Laura Bailey, Elizabeth Tascione, and Ruth David. Another former student, Sarah Schumacher, conducted important 1897-related research in Chicago. Fran Fuensalida tirelessly scoured archives in Madrid for materials about the year's most dramatic episode in activist journalism—the *New York Journal*'s rescue of Evangelina Cosío y Cisneros from jail in Spanish-ruled Cuba. Kristen Grinager translated passages from Spanish that were crucial to understanding the stealthy and obscure dimensions of the Cisneros case.

My faculty colleagues at American University—including Larry Kirkman, Rodger Streitmatter, John Doolittle, John Watson, Amy Eisman, Wendell Cochran, Barbara Diggs-Brown, and Glenn Harnden—deserve special thanks for their support and suggestions. Mary Evangeliste, formerly of the interlibrary loan department at American University's library, earnestly tracked down a succession of obscure and otherwise hard-to-find books and articles related to 1897.

I am grateful to Ivy Broder, the university's interim provost, for the grant that helped finance an important research trip to Cuba in 2002. Richard R. Cole, former dean of the School of Journalism and Mass Communication at the University of North Carolina at Chapel Hill, generously allowed me to join him and his undergraduate class in traveling to Cuba. In Havana, Leal Spengler and Jorge Macle were very helpful in offering insights and leads about the Cisneros jailbreak.

xii • The Year That Defined American Journalism

Geoff Chester of the U.S. Naval Observatory provided important data about lunar phases in October 1897—data that helped confirm forensic details related to the jailbreak. Specifically, the moon over Havana probably was shining brightly at the time of the jailbreak, much as Cisneros and her rescuer recalled.

Undergirding this project is the considerable research conducted at the Newspaper and Current Periodical Reading Room of the Library of Congress, where Georgia Higley and her staff provided unstinting and ever-gracious support. I am deeply grateful for their help on this and other research projects.

Special thanks are due to Keith Saunders, the executive director of Kappa Tau Alpha, the national honor society in journalism and mass communication. This project was supported by a KTA chapter adviser's research grant, which helped finance my trips to New York City and upstate New York. James Temple was generous with his time and hospitality during my visit to North Chatham, New York. Temple is the grandson of Virginia O'Hanlon Douglas, who as an eight-year-old wrote the letter that prompted the *New York Sun*'s famous 1897 editorial, "Is There A Santa Claus?" Temple's insights and recollections were invaluable in resolving a modest mystery about why the *Sun* published "Is There A Santa Claus?" three months before Christmas in 1897. I am grateful for the generosity of George Vollmuth of the historical society in North Chatham, which works to keep alive the memory of Virginia O'Hanlon.

This project also benefited from the thoughtfulness and earnest interest of Karl Gurcke, an historian at the Klondike Gold Rush National Historical Park in Skagway, Alaska. His help was vital in clarifying aspects of what Gurke called Sylvester Scovel's "romp through Gold Rush Skagway" in 1897, on assignment for the *New York World*.

I am grateful to Charles Overby, chairman and chief executive of the Freedom Forum foundation, for the encouragement and enthusiastic support he has given to my research. Don Ross of the Freedom Forum offered invaluable suggestions about this project.

My wife, Ann-Marie C. Regan, heard more about 1897 and the developments that year than anyone should be expected to bear. Ann-Marie invariably was patient, kind, and supportive during the years I was working on *The Year That Defined American Journalism*.

AN 1897 TIMELINE

Pivotal Moments of a Decisive Year

January 1—The new year is celebrated at midnight in New York City with the traditional pealing of the chimes at Trinity Church on lower Broadway.

January 21—The *New York Tribune* publishes on its front page a halftone photograph of Thomas Platt, New York's U.S. Senator-elect—demonstrating that the halftone process can be applied on the high-speed web perfecting presses at large-circulation newspapers. The *Tribune*'s portrait "startled New York" journalism, says the trade journal *Fourth Estate*.

January 31—The epithet "yellow journalism" first appears in print, in a small headline near the bottom of page six of the *New York Press*.

February 2—The *New York Journal* publishes Richard Harding Davis' evocative, detail-rich dispatch about the firing-squad execution of a twenty-year-old Cuban who had joined the island-wide rebellion against Spanish rule. Davis' report stands as American journalism's finest example of foreign correspondence in 1897.

February 4—Trustees of the Newark Free Public Library in New Jersey vote to remove the *New York Journal* and the *New York World* from its reading room—the opening move in a bitter campaign to ban the leading exemplars of yellow journalism from libraries, social clubs, and reading rooms in metropolitan New York.

February 5—Sylvester Scovel, a war correspondent for the *New York World*, is arrested and jailed in Sancti Spíritus, Cuba. He is held on four counts, including communicating with the Cuban insurgents and traveling with forged papers. The *World* declares Scovel to be "in imminent danger of butchery."

February 10—Without fanfare, the *New York Times* places its slogan, "All the News That's Fit to Print," in the upper left corner of its front page. The slogan will appear there permanently.

February 17—The annual meeting of the American Newspaper Publishers' Association is convened at the Hoffman House in New York City.

February 18—The *World* publishes a dispatch written by Sylvester Scovel and smuggled from his jail cell in Cuba. In it, Scovel calls himself a "prisoner of war." In fact, the conditions of Scovel's detention border on the luxurious.

March 4—William McKinley is sworn in as the twenty-fifth U.S. president, ushering in a prolonged period of Republican domination of national politics. McKinley's is the first U.S. presidential inauguration to be captured on film.

March 10—The *World* reports that Sylvester Scovel is to be released without trial and will soon leave Cuba for the United States. The newspaper's high-profile efforts to win his freedom have helped make Scovel the best-known journalist in America.

March 17—Robert Fitzsimmons defeats James Corbett in a much-anticipated heavyweight boxing match in Nevada. The fight is staged with the motion-picture camera in mind. Beginning in May, flickering footage of the bout is shown in theaters across the country, attracting large audiences.

April 19—The first Boston Marathon is run, and won by John J. McDermott of the Pastime Athletic Club in New York.

April 22—First issue of the Yiddish-language daily newspaper, For-verts, appears. The newspaper is still published, as a weekly, in English and Yiddish.

June 10—The *Chicago Tribune* marks its fiftieth anniversary and reports vigorous demand for its "golden jubilee" souvenir edition.

June 22—Queen Victoria's silver jubilee is celebrated in London. In his dispatch to the *New York Journal*, Mark Twain says, the event was "a spectacle for the kodak [camera], not the pen."

June 27—A man's headless torso washes up in the East River in New York. Other body parts are found in the river on following days, creating a lurid murder mystery that grips New York.

July 3—The *New York Journal* solves the East River murder mystery, identifying the victim as William Guldensuppe and leading authorities to the chief suspects in the crime. The newspaper later declares: "But for the Journal, the arm of the law would have been palsied."

July 4—The *New York Times* publishes in its Sunday magazine thirty-seven halftone photographs of Queen Victoria's silver jubilee in London. The *Times* says anyone who "looks over these pictures will really see more of the jubilee than any one visitor could have seen, and more than the Queen herself could possibly have witnessed." Meanwhile, the *New York Journal* publishes details of labor journalist Eva McDonald Valesh's interview with President McKinley.

July 17—The steamer *Portland* arrives in Seattle carrying sixty-eight passengers and a ton of gold from Canada's subarctic Klondike region. The vessel's arrival helps ignite a continent-wide stampede to the Klondike's goldfields.

July 20—Guglielmo Marconi establishes the Wireless Telegraph and Signal Company Ltd., near London. It is the world's first electronic communications wireless company.

August 17—The *New York Journal* discloses that a young Cuban woman, Evangelina Cosío y Cisneros, has been imprisoned for more than a year in Havana's wretched Casa de Recogidas. The *Journal's* calls her the "Cuban Girl Martyr" and begins a noisy but ultimately unsuccessful petition drive to force Spain to set her free.

August 28—Karl Decker, a Washington-based reporter for the *Journal*, arrives in Havana on a secret mission to free Cisneros and send her to the United States.

August 29—The first Zionist Congress is convened in Basel, Switzerland. The principal organizer, Theodor Herzl, soon after confides to his diary: "At Basel, I founded the Jewish State. If I said this out loud today, I would be answered by universal laughter. Perhaps in five years and certainly in fifty, everyone will know it."

August 31—Six years after applying, Thomas Edison receives a patent for the kinetograph, a motion-picture camera.

September 1—The first section of America's first subway system opens in Boston. Enthusiastic passengers on the first trolley car to enter the subterranean tunnel yell themselves "to the verge of apoplexy," according to the *Boston Globe.*

September 10—Nineteen protesting coal miners are shot to death by sheriff's deputies near Lattimer, Pennsylvania. The sheriff is acquitted of murder charges at a trial six months later.

September 21—The *New York Sun* publishes an editorial titled, "Is There A Santa Claus?" The commentary, written by Francis P. Church in reply to the inquiry of an eight-year-old girl, appears in the third of three columns of editorials. In time, "Is There A Santa Claus?" becomes a classic in American journalism.

October 2—The Boston Beaneaters win the National League pennant, edging the Baltimore Orioles in the tightest pennant race of the 1890s. The professional baseball season was marred by frequent run-ins among players, umpires, and fans.

October 7—With help from Karl Decker and his accomplices, Evangelina Cisneros escapes from the Casa de Recogidas. She is hidden at the home of a Cuban-American banker, just a few blocks from the jail, before being smuggled aboard a passenger steamer to New York.

October 10—In headlines four lines deep, the *New York Journal* takes credit for organizing the escape and flight of Evangelina Cisneros. It calls the jailbreak the "greatest journalistic coup of this age." Cisneros arrives in New York City on October 13.

October 16—The *Journal* stages an enthusiastic welcome to Cisneros, and calls the event the city's largest public reception since the end of the Civil War.

October 17—Charles A. Dana, the brilliant but ill-tempered editor of the *New York Sun*, dies at his country home on Long Island. Dana edited the *Sun* for nearly thirty years and his death underscores the transitory nature of the year in journalism.

November 1—The ornate Library of Congress building is opened on Capitol Hill in Washington, D.C. The edifice is a spectacular assertion of expanding American self-assuredness.

November 3—Sylvester Scovel arrives in Cuba, accompanied by his wife. His principal assignment for the *World* is to chronicle the ravages of Spain's reconcentration policy, in which Cuban noncombatants were ordered into garrison towns. Thousands of them died from malnutrition and disease.

December 12—The Katzenjammer Kids comic makes its debut in the *New York Journal*. It will become the longest-running newspaper comic strip.

December 23—Joseph Pulitzer, proprietor of the *New York World*, privately acknowledges that his archrival, the *New York Journal*, has become "a wonderfully able & attractive and popular paper." Sylvester Scovel of the *World*, in a capstone to a remarkably full and energetic year of reporting, interviews the Cuban insurgent leader, General Máximo Gómez, who reasserts his opposition to Spain's offer of limited home rule in Cuba.

December 31—The *New York Journal* stages a lavish New Year's Eve party to commemorate the consolidation of the five boroughs of New York City, which officially takes place January 1, 1898. Some 100,000 merrymakers defy rain and snow to make their way to lower Manhattan and celebrate what the *Journal* calls the "luminous starting point from which the history of the expanded New York will be dated."

PREFACE

Anyone browsing a good secondhand bookstore won't need much time before encountering a succession of titles devoted to decisive and exceptionally important years. Some of these works are about years of undeniable consequence: *1776*[1] and *1929: The Year of the Great Crash*,[2] for example. Others consider years whose importance is less immediately apparent: *1831, Year of Eclipse*;[3] *America in 1857*,[4] and *American Nervousness, 1903*,[5] are examples. Some year studies inevitably are pegged to anniversaries.[6] And more than a few year studies are splendidly written: *Paris 1919*[7] is a notable example.

Quite absent from this flourishing and diverse genre are works in journalism and mass communication. Until now, journalism scholars have neither tested nor adopted the year-study approach—a methodological deficit that is addressed with this work, an exploration of the exceptionality of 1897, the year when the contours and ethos of modern American journalism began to take shape. Eighteen-ninety-seven was a time when powerful transformative forces were at work—forces that gave rise to innovation, intolerance, vigorous competition, and much uncertainty in American journalism. Revisiting that defining and pivotal year offers intriguing and relevant insights into the forces that promise to reshape American journalism in the early twenty-first century. Echoes and parallels are not difficult to detect. The mainstream news media's scorn of innovative Web logs of the early twenty-first century certainly evokes the fierce hostility directed at the practitioners of what was called the "new journalism" in 1897. Then, as now, American journalists were susceptible to charges of injecting bias and ideology into their reporting.

More significantly, revisiting 1897 offers keener understanding about the emergence of standards and norms that still define mainstream American journalism. Eighteen-ninety-seven was the year three headstrong journalists in their thirties developed and pursued clashing, dramatically different visions for the future of newsgathering in America. One of them, Adolph Ochs of the *New York Times*, ultimately prevailed, establishing the normative standard of authoritative detachment that defines and, some critics are prone to say, restricts[8] American journalism of the early twenty-first century.

This study of American journalism's defining year had its origins in 2001, as I completed the research for *Yellow Journalism: Puncturing the Myths, Defining the Legacies*, a work that confronted the mythology about the yellow press of the late nineteenth century. *Yellow Journalism* dismantled what is arguably American journalism's best-known tale—that of the purported exchange between the artist Frederic Remington and the publisher William Randolph Hearst. According to legend, Remington wanted to cut short an assignment to Cuba, which at the time was rebelling against Spanish rule. Hearst supposedly told Remington, "Please remain. You furnish the pictures, and I'll furnish the war." As is described in *Yellow Journalism*, the purported exchange is almost certainly apocryphal.[9] But the anecdote does suggest the centrality of Hearst and his *New York Journal* to *fin-de-siècle* American journalism.

The exceptionality of 1897 became apparent to me as I spent hours at the Library of Congress, reading microfilmed issues of the *Journal*. In 1897, the *Journal* was easily the most ambitious, enterprising, and free-spending newspaper in America, routinely besting its competitors in New York and even winning the grudging respect of its fiercest rival, Joseph Pulitzer's *New York World*. If measured by his newspaper's successes and by the development of a coherent paradigm for the practice of journalism, 1897 may have been Hearst's most accomplished year. He was thirty-four then, and his *Journal* that year solved a gruesome, mid-summer murder mystery that captivated New Yorkers; organized the successful jailbreak and flight of a Cuban political prisoner named Evangelina Cisneros; filed a succession of injunctions to thwart the grant of dubious municipal public-works contracts, and single-handedly organized the extravagant New Year's Eve celebration to mark the political consolidation of New York City's five boroughs. "Damn," I recall saying to myself as I finished reviewing microfilm of the *Journal* of 1897. "They really had one hell of a year." It was then when I began contemplating a study of the year 1897.

This study offers more than a dose of methodological freshness in journalism and mass communication research. It suggests a new way of thinking about a defining period in American journalism. The mid- and late-1890s often are dismissed by scholars as a dismal time of excess and sensationalism in American journalism, when Hearst not only vowed to "furnish the war" with Spain but supposedly went ahead and did so, through the *Journal*'s hyperbolic reporting.[10] Such claims are absurd, of course—a classic case of mistaking presence for influence. The Spanish-American War was the consequence of forces far more powerful than Hearst and his rambunctious brand of activist, self-congratulatory journalism. Indeed, the *Journal*'s flawed reporting in the run-up to the war was surely a factor in its eventual eclipse by Ochs and the *Times*' model of detached, even bloodless, treatment of the news. This study considers *fin-de-siècle* journalism in complex and dynamic ways, exploring how broad evolutionary forces combined in 1897 to produce developments of enduring significance—in the emergence of journalistic identity, in the application of innovative technologies, and in the development of standards that have shaped and defined American journalism for more than a century. Eighteen-ninety-seven was an exceptional year of experimentation and transformation—and a most fitting year for extending the year-study genre to journalism and mass communication research.

W. Joseph Campbell
Kensington, Maryland
December 2005

INTRODUCTION

On the agenda when the American Newspaper Publishers' Association convened its annual meeting in New York City in February 1897 were questions such as: "Should a newspaper furnish members of the editorial staff with stationery supplies, especially lead pencils?" Do typewriters "lower the literary grade of work done by reporters?" And: "What is the rule in regard to paying car fare for reporters on the local staff of newspapers?"[1]

While offering a glimpse into late nineteenth-century journalism, the mundane agenda items[2] were inadvertently deceptive: they contained no hint that the year 1897 was unfolding as an important moment of transition in American journalism. The topics before the publishers in early 1897 seem quaint and trivial now; that year in journalism was anything but.

As the publishers gathered in New York, evidence of the exceptionality of 1897 was slowly emerging. Shortly before the publishers convened, the *New York Tribune* published a halftone photograph on its front page, an image that "startled New York" journalism[3] and signaled a breakthrough in newspaper illustration.[4] The *Tribune*'s halftone was printed on newsprint, on web perfecting presses running at full speed—a combination long thought improbable. But on January 21, 1897, there it was—evidence of an unambiguous advance in halftone technology, which ultimately contributed to a dramatic recasting of the appearance of the daily newspaper.

Not long after the *Tribune*'s breakthrough, the scathing pejorative—"yellow journalism"—first appeared in print, in the *New York Press*. The newspaper had seized on the term to censure the aggressive, self-promoting "new journalism" of William Randolph Hearst's *New York Journal* and Joseph Pulitzer's *New York World*.[5] The emergence of "yellow journalism" was emblematic of name-calling in print that was commonplace among newspapers of the time—and not unlike the sneers often directed at Web logs and other "new media" of the early twenty-first century.[6] But "yellow journalism" was singularly evocative and colorful, a pejorative that was immediately and forever linked with the *Journal* and the *World*. The epithet spread rapidly; newspapers across the country began invoking "yellow journalism" in 1897. And it lives on, as shorthand for journalistic misconduct of all kinds.

Just days before the publishers met, Adolph S. Ochs, the new publisher of the *New York Times*, placed the smug motto, "All the News That's Fit to Print," on the front page of his fledgling newspaper. The phrase thereafter would occupy a permanent place adjacent to the *Times'* nameplate. In time it became the most famous and most-recited slogan in journalism. A few days before that, Hearst's *New York Journal* published the year's finest work of foreign correspondence—Richard Harding Davis' moving and detail-rich account of the firing-squad execution of a Cuban insurgent captured during the rebellion against Spain's colonial rule. The Cuban uprising was to give rise in 1898 to the Spanish-American War, a conflict that confirmed America's rise as a global power. In October 1897, only six months before the war began, the *Journal* organized a stunning escape from jail of Evangelina Cosío y Cisneros, a political prisoner in Havana. For lawlessness and breathtaking audacity, the case of "jail-breaking journalism"[7] was never again matched or rivaled in American journalism. For its part, the *Journal* declared the Cisneros rescue "the greatest journalistic coup of this age."[8]

Eighteen-ninety-seven was the year of publication of American journalism's most famous editorial[9]—the *New York Sun*'s timeless paean to childhood and the Christmas spirit, "Is There A Santa Claus?"[10] No single artifact of American journalism has been so often reprinted as that editorial. Eighteen-ninety-seven was also the year of origin of the "Katzenjammer Kids" cartoon. The hell-raising Kids made their debut in the *New York Journal* in December 1897, and the strip has since become America's longest-running newspaper comic. The *Jewish Forward* of New York first appeared in April 1897 as the *Forverts*, a Yiddish daily devoted to socialist causes.[11] The *Forward* is still published, as a weekly, in Yiddish and English.

The emergent cinema was in its "novelty year" in 1897.[12] The presidential inauguration of William McKinley in March 1897 was the first to be captured on film. The heavyweight prizefight in Carson City, Nevada, that month between Robert Fitzsimmons and James Corbett was staged with the motion-picture camera in mind, and film footage of the bout attracted sizable audiences across the country.[13] In the spring of the year, a motion-picture camera was taken to war for the first time: Frederick Villiers lugged a crank-operated camera to the theater of the brief conflict between Greece and Turkey, and shot images that afterward were described as "foggy."[14]

The forerunner of broadcast journalism was taking shape. In July 1897, Guglielmo Marconi incorporated the Wireless Telegraph and Signal Company Ltd., an important step in wireless telegraphy's move "from the scientific-academic sector to the marketplace."[15] Eighteen-ninety-seven was the year, say some scholars, of the first modern use of "public relations." The phrase appeared in the preface to the *Yearbook*

Figure 1   The heavyweight boxing match in March 1897 between Robert Fitzsimmons and James Corbett was staged with motion pictures in mind. Film footage of the bout was shown across the country, attracting large audiences of men and women. The *New York Journal's* Winifred Black attended a showing and reported: "The whole thing was so shadowy—yet real, vividly, dreadfully real." (Library of Congress.)

Figure 2 William McKinley's presidential inauguration in March 1897 ushered in a prolonged period of Republican dominance in American political life. It was also the first U.S. presidential inaugural ceremony to be captured by a motion-picture camera. The *New York Journal* thoroughly covered the inauguration, arranging for a special, high-speed train to rush its artists back to New York with illustrations of McKinley's swearing-in. (Library of Congress.)

of Railway Literature.[16] Other scholars have traced the origins of the modern White House press corps to 1897, the first year of the McKinley administration.[17] The president went out of his way in 1897 to develop cordial ties with reporters. He refused, for example, to enter the Vanderbilts' Biltmore mansion in North Carolina unless correspondents who accompanied him also were admitted. And they were.[18]

This work considers these and other moments in positing that 1897 merits recognition as a year pivotal in the trajectory of American journalism. That these events and developments took place in 1897 signals unequivocally that the year was a time of great ferment and experimentation in the field. Journalists then grappled with new technologies in ways that evoke the sometimes-uncertain embrace of new technologies these days. As this study will make clear, however, the exceptionality of 1897 was defined by more than notable accomplishments and breakthroughs.

Figure 3 This is the first page of Lincoln Steffens' in-depth assessment of *fin-de-siècle* American journalism. The article appeared in *Scribner's Monthly* in October 1897 and focused on the changes wrought by the commercialization of journalism. "The magnitude of the financial operations of the newspaper," Steffens wrote, "is turning journalism upside down." (From *Scribner's*.)

THE CLASH OF PARADIGMS

Significantly, 1897 was the year when American journalism came face-to-face with a choice among three rival and incompatible visions, or paradigms, for the profession's future. The emergence of these rival visions is central to the exceptionality of 1897. The choices that materialized then were to set a course for American journalism in the twentieth century and beyond.

The most dramatic of the three paradigms was the self-activated, participatory model of Hearst's yellow journalism. Hearst called it the "journalism of action" or the "journalism that acts." It was a paradigm of agency and engagement that went beyond gathering and publishing the news. Hearst's *New York Journal*, the leading exemplar of the activist paradigm, argued that newspapers were obliged to inject themselves, conspicuously and vigorously, in righting the wrongs of public life, and in filling the void of government inaction and incompetence. There was no more dramatic or celebrated manifestation of the "journalism of action" than the Cisneros jailbreak in Havana.

The antithesis of the "journalism of action" was the conservative, counteractivist paradigm represented by the *New York Times* and its lofty commitment to "All the News That's Fit to Print." The *Times* model emphasized the detached, impartial, yet authoritative treatment of news. Unlike its conservative counterparts such as the *New York Sun*, the *Times* was not reluctant to adapt innovative technologies of the 1890s. The *Times* in 1897 made memorable use of halftone photographs in its upscale Sunday magazine supplement, presenting the images in a sober, restrained manner quite unlike the flashy treatment typical of Hearst's newspapers.

The most eccentric of the three paradigms was non-journalistic, even anti-journalistic: it was a literary approach pursued by Lincoln Steffens upon his becoming city editor of the *New York Commercial Advertiser* in late 1897. Deliberately, and even demonstratively, Steffens shunned veteran newspapermen and instead recruited college-educated writers who had little or no experience in journalism. He then sent them out to write, to hone their talent by telling stories about the joys, hardships, and serendipity of life in New York City.

Resolution of the three-sided clash of paradigms would take years and result ultimately in the ascendancy of the *Times*' detached, counteractivist model—which still is the standard that undergirds mainstream American journalism. Journalists are trained and expected not to participate in the events and topics they cover; they are to treat the news impartially, in an even-handed manner. Those normative values are fundamental to the orthodoxy of American journalism and they can be traced to the Ochsian vision for the *New York Times*. His counteractivist model proved best able to absorb and accommodate the multiple stresses and pressures that were reshaping American journalism at the end of the nineteenth century, transforming it into a decidedly big business that attracted well-educated professionals to its editorial and reporting ranks. In 1897, though it seemed highly unlikely that the *Times*' emergent model had any chance of prevailing, given the newspaper's modest circulation and its precarious financial status. In any event, the choice among the three rival paradigms was clearly laid down in 1897. During that crowded year, the character and future of American journalism were put in play.

This is not to say that no other models were contemplated or developed in 1897. Several were. A small, struggling newspaper in Bloomfield, New Jersey, announced at the end of the year that its editorial positions would thereafter be "'guided and controlled'" by the vote of paying subscribers.[19] In some ways, the Bloomfield experiment anticipated the "civic journalism" experiment of the late 1990s, in which editors and publishers of a number of small newspapers enlisted nonjournalists to help shape editorial decisionmaking. Also contemplated in the late nineteenth century was the notion of "endowed journalism," in which a wealthy philanthropist would establish and bankroll a newspaper, allowing it to appear without the support and presumed taint of advertising. William T. Stead, a prominent British editor who advocated activism in journalism, was a prominent exponent of advertising-free "endowed" newspapers.[20]

But the paradigms developed and tested by Hearst, Ochs, and Steffens were by far the most significant and vital. Each was rolled out in New York City, the widely acknowledged "Mecca" of American journalism,[21] where the field was at its most competitive, demonstrative, and alluring.[22] The *Journal* was the most emphatic in asserting the originality and inevitability of its vision. The "journalism of action," it declared, represented "the final state in the evolution of the modern newspaper"[23] and that a participatory ethos would "likely ... become an accepted part of the functions of newspapers of this country."[24] Ochs offered no similarly bold claims in 1897 about the *Times'* standard. Because he had recently acquired the newspaper at a foreclosure, such an assertion would have seemed strained, even ludicrous. But in the *Times'* persistent criticism in 1897 of the techniques and practices of the yellow press, Ochs sensed that his emergent model possessed wide appeal. Soon enough, Ochs was touting his newspaper as the best in America—long "before it was true."[25] Steffens for his part claimed that he and his staff at the *Commercial Advertiser* were "doing some things that were never done in journalism before...."[26] One of his biographers, Justin Kaplan, called the Steffens model "a new kind of daily journalism, personal, literary and immediate."[27]

The depiction of a three-sided clash of paradigms may invite criticism for its decided New York focus. But it should be kept in mind that Hearst and Ochs developed their respective paradigms after lengthy experience in journalism outside of New York City. Hearst had run the *San Francisco Examiner* for eight years before entering the New York market in September 1895. Ochs had been publisher of the *Chattanooga Times* for eighteen years before gaining control of the *New York Times* in August 1896. The formative years preceding the emergence of their respective models were spent in the American hinterland. While Steffens had worked for several years on the *New York Evening Post* before joining the *Commercial Advertiser*, his iconoclastic, anti-journalistic model was in part an answer to the effects of the commercialization of the American press, which in 1897 were rippling through newspaper markets in New York and beyond.

Figure 4   Newspaper Row in lower Manhattan was the nerve center of American journalism in the late nineteenth century. The domed edifice at far left was the *New York World's* headquarters. The squat structure next to it was home of the *New York Sun*. The Tribune Building in the center housed the *New York Tribune* and the *New York Journal*. New York's remaining daily newspapers have long since moved uptown. (Library of Congress.)

That new paradigms would present themselves in 1897 is scarcely surprising. American journalism of the late 1890s reflected the activism, ferment, and "clamorous vitality"[28] at large in the country. As will be discussed in Chapter 1, a sense of novelty, the appeal of things "new," imbued the *fin-de-siècle* years. "Not to be 'new' is, in these days, to be nothing," Henry D. Traill, a British journalist and literary critic, said of the 1890s.[29] By 1897, Hearst had borrowed from Britain the term "new journalism" to describe the aggressive, sometimes manic, and usually self-congratulatory character of his *Journal*. The emergent clash of paradigms called attention to the new possibilities and directions in American journalism. The time of the dominant editor, the "one-man-ruled-press,"[30] was fast giving way to the forces of commercialization and the enormous capital investment required of big-city dailies. The organizational structure and the mechanized equipment required to publish a metropolitan daily newspaper—from circulation managers to batteries of linotype machines and multiple high-speed presses—prompted Steffens to write in 1897: "The magnitude of the financial operations of the newspaper is turning journalism upside down."[31]

The three-sided clash of paradigms took shape at a highly competitive and challenging time in American journalism. Newspaper editors and publishers across the country grappled with strategies and methods of reaching audiences that were increasingly urban, educated, and literate. As they grappled, editors quarreled and fought among themselves. They eagerly traded insults in print. The *New York Journal*, for example, had few more persistent critics in 1897 than the *New York Times*, which deplored the "freak journalism"[32] of Hearst's newspaper. The *New York World* in March 1897 assailed nearly all of its local competitors as the "derelicts of journalism," dismissing them as "syndicate-owned and sinking newspapers."[33]

The enthusiasm with which newspapers exchanged insults and brickbats seems strange and oddly humorous today. But in the 1890s, they were exchanged in decided seriousness. *Fin-de-siècle* American newspapers took themselves seriously, notably as agents for mass education and cultural refinement. The trade journal *Fourth Estate* called the press "the great engine of modern civilization and its efforts are equally effective for good or for evil."[34]

At the same time, evidence was gathering that the influence of the press was vastly overstated. One disturbing example came when the U.S. Senate failed in 1897 to ratify a proposed treaty of arbitration with Britain, even though the pact had won wide editorial support among American newspapers. In the 1897 mayoral election in New York, nearly all the city's newspapers backed losing candidates. Such embarrassments prompted *The Journalist* to scoff: "what a hollow sham the boasted power of the press is." It added: "'The Power of the Press' is a myth and the sooner we hunt up some other new delusion to hug [to] our bosoms the more quickly will we avoid making ourselves ridiculous."[35]

THE CENTRALITY OF NEWSPAPERS

Evidence of declining influence notwithstanding, American newspapers probably were never more popular or integral than they were in the late 1890s. In his study of newspaper penetration in urban America, historian Ted Curtis Smythe found that, on average, 2.61 newspaper copies circulated within an urban dwelling unit in 1900—compared with 0.72 copies in 2000. Those averages were much greater in the country's largest cities in 1900, Smythe reported.[36] Such penetration rates can be attributed in part to widespread per-issue price-cutting in the late nineteenth century, which was made possible by dramatically lower costs of newsprint.[37] And of course, newspapers in the late 1890s faced no competition from the likes of radio, television, or the Internet.

In ways that are difficult to fathom now, newspapers in 1897 were integral, even organic, to American life, which visitors from abroad found striking. In his *America and the Americans: From A French Point of View*, Price Collier wrote: "The Americans are such voracious readers of their own newspapers, that the newspapers must be taken into account as an important—not to say the chief—factor in what may be termed the secondary education of the mass of the people."[38]

The centrality of newspapers[39] was evident in the apparently spontaneous enthusiasm that greeted publication of the *Chicago Tribune*'s fiftieth anniversary edition on June 10, 1897. So keen was the demand for the *Tribune*'s superbly illustrated, forty-eight page "golden jubilee" issue[40] that blocks-long lines of customers formed near the newspaper's offices on the morning of the anniversary. Newsboys shouting "'strated jubiloo" and "lustrous Trib" quickly raised the price of the souvenir edition from a penny to five cents. Before the morning was out, they had doubled the price again, to ten cents. Some shrewd street vendors in the city were asking twenty-five cents a copy.[41]

"The *Tribune* was everywhere," the newspaper said of its anniversary issue, which offered readers stunning color lithography as well as detailed articles about the rise of the newspaper and the city. "Its handsome colors flashed in every store," the *Tribune* exulted. "It was carried by nearly every shopper on State and the other retail streets. It was in sight in every passing [street] car."[42] For "artistic excellence," the newspaper declared, the jubilee issue "has never been equaled by any daily newspaper in the world."[43]

Hyperbole certainly marked the *Tribune*'s account of its fiftieth anniversary issue. But the self-congratulatory tone was neither out of place nor uncommon among newspapers of 1897. It was, notably, a defining feature of the yellow press. The *New York Journal* and the *New York World* were relentless in announcing their exploits and calling attention to their accomplishments.[44] Self-promotion was a way for newspapers of the 1890s to differentiate themselves in highly competitive urban markets. Self-promotion was also a way for newspapers to assert an attachment with the communities in which they circulated. By boasting and promoting themselves, newspapers sought to project a sense of irresistibility, which readers could ill afford to miss. The *Chicago Tribune* clearly used its fiftieth anniversary to project an irresistibility. "It has not been an accident," the newspaper declared, "that the Tribune has grown into the heart of the people" through "unflagging loyalty to the best interests of the whole people of Chicago."[45]

Another common way in which newspapers of the 1890s asserted their local attachment was by acting as agents of charity. The *New York*

World, for example, prepared thousands of Thanksgiving and Christmas dinners for the poor of New York and helped establish schools for newsboys.[46] The *New York Tribune* offered summer outings for the city's poor children.[47] Hearst's *Journal* set up soup kitchens to ease the harsh consequences of winter snowstorms.[48] *The Journalist* attributed the *Journal's* popularity in part to the newspaper's big-heartedness—to the sense "that behind and through the paper there beats a warm, generous, human heart alive to the troubles and miseries of humanity and anxious to alleviate them."[49] More conservative newspapers would do well, *The Journalist* said, to "bring themselves in closer touch with the hearts of the people."[50]

The centrality of newspapers in the life of Americans in the late 1890s would seem alien today. Few large-city newspapers of the twenty-first century speak in their columns of the importance of winning their readers' heartfelt affection. Given that newspaper circulation has been in nearly unbroken decline for many years, few readers nowadays regard newspapers as organic, or as essential to the fabric of American society.

Other aspects of the journalism of 1897 would seem peculiar and even off-putting today. Some leading regional newspapers, such as the *Boston Globe* and *Cleveland Press*, routinely devoted large portions of their front pages to display advertising, for products such as patent medicines, men's suits, and the latest models of bicycles. The front page of the *New York Herald* in the 1890s contained no news at all. The first two or three pages of the *Herald* were typically devoted to classified advertising, including personal advertisements that were sometimes fairly *risqué*.

Newspapers in 1897 often crammed twenty to thirty articles—many of them a paragraph or two in length—onto their front pages. On February 10, 1897, the day "All the News That's Fit to Print" first appeared adjacent to the newspaper's nameplate, the *New York Times* offered twenty-seven articles on its front page. These included brief, oddball stories such as "Dying of Hiccoughs," "Tin-Plate Factory to Start Up," and "Indicted for Making a Bet." A detailed index stretching for a column and a half also appeared on the *Times*' front page that day, as it did on most days in 1897. But neither pictures nor illustrations graced the front page of February 10, 1897—another feature of a newspaper which, for ample good reason, came to be called "the gray lady."

The crowded, chaotic makeup of the *Times* was fairly common among U.S. newspapers in the late 1890s. Foreign visitors were known to sneer at the newspapers' disorderly appearance. "There is a lack of discrimination in the daily bill of fare served up by the American press that cannot but disgust the refined and tutored palate," declared James Fullarton Muirhead, a fastidious British travel writer who visited the United States in the mid-1890s and wrote a handbook for visitors to the United States.[51] "The very end for which the newspaper avowedly exists," Muirhead added, "is often defeated by the impossibility of finding out what is the important news of the day."[52]

Another feature of the American press of 1897 that would seem quaint and alien today were the newsboys who loudly and aggressively hawked newspapers on city streets. More than a few people thought them nuisances, and the city commissioners of Washington, D.C., adopted a measure in 1897 forbidding newsboys from calling out on Sundays. The so-called "crying ban" was advocated by a group of Protestant clergy who claimed that the yelling of newsboys disturbed worship services.[53] The Secular League of Washington opposed the ban as an attack on "the poor newsboy's ... attempt to earn an honest living." The organization claimed that the crying of newsboys was no less disruptive than "the clanging of church bells" on Sunday mornings.[54] One dissident clergyman, the Rev. A. G. Rogers, suggested the ban was sought because Sunday newspapers had become more popular and entertaining than church-going. "If it comes to a contest for popular favor between the Sunday newspaper and the church, ... the only way in which the church can come out on top is to offer the most inducements for a pleasant time," he said. "Make the church entertaining and people will come to them."[55]

But the crying ban remained in force. Four newsboys were arrested in a test case in early 1897 and an appellate judge upheld the ordinance.[56] Police occasionally brought in a law-breaking newsboy.[57] By early 1898, Washington was said to be more quiet on Sundays than any other American city.[58]

PARALLELS, THEN AND NOW

Yelling newsboys and the mild controversies they prompted long ago disappeared from urban America. But other issues and controversies that percolated in American journalism in 1897 would seem very familiar in the early twenty-first century. Then, as now, New York was the nerve center of American journalism, home to the most prestigious news outlets, the city where many journalists aspired to work.[59] So alluring was New York in 1897 that the *Fourth Estate* spoke of "a veritable deluge of talent" that had reached New York in recent years. But the city proved rudely inhospitable to many job-seekers in journalism, and *Fourth Estate* felt compelled to offer this blunt advice: "Go anywhere, but leave New York. It is today the poorest field for anything but the highest talents, and these are often crowded into insignificance."[60]

Newspapers of the late 1890s were known to inflate their circulation figures, not unlike the deceptive practices one hundred or so years later of *Newsday*, the *Chicago Sun-Times*, and a few other titles.[61] Newspaper circulations were not audited in the late nineteenth century, which allowed for egregious exaggeration, despite the insistence of many newspapers that their books were open to anyone who wished to inspect them. *Fourth Estate* said such claims served as a reminder "that perjury is not a forgotten vice."[62] As will be discussed in Chapter 2, Adolph Ochs' inflated claims about the circulation of the *New York Times* precipitated a crisis at the newspaper in 1898, when a former employee threatened to tell advertisers of the exaggerated figures. Ochs escaped the quandary by trimming the newspaper's daily price to a penny from three cents to boost circulation.[63] This desperate move also had the unexpected effect of ensuring the *Times*' survival and ultimately establishing its counteractivist paradigm as the gold standard of American journalism.

Then, as now, the use and protection of anonymous sources by reporters gave rise to messy controversies and threats of jail. Two reporters were brought to trial in June 1897, three years after they had refused to tell a U.S. Senate committee the source for their reports that senators had been improperly speculating in sugar stocks. The reporters, John S. Shriver of the *New York Mail and Express* and E. J. Edwards of the *Philadelphia Press*, were acquitted separately on technicalities about whether the Senate committee had properly summoned them and whether the questions they were asked were pertinent.[64] In his directed verdicts clearing the reporters, the judge made clear the verdicts were not meant to be extensions of journalistic privilege. Even so, the *Fourth Estate* hailed the outcomes as indirect support for allowing journalists "to hold inviolate confidences"[65] akin to those of lawyer and client and doctor and patient. Such broad interpretations of journalistic privilege have never been recognized, and even in the early twenty-first century journalists face time in jail if they refuse to testify before grand juries.[66]

Then, as now, newspapers stood accused of barely concealing their partisan ways. The political preference or party orientation of major newspapers in 1897 was readily apparent, and that prompted press critic Harry Thurston Peck to write: "The most fundamental defect ... in our American journals is an absolute and lamentable lack of fairness in everything that touches upon political opinion." Peck asserted that "political news reports are tinctured with a partisanship that destroys their value as news, and that does more than any other thing to discredit the claim of our journalists to be taken seriously."[67] Peck, a Columbia University professor and sometimes press critic, was scarcely alone in charging of partisanship. Muirhead, the fussy British travel writer, said "the want of impartiality" in U.S. newspapers was "another of the patent defects of the American daily press." He said the press in America was so "unscrupulous" in its partisanship that it more resembled "the ethics of the ward politician ... than the seeker after truth."[68]

As it is today—when books are written about the urgent obligation of "saving journalism"[69]—the American press in 1897 was the target of harsh and withering critiques. In a lament that would be familiar today, a magazine called *The Dial* published in 1897 an assessment of what it called the "decay" of American journalism. *The Dial* said it was an "undeniable fact that most of the newspapers published in our large cities are so devoid of principle that they constitute a perpetual menace to every genuine interest of our civilization."[70] Then, as now, the critiques of American journalism sprang partly from the demands and uncertainties associated with new techniques and technologies. In 1897, "the fad for illustrations"—the expanding use of engravings and halftones—was seen as contributing to the "decadence of newspapers" and a decline in their literary quality.[71] Then as now, technology was seen as contributing to lowered standards. The Linotype typesetting machine was blamed for what *The Journalist* called a "deteriorating effect of modern journalistic methods. ... Never before were sheets which made a pretense to respectability so slouchily printed as now."[72] But for all the qualms of traditionalists, Linotypes were in wide usage in 1897—4,150 of them were in use at 600 places across North America.[73] The *New York Herald* owned the country's largest Linotype battery in 1897—52 machines. The *New York World* had 51 linotypes and the *Journal* 50.[74]

Other innovations were catching on in 1897. Newer models of the typewriter had passed the threshold of reliability and ease of use, and were gaining favor in American newsrooms. Trade journals of 1897 noted the "marked increase in typewriter usage among literary workers and journalists"[75] and waxed enthusiastic about the machine's capabilities. "There is no modern invention except, perhaps, the bicycle, which has so evidently filled a long-felt want and taken its position in the economy of modern business life as the typewriter," Allan Forman, the editor of *The Journalist*, wrote in May 1897.[76] Forman said his first piece of advice to any novice in journalism would be: "'Get a typewriter and learn how to use it.' It is easy, and anybody who has brains enough to write anything worth reading can learn to put it into good shape on a machine in a week."[77] Forman figured that learning to use a typewriter could enhance a journalist's earning capacity by perhaps one-third.[78]

But the typewriter was not unanimously received with warmth and enthusiasm in American newsrooms. Just as some journalists expressed skepticism about the Internet and emergent media technologies in the mid-1990s,[79] some veteran reporters of the 1890s resented the noisy, intrusive typewriter. They preferred to compose articles by longhand while seated at sloped desks, and they greeted the typewriter with hostility and disdain. At the *New York Times*, typewriters were set up on a "felt-covered table in a remote part of the city room" so that their clatter "wouldn't drive the older men nuts."[80]

Expense was another barrier to adopting the typewriter. A reliable model cost about $100 in 1897, which *The Journalist* acknowledged was almost prohibitively expensive for most young writers.[81] But *Fourth Estate* argued that price should be no barrier and advised journalists to regard the typewriter as a "good friend":[82]

> Though it is unfortunately true that many of the best reporters fail to save enough to begin a bank account, yet there is no reason why any man earning a decent salary should not possess a typewriter. It is more than a mechanical connivance, for it is a stimulus to extra work while it is a reliever of much manual labor. It is the good friend who eases regular work and incites ambitions above receiving a salary.[83]

The typewriter's convenience as a time-saving device[84] was well-suited to the "rush and hurry" pace[85] of *fin-de-siècle* America—and was an important factor in what *Fourth Estate* described in 1897 as the "rapid introduction of the typewriter into newspaper offices."[86] The typewriter's capacity to accelerate the flow of copy from reporter to editor to typesetter was vital to its adoption in newsrooms, a factor particularly important in deadline writing. It was not at all hypothetical for a reporter using a typewriter to compose the day's most important story only minutes before the presses would roll. "The sharp click of the machine sounds like a telegraph instrument wildly out of order," *Fourth Estate* said in describing such a scenario. "Bits of copy are cut off without interrupting the writer, and the whole story is in type before he has had time to get his breath. The seemingly impossible has been accomplished ... and the newspaper presents the very latest news to its readers."[87]

By 1897, famous correspondents, including Sylvester Scovel of the *New York World*, had begun carrying typewriters on their assignments.[88] Typewritten manuscripts for books and magazines were becoming *de rigueur.* "A modern Thackeray," said *Fourth Estate*, "would in all probability be overlooked unless he handed in his manuscript in type-written form."[89]

INTRODUCING THE YEAR STUDY

In presenting the case that 1897 was a pivotal year in American journalism, this work pursues a methodological frame—the single-year study—that has been neglected or overlooked in journalism history,[90] a field that leading scholars periodically have criticized for its "restrictions on methodological approaches"[91] and its resistance to "new and better ways to study [journalism's] past."[92] Thus, another important objective of this work is to introduce the year study to journalism history.

Year studies have been common enough in other fields. Recent and popular year studies have focused, for example, on 1000,[93] 1215,[94] 1759,[95] 1776,[96] 1777,[97] 1912,[98] 1919,[99] and 1968.[100] On occasion a single month,[101] or even a single day,[102] has been the subject of book-length treatment. An important reason for the popularity of year studies is that they are intriguingly flexible and inclusive—"durational and punctual at the same time." [103] As Michael North, the author of *Reading 1922*,[104] has observed, "In the telling of history … a year can be used as a date, as if it were punctual and precise, or as a period containing a great many other dates."[105] Such versatility is apparent in the single-year works that have examined the world on the cusp of modernity,[106] the United States at a critical moment thirty years before its civil war,[107] and the United States on the eve of the "American century."[108]

While year studies notably have been missing from journalism research, occasional attempts have been made to identify and celebrate the profession's pivotal moments. Perhaps the best example of such an effort was the 1997 issue of the now-defunct *Media Studies Journal* that offered short essays on "defining moments in journalism" since the 1940s. The collection was topical, anecdotal, and fairly predictable. It included discussions about "Vietnam and War Reporting,"[109] "The Weight of Watergate,"[110] and "Covering Politics—Is There a Female Difference?"[111]

Although not in the form of year studies, American journalism of the late 1890s has attracted considerable and sustained interest from scholars over the years, many of whom have focused on the press and the Spanish-American War,[112] or on the personalities of Hearst and Pulitzer. These works often have presented the seriously misleading characterization of the yellow press as wretched and trivial, prone to trafficking in lurid sensation and fabrication.[113] Nearly all of Hearst's biographers have been harsh and unforgiving,[114] while Pulitzer's have been largely sympathetic and often fawning.[115] W. A. Swanberg, who wrote biographies about both men, disparaged Hearst's newspapers of the late 1890s as little more than "printed entertainment and excitement—the equivalent in newsprint of bombs exploding, bands blaring, firecrackers popping, victims screaming, flags waving, cannons roaring … and smoke rising from the singed flesh of executed criminals."[116]

More recent and dispassionate studies—written by scholars who clearly spent considerable time *reading* Hearst's newspapers—have rejected such simplistic and unrevealing characterizations. They have instead identified earnestness and a degree of sophistication in Hearst's newspapers, especially the *New York Journal*. In his admirably even-handed biography, *The Chief*, David Nasaw said of the 1895–1897 period at Hearst's *Journal*:

> Day after day, Hearst and his staff improved on their product. Their headlines were more provocative than anyone else's, their drawings more lifelike; the cartoons by Homer Davenport were sharply focused and brilliantly drawn, the writing throughout the paper outstanding, if, at times, a bit long-winded. Equally important in attracting new readers, the newspaper's layout was excellent, with text and drawings breaking through columns to create new full-page landscapes, and sensational bold headlines that seized the eye and quickened the imagination.[117]

John D. Stevens, in his insightful study of sensationalism in the New York City press, similarly identified an intensity and industriousness in the yellow press which, he argued, was probably "read by people in all social classes."[118] Stevens also wrote: "If they titillated, the yellow papers also told New Yorkers what was going on, what forces were shaping their lives. Each issue bulged with news accounts and feature stories which were little parables about life in the big city."[119] However, neither Nasaw nor Stevens recognized the clash of paradigms that took shape in *fin-de-siècle* New York journalism. Other writers and scholars have hinted at something resembling that clash, but have defined it narrowly, usually as a dichotomy of "journalism-as-information" against "journalism-as-entertainment."

An early expression of this dichotomy appeared in 1932, in a *Vanity Fair* essay that reviewed the long careers and contributions of Ochs and Hearst.[120] The essay, which was notably sympathetic to both men, declared that "Ochs specialized in information, Hearst in entertainment."[121] In his 1978 study, *Discovering the News*, the sociologist Michael Schudson took up and modified the information-*versus*-entertainment dichotomy. Schudson called the dichotomy "the two journalisms of the 1890s," and he substituted Pulitzer for Hearst as the most prominent representative of "journalism as entertainment." Pulitzer's *World*, Schudson wrote, "may have set the pace for modern mass-circulation journalism, but after 1896 the *New York Times* established the standard."[122] According to Schudson, Ochs best represented "journalism as information."[123]

Schudson's was an intriguing and thoughtful construct, but was encumbered by a focus on class. The *Times*' "information" model appealed to "wealthier people in New York," Schudson wrote,[124] while the *World*'s storytelling approach resonated with "the working class reader."[125] This part of his analysis rests more on conjecture than persuasive evidence. Indeed, the best evidence suggests that the *Times* and the *World* sought and doubtlessly attracted readers across the social and economic strata, as Stevens and others have noted.[126]

Moreover, the construct of "the two journalisms" is fuzzy, imprecise, and contradicted by a fair amount of evidence.[127] As readers readily discern in moving from the news sections to the sport pages, newspaper content is, and long has been, an amalgam of news *and* entertainment. This certainly was true of the yellow press of Pulitzer and Hearst of the late 1890s, as critics of the time pointed out. Hearst "would have one of the best papers published in the English language," *The Journalist* observed, were he to "cut his newspaper in two, and publish the real, vital news in one part, and the sensations, rot, and nonsense in the other."[128] While Pulitzer was notoriously tight-fisted, the *World* was known to devote considerable resources to gathering the news. The commitment to far-flung newsgathering was suggested by the assignments that the *World*'s Scovel—perhaps the most prominent foreign correspondent of the time—took on in 1897. As will be discussed in Chapter 3, Scovel's reporting that year traced the arc of the most important international events—from the insurrection in Cuba, to the brief war between Greece and Turkey and the mad rush to the gold fields of the subarctic Klondike.[129]

Not only did the *World* devote resources to gathering news, it moved in 1898 to *de-emphasize* its sensational content (or "journalism-as-entertainment"). Pulitzer instructed his editors to tone down the *World*, typographically—a decision announced at a staff meeting in November 1898.[130] Thereafter, the *World* became steadily more conservative in appearance and in content. The *Times*, meanwhile, was not above frivolity and entertainment in promoting itself. During his first months as the newspaper's publisher in 1896 and 1897, Ochs "promoted the *Times* with every gimmick he could think of," according to Susan Tifft and Alex Jones in their revealing study of Ochs and his heirs.[131] As will be discussed in Chapter 2, Ochs pursued a variety of schemes—including a contest for a new motto—to call attention to his newspaper and attract badly needed readers.[132]

Schudson's "two journalisms" construct not only draws sharper contrasts than are warranted, it ignores the *Journal's* ascendancy as America's most compelling and energetic newspaper and fails to identify the elaborate nature of the *Journal's* activist paradigm. One of the few scholars who explicitly considered the implications of the *Journal's* activism was Gerald Linderman in *The Mirror of War: American Society and the Spanish-American War*. While noting that Hearst believed the newspaper could be "an instrument of government vis-à-vis government," Linderman inaccurately characterized the "journalism of action" as an irregular and inconsistent force which, "in limited categories of action would rival and occasionally displace government."[133] As will be explored in Chapter 2, the "journalism of action" was far more complex than that characterization. The paradigm, as Hearst saw it, was hardly self-limiting or constrained, and it certainly was not meant to be episodic. The "journalism of action" was defined by a panoply of strategies through which Hearst's *Journal* would inject itself as a *participant*, ranging widely to "fitly render any public service within its power."[134] The *Journal* insisted that a "newspaper, hardly less than a government, is the guardian of the people's rights."[135] As we shall see, the *Journal's* activism was seldom at rest in 1897.

While no work of American journalism has specifically identified or analyzed the watershed character of 1897, a few studies have focused on the exploits of Scovel and other journalists at that time. For example, Joyce Milton's engaging, if flawed, work, *The Yellow Kids: Foreign Correspondents in the Heyday of Yellow Journalism*, devoted considerable attention to Scovel and Richard Harding Davis. Their exceptional reporting in 1897 will be considered in Chapter 3. David Traxel's insightful year study, *1898: The Birth of the American Century*, explored the lasting political and military significance of 1898—notably, the decisiveness of the Spanish-American War to American foreign policy and the country's emergence as a global power.[136] Traxel, however, offered only passing reference to Hearst's activist vision[137] and instead embraced the conventional and misleading critique that the yellow press sought "to entertain and inform an audience of the imperfectly literate and barely educated."[138] Its readership was certainly much more diverse than that. Traxel in any case did not explore in detail the ferment and tensions the roiled American journalism in 1897.

This is not to say that 1897 has no prospective rival as American journalism's exceptional year. There are other candidates, including: 1798 and the promulgation of the Alien and Sedition Acts, under which ten journalists eventually were convicted;[139] 1833 and the emergence (disputed by some scholars) of innovative techniques associated with the penny press;[140] 1972 and the *Washington Post's* disclosures about the Watergate scandal, a constitutional crisis that led to the resignation of President Richard M. Nixon,[141] and 1995 and the popular embrace of the Internet and its World Wide Web.[142] Each of those years was significant, even extraordinary, in the historiography of American journalism. But none of them offered the rich variety of salient, decisive moments that so distinguished 1897.

THE MERITS OF YEAR STUDIES

While critiques of journalism history have not specifically identified single-year studies as representative of methodological freshness, such approaches offer "a manageable way to narrow the scope, deal in specifics, yet still work with a beginning, middle, and end."[143] Because they are sharply focused, year studies can clarify trends, issues, and developments that otherwise might be obscured in the sweep of historiography. For example, the intense if ultimately passing interest among many newspapers in Hearst's "journalism of action" is rarely recognized by historians. But a detailed examination of 1897 reveals that the "journalism of action" won considerable interest and even admiration among journalists, including some of Hearst's many rivals and foes. For a time, the "journalism of action" was regarded as a promising agent, as "honest, fearless, unpurchaseable journalism"[144] that seemed powerful enough to take on official corruption and the excesses of monopoly interests that were gathering strength in *fin-de-siècle* America. "It is not too much to say," Henry A. Crittenden, a reform-minded commentator wrote in *The Journalist*, "that the vital interests of the national progress and of the civilization demand that Mr. Hearst and the new journalism shall win in this titanic battle"[145] against trusts and corruption.[146]

Year studies, moreover, can yield insight into what are regarded as familiar, even mundane topics. Chapter 2 of this work, for example, will revisit the emergence of the *New York Times'* famous motto and describe how "All the News That's Fit to Print" was first an advertising and marketing tool before being assigned to a permanent and prominent place on the newspaper's front page.

Year studies of course are not without risks, the most acute of which is reductive—claiming too much significance for a single year while ignoring the broader, evolutionary context. And indeed it would be erroneous to characterize the succession of decisive developments in American journalism in 1897 as solely the harvest of sudden inspiration. Some of those developments were, to be sure. The *New York Sun's* classic Santa Claus editorial was, according to an account by the newspaper's editor, quickly written, in the course of a day's work.[147] But other pivotal moments in 1897 were the result of extended periods of testing. A year study can capture or freeze-frame key moments amid the trajectory of long-term change, and then consider those moments in detail. An example of the flexibility of this approach is apparent in considering the breakthrough in halftone technology—the development of the mechanical process allowing photographic images to be printed in the main section of a newspaper as it was published on a high-speed web perfecting press. While a method for printing halftones on flatbed presses had been developed by 1880, it had been thought "an impossible method" to apply the technology to a large daily newspaper that was published on high-speed web presses, which were becoming ever more sophisticated.[148] But in January 1897, the *New York Tribune* demonstrated that it could be done—becoming "the first mass circulation newspaper to publish a halftone photograph" in its news pages. [149]

The subject of the *Tribune's* photograph was not particularly memorable: the image was a profile view of Thomas Platt, the New York Republican party boss and a U.S. senator-elect.[150] But the significance of the Platt photograph was readily apparent. *Fourth Estate* called its appearance "a new step in the art of newspaper illustration, proving that a half-tone could be used successfully, not only in a supplement but in the news pages."[151] The *Tribune* later congratulated itself on becoming "the first of all the metropolitan newspapers to make and print a satisfactory half-tone picture in its main sheet with its rapid, web perfecting presses, running at full speed, and using simply the regular everyday quality of printing paper." The newspaper asserted: "We do not say The Tribune's half-tones cannot be improved. ... But the mechanical difficulty, hitherto deemed insuperable, has been at last overcome."[152] Within six weeks, the *Fourth Estate* reported a "distinct passion for half-tones" had taken hold "throughout the country."[153]

Although his name was nowhere mentioned in the reports about the *Tribune's* success, the breakthrough was a personal triumph for the newspaper's art manager, Stephen H. Horgan.[154] For years, Horgan had maintained that a process for printing halftones on high-speed presses was practical and could be developed. His enthusiasm was not widely shared, however, and it reportedly cost him his job at the *New York Herald*. Printers there scoffed at Horgan's advocacy of the halftone process. They regarded it as preposterous, especially after the *Herald's* experiments with halftones turned out to be little short of miserable.[155] The publisher, James Gordon Bennett Jr., was said to have ordered Horgan dismissed.[156] Horgan subsequently joined the *Tribune*.

Long before photojournalism was fashionable, or imaginable, Horgan recognized the importance of marrying photography and journalism. "The newspaper aims to give a faithful picture of current history," he said in 1886. "How much more truthful would that record be if it were made by the unprejudiced and impartial camera[?]"[157] By then, he and others had pioneered the use of halftones in illustrated newspapers and weeklies, including the *New York Daily Graphic*, where Horgan had worked as a photographer.[158] He helped develop the process by which halftones appeared in that newspaper—among them the famous upper Fifth Avenue "Shantytown" image, published March 4, 1880, on the *Graphic's* eighth anniversary.[159] It was among the first halftones ever published in a newspaper. But the process used by the *Graphic* was rudimentary compared to the technique Horgan successfully demonstrated in 1897, to embed halftones in the curved stereotype plates used on the *Tribune's* presses.[160] The *Tribune's* application of the halftone process to high-speed presses was soon recognized as signaling a "wonderful revolution … in the illustration of great metropolitan daily papers."[161] In his social history of photography, Robert Taft wrote: "The year 1897 really marks the advent of half-tone illustration as a regular feature of American newspaper journalism."[162]

The most significant aspect of Horgan's breakthrough was not the process but its promise of rapidly transferring high-fidelity photographic images to the printed page. The ready application of the halftone process in daily journalism led to nothing less than a realtering of the appearance of American newspapers—a development that *Fourth Estate* detected as early as 1899.[163] The halftone process allowed the newspaper to become a more vivid and more visual medium, and encouraged the eventual ascendancy of graphic illustrations (or "visuals") in newspaper design. The contemporary formula for American newspapers favors fewer articles and more "visuals"—a dramatic reversal of the equation that prevailed in 1897. For confirmation, one need only compare the front pages of the *New York Times* in 1897 with those of today. Instead of twenty to thirty articles crowded onto page one, the *Times'* front page is striking in its use of color photographs. Fewer than a dozen articles appear on the *Times*' front "cover." Other newspapers in the early twenty-first century—among them the *St. Louis Post-Dispatch*, which Pulitzer and his heirs owned for decades—usually offered two or three articles on front pages that were dominated by large color photographs.[164] The altered appearance of the newspaper's front page was not necessarily a direct and inevitable consequence of Horgan's breakthrough of 1897. But his accomplishment was vital in making possible the graphic transformation of newspapers.

DEATH OF THE "POPE"

The transitory nature of 1897 was underscored in October that year by the death after a months-long illness of Charles A. Dana, the "pope" of American journalism.[165] Dana was the brilliant but ill-tempered editor of the *New York Sun*. He ran the *Sun* for nearly thirty years and the newspaper thoroughly bore his imprint. Dana's spectacles, bald pate, and long beard made him one of journalism's instantly recognizable figures. He was as cerebral as he looked, and he cultivated an intellectualism at the *Sun*.

Dana was an accomplished linguist who spoke French, knew Gaelic, was familiar with Russian and Norwegian, and read Dante in the original Italian.[166] He impressed visitors with his powers of concentration. Even late in life, Dana was known to absorb the contents of a book or magazine while carrying on a conversation.[167] He developed one of the world's finest private collections of ceramics and objets d'art, and spent upwards of $400,000 in doing so.[168]

The *Sun* during Dana's long stewardship became known as a writer's paper. In its newsroom, the author of a particularly fine story was held in higher esteem "than he who conquers kingdoms," according to the press critic Will Irwin.[169] By 1897, however, Dana's prominence in American journalism had slipped into eclipse. He was then seventy-eight-years old and the last of the nineteenth-century's famous "old-time American editors."[170] Better than any editor, Dana represented the fading concept of "personal journalism," in which the editor's voice, experience, intellect, and opinion infused the newspaper with singular character and personality.[171] The decline of "personal journalism" sometimes was a topic of debate in 1897. *Fourth Estate* insisted, for example, that "personal journalism" was not *passé*, writing:

> It is our belief that individuality still counts and that the people like to feel the personality of the editor. They agree or disagree with him as they see fit, and in either case they still demand

a personal head distinct from the business office, though they often care most for papers whose editors are also proprietors. The day of the editor is not gone. His training and intimate acquaintance with men and affairs make him an authority on many subjects. His power as an educator and instructor is not gone. He is still a leader among men.[172]

But that was a romantic view. The intimacy of "personal journalism" was untenable and even implausible as newspapers of the late nineteenth century inexorably grew into capital-intensive big businesses sustained increasingly by advertising revenues.[173] A large-city American daily newspaper in 1897 could expect to raise two-thirds of its revenues by selling space to advertisers.[174]

Dana tried to hold out against the changes sweeping American journalism of the late nineteenth century. He likened himself as "an old-fashioned expert," but was more hopeful than prescient in predicting that illustrations in newspapers would prove "a passing fashion."[175] Dana conceded never having taken a liking to the Linotype machine "because it didn't seem to me to turn out a page as handsome, in a typographical point of view, as a page set by hand."[176]

In death, Dana was not deeply mourned. Many leading journalists of New York were conspicuous by their absence from his funeral. The old editor, as *Fourth Estate* noted, had accumulated "hosts of admirers and legions of enemies."[177] In an editorial eulogizing Dana, the *Los Angeles Times* characterized him as "a born fighter who was wont to slay and spare not."[178] He had made many enemies during the bitter war that pitted the Associated Press news cooperative against the privately owned United Press, of which Dana was president.

That war had broken out in 1893 and both news agencies raided the other's clients.[179] Slowly, the Associated Press began to gain the upper hand, thanks largely to its membership in a cartel of international news agencies. Cartel membership allowed the Associated Press to send its subscribers a steady diet of news from abroad, including reports of the Sino-Japanese War in 1894.[180] The defection in early 1897 of several prominent United Press clients, including the *New York Herald* and *New York Tribune*,[181] signaled the end of the bitter struggle. By early April 1897, United Press had declared bankruptcy and Dana filed the documents that formalized the agency's collapse.[182]

It was a staggering defeat for the old editor, the humiliation of which deepened a few weeks later when the *Sun* was obliged to publish an apology[183] to Frank B. Noyes, an Associated Press director and publisher of the *Washington Evening Star*, to settle a case of criminal libel.[184] Noyes had sued the *Sun* over an editorial in 1895 that described him as "a thoroughly dishonest director" of the Associated Press.[185] In apologizing to Noyes, the *Sun* said it retracted "any remarks reflecting either upon his personal or business integrity."[186]

During Dana's last months, the *Sun* was at the forefront of two other failed campaigns, both of them widely publicized if clumsy assaults on what the *Sun* termed the "leprous new journalism"[187] of Hearst and Pulitzer. One campaign sought to destroy the *Journal* and the *World* by expelling them from social clubs, reading rooms, and libraries across metropolitan New York. The other was legislation—aimed principally at the *Journal*—to outlaw the unauthorized publication of caricatures in newspapers in New York state. Although both campaigns were ill-conceived and had little lasting effect, they nonetheless demonstrated how the transformations in American journalism in 1897 troubled and unnerved not only journalists but politicians as well.

The boycott against the *Journal* and the *World* was an amorphous campaign that gathered considerable momentum in late winter 1897. The Newark Free Public Library was the first institution to ban what the *Sun* called "the chronicles of crime, of lust and of general nastiness."[188] The library's trustees voted on February 4, 1897, to cancel subscriptions to the *Journal* and the *World* and remove back issues of the newspapers from the library's files.[189] The *Sun* devoted more than two columns of newsprint to a glowing and approving report about the library's rebuke. It quotes the young woman in charge of the library's reading room as saying:

> Many times every day, ladies and gentlemen, young and old, come in here and say: 'Oh, what a relief it is to come in here and not find that horrible *World* and *Journal*! It is safe now for boys and girls to come here and read now. Those papers ought to be kept out of every public library in the country!'

The boycott spread quickly and by May 1897, the *Journal* and *World* had been banned by nearly ninety institutions,[190] including the Century Club and Merchants' Club in New York City, the New York Yacht Club, the Harlem Branch of the YMCA, the Montauk Club of Brooklyn, the Flatbush Young Republican Club in Brooklyn, public libraries in Bridgeport and New Haven, Connecticut, [191] as well as the library reading room at Yale University Library.[192] Clubs and organizations in Syracuse [193] and Portland, Oregon, [194] also joined in what the *Sun* called "the protest of decency."[195]

Other New York newspapers joined the *Sun* in welcoming the boycott. The *New York Times* approvingly declared it "a moral revolt against the unclean and sensational examples of the 'new journalism.'"[196] Essential to the boycott's success, the *Times* said, must be an element of shame. "Respectable men must be made to blush and hang their heads when caught reading these polluting sheets or having them in their houses," it said.[197]

The inchoate protest—which evoked the "moral war" in 1840 against the *New York Herald* of the elder James Gordon Bennett[198]—tended to be long on denunciation and short on explicit grievance. Rarely did the *Sun* or other newspapers cite examples of the vulgar and reprehensible content of the *Journal* or *World*, both of which were certainly more flamboyant in appearance than their conservative rivals. It was vaguely asserted that in their coverage of crime and corruption, the yellow journals abetted even more crime and corruption.[199] But for the most part, the assaults against the yellow press were invective-filled generalizations.[200] Typical was this passage from the *Sun*: "The procuress corrupting her sex is not more an enemy to society than the 'new journalism,' with its prurient wares—the suggestiveness of the pencil and the salaciousness of the pen."[201] As the boycott gathered momentum, the *Times* declared: "The moral disease germs of the new journals are as big and hideous as rattlesnakes. Every eye sees them, every mind comprehends their poisonous nature."[202]

The "protest of decency" also won support among conservative clergymen who, like the *Sun* and *Times*, invested great hope in the boycott. "Would to God the exclusion might become universal and extend to every family in the land," declared the Rev. W. H. P. Faunce of Fifth Avenue Baptist Church. "The man who allows [the yellow press] in his family opens a connection between the cradle and the sewer, the nursery and the swamp, and is inviting the germs of moral typhoid."[203]

That was the hope, that the boycott would "become universal and extend to every family," and thus kill off the yellow press. Such an outcome would "cleanse" the American press and ease the ferment roiling the profession. Such expectations were hopelessly naïve, however, and the boycott against the yellow press collapsed by mid-1897. The prospect of shaming people for reading "polluting sheets" proved to be no match for the energy and enterprise of the *Journal* (and, to a lesser extent, the *World*). The content of the yellow press proved irresistible—too exciting and engaging to shun for very long.

The boycott also suffered the inevitable effects of a self-limiting protest: after banning the yellow journals, there was no other way in which a library, reading room, or social club could register its disapproval.[204]

Moreover, the boycott had the unexpected consequence of modestly *stimulating* the circulation of the *Journal* and the *World*. Unable to find the newspapers at clubs, reading rooms, and libraries, untold numbers of readers bought their own copies. "The crusade was waged with great fury" in the first months of 1897, *Fourth Estate* said, but "there has been nothing ... heard of it in a long time."[205]

As the boycott began spreading in metropolitan New York, legislation was introduced in the state legislature that also aimed at curbing the perceived excesses of Hearst's *Journal*. The legislation sought to prohibit publication of portraits and cartoons without the subjects' prior consent, and called for penalties of $1,000 in fines and sentences of up to one year in prison.[206] The measure was sponsored by the state senate's mirthless president *pro tempore*, Timothy E. Ellsworth, an obscure Republican legislator from Lockport, who gained a reputation for introducing bills that attracted little notice[207]—and for "never having smiled in public."[208] It was widely believed that the drab and uninspiring Ellsworth was cynically doing the bidding of Platt, the state's Republican leader.[209] It even was speculated that Dana's *Sun* had quietly encouraged Platt to press ahead with what came to be called the Ellsworth Anti-Cartoon Bill.[210] The measure eventually won the backing of the state Senate[211] before dying without a vote in the lower house.[212]

The Ellsworth Bill was a heavy-handed response to the expanding use of illustrations and caricatures—and an attempt to exert control over an increasingly popular, if controversial[213] feature of American newspapers. There was little doubt that the measure was aimed at the *Journal*, which rightly claimed to have "made more extensive use of pictorial journalism than any other" newspaper.[214] The measure took inspiration[215] in the *Journal*'s irreverence, particularly a gossipy article published in its Sunday supplement in early October 1896. The article fairly oozed with insouciance in discussing the pregnancies of the wives of some of the world's wealthiest men. The *Journal* published the likenesses of several of the women, including the Duchess of Marlborough and the Countess Castellane. "This is to be the biggest Winter for big babies in the history of the United States," the *Journal* declared. "Eight babies, all told, literally worth ten billion times their weight in gold!"[216] Such an article these days would be hardly shocking, not with the publicity and scrutiny routinely given to celebrities and the well-to-do. But genteel society in the late 1890s usually was distanced and the *Journal*'s article was seen as indecent, intrusive, and far outside the bounds of good taste.

The Ellsworth Bill did attract one unlikely ally—Pulitzer's *World*, which endorsed the measure as a much-needed vehicle for curbing the wayward and irresponsible newspapers. While conceding the measure's dubious constitutionality, the *World* declared that "certain newspapers have carried this abuse of the art of illustrating news to a point which justifies legal interference. ... The World is not only willing but anxious to do its share in ridding respectable journalism of this evil."[217] It was a thoroughly transparent, disingenuous argument, allowing the *World* to characterize itself smugly as a newspaper beyond reproach while conveniently hammering at the *Journal*, its keenest rival.

Dana's *Sun*, which largely eschewed cartoons and other illustrations, energetically backed the Ellsworth Bill as "a wholesome, enlightened, and proper measure."[218] The *Sun* justified the measure's severe restrictions by stating:

> No one can now be summoned into public view without the certainty of having not merely his portrait flaunted to the rabble, but of having the same subjected to every conceivable distortion and deformity. No more outrageous assault upon the privacy of a citizen can be devised than is implied in these infamous publications. Their purpose and effect is to hold him up to ridicule by the most vulgar and offensive expedients; to prejudice him permanently in the eyes of the community at large, and to wound with undisguised brutality the sensibilities of his family. If there ever was an evil that called for whole restraint by law, it is surely this.[219]

Unlike the *World* and the *Sun,* most New York newspapers condemned the Ellsworth Bill as legislative overreach, as a shield for political bosses, and as a disconcerting assault on press freedom.[220] To the *Times* it was "an ill-contrived sort of trip-hammer for crushing a loathsome but rather puny reptile, which it might miss after all while smashing a lot of harmless if not useful things that might fall in its way."[221] The *Herald* said "the measure would tend to check the development of the graphic arts [and] would deprive the public of one of the most attractive and innocent features they enjoy in legitimate and cleanly newspapers."[222]

The Journalist likened the Ellsworth Bill to "the man who burned down his house in order to get rid of a flea in his bedroom." But it said that illustrations often were published in newspapers "not because they look like anybody, but because, in the minds of the editors, they ornament the papers."[223] *Fourth Estate* assailed the Ellsworth Bill as "damfoolmania,"[224] a "vicious species of class legislation,"[225] and declared it "certainly not wise for cap-and-bell legislators to try to correct the follies of even the most foolish of enterprising newspapers."[226] For its part, the *Journal* claimed that its daily circulation of 500,000 stood as persuasive evidence that readers wanted illustrations with their news —and thus wanted nothing akin to the restrictions promised by the Ellsworth Bill.[227]

Though crude and blunt, the Ellsworth Bill and the boycott against the yellow press represented an anxious backlash—rear-guard actions that sought to calm the ferment and channel or regulate it in familiar ways. The failure of the Ellsworth Bill and of the boycott served to underscore the power of the forces reshaping the *fin-de-siècle* press, forces that promised to make American journalism more graphically vivid, more searching, and even more impertinent.

The ferment roiling American journalism was at once stimulating and bewildering. It reflected the broader sentiment of the late 1890s of *épater le bourgeois*,[228] of shocking or shaking up established values. In 1897, no news organization was more inclined to challenge and shake up established norms than the *New York Journal* with its "journalism of action." As suggested by the agenda of the 1897 publishers association meeting, however, the implications of the ferment in journalism were not well understood or well articulated at the time. In its year-end review, *Fourth Estate* identified the triumph of the Associated Press and the bankruptcy of the United Press as the most significant events in American journalism in 1897.[229] The *Fourth Estate*'s year-in-review had little if anything to say about the "journalism of action," or "All the News That's Fit to Print," or "Is There A Santa Claus?" That is scarcely surprising, given that significance is usually identified, clarified, and best understood only with the passage of time.[230] The *Journalist* probably came closest to grasping the importance of the transformations afoot in 1897. "Be the causes what they may," The *Journalist* said, the "methods of journalism are at present changing. Whether they have yet reached the limit of that change … is a question no man can answer."[231]

There is little doubt that 1897 was an exceptional year in American journalism—a critical moment of experimentation and transition that helped reshape the profession and define its modern contours. No other year, arguably, has produced more memorable and singularly important moments than 1897. This study is guided not only by a recognition that 1897 was exceptional and consequential, but that it embraced moments when broader evolutionary forces combined to produce breakthroughs of enduring significance, as well as moments of extraordinary individual accomplishment. This work seeks to make more coherent and understandable this defining moment in American journalism and pursues a methodology never previously utilized in media history. As such, this study has the decided merit of offering a fresh perspective and a fresh assessment about a pivotal time in American journalism.

An orthographic note is in order here. Excerpts of articles, editorials, and correspondence are presented in this study as they appeared in the original version—a decision that accounts for the occasional appearance of such constructions as "half-tone," "Klondyke," "kodak," and "to-day." Newspapers in the 1890s generally did not italicize the names of periodicals, which is why the Roman version of those names is used in direct quotations.

This study is buttressed by, and built around, extensive archival research including the manuscript collections of journalists, political leaders, and diplomats, kept at the Library of Congress in Washington, D.C., Columbia University, Cornell University, Syracuse University, the University of Virginia, the Missouri Historical Society, the Cuban National Archives in Havana, and the Spanish archives in Madrid. The study also draws upon the contents of numerous period newspapers, including the *New York Journal, New York World, New York Times, New York Commercial Advertiser, New York Sun, New York Herald, New York Tribune, New York Evening Post, New York Press, Brooklyn Daily Eagle, Chicago Tribune, Chicago Times-Herald, Boston Globe, Boston Post, Philadelphia Inquirer, Philadelphia Times, Philadelphia Press, Philadelphia Daily Item, Richmond Times, San Francisco Examiner, Washington Post,* and *Washington Evening Star.* Other important primary sources include trade journals such as *Fourth Estate* and *The Journalist* as well as period publications including *Atlantic Monthly, Harper's Weekly, The Independent, Literary Digest, Public Opinion, Self Culture,* and *Scribner's Magazine.*

As those and other sources make abundantly clear, the pivotal developments in American journalism in 1897 took place in the context of broader upheaval and innovation. Profound change was stirring in American life in 1897, a crowded and remarkable year when heavier-than-air flight was declared accomplished, when the horseless carriage had "apparently come to stay,"[232] when the last great international gold rush unfolded, and when the United States reached the threshold of emerging as a global power. The crowded year of 1897 is the subject of the first chapter, which will serve as context for the chapters beyond.

1

1897

America at an Hour of Transition

To appreciate the remoteness of the 1890s, one needs only to flip through the 1897 Sears, Roebuck Catalogue, which was reissued several years ago as a novelty item. The pages of the 1897 volume abound with illustrations of artifacts alien to the twenty-first century—merchandise such as dog-powered cream separators, Queen Victoria perfumes, coal-burning laundry stoves, abdominal corsets, arsenic complexion wafers, horse-drawn carriages, and Pink Pills for Pale People.

Eighteen-ninety-seven indeed was a time far different from our own. But in considering the year from perspectives beyond the artifacts, some striking similarities across time emerge. For example, Americans in 1897 reproved themselves in ways that would be familiar today—for having grown reckless, for tolerating moral decay,[1] for saving too little,[2] for eating too much meat,[3] for failing to appreciate their spouses,[4] for lagging in matters of public health,[5] for assuming too readily the problems of the world,[6] and for indulging a taste for sensationalism in the news media.[7]

More significantly, 1897 offered a first glimpse of the unfolding modern age. The automobile became conspicuous if not quite yet commonplace in major U.S. cities in 1897. E. S. Martin, a columnist for *Harper's Weekly*, wrote in March 1897 that the automobile in New York

Figure 1.1 The late 1890s were hardly quaint and unhurried times in urban America. As this 1897 Philadelphia street scene suggests, trolley cars, horse-drawn carriages, and wary pedestrians all vied for space in the crowded city center. At that time, the automobile was becoming more conspicuous in U.S. cities. (Library of Congress.)

was "a rare sight still, and people pay attention when it passes. Pedestrians stop and gawk at it. Streetcar passengers rise and look out of the windows. No one hesitates to show interest."[8] By years' end, the *New York Tribune* declared, the "horseless carriage has apparently come to stay."[9] The implications of the automobile's emergence were not lost on perceptive observers. The *New York Times* said "sooner or later," automobiles "will deplace the fashionable carriage of the present hour, and the horse will cease to be an important factor in the transportation of human beings for pleasure or business."[10] The *Los Angeles Times* was even more sanguine. "The era of horseless carriages is obviously not far distant," the *Times* said in the autumn of 1897. "And with it will come the era of good roads, a higher civilization, and the more general distribution of the comforts, conveniences and luxuries of life."[11]

In 1897, Samuel P. Langley, the director of the Smithsonian Institution, reported on the successful test flights of his unmanned, steam-powered "aerodrome," a double-winged flying machine that rather

Figure 1.2 The automobile, or "horseless carriage," became increasingly conspicuous in major U.S. cities in 1897. Its emergence inspired the antics of the "Yellow Kid" (center, atop the automobile's roof) and his friends in this cartoon panel drawn by R. F. Outcault for the *New York Journal*. Outcault's "Yellow Kid" was a wildly popular character who, indirectly, gave rise to the epithet "yellow journalism." (Library of Congress.)

resembled an oversized and ungainly dragonfly. "Aerial navigation at last," the *New York Journal* exclaimed in an editorial saluting Langley's accomplishments.[12] The *New York World* rhapsodized in 1897 about the young Italian inventor, Guglielmo Marconi, and his successful demonstrations in London of wireless telegraphy. "A boy of 23 years old appears to have revolutionized telegraphy," the *World* declared. "What he does is to transmit telegraphic messages from sender to receiver without wires, using air as the medium of passage."[13]

Then as now, Americans were enthralled by the promise and the gadgetry of new technologies. "The Americans have far more mechanical devices, and make more use of them, than any other people," Price Collier wrote in his breezy and anonymously published 1897 work, *America and the Americans: From A French Point of View.* He was referring to devices such as the telegraph, typewriter, and the telephone. Although it had been invented in 1876, the telephone's popularity and intrusiveness had become striking by 1897, prompting complaints not unlike those associated with cellular phones in the early twenty-first century. The *New York Tribune* in 1897 lamented the spread of "telephone mania," an affliction the newspaper ranked high "among the latest negative results of modern inventions." The symptoms of "telephone mania," according to the *Tribune*, included "senseless chatter," "constant 'helloing'" and "a desire to talk to people at distant points about all sorts of things at all hours of the day or night"[14]—irritants all that can be ascribed to cell phones.

It is tempting nowadays to think of the late 1890s as a quaint and unhurried time: It *must* have been so, before airplanes, television, air conditioning, the Internet, and cellular phones. But quaint and unhurried was scarcely how Americans of 1897 regarded their lives. They were active, engaged, and altogether too short on leisure time. Theirs was a "hustling, high-tension age."[15] The pace of urban journalism was said to have been so intense that it made "men old at forty."[16] The ceaseless noise, the "continual clatter" of robust big-city life was suspected to be a life-shortening hazard.[17] The idiom, "busy modern public," was much *en vogue*. No other phrase, said the *New York Tribune*, was invoked more often "in describing present-day conditions of social existence. No other [phrase] is as often used as an apology for social and even individual shortcomings."[18]

The consequences of a busy society often were to be lamented, the *Tribune* said in a critique that would have meaning today. "Men do not observe the niceties of deportment toward women and toward each other, because they are too busy," the newspaper said. "They are slangy or careless in their speech and letter writing, because they are too busy … They want nothing but trashy variety shows at the theatres, because they are so busy all day that they cannot endure the labor of witnessing a serious performance at night. They must have all their information put in the briefest and most superficial form, because they are too busy for long and thorough reading." In literature, science, and "even religion," the *Tribune* added, "everything must be 'summarized,' which means made superficial and probably inaccurate. Men are too busy to be accurate. Their minds and souls must be fed, as are their bodies, at the quick-lunch counter."[19]

Foreign visitors noted this phenomenon, too. Collier in his *America and the Americans* identified the "peculiar American trait of itching to be busy."[20] In America in 1897, he wrote, it was "symbolic of success to 'have no time!'"[21] It was fashionable "to be busy," he wrote, fashionable "to be overwhelmed with engagements, to be pressed for time, to be driven to death, in short, by one's terrible social, professional, or business responsibilities. In some cases it is true, but true because the sufferers are incompetent to control their own affairs; but in the great majority of instances it is a huge joke or a seriously assumed affectation."

Being unrelievedly busy in 1897 signaled something far more profound than an affectation or mismanagement of one's personal calendar. There was meaning and virtue in being active, engaged, busy. The busy Americans of 1897 projected a mood of expectation, a sense that their *fin-de-siècle* days represented an exceptional hour of transition. They were at the cusp of what would be called the American century. If vaguely, American newspapers sensed that powerful transformations were afoot. In a retrospective published on New Year's Eve 1897, the *New York Tribune* said the world was "probably on the threshold of more stirring scenes and more important changes than have occurred in the year now closing."[22] Within months, the *Tribune's* prophecy was proved correct, as America "irrevocably entered the world"[23] in projecting its military power to humble the decaying Spanish empire in the Caribbean and the Philippines.

The war with Spain—fought principally to resolve a deepening humanitarian crisis in Cuba—lasted 114 days. When it ended, U.S. forces claimed or controlled territories beyond the North American mainland. The war's outcome confirmed America as a global power, a role and status from which the country would never fully retreat. That war would bring America an empire was unimaginable at the end of 1897. Indeed, few people then expected to go to war with Spain over Cuba.

But by year's end, the sense that change was afoot was palpable and conspicuous. The first section of America's first subway—running a little more than a mile beneath Tremont Street in the heart of Boston—was opened, without notable ceremony,[24] on September 1, 1897. The first trolley car to enter the subterranean tunnel at Boylston Street carried more than one hundred eager passengers who, the *Boston Globe* reported, "yelled themselves to the verge of apoplexy," cheering the inaugural, four-minute run.[25] As many as 200,000 passengers were said to have ridden the subway on its first day of business[26] and the subway soon brought relief to the snarled and congested streets of Boston's city center.[27] That such a "conservative an American town" as Boston was the first city in America to build and operate a subway prompted no small amount of commentary. This, the *New York Times* said, "is viewed as remarkable."[28]

Two months later in Washington, D.C., the ornate Library of Congress was opened—a grand and unmistakable expression of America's growing self-assuredness. "In construction, in accommodations, in suitability to intended uses, and in artistic luxury of decoration," the *Philadelphia Telegraph* declared in 1897, "there is no building that will compare with it in this country and very few in any other country."[29] It was, and remains, an awe-inspiring edifice.

Figure 1.3 The ornate Library of Congress building was opened on Capitol Hill in Washington in November 1897. It was a grand and unambiguous expression of America's growing self-assuredness. The rotunda of the library's main reading room is perhaps its single most spectacular feature. (From *Scribner's*.)

"SOMETHING OUT OF THE COMMON"

No expression better captured the energy, the exuberance, and even the folly of 1897 than "doing something out of the common." The phrase predated 1897, having been coined a few years earlier by Ambrose G. Bierce, a columnist for William Randolph Hearst's *San Francisco Examiner*. "The *fin de siecle* spirit," Bierce wrote in the *Examiner*, "is fairly expressible by an oath to make the most of a vanishing opportunity by doing something out of the common."[30] For Bierce, a prickly, acerbic commentator, "doing something out of the common" was offered not in a spirit of hopefulness or generosity but as a dark assessment of the upheavals during the first half of the 1890s. "Nearly everywhere," Bierce wrote, "we observe this [*fin-de-siècle*] spirit translating itself into acts and phenomena. … In politics it has overspread the earth with anarchism, socialism, communism, woman suffrage and actual antagonism between the sexes. ... In literature it has given us realism, in art impressionism, and in both as much else that is false and extravagant as it is possible to name."[31] He added, "Everywhere is a wild welter of action and thought, a cutting loose from all that is conservative and restraining, a 'carnival of crime,' a reign of unreason."[32]

Bierce's gloomy characterizations were rooted, at least in part, in the Panic of 1893, a severe economic recession that struck America like no other previous downturn. By the end of 1893, more than 600 banks had failed and more than thirty iron and steel companies had declared bankruptcy.[33] Twenty-five percent of the country's railroads were insolvent,[34] including all the large systems in the South Atlantic seaboard.[35] Miners in bituminous coalfields from western Pennsylvania to Illinois went on strike in the spring of 1894, in a failed attempt to boost, or in some cases, restore their pay scales.[36] An Ohio businessman named Jacob Coxey organized a march on Washington in 1894 to prod the federal government to ease the recession's harsh effects. Soon after arriving at the capital Coxey was arrested and his followers dispersed.

Unemployment topped 18 percent in 1894, and had eased only to 14.5 percent by 1897, when economic recovery, fueled by demand abroad for America's agricultural products, began to take hold. Average annual earnings dropped by nearly 7 percent during the recession, from $495 in 1892 to $462 in 1897. Hard economic times framed the bitterly contested presidential election of 1896, which was fought largely over the question of retaining a gold-backed monetary standard or adopting an inflationary policy of coining gold and silver at a ratio of 16-to-1. The Republicans, who favored the gold standard, swept to victory and their candidate, William McKinley of Ohio, became president in March 1897. McKinley's inauguration ushered in a thirty-six-year interregnum of Republican dominance in American political life, a reign interrupted only by Woodrow Wilson's electoral victories in 1912 and 1916.

By the end of 1897, a sense of renewed vigor and vitality were coursing through the American economy. What the *New York Herald* called "the Slough of Despondency"[37] was easing, business failures were declining, and farm exports were expanding.[38] By year's end, many newspapers had placed new orders for presses and other machinery, which, according to the trade journal *Fourth Estate*, represented "the strongest kind of evidence that prosperity has come."[39] The *St. Paul Pioneer Press* said in a year-end review: "In contrast with the four preceding years, 1897 was as the genial spring which follows the long,

Figure 1.4 A bicycling craze swept America in the mid-and late-1890s, following a series of design improvements that made the wheel a safe and enjoyable form of recreational exercise. "The bicycle has coaxed us all out of doors," the *New York Herald* said in 1897. Both men and women took eagerly to cycling, the benefits of which included the paving of many miles of streets and roadways across the country. (Library of Congress.)

cold, dead winter, and sets aflow the currents of a new life in stream and tree and plant."[40]

As times turned for the better, Bierce's characterization took on fresh meaning. The turn of phrase—"doing something out of the common"—can be seen as a defining metaphor for 1897. They may not have used the exact words, but Americans in 1897 believed quite thoroughly they were participating in "something out of the common." That impulse perhaps found keenest expression in the frenzy of the Klondike gold rush. Thousands of Americans, many of them ill-prepared for the rigors that awaited them, set off for the Klondike goldfields of Canada's subarctic Yukon Territory. It was North America's last great, frenzied gold rush and, for a time in late summer 1897, Klondike fever set "the whole world agog."[41] The sense of "doing something out of the common" was apparent in more popular ways. The streets of American cities teamed in 1897 with bicyclists enjoying the freedom of movement offered by the wheel. It was the first and only time a generation of Americans was introduced to the bicycle as adults,[42] and the adults took to it enthusiastically.

There were more extreme and imprudent manifestations of "doing something out of the common" in 1897, such as the much-anticipated

Figure 1.5 New York's high society indulged in the lavish and controversial Bradley Martin costume ball in February 1897. As many as 800 guests, all richly attired in costumes of the sixteenth, seventeenth, or eighteenth centuries, attended the dazzling affair at the Waldorf Hotel. The ball was condemned by some clergymen and newspapers as an ill-timed extravagance, given that the country was still recovering from a severe recession that began in 1893. (Library of Congress.)

expedition of Solomon A. Andrée. He was a Swede who attempted to fly a huge hydrogen balloon over the North Pole.[43] Andrée and his two traveling companions set off in July 1897 from a base on Dane Island in Norway's remote Spitzbergen group—and never came close to their objective. Their balloon, christened the *Eagle*, rose sluggishly on lift-off and large sections of the draglines, which were to help guide the balloon, were torn away.[44] After its inauspicious launch, the balloon performed erratically during its sixty-five hours aloft and finally came down on an ice floe far from the pole. According to their diary entries and other notes, Andrée and his companions spent the next three months in a desperate effort to cross the Arctic pack ice and reach an outpost of civilization on Franz Joseph Land. Their remains were discovered thirty-three years later at their last camp on uninhabited White Island.[45]

High society in New York City indulged extravagantly in the impulse to do "something out of the common" at the famous Bradley Martin costume ball in February 1897. As many as eight hundred guests—all attired in rich and colorful costumes evoking characters from the sixteenth, seventeenth, or eighteenth centuries—attended the dazzling affair at the Waldorf Hotel. "The eye scarcely knew where to look or what to study," a *New York Times* reporter said of the lavishly decorated grand ballroom, "it was such a bewildering maze of gorgeous dames and gentlemen on the floor, such a flood of light from the ceiling, paneled in terra cotta and gold, and such an entrancing picture of garlands that hung everywhere in rich festoons. The first impression on entering the room was that some fairy god-mother, in a dream, had revived the glories of the past for one's special enjoyment."[46] At least a dozen guests were dressed as Marie Antoinette. Others came as Cardinal Richelieu, Henry of Navarre, Catherine the Great of Russia, the Marquis de Lafayette, and as court ladies in the time of Charles VI.[47] The costume of the hostess, Mrs. Bradley Martin, was reportedly "a surprise to many of her guests." She dressed in velvet and satin as Mary Queen of Scots.[48]

Newspapers described the Bradley Martin ball as "the crowning glory of the social life of New York of this century,"[49] but the times were still too harsh for many people to countenance such staggering and unabashed displays of wealth. Among the critics was the Rev. William S. Rainsford, the rector of St. George Protestant Episcopal Church in New York, who urged socialites to boycott the ball, saying it served only to "draw attention to the widening chasm between" the rich and poor.[50] The *New York World* deplored the "ill-timed ostentation and extravagance of the ball"[51] and invited newspaper editors in the American heartland to heap scorn on the whole affair. The editor of the *Wichita Beacon* cabled the *World* to say the ball suggested that "we are fast drifting towards a moneyed aristocracy in this country." But not all editors were so alarmed. The editor of the *Commercial Tribune* in Cincinnati told the *World* the event attracted little comment or notice in his city, and the editor of the *Detroit Free Press* pointed out that "every cent" spent on the ball "went to the employment of labor in some form, and was in that way a benefit to the working people."[52]

The hostess had spent months planning the masked ball, but her timing was hardly impeccable. Less than two weeks before the ball, New York City and much of the country was locked in a severe cold snap that dropped temperatures to near or below zero for a few bitter days.[53] As the temperatures fell, poor people suffered severely. "Hundreds of families are without fuel to warm the freezing air that blows freely through the flimsy walls of their poor houses," said the *Washington Evening Star*. "Many of them are without food or the money to buy it."[54] Pitiable stories circulated as the cold spell deepened. In Brooklyn, a baker told a reporter about the thinly clad little girl who came to his shop on an errand for her mother. The girl handed the baker an envelope and said, "Please, sir, ma says won't you give me a loaf for that?" In the envelope the baker found a 2 cent stamp. He filled a basket with loaves of bread and told his assistant to carry it to the little girl's home.[55]

Scores of fires were reported in Chicago, where temperatures plunged well below zero.[56] Many fires were the result of stoves and furnaces run "at full blast, without regard for the danger of overheating flues and setting fire to the encasing woodwork," the *Evening Star* reported. "In many cases, too, the careless use of heat for thawing out frozen water pipes resulted in conflagrations."[57] The deep freeze forced unemployed and homeless men to take refuge at Chicago's police stations. The cells were "packed full of lodgers, lying on the floor just as close as they could be squeezed," E. S. Martin wrote in his column in *Harper's Weekly*. "Most of these vagrants are said to be decent men out of work."[58]

Eighteen-ninety-seven had its share of weather that was certainly "out of the common." Early June, for example, brought exceptionally cool weather to New York and Washington,[59] ground-covering snow to northern New Jersey, and killing frosts in the upper Midwest.[60] The prolonged chill of late spring baffled weather forecasters. Willis L. Moore, the chief of the U.S. Weather Bureau, told the *New York Journal*: "In the present state of meteorological science we do not know the cause of such extremely long, cool spells as is now undergoing. ... Not even a satisfactory theory can be formulated, although scientific weather forecasting is now a quarter of a century old."[61] About a month later, a heat wave staggered the Midwest, causing thirty-five deaths in Chicago,[62] and thirty-six in Cincinnati.[63] Heat-stricken work horses died by the score in Chicago, many of them overcome as they stood in their stalls.[64]

The *Chicago Tribune* reported that at least 200,000 "heat-tortured" Chicagoans[65] took to the city's parks in search of a small measure of relief as temperatures approached 100 degrees. "Young and old alike seem to have but one desire," the *Tribune* said, "and that was to get into a shady place and keep as quiet as possible. Nearly every face bore evidence of the terrible strain which the excessive heat is bringing upon nerve and heart, and the expression upon the faces of some of the poorer class of people was absolutely ghastly."[66]

NEW JOURNALISM, NEW WOMAN

Doing "something out of the common" both acknowledged and confirmed the sense of novelty that broadly characterized the 1890s. In *fin-de-siècle* nomenclature, the adjective "new" was widely, generously, and even excessively applied. But "new" was more than a conceit. It imbued the decade's thinking, styles, experiments, and morals.[67] The 1890s gave rise to *l'Art Nouveau*, the New Fiction, the New Drama, the New Humor, the New Realism, the New Hedonism, the New Woman, and the New Journalism, among other variations.[68] "New" was even applied redundantly—as in "New Inventions."[69]

"New Journalism" was coined in Britain during the mid-1880s but not applied to the American press until the mid-1890s. William Randolph Hearst embraced the term to distinguish his activist style of journalism from the stodgy, standoffish approach of his competitors. "The new journalism gives brains and money to the task of getting the news always and everywhere," Hearst's *New York Journal* declared. "The old journalism expends neither. ... The new journalism does things; the old journalism stands around and objects."[70]

No aspect of novelty in the 1890s attracted more comment than the phenomenon of the "New Woman." She was politely assertive, independent-minded, and increasingly educated. In 1897, 4,600 women received undergraduate degrees, nearly twice as many as in 1887. The "new woman" was also increasingly visible in the American workplace. U.S. census data released in 1897 showed the number of women in the workforce had more than doubled, to 3.9 million in 1890 from 1.8 million in 1870.[71] Commenting on those data, the *New York Sun* declared that the country's nearly "4,000,000 women breadwinners" deserved to be "congratulated on the headway they have made on the road to independence; and may their efforts be crowned with even greater success by the close of the present century."[72] Veteran activists such as Susan B. Anthony similarly cheered the progress of American women. In an article for the reform-minded *Arena* magazine in 1897, Anthony reviewed the progress of the previous fifty years, and stated:

> The close of this nineteenth century finds every trade, vocation, and profession open to women, and every opportunity at their command for preparing themselves to follow these occupations.

The girls as well as the boys of a family now fit themselves for such careers as their tastes and abilities permit. A vast amount of household drudgery that once monopolized the whole time and strengths of the mother and daughters, has been taken outside and turned over to machinery in vast establishments. A money value is placed upon the labor of women. The ban of social ostracism has been largely removed from the woman wage-earner. She who can make for herself a place of distinction in any line of work receives commendation rather than condemnation. Woman is no longer compelled to marry for support, but may herself make her own home and earn her own financial independence.[73]

A more melancholy measure of independent-mindedness was the prevalence of divorce in *fin-de-siècle* America. In 1897, divorce was said to be "rampant in the United States,"[74] although specific data to support such claims were elusive. Nonetheless, as many as 80 percent of divorce proceedings then were initiated by women, typically for cruelty, infidelity, intemperance, failure to provide, and desertion.[75] Rather than being "divorce-mad," women were understood to "bear their burdens as long as they can, consistently with self-respect. But when they do act [and seek a divorce,] it is with the uncompromising directness of their race."[76] The stigma seemed to be lifting for women who never married. The *Sun* in 1897 dismissed as *passé* the image of the pathetic "old maid," fettered to and dependent upon the generosity of her relatives. She had been "emancipated," the *Sun* said, replaced by the "woman bachelor," who was keen to demonstrate a sense of "stern purpose in her life and the will to show the world how well she can get along without certain things long believed indispensable to [a woman's] nature."[77] While the *Sun*'s sweeping assertions surely were infused with hyperbole, they also carried a ring of veracity, given that women of the 1890s were pursuing careers and college degrees. But public life remained largely off limits to American women. Only four states in 1897 had granted women universal suffrage: Colorado, Idaho, Utah, and Wyoming.

"If women could make the laws or elect those who make them," Anthony wrote in 1897, "they would be in the position of sovereigns instead of subjects. Were they the political peers of man they could command instead of having to beg, petition, and pray. Can it be possible it is for this reason that men have been so determined in their opposition to grant to women [political] power?"[78] But even the political kingdom was slowly beginning to open to women, Anthony said,[79] and 1897 offered few more striking examples of female political agitation than the efforts of New Hampshire's lawyer-activist Marilla M. Ricker. Ricker had tried to vote as early 1870, but was kept from doing so by Democratic poll watchers.[80] She had been admitted to practice law in Washington, D.C., in 1882 and in New Hampshire in 1890. In 1897, Ricker declared her intention to run for the congressional seat occupied by fellow Republican Cyrus A. Sulloway, saying, "Why should not women go to Congress? There is no valid reason why they should not. Mark you, the time is not far distant when it will not be possible for men to prevent their going as representatives of the people."[81] In the end, Ricker never reached Congress. She lived until 1920, the year when female suffrage became a reality in the United States.

Political agitation aside, 1897 offered no more striking symbol of the push for gender equality than the bicycle. What once was dismissed as a dangerous toy[82] had become wildly popular by 1897. "Everyone rides now," Ellen Maury Slayden, the wife of a Texas congressman, wrote in her journal in 1897. The streets of Washington, D.C., "swarm with cyclists, and they are especially pretty at night when clubs, sometimes of hundreds, go out for a spin. There is no sound but the faint chatter of the riders, and each wheel carrying a light, they look like a parade of will-o'-the-wisps. All the big shops, theaters and churches have rows of stalls where you can stable and lock your wheel while you go about your business or pleasure."[83] A series of design improvements in the 1880s and early 1890s—notably wheels of equal size; sturdy, diamond-shaped framing, and shock-absorbing pneumatic tires[84]—as well as softening prices for top-of-the-line models[85] had rendered the bicycle widely accessible. For the men and women of the mid- and late-1890s, the wheel certainly represented "something out of the common"—notably the unprecedented thrill of the freedom of individual movement at controlled speeds.[86] And women took readily to the wheel, and "demonstrated by skill and perseverance that the exercise [from cycling] is every bit as good for them as it is for their brothers," according to the *New York Sun*.[87]

The bicycle nowadays is so unremarkable and commonplace that it is almost impossible to understand the marvel that cycling conjured up in the mid- and late-1890s. The wheel was seen as possessing "magic powers,"[88] as having "annihilated distance,"[89] as occupying a singular place among the inventions and improvements of the late nineteenth century. The 1890s, declared the *New York Tribune*, were truly, "The Age of Wheeling." The *Tribune* said:

Among all our modern improvements there are few that would have seemed more marvelous to the people of a generation or two ago than the bicycle. There are few if any that are effecting so important a social revolution. ... The steamship and railroad and telegraph and electric light are merely doing what used to be done by the sailing ship and stagecoach and mails and oil lamp. They are doing them far better, no doubt; but they are, after all, nothing but improvements upon those older and simpler things. But there was nothing that ever undertook to do what the bicycle is doing. There has been nothing upon which it is merely an improvement. More than almost anything else in this age it is a new thing, doing new work, creating new departments of human industry and human pleasure, and bringing into the economy of the social organization a new factor.[90]

The salutary effects of the wheel were many. Its popularity led to paving and improving of roads and pathways across America.[91] "Fortunately, the bicycle is invading the country districts," the *Philadelphia Item* observed, "and every one sold makes a new advocate of good roads."[92] Invigorating exercise was another decided benefit. "The bicycle has coaxed us all out of doors," said the *New York Herald*. "This glorious exercise, followed by a glorious appetite three times a day and sound sleep at night is making us all over again."[93] The wheel was of great value to businesses, including newspapers. *Fourth Estate* noted in 1895 how "in cases of emergency a reporter could mount his wheel and reach a distant part of the city in less time than would be consumed in going by street car or even with horse and carriage. ... During the past year many newspapers have purchased bicycles as part of the necessary equipment of the force, and in some cases clubs have been formed among the employes of newspaper offices."[94]

Not everyone was thrilled by the bicycle's popularity. Some clerics disapproved of Sunday bicycling, except as a means of traveling to church. "It is very wise for churches to make provision for the care of bicycles, which people ride to church," said the Reverend H. P. Faunce of the Fifth Avenue Baptist Church in New York. "But if a member of a church is asked to join a party of bicycle riders on Sunday, he should decline, just as he would decline ... to indulge in any other form of sport, and it is for the interest of the community not to encourage sports and pasttimes on the Sabbath."[95] The popularity of the wheel prompted a good deal of scapegoating. The bicycle was a suspected culprit in a falloff in beer consumption in Midwestern states[96] and in the drop in sales of Sunday newspapers in Boston.[97] Carriage-makers, jewelers, and furniture dealers were "particularly vociferous" in complaining about business lost to cycling's popularity, E. S. Martin wrote in his *Harper's Weekly* column.[98] The wheel also was suspected as depressing prices for horses—and for the oats they ate.[99]

Perhaps inevitably, bicycling gave rise in 1897 to what nowadays would be considered extreme sport. The six-day marathon race at Madison Square Garden in New York was an example. Charles Miller of Chicago pedaled more than 2,000 miles around and around the arena's track to win the contest, which the *New York Journal* criticized as "ruinous to the proper use of the wheel"[100] and the *New York Herald* deplored as an exhibition "of inhumanity under the name of 'sport.'"[101] Far more popular were "century runs"—day trips in which groups of cyclists would cover one hundred miles.[102] By the spring of 1897, century runs had become so common as to be unremarkable, according to the *Philadelphia Item*.[103] Double centuries, even triple centuries—outings of two and three hundred miles—were not unheard of, and journalists sometimes waxed vivid in reporting these long-distance excursions. The *New York Herald*, for example, described the start of a midsummer double century run this way: "Out under the blistering, broiling sun, with the hot dust of the hot roads burning in their eyes and choking in their throats, a company of riders on scorching wheels scurried away from the metropolis on Saturday. Little they minded the heat or dust. There were both wheelmen and wheelwomen in the company, and the latter were quite as eager as the former."[104]

Female cyclists often were eager participants in these extended outings. Mrs. A. E. Rinehart of Denver was a particularly remarkable "century rider." She took up cycling only in mid-1895. In 1896, Rinehart completed 116 century runs, proving "that wheelwomen have great endurance, which the men say they have not," the *New York Sun* said.[105] But the *Herald* worried that century runs were too taxing for women, insisting "there is probably nothing that will sooner and more utterly wreck a woman's constitution than a bicycle if she persists in long distance riding." Nothing, the *Herald* said, "can be worse for them than these century runs. And as for the greater distance contests, they are simply invitations to suicide—an overtaxing of physical strength that no woman can long withstand."[106] Such admonitions were little heeded, though.[107] As Richard Harmond has noted, female cyclists of the 1890s "doffed their confining whalebone corsets, and donned shorter dresses, split skirts and even bloomers" and pursued the thrilling new pastime. "By doing so," Harmond wrote, they "conquered their inhibitions, improved their health, and enlarged their sense of physical freedom."[108]

The mobility and popularity of the bicycle anticipated and quite literally paved the way for the automobile, which decisively entered the public consciousness in 1897.[109] The "extensive adoption" of the automobile was on the way.[110] "If such vehicles are or can be made in such a manner that they will do their work with certainty and economy, and can be cared for and handled by an ordinarily intelligent man, there can be little doubt of their extensive adoption for business and pleasure, especially in cities," the *New York Sun* said, adding: "They can be stabled in less than half the room needed for horses and in places where horses could not be kept."[111]

Various models and prototypes of the "horseless carriage"—also known variously as the "automotive," the "motor carriage," and the "new mechanical wagon"—made inaugural appearances on American streets in 1897. On April 3, the *Washington Post* reported the appearance of the "first horseless carriage ever seen upon the streets in Washington." It was a prototypical delivery wagon that ran on compressed air. In its debut outing, the *Post* said, the vehicle covered ten miles over asphalt-paved streets, reached speeds of ten miles per hour, was followed nearly everywhere by bicyclists—and on the whole "caused more excitement than a circus."[112]

In late May 1897, the *Los Angeles Times* reported on the successful test drive of "the first horseless carriage seen in Los Angeles." It was a four-cylinder, gasoline-powered vehicle that the *Times* called a "motorcycle." But clearly it was a prototypical automobile[113] and it made its first trial run a little after 2 a.m. on May 30, 1897, a Sunday. That hour was chosen, the newspaper said, because "the inventor, J. Philip Erie, knew that if it were at any less unearthly hour the spectacle would attract a crowd which would interfere seriously with the program of affairs."[114] In the heart of a city that ultimately would be defined by the automobile, Erie's "gasoline carriage" trundled along, crossing streetcar tracks and innumerable potholes "without any trouble. ... The trial was a gratifying success in every way," the *Times* reported.[115] Fears that the new vehicle's gasoline engine would frighten horses proved groundless, the *Times* said. "A number of teams [of horses] were passed during the trial, but they showed not the slightest fear of the novel spectacle."[116]

That the automobile would panic horses was of no small concern in 1897. The commissioners of Washington, D.C., refused a deliveryman's request to operate a gasoline-powered "horseless wagon" on the district's streets because even brief experience with similar self-propelled vehicles had shown they could "cause serious danger by frightening horses."[117] Besides, the deliveryman's vehicle made "a puffing noise while running," which nervous horses might confuse with "a steam street roller," the *Washington Post* said.[118] But as 1897 unfolded, it became increasingly apparent that the horse was doomed.[119] At mid-year the *New York Sun* predicted that "the new craze" for horseless carriages would expand until the vehicles were "in common use in every part of the civilized world."[120] That diffusion was well underway, the *Sun* noted: "From France, the use of these new vehicles has spread into Germany ... and now England is full of interest for the horseless carriages, and New York is learning to use and like them."[121]

The certain passing of the horse and carriage gave rise to some melancholy reflection. "Sensitive and sentimental folk cannot view the pending change without conflicting emotions," the *New York Times* said. "There are reasons why the departure of the horse from the streets and park drives should be considered gratifying. But it must be confessed that he will take with him a kind of picturesqueness which the self-moving wagon will never supply." [122] Moreover, the *Times* said, "man loves the horse, and he is not likely ever to love the automobile."[123] The *Times* groused about the adoption of "automobile" into vernacular, deploring it as "a dreadful word," of which the French who coined it "ought to be ashamed."[124]

No less momentous than the emergence of automobiles in American cities were Samuel Langley's successful experiments in unmanned, steam-powered, heavier-than-air flight. Langley reported at length in 1897 on the test flights of his double-winged flying machine he called the aerodrome. "Langley's steam-bird"[125] was another name for the ungainly craft, which was launched by catapult from atop a houseboat on the Potomac River, south of Washington. The aerodrome had flown twice in May 1896, covering about a half a mile both times before touching down on the Potomac.[126] A later model had flown about three-quarters of a mile in November 1896.[127] Though unmanned and tentative, the flights of Langley's aerodromes were important, encouraging steps toward manned flight.[128] Alexander Graham Bell, the inventor of the telephone and one of Langley's few close friends, had witnessed the aerodrome's two maiden flights and reported to the French Academy "that no one who was present on this interesting occasion could have failed to recognize that the practicability of mechanical flight had been demonstrated."[129] Langley described his experiments in an article in *McClure's* magazine in June 1897, declaring: "This has been done: a 'flying machine,' so long a type for ridicule, has really flown; it has demonstrated its practicability in the only satisfactory way—by actually flying, and by doing this again and again, under conditions which leave no doubt."[130]

Langley also predicted that when perfected, the flying machine would "hasten ... the coming of the day when war shall cease," given what he thought would be the insurmountable "difficulties of defending a country against an attacking enemy in the air."[131] Hearst's *New York Journal* hailed Langley's account, declaring a bit prematurely that "Professor Langley has the distinction of having produced the first flying machine in the history of the world that has actually flown for more than a few seconds at a time. ... The man of science has shown the way; it remains for the man of commerce and industry to open up the aerial highway to the common service of mankind."[132] But aerial navigation had more than a few skeptics and doubters in 1897. E. S. Martin, the *Harper's Weekly* columnist, declared himself unconvinced and unimpressed. "It does not appear," Martin wrote, "... that as yet there is any ground for expecting to see within any definite period a flying-machine on which a man may cruise in the air."[133]

Langley's 1897 report in *McClure's* represented a rare moment of personal triumph in his work in heavier-than-air flight. If Langley is remembered at all, it is usually for a spectacular failure on December 8, 1903. Late in the afternoon that day, Langley attempted to a launch a manned, gasoline-powered aerodrome from the Potomac River houseboat. The frail craft began to fall apart as it took off. It thrust itself upward, hovered like a helicopter for a few moments, flipped over, and plunged into the icy river.[134] The flight was a disaster, another personal humiliation for Langley. A manned test flight had also failed in October 1903. This time, the pilot narrowly escaped death. He swam clear of the wreckage and was pulled from the frigid waters alive but almost unconscious.[135]

Newspaper critics heaped ridicule on Langley. The *Newark News* snidely suggested that a "little dynamite placed under Prof. Langley's machine and judiciously touched off at the proper moment might get more flying out of it than the launching apparatus hitherto used so disastrously."[136] The *Boston Herald* sneered: "How insignificant and inferior Prof. Langley must feel every time he sees a little English sparrow fly across his path."[137] And in an editorial that proved breathtaking for its short-sightedness, the *Chicago Tribune* asserted on December 10, 1903: "Even if a machine could be made to fly no one would wish to fly with it. Nature has fitted us with appliances for getting short distances through water, also with appliances for getting over the ground short and long distances, but no trace of a wing can be found or anything that indicates nature intended us to navigate the air. There is little possibility of that until we become angels."[138] Seven days later, the brothers

Orville and Wilbur Wright inaugurated manned flight at Kitty Hawk, North Carolina.

Langley's aerodrome experiments coincided with a growing fascination with aerial navigation, which in turn may have contributed to the spate of what today would be called mass UFO sightings. The spring of 1897 brought numerous reports of airships and mysterious lights in the skies over the Midwest. Hundreds of people[139] reportedly watched an airship "skylarking about by night" in the skies near Omaha.[140] Another report told of an airship blowing up near Kalamazoo, Michigan.[141] As a skeptical report in the *Chicago Tribune* pointed out, the airship seemed to alter its form with every city or town it passed. In Topeka, Kansas, the airship "resembled a fish composed of a complex frame of steel rods." It was of oblong shape and moving at a terrific speed when it passed over Mount Carroll, Illinois. In Evanston, Illinois, it appeared to be "a veritable ship of the air, with masts and yards, sailing under a cloud of canvas," with colored lights suspended from rails. In Wisconsin, the airship was egg-shaped, "doubtless in deference to the approaching festival of Easter," the *Tribune* said.[142] With tongue decidedly in cheek, the *Tribune* added: "These varied aspects of the airship, as depicted by numerous and trustworthy correspondents, seem to lend color to the statement of a prominent Chicago aeronaut that the ship is made of paper, probably newspaper."[143]

Thomas A. Edison brusquely dismissed the reported sightings, correctly noting that it was "absolutely absurd that a man would construct a successful airship and keep the matter secret." Edison speculated that the sightings were nothing more than helium-filled balloons that had escaped their owners. "When I was young," he said, "we used to construct big colored paper balloons, fill them with gas, and they would float about for days. I guess some one has been up to the same game out West."[144] Large cellular kites, capable of reaching considerable heights and floating for great distances, were also identified as a likely source of the strange, moving lights.[145] But the notion that the mysterious airships were of extraterrestrial origin was not to be completely ruled out. That life existed on Mars was not such a far-fetched idea in the late nineteenth and early twentieth centuries. After all, the noted astronomer Percival Lowell maintained that the Martian surface was crisscrossed by a network of canals.[146] At about this time, H. G. Wells was completing his science-fiction thriller, *The War of the Worlds*, which depicted the catastrophic invasion of Britain from Mars. *War of the Worlds* appeared in 1898 but the *New York Evening Journal* carried excerpts of the work beginning in late 1897. The newspaper's version was localized to metropolitan New York and included sensationalized

Figure 1.6 Confirmation of gold strikes in Canada's Klondike region prompted a stampede in late summer 1897. The dreams of many goldseekers shattered in face of the hardships encountered in crossing the narrow mountain corridors such as the Chilkoot Trail (shown here) that were gateways to the Klondike. The Chilkoot led from southeastern Alaska into Canada. (Library of Congress.)

passages describing the destruction of churches, libraries, Fifth Avenue mansions, and the Brooklyn Bridge.[147]

No less illusory than airship sightings was the promise of great wealth in the Klondike, where "large fields of marvelous richness" allowed men to grow "fabulously rich in a single night," as the *New York Times* reported in the first blush of gold fever.[148] By the thousands, Americans in late summer 1897 set off for the Klondike, where alluvial gold had been discovered in the creeks of the vast and uninviting watershed east of the Alaska border. Klondike fever took hold and became the most intense and delirious expression in 1897 of "doing something out of the common." But careful readers of American newspapers would have noted, well before mid-summer 1897, the occasional

Figure 1.7 Packhorses died by the hundreds along the White Pass Trail, another corridor that took Klondike gold-seekers into Canada. So many horses fell victim to abusive handlers, excessive loads, and terrible falls that the White Pass came to be called Dead Horse Trail, an epithet immortalized by the novelist Jack London. "The horses died like mosquitoes in the first frost," he wrote. (Library of Congress.)

reports of gold discoveries in the faraway Klondike. "Pay dirt is found in large quantities, and fortunes are made by many," the *Washington Post* reported in May 1897.[149] Early in the year, the *New York Tribune* had taken note of a U.S. Geological Survey report about gold in the Yukon and declared: "It is by no means improbable that it will one day rank with California, Australia and South Africa as a land of gold."[150] And the *New York Sun* reported from Juneau, Alaska, in April 1897, that miners were "swarming in here and outfitting for the Yukon. ... The reports of wonderful strikes on the Klondyke are turning most of the travel toward the interior. ... Every steamer that comes up from down below is crowded to the limit of its capacity."[151]

Gold had been discovered in the Klondike in August 1896, but it took tangible evidence to precipitate a stampede. Unambiguous proof that men had become rich panning for Klondike gold came in mid-July 1897 with the arrivals of the *Excelsior* in San Francisco[152] and the *Portland* in Seattle. Both vessels carried dozens of hard-bitten, now-rich Klondike prospectors back to the United States. The *New York Herald* said that not one of the sixty or so prospectors aboard the *Portland* had brought back less than $30,000 in gold dust and nuggets.[153] A correspondent for the *New York Sun* went aboard shortly after the *Portland* landed in Seattle and saw "piles of buckskin sacks bulging out with coarse gold and nuggets. A small safe contained the sacks of a number of the more suspicious miners." Those sacks, alone, contained gold worth $750,000, the correspondent figured.[154]

The *Portland*'s arrival created an immediate sensation. The front page of the *Seattle Post-Intelligencer* on July 17, 1897, proclaimed: "Gold! Gold! Gold! Gold!" The news was electrifying and Klondike fever soon swept the continent. It was to be "the last and most frenzied of the great international gold rushes," according to Pierre Berton's engaging study, *The Klondike Fever*[155]—a stampede "out of all proportion to the amount of gold that actually existed on the Klondike watershed."[156] Frederick Palmer, a newspaper correspondent who went to the Klondike early in 1898, figured that the stampeders of 1897–98 "must have spent" $30 million to $40 million on outfits and transportation to extract perhaps $11 million in gold from the Klondike.[157] But the likelihood that extraordinary effort would bring disproportionately small returns was dimly perceived in mid-summer 1897. The *Herald* declared Seattle had gone "stark, raving mad on gold"[158] and offered as evidence the frenzy surrounding the departure of the *Alki*, a little passenger steamer that left for Alaska a day after the *Portland*'s triumphant arrival.

Hundreds of people gathered on the docks, awaiting the *Alki*'s departure. Word went out that the captain might take the *Alki* out at night, to keep the vessel from being overwhelmed by goldseekers. The rumor proved unfounded, but many would-be adventurers waited at the dock through the night just in case, their outfits of clothing and provisions at the ready.[159] When the *Alki* left port on July 18, 1897, it was loaded well beyond its limit with 125 passengers, eighty sheep, fifty horses, and many tons of provisions. "There was not one inch of idle room," the *Herald* said. "Excited humanity, sheep, horses, baggage, all were together. ... One might have thought that the main deck of the steamer would have been kept clear so that the gold seeking passengers would have a chance to stroll about. But space was too valuable."[160] Similar scenes were repeated over the next several weeks as steamers left for Alaska, all overloaded with people, horses, mules, sheep, and tons of provisions.

Stories about suddenly rich gold prospectors were the stuff of many newspaper reports, particularly in the first rush of Klondike fever. One of the rich and lucky argonauts, as they were called, was Clarence Berry of California. He and his wife and two children arrived on the *Portland* with four sacks of nuggets and other containers filled with gold.[161] "Yes, it is true that ten months ago I was a poor miner, cast down and discouraged with three years' unrewarded prospecting," he told a correspondent for the *New York Times*. "To-day, my wife and I are returning to San Francisco with over $130,000 worth of gold in our possession, most of it in nuggets."[162] American newspapers of 1897 have been criticized for stoking Klondike fever by playing up such get-rich-quick stories and indulging in eye-popping descriptions of fabulous wealth waiting to be extracted from the goldfields. "Anxious to sell their product and to maintain readers' interest, the North American newspapers plugged the Klondike story shamelessly, doing their best to find or create human interest stories," wrote a recent critic of the 1897 Klondike coverage. "They correctly identified widespread fascination with the Klondike experience and then did their best to sustain the level of appeal."[163] Such critiques, however, are more than a little unfair. Close reading of leading U.S. newspapers shows that their reports about the unfolding gold rush were excited *and* cautionary. Even as gold fever spread, newspapers emphasized the hazards and hardships of traveling to the Klondike.[164] The *Times* story about Berry's good fortune, for example, quoted the prospector as saying: "The country is wild, rough, and full of hardships for those unused to the rigors of artic Winters. If a man makes a fortune, he is liable to earn it by severe hardship and suffering."[165]

Hearst's *New York Journal* covered the gold rush in typically aggressive fashion—but made it clear that prospectors who found wealth in the Klondike typically did so after many months, and even years, of toil. The Klondike was not prone to yield its riches readily or without great effort.[166] If anything, American newspapers could be faulted for *overstating* the prospect of famine in the Klondike's hardscrabble boomtown, Dawson City, during the winter of 1897–98.[167] The fears of famine did not materialize, in large measure because many goldseekers left Dawson in the autumn and even the winter.[168] The newspapers also focused on the severity of the Yukon's climate,[169] where summers are brief and winters long and icy. They made clear the enormous distances to Dawson City, at the confluence of the Klondike and Yukon rivers. The all-water route to Dawson City from San Francisco was about 4,500 miles—up the Pacific Coast to the Bering Sea and the Yukon River delta at St. Michael, Alaska. From there, prospectors would travel up the boiling Yukon to Dawson City, during the few months the river was navigable. A less expensive and more popular route—shorter by about 3,000 miles—was by steamer from Seattle to Dyea or Skagway, Alaska, northeast of Juneau. From Dyea and Skagway, stampeders negotiated miles of treacherous mountain passes to reach Canada and the headwaters of the Yukon. From there, they could build or buy a boat and navigate the waterways to Dawson City. During the long winter, the lake and rivers froze solid, and dogsled teams made the run from Dawson City to Dyea or Skagway in about twenty-five to thirty days.

"People talk about the journey [to the Klondike] … as if it were walking across the street," the *New York Herald* said dismissively in a dispatch from Seattle in July 1897. "They don't realize what the Yukon is."[170] The magazine *Self Culture* noted that "considerations of prudence do not usually weigh with the adventurer of fortune. All he cares to know is the location where treasures may be found, as he fondly thinks, for the picking up."[171] Similarly, *Harper's Weekly* observed at the end of July 1897:

> It is characteristic of the speculative nature of the American that he is willing to take chances of extreme hardship, and even of death, for the remote possibility of quickly found fortune. How remote that possibility usually is has been illustrated at the opening of every new mining country, and it has been proved again and again that the proportion of men who grow wealthy in mining is almost as small as that of the men who break the bank at Monte Carlo. … Provisions [in the Klondike] are scarce and dear; hardships are great; the promising placer territory is limited, and already there are enough eager workers in the field to exhaust its capacity.[172]

The gold-seekers' motives were at once straightforward and complex. In some respects, Klondike fever was akin on an epic scale to a sustained, continent-wide bout of lottery fever, in which an immense and unprecedented jackpot grows and grows, steadily building excitement and attention. The odds of winning such a bonanza are unimaginably remote. But the chances are real enough to lure many thousands of players. The Klondike likewise offered the extraordinarily slim but undeniably real prospect of winning a fortune. Also accounting for Klondike fever were the harsh, lingering effects of the Panic of 1893 and the years of despair that followed. The economic downturn had begun to lift by mid-1897, but recovery was uneven, halting, and uncertain. In the context of hard economic times, the enticement of sudden wealth in the Klondike was very strong. A related factor was a broader *fin-de-siècle* taste for adventure, for "doing something out of the common." For thousands of Americans, to head to the Klondike was "doing something out of the common" on the grandest scale imaginable. Many Klondike stampeders were men in their twenties—just "young enough to be gullible, young enough to be foolhardy, young enough to be optimistic, young enough to be carefree," as Berton has written.[173]

Hints and reminders of the stampeders' adventurous spirit, their hardiness, and their risk-taking character can still be detected in the Pacific Northwest. In a perceptive account published in 1997 as the gold rush centennial approached, the *Economist* magazine of London observed that stampeders left at least an indirect legacy of risk-taking in a region that now is home to Microsoft, Starbucks, and Nordstrom. "At Microsoft, for example," the *Economist* noted, "risk-taking is part of the ethos: if a particular project does not work out, you move on to the next one. The company aims to hire people who are not only clever and hard-working but assertive and persistent too—modern-day pioneers, you might say."[174]

The magazine acknowledged, "Direct connections between today's corporate successes and the 1897 gold rush are few (though some exist: John W. Nordstrom, an immigrant from Sweden, struck gold in Alaska, and the shoe store he founded with his riches was the beginning of today's fashion-retail empire). Indirectly, however, the influence is great," the *Economist* said,[175] adding: "It was through the gold rush that Seattle learned the marketing flair it now applies to selling computer software or persuading people to pay $2-odd for a cup of coffee. The city's first marketing wizard was a failed newspaper editor, Erastus Brainerd, who set out to persuade prospectors that Seattle was the gateway to the Alaskan gold fields 1,600 miles away. He advertised, wrote articles, [organized] letter-writing by newcomers to their hometown papers, and bombarded mayors and governors and foreign governments with propaganda."[176]

It would be misleading, of course, to valorize the stampeders of 1897 as singularly imbued with the spirit of risk-taking and adventure. A keen sense of the absurd characterized the gold rush as well. Some would-be goldseekers dreamed up improbable plans for reaching the Klondike, few of which came close to realization. For example, a company in San Francisco announced plans to build an airship capable of transporting passengers and freight to the Klondike.[177] An entrepreneur in New York raised $150,000 to build what he promised would be the world's largest balloon, to make regular runs from Juneau to the Klondike.[178] There were more than a few reports in U.S. newspapers of cyclists who planned to ride at least part of the way to the goldfields.[179]

Beyond such foolhardy ideas, the gold rush also exposed the raw and brutal side of human nature, evident most notably when stampeders finally came face-to-face with the enormity of their task. For thousands of stampeders, that realization struck when they confronted the forbidding mountain corridors above Dyea and Skagway. Both were inconsequential villages before the gold rush. But because they were the terminal points for passenger steamers plying the coast from Seattle, they became booming gateways to the Klondike in the summer of 1897 to the Klondike. Within two months of the start of the gold rush, Skagway was remarkably transformed from a village of mud and tents into a robust and substantial-looking town of "wooden houses and straight streets."[180]

At Dyea or Skagway, where the steamers unceremoniously discharged them and their gear, stampeders faced the unappealing choice of crossing the Chilkoot Trail above Dyea or the White Pass Trail near Skagway. While longer, the White Pass Trail crossed the mountains at a lower altitude than the Chilkoot and, for a time, was the preferred route into Canada. The volume of goldseekers soon overwhelmed the trail and by late August 1897, it was impassible—an obstacle course of boulders, rock outcroppings, and mudholes that all but swallowed up horses and mules. Tappan Adney, a journalist sent to the Klondike by *Harper's Weekly*, wrote that the "opening of the White Pass as a summer trail was not a blunder—it was a crime."[181] Berton estimated that of the 5,000 stampeders who attempted to cross the White Pass Trail in late summer and fall 1897, only a small percentage made it through.[182] The ambitions of many stampeders were shattered in mind-numbing despair along the trail. Halfway up, Adney wrote, "goods were actually given away, the unfortunate owners having neither money nor strength to pack them either ahead or back."[183]

Packhorses suffered most acutely. Adney and others have estimated that 3,000 horses died or were killed on the trail[184]—many of them the victims of inexpert packing, abusive handlers, and terrible falls from the narrow and congested corridor. The White Pass came to be called Dead Horse Trail, an epithet immortalized by the novelist Jack London. He joined the Klondike rush in 1897 as a fledgling writer and witnessed the mistreatment of horses on the White Pass Trail. "The horses died like mosquitoes in the first frost," London wrote. Stampeders "shot them, worked them to death. ... Some did not bother to shoot them, stripping the saddles off and the shoes and leaving them where they fell. Their hearts turned to stone—those which did not break—and they became beasts, the men on the Dead Horse Trail."[185]

Gold fever eased in the United States during the autumn of 1897, and never again reached the intensity and frenzy of mid-summer. Reports of new rich strikes in the Klondike occasionally reached American newspapers during the winter of 1897–98,[186] and reminders of the great wealth a few Klondike prospectors had made sometimes found their way into print. For example, James Clements, a brakeman for the Southern Pacific Railroad who struck it rich in the Klondike, treated his family to a trip to New York City in December 1897. Clements hung branch-bending gold nuggets on a Christmas tree in their room, and surrounded the tree with small piles of freshly minted gold coins. "Mrs. Clements rubbed her eyes ... and wondered if it was all a dream," the *Chicago Times-Herald* said in reporting on the extravagant display. On the carpet, the Clements children played marbles with gold nuggets.[187]

The remoteness of the Klondike also contributed to the easing of gold fever. The region's isolation meant that reliable reports from the goldfields arrived irregularly, making it impossible to sustain the thrill of the discovery. More significantly, the gold rush was supplanted in early 1898 by a preoccupation with the deepening tensions between Spain and the United States over Spain's failure to quell the island-wide rebellion on Cuba. The destruction of the U.S. battleship *Maine* in Havana harbor in February 1898 was a trigger for the United States to intervene militarily in Cuba in April 1898. The Spanish-American War was the first U.S. conflict in thirty-three years, and it shouldered aside the Klondike as the most compelling, most important international news.

But at the end of 1897, war with Spain over Cuba had seemed unlikely. Crises had periodically flared over Cuba, only to die down without forcing a rupture in U.S.-Spanish relations. These episodes included the mysterious death in Spanish custody of a Cuban-American dentist named Ricardo Ruiz, the *New York Journal*'s rescue of Evangelina Cisneros from a Havana prison, and the filibusters that illegally ran guns and supplies from the United States to the Cuban insurgents. American popular sentiment sided reflexively with the insurgents who demanded political independence from Spain. But their slash-and-burn tactics had destroyed millions of dollars in American-owned property, diminishing enthusiasm for their cause.[188]

By year's end, the signs from Cuba were hopeful indeed. The much-despised Spanish commander, Captain-General Valeriano Weyler y Nicolau, had been recalled to Spain and a new government in Madrid had offered the Cubans limited political autonomy. The sporadic fighting between the ragtag insurgents and the ponderous Spanish military had settled into a stalemate. The insurgents controlled much of the countryside, especially in eastern Cuba, and Spanish forces held and stayed close to the ports and cities. President William McKinley in his annual message to Congress in December 1897 said the Spanish government deserved to be given time to pursue its political reforms in

Cuba. But McKinley held open the prospect of "action by the United States" should the reforms fail,[189] as they did in early 1898. Reflecting the transient optimism about Cuba, the *New York Herald* declared in its outlook for the new year: "Hope already appears in the horizon of Cuba. The long and deadly contest seems nearing its end. Whether the close be autonomy under Spain or absolute independence, the havoc and disaster which have preyed upon the resources of the island will cease and a new era of prosperity will dawn."[190] The *Herald* further predicted that the United States would "remain at peace with the world" in 1898.[191]

The insurrection in Cuba was not the only international conflict to command attention in 1897. Greece and Turkey declared war in the spring of 1897, after Greece tried to assert claims of sovereignty over Crete. Although they had provoked the war, the Greeks were ill-prepared for a fight. One correspondent wrote that they "plunged into the campaign without an intelligence department, without maps, without field-glasses, without sufficient provision for signaling, and with the most incompetent body of officers that ever troops had set over them."[192]

The war lasted about a month. It was fought mostly in northern Greece and was characterized by the frequent retreat of Greek forces, which were commanded ineptly by the Crown Prince Constantine. "Their fiercest fighting has been rewarded, not with victory, but with orders to retreat," the novelist Stephen Crane wrote of the Greek troops. "They have had a fierce, outnumbering enemy before them and a rear fire from the vacillating Crown Prince,"[193] who repeatedly and unaccountably ordered them to fall back.

The Greco-Turkish War was intensively covered by American journalists—Crane, Palmer, Richard Harding Davis, and Sylvester Scovel, among others—in a sort of trial run for reporting from the Caribbean theater during the Spanish-American War. Some American newspapers depicted the Greco-Turkish conflict in terms that would be familiar today—as a struggle or religious war against the specter of fanatical Islam.[194] The *New York Times* stated after the brief war: "Whatever may be the differences of the Mohammedan nations among themselves, the news of a new victory of the crescent over the cross is hailed with delight in every mosque in Asia and in Africa in which the faithful are gathered. ... The tradition of the great days of the Mohammedan conquests undoubtedly survives in Mohammedan countries, and a desire to repeat those conquests is naturally awakened by such a signal defeat of a Christian power as Greece has undergone."[195]

AN INSTRUMENT OF SOCIAL CONTROL

Eighteen-ninety-seven was one of the many years of the late-nineteenth century when lynchings—the extrajudicial killing of suspected criminals—outnumbered legal executions in the United States. According to the *Chicago Tribune*'s annual compilation, 166 people were lynched in 1897, 146 of them in Southern states.[196] There were 128 legal executions in 1897, most of them for murder.[197] Texas, with twenty-five, was the lynch leader, followed by Alabama (nineteen) and Mississippi (sixteen). Nearly three victims in four were black (N = 122), and the most common suspected offenses were rape and attempted rape (N = 32).[198]

More than a few lynchings in 1897 were carried out to punish trivial offenses,[199] such as the theft of a mule,[200] or writing insulting letters.[201] The *Tribune*'s roster included two cases of lynching for "elopement," one for "disobedience of regulations," and one for "train-wrecking."[202] It was not unheard of that innocent victims were lynched, as reportedly was the case of Henry Wall, a white man wrongly accused of sexually assaulting a white woman in Patrick County, Virginia.[203] Rarely were the participants in lynchings punished[204] and impunity assuredly fueled the lawlessness. Northern states were hardly immune from what the *Tribune* called the "criminal work of mob-murderers."[205] Five lynchings were counted in Indiana, three in North Dakota, and one each in California, Illinois, Ohio, and Maryland.[206]

Lynching was an ugly side of *fin-de-siècle* America, an appalling practice that persisted well into the twentieth century[207] despite the condemnation of many leading newspapers. The *Philadelphia Inquirer*, for example, deplored what it termed "these barbarous exhibitions of insane frenzy."[208] The *New York Times* asked: "Can it be that our boasted civilization has not yet reached the point at which it eradicates the unreasoning bloodthirstiness of the primeval, barbarian man?"[209] Lynching was clearly an instrument of social control, especially in the South,[210] where the threat of violence was prominent among the tactics employed to deny civil rights to African Americans. Disfranchisement and Jim Crow social segregation were others.[211]

Some leading Southerners in 1897 openly advocated or justified lynching, as an effective remedy to the perceived threat of black-on-white crime.[212] A leading Southern suffrage advocate, Rebecca Lattimer Felton, told an audience in Savannah, Georgia, in August 1897 that so long as men in Georgia could find sufficient lengths of rope, they should defend their wives and daughters from assailants.[213] The Tennessee governor, Robert L. Taylor, told the *New York Journal*: "There have always been lynchings. There always will be until the dawn of the millennium. ... They occur now and then when the most horrible of all crimes is committed, and when an infuriated community refuses to wait for the law ... There is not a more law-abiding people on the face of the earth than the people of the South ... and yet when the black fiend steals into some happy home and destroys its peace and joy forever our people do not put on mourning when the neck of the destroyer is broken."[214]

Few Northern newspapers in 1897 addressed or focused on the social-control aspects of lynching, however.[215] Many of them argued instead that the lynch mob could be thwarted only by strengthening criminal penalties. "It is the uncertainty that the death sentence really means death that is largely responsible for lynch law," said the *Philadelphia Item*. "And until this cause is removed lynchings will continue when an outrageous crime thoroughly arouses public indignation."[216] "Lynch law usually becomes the resort of people who believe that properly enacted laws do not adequately punish malefactors," said the *New York Times*.[217] Similarly, the *New York Journal* observed: "All through the West and South it seems to be an admitted principle that assaults on women call for the infliction of the death penalty in the most summary possible way. Yet in hardly any of these States is this principle embodied in the laws. ... It is strange that men who feel so intensely on this subject as to be willing to take their lives in their hands to avenge the crime do not think enough of it when their Legislatures are in session to secure the passage of laws making the deed a capital offense."[218]

No lynching in 1897 stirred more comment and outrage than that of Charles (Click) Mitchell in Urbana, Ohio. "There has not been and could not be a more inexcusable lynching," the *New York Times* said of Mitchell's violent death.[219] Mitchell was a twenty-three-year-old black man accused of sexually assaulting Eliza Gaumer, a widowed white woman, at her house in Urbana. According to news reports about the case, Mitchell, a hotel porter, was promptly arrested and taken to face Mrs. Gaumer, who was bedridden after the attack. She reportedly exclaimed, "Hang the brute. How dare he face me?"[220] Mitchell was quickly brought to trial, where he pleaded guilty to criminal assault. He was sentenced to prison for twenty years, the state's maximum penalty for the crime. During the brief trial, scores of angry townspeople gathered outside the courthouse. News of Mitchell's guilty plea and sentencing spread quickly.

According to the *New York Journal*'s detailed account of the lynching, "an excited mob surged around the Court House and jail" and vigilantes guarded every street leading from the jail,[221] thwarting plans to transfer Mitchell that night to the state penitentiary in Columbus,

Ohio. A local unit of the Ohio National Guard was summoned to support the sheriff's deputies protecting the Urbana jail. When the surging mob moved on the jail, battering the rear door with sledge-hammers,[222] the National Guard troops opened fire.[223] Two men in the mob were killed and eleven others were wounded. The mob fell back, but remained a seething, threatening presence. A separate detach-ment of National Guardsmen was dispatched to Urbana from Spring-field, Ohio. But almost as soon as they had arrived, the Urbana mayor ordered the reinforcements to leave.[224]

The mob soon moved again on the thinly defended jail. This time, the local National Guard unit stacked its arms, refusing to fire on the enraged townspeople. The mob needed only minutes to batter down the jailhouse door and break the steel lock on Mitchell's cell. "Then began one of the most terrible scenes which have ever disgraced a com-munity in this country," the *Journal* said.[225] A "frightful shriek of tri-umph" rose from the mob as several men seized Mitchell and dragged him outside. "Men, crazed with passion, attempted to tear one another down in order to reach" Mitchell and beat him, the *Journal* reported. "Those who succeeded in kicking him in the head or about the body afterward boasted of it gleefully."[226]

Mitchell was battered, bleeding, and half-conscious as he was dragged to a maple tree in the courthouse square. As a noose was tied around his neck, the howls and screams from the mob intensified. The end of the rope was tossed over a tree limb, and men in the mob took turns jerking it "with terrible force, knocking the negro's head against the limb. ... The crowd seething beneath the swaying form of the negro kicked and struck at the body. Men hacked at it with clubs and ham-mers, and when the body was taken down and laid on the grass, it was almost unrecognizable."[227]

Hundreds of curiosity-seekers flocked to Urbana, many in search of mementos of the Mitchell hanging. The bark of the lynching tree was almost entirely chipped away for souvenirs. Mitchell's shoes were taken, as were fragments of his coat[228] and bits of the lynch rope.[229] The mayor, the sheriff, and the local guardsmen who had fired on the mob all fled.[230] Four inmates at the Urbana jail escaped after the mob broke in to seize Mitchell.[231]

Northern newspapers reacted with horror and outrage to the Urbana lynching. "The riot was an outbreak of barbarism without excuse," the *New York Tribune* declared. "It was not an impatient attempt to do justice, but a bloodthirsty attempt to thwart it. ... No republican government can command respect when its citizens refuse to obey the laws of their own making."[232] The *Los Angeles Times* called the Urbana lynching "a triumph of lawlessness over law" and declared: "There is no crueler despotism under the sun than the despotism of mob rule."[233] But some Southern newspapers were quick to say that lynching was a instinctive response that knew no boundary, neither North nor South. The *New Orleans Times-Democrat* declared, smugly: "Human nature is pretty much alike both in North and South, when crimes like the one of which 'Click' Mitchell was guilty are in question; and it is questionable whether the very strictest administration of justice will ever be able to dispense with the rough-and-ready services of Justice Lynch in cases in which Caucasian women are assaulted by ruffian Senegambians. The Ohioans of Urbana are not law abiding enough to allow a brute like 'Click' Mitchell to escape the noose, court or no court."[234]

Labor unrest in the anthracite coalfields of northeastern Pennsylvania brought the year's single bloodiest confrontation. That came on September 10, 1897, when striking miners, marching from Hazelton to Lattimer, Pennsylvania, refused orders to disperse. Deputy sheriffs opened fire and nineteen miners were fatally wounded. The Lattimer sheriff, James Martin, was accused of murder and felonious wounding and in early 1898 went on trial in Wilkes-Barre, Pennsylvania. Although the proceedings lasted a month, little persuasive evidence was produced to demonstrate the sheriff and his subordinates had exceeded their authority in shooting the stone-throwing miners, many of whom were immigrants from eastern and southern Europe. Martin was acquitted, an outcome the *Chicago Tribune* said was "not a surprise, as everybody, including the prosecuting committee and the attorneys for the commonwealth [of Pennsylvania], rather expected such a verdict."[235]

VIOLENCE IN SPORT

Violent encounters were not uncommon features of collegiate football and professional baseball, America's two most popular sports in 1897. Football was played widely—"in every vacant lot," the *Chicago Times-Herald* said[236]—and followed avidly. On the eve of the Yale-Princeton football game in late November 1897, the *New York Times* said of New Haven, Connecticut: "This city became football wild to-day, and every hour adds to the enthusiasm and the crowds. ... The demand for tickets for the big game has developed into a fight between the would-be purchasers and the speculators. The most exorbitant prices are asked, and in many cases paid. The prevailing figures are $15 for two-dollar seats and $8 and $10 for dollar-and-a-half seats."[237] About 18,000 people

Figure 1.8 Sports journalism became increasingly important in the 1890s as Americans took to the outdoors to ride bicycles and play golf. In the spring of 1897, the *Daily Item* of Philadelphia took to calling one of its late editions the *Sporting Item* because it carried the latest baseball scores and race results. Note the lavishly illustrated nameplate. (Library of Congress.)

attended the game, which Yale won, 6–0, to complete an undefeated season.[238] But the national collegiate champion in 1897 was the University of Pennsylvania, which compiled a 15–0 record. The Penn juggernaut scored 463 points while allowing just 20. Twelve of its opponents never scored.[239] But mighty Penn nearly stumbled in the season-ending game against Cornell, played Thanksgiving Day before 20,000 spectators at Franklin Field in Philadelphia. After a scoreless first half, the Penn team prevailed, 4–0, by scoring a touchdown late in the game.[240]

Football was brutally played in the 1890s[241] and far more resembled rugby than the passing-oriented game it became during the twentieth century. According to the *Chicago Tribune*'s count, eight collegiate and amateur football players died in 1897 from injuries suffered on the gridiron.[242] The year before, three players died from injuries, which prompted the *Tribune* to declare football "is the game of the century, yet in its roughness it suggests the gladiatorial contests ... of the Roman Empire; in its bloodiness, the bullfights of Spain and Mexico."[243] The *Tribune* and the *New York Journal* were leaders in newspaper campaigns that sought to ban or modify mass-formation plays, which aligned no fewer than five blockers for the ball carrier.[244] "Football under this system," said the *Journal*, "becomes a question of the weight and mere brute force of the opposing team."[245]

No fatal injury on the gridiron in 1897 caused a greater outcry than that of Richard Von Gammon, an imposing fullback who gained a national reputation while playing for the University of Georgia. Gammon struck his head while being tackled during a game in Atlanta against the University of Virginia, suffering a brain injury that killed him. The thousands of people at the game knew Gammon had been badly injured. Nonetheless, a substitute was sent in for him and the game went on.[246] The state legislature shortly afterward voted to outlaw the sport in Georgia, despite the plea of Gammon's mother who asked legislators not to ban the game her son so deeply loved.[247] The Georgia governor vetoed the measure, which would have made football-playing a misdemeanor punishable by a fine or prison sentence.[248]

Despite the violence, crackdowns against the sport were unthinkable at leading football institutions of the time—places like Harvard and Princeton. At Harvard, the *New York Herald* reported, there was "no disposition ... to abolish ... the manliest of college sports."[249] Princeton undergraduates, the *Herald* said, "would rise in arms if such a thing as the abolishing of football was proposed ... and there would be a large number of faculty members in the ranks, too."[250] But the sport was under attack from many quarters in 1897. A conference of Methodist clergy in Philadelphia denounced football as violent and degrading[251] and the *Chicago Tribune* predicted that unless reforms were adopted that opened up the game and made it less perilous to players, American colleges and universities sooner or later would move to "end ... the dangerous, barbarous, and degrading" pastime.[252] Not until early in the early twentieth century were rule changes implemented that decisively opened up the game by legalizing the forward pass and establishing a neutral zone between opposing linemen.[253]

The 1897 pennant race was easily professional baseball's most competitive of the decade. It pitted the two dominant teams of the National League, the Boston Beaneaters and the Baltimore Orioles, in a battle not decided until the season's last week. Boston, which began the season poorly and dropped into last place during the season's first weeks, played splendidly through the summer and moved into first place in June. The Beaneaters and the Orioles vied for the top spot the rest of the season. Both teams compiled extended winning streaks—Boston won seventeen games in a row in late May and June, and Baltimore won nine in a row in June and eight straight in August. In September, the teams seldom were separated by more than one game in the standings.

In late September, Boston traveled to Baltimore for a three-game series that was to determine the league champion, the most dramatic series of the decade.[254] The teams split the first two games. The third game attracted 25,390 fans (usually called "cranks" in 1897)—not counting the 1,500 or so who got in by breaking through a fence.[255] The spectators overflowed the stands and sat as close as a few feet from home plate.[256] The game was a slugfest, one requiring "nerves of steel and hearts of oak," according to the *Boston Globe*'s account.[257] Boston hammered out twenty-four hits, scored nine runs in the seventh inning, and won, 19–10.[258] In celebration, the Boston fans tossed pocketfuls of beans into the air.[259] The victory left the Beaneaters in first place, with three games to be played in the season. They won the pennant by a two-game margin.

The games between the Beaneaters and the Orioles in 1897 were fiercely contested and marred on occasion by fisticuffs and brawls that would rival any of the sport's ugly explosions these days. The game at Boston's South End Grounds in early August was notable for a melee sparked by the game's umpire, Tom Lynch. Throughout the game, the Baltimore first baseman, Jack Doyle, had directed at Lynch an unbroken stream of insults and obscenities. The umpire finally had enough. He turned "mad with rage" and landed a blow on Doyle's jaw. "Instantly," the *Boston Post* reported, "the ground before the grand stand became the scene of a fierce conflict. The players from both sides swayed to and fro in a savage melee … and down from both bleachers a yelling mob rushed into the fight. From all quarters of the field the police left stations and ran for the riot."[260] The police needed ten minutes to separate the players and restore a measure of order. As the row subsided, Baltimore's best pitcher, Joe Corbett, "staggered out of the melee with his arm hooked in a 'half-Nelson' around Lynch's neck," the *Post* said. "Swearing, cursing, shaking their fists at each other, the players backed away."[261] Doyle was immediately fined $300 and ejected from the game,[262] which the Beaneaters won, 6–5.

On the game's last play, Lynch called out a Baltimore player who tried to score on a base hit. Boston fans again rushed the field, clapping Lynch on the back and congratulating him for his game-saving call.[263] But the ugliness was far from ended. As the Orioles tried to leave the park for their hotel downtown, Boston fans swarmed around the team's horse-drawn bus, blocking its departure. John McGraw, one of the Orioles' most aggressive players, emerged, swinging a bat to clear the crowd. With that, the team bus sped down Tremont Street, "pursued by curses and obscenity and howls."[264]

As that Beaneaters-Orioles encounter suggests, professional baseball was an aggressive, often unattractive game in the 1890s. "Rowdyism" and hostile encounters were so numerous that newspapers such as the *New York Herald*[265] and *New York Sun*[266] despaired for the sport's future. As the 1897 season neared its end, the *Philadelphia Times* declared:

> For three or four years things have been going from bad to worse until now rows on the ball field and the mobbing of umpires are almost a matter of daily occurrence. ... Players engage in altercations not only among themselves, but with the umpires as well, and the conversation carried on is simply vile. This, of course, does not redound to the credit of the game, and it has been and is fast losing caste with the respectable element. ... All this is no news to any who are at all familiar with base ball as it is played to-day, but if the national game is to remain such something must be done to drive out the ruffians of ball players, and thus win back those [fans] who have been driven away by their actions.[267]

There was ample evidence to support the gloomy appraisals. Players and managers routinely "kicked," or quarreled with, umpires despite rules clearly prohibiting such challenges. As a writer for the *New York Journal* so colorfully put it, players in 1897 were known to assail the umpire "with fire in their eyes and tabasco sauce on their tongues. Fiercely they argued and loudly they hurled expletives." The disputes sometimes became so heated and menacing that fans would rush onto the playing field, surrounding the umpire and the visiting team.[268]

The conduct of umpires was not always above reproach. When a Cincinnati player named Henry (Heinie) Peitz rushed the umpire, Tim Hurst, to dispute a call, Hurst shoved his mask into the player's midsection. Peitz wheeled and struck Hurst in the mouth, drawing blood.[269] A few days after his encounter with Peitz, Hurst dodged a beer glass lobbed from the stands in Cincinnati. The pugnacious umpire hurled the glass back into the stands, striking a fan in the head.[270] A police wagon was summoned and Hurst was arrested, and charged with assault and battery.[271] He was fined $100[272] and later dismissed as an umpire.

The fiercely competitive nature of American sports was striking to visitors from abroad. In his *America and Americans*, Collier observed that Americans seemed to play sports "not for the mental and physical refreshment so much as for the excitement of surpassing someone else."[273] That spirit certainly seems to have animated collegiate football and professional baseball in 1897. But it does not fully explain one of the year's landmark moments—the inaugural Boston Marathon, now the most famous and prestigious race of its kind in the United States.

The first Boston Marathon was run April 19, 1897. The founding organization, the Boston Athletic Association, was inspired by the revival of the marathon race at the first modern Olympic games in 1896.[274] The Boston course began near Metcalf's Mill in Ashland, Massachusetts, and was 24.5 miles long, or about 1.5 miles shorter than that of a contemporary marathon. Fifteen men entered the race, some of whom "looked as if they could spare a few pounds," the *Boston Post* reported.[275] Along the course, the runners answered the cheers of spectators with bows and waves.

The winner was John J. McDermott of the Pastime Athletic Club in New York, who finished the course in 2 hours, 55 minutes, and 10 seconds, which the *Boston Globe* said exceeded the record time of the 1896 Olympics.[276] McDermott dropped nine pounds, suffered severe leg cramps, and was forced to cut through a funeral procession on the last leg of the race. Some 3,000 spectators awaited at the finish line.[277] "This probably will be my last long race," McDermott said afterward. "I hate to quit now, because I will be called a quitter and a coward, but look at my feet. Do you blame me for wanting to stop it? I only walked about a quarter of a mile in the whole distance and it was 20 miles before I lagged a step. I think I shall be all right tomorrow."[278]

Inevitably, the year of "doing something out of the common" would embrace the journalism of the day. It was scarcely surprising that the American press would be shaped by and reflect the vigor, upheaval, and transitions that broadly defined the country in 1897. As it was in American sports, competition was fierce among American newspapers. More than 2,200 daily newspapers—an increase of nearly 40 percent from the start of the decade—were published in the United States at the end of the 1890s.[279] Fifty-eight dailies were published in New York City and thirty-seven in Chicago.[280] Never before had American journalism been defined by such intense competition. The rivalries made for a remarkable time of ferment, innovation, and transformation in journalism—a time when fresh models for the future were developed and advocated. We turn now to explore the clash of paradigms that defined American journalism's exceptional year.

2

THE CLASH OF PARADIGMS

The most famous slogan in American journalism made its debut in October 1896, in a row of red lights arrayed across a huge advertising sign at Manhattan's Madison Square. The slogan was part of a marketing campaign of the beleaguered *New York Times* which, two months before, had been acquired for a pittance in bankruptcy court. For the owner, a newcomer from Tennessee named Adolph S. Ochs, securing space on the electric sign at Madison Square was nothing less than a coup. The bright, multi-colored lights could be seen for many blocks away. Nowhere in the country, or in Europe, the *Times* immodestly crowed, was there "so large and perfect a display."[1]

The *Times'* advertisement was illuminated by four rows of lights. The white lights of the top and bottom rows spelled out the newspaper's name and the question, "Have You Seen It?" A row of blue, white, and green lights spelled out "Sunday Magazine Supplement." The red lights, which formed the second row of illumination, announced the smug and tidy slogan, "All the News That's Fit to Print."[2] That row of red lights would glow, figuratively, through the decades.

"All the News That's Fit to Print" became much more than a marketing vehicle. It appeared in advertisements in the trade journal *Fourth Estate* in mid-October 1896,[3] and by month's end had taken a place in the upper-left corner of the newspaper's editorial page. On February 10, 1897—without notice or fanfare—"All the News That's Fit to Print" appeared in a box at the upper-left corner of the *Times*' front page. The slogan has been there ever since, an enduring statement of guiding principle for what has long been recognized as the best newspaper in America.[4]

The *Times*' slogan has been parodied, praised, and analyzed in countless ways since 1897. Even admiring chroniclers of the *Times* have called it "overweening"[5] and "elliptical." But no other seven words in journalism have attracted more attention.[6] At its fiftieth anniversary in 1901, the *Times* referred to "All the News That's Fit to Print" as its "covenant."[7] One-hundred years later, a columnist for the *Wall Street Journal* aptly identified the motto as the "leitmotif not merely for the Times, but also, by a process of osmosis and emulation, for most other general-interest papers in the country, as well as for much of the broadcast media."[8] Indeed, "All the News That's Fit to Print" has long been American journalism's guiding *leitmotif* —a summation and a celebration of the detached, restrained, yet authoritative journalism that the *Times* has promoted since the late nineteenth century. The motto is also a daily and lasting reminder of the *Times*' triumph in a momentous, three-sided clash of paradigms that took shape in 1897—a clash that helped define the modern contours of American journalism.

The struggle pitted three rival, incompatible models. As suggested by its slogan, the *Times* offered a detached, impartial, fact-based paradigm that embraced the innovative technologies emergent in the late nineteenth century but eschewed extravagance, prurience, and flamboyance in presenting the news. Extravagance, prurience, and flamboyance were features typically associated with yellow journalism, a robust genre which, despite its controversial and self-indulgent ways, seemed to be irresistibly popular in 1897. The leading exemplar of yellow journalism was William Randolph Hearst's *New York Journal*, which in 1897 claimed to have developed a new kind of journalism, a paradigm infused by a self-activating ethos that sidestepped the inertia of government to "get things done."[9] The *Journal* called its model the "journalism of action" or the "journalism that acts," and declared that it represented "the final state in the evolution of the modern newspaper."[10]

The third rival paradigm was more modest and idiosyncratic than those of the *Times* and *Journal*. While improbable, it was also an imaginative response to the trends of commercialization in journalism. The paradigm was an anti-journalistic literary model devised and promoted by J. Lincoln Steffens, who in late 1897 became city editor of the

Figure 2.1 Before winning fame as a leading muckraking journalist in the early twentieth century, Lincoln Steffens was city editor at the *New York Commercial Advertiser*. In that position, he pursued an intriguing if eccentric experiment in literary journalism by sending young, would-be writers out to report stories about life in the big city. (Library of Congress.)

New York Commercial Advertiser, then New York's oldest newspaper. Steffens kept few professional reporters on his city staff and recruited recent college graduates—novices in journalism who shared a flair and an eagerness to write. "I wanted fresh, young, enthusiastic writers who would see and make others see the life of the city," Steffens wrote in his memoirs.[11] The *Commercial Advertiser* city staff, he said, "had use for any one who, openly or secretly, hoped to be a poet, a novelist, or an essayist."[12] Steffens' model was predicated on the notion "that anything that interested any of us would interest our readers and, therefore, would be news if reported interestingly."[13] Steffens considered the model a unique experiment. It was also a modest protest against the forces turning American journalism into a big business.

The three-sided clash of paradigms that emerged in 1897 was framed by an exceptional convergence of personality and opportunity.

The respective advocates were each in their thirties in 1987, and all were fairly new in their positions. Ochs was thirty-nine and in his first full year as publisher of the *Times*. Hearst turned thirty-four in 1897 and was in his second full year as the *Journal*'s publisher. Steffens was thirty-one when he became city editor of the *Commercial Advertiser*. Though comparatively young, the three men were experienced journalists with records of success elsewhere. For eighteen years before coming to New York, Ochs had been publisher of the *Chattanooga Times*. Hearst had resuscitated the *San Francisco Examiner*, a money-losing daily that his father, a millionaire miner-politician, had acquired in 1880.[14] The younger Hearst began running the paper in 1887[15] and turned it into one of the liveliest dailies in the American West. Steffens, before joining the *Commercial Advertiser*, was assistant city editor at the *New York Evening Post*, a venerable daily run by an irascible Briton, Edward L. Godkin.

The models that Ochs, Hearst, and Steffens proposed for American journalism were not the results of sudden inspiration but were, rather, the consequence of considerable thought, practice, and experimentation. Each man, moreover, exploited what was an exceptional opening. *Fin-de-siècle* journalism in America was badly in need of inspiration. In July 1895, *Fourth Estate* declared the sense of "glamor of romantic adventure" had been bled from newspapering in New York.[16] It deplored that "conscientious work does not count in the frequent reorganizations [at newspapers], and loyalty is at a discount, if not a forgotten sentiment. It all comes down to how much is given per column, and how many columns the reporter can squeeze in."[17]

About three months after the *Fourth Estate*'s commentary, Hearst arrived in New York—a seismic event in the city's journalism.[18] A year after that, Ochs took over the *New York Times*, and some two years later, Steffens became city editor at the *Commercial Advertiser*. Their principal rivals in New York journalism—Charles A. Dana of the *Sun*, Whitelaw Reid of the *Tribune*, James Gordon Bennett Jr. of the *Herald*, and Joseph Pulitzer of the *World*—were all older, and past their prime. Their respective newspapers were in decline, suffering from the "decay implanted by complacency"[19] that had overtaken New York City journalism. While Dana worked tirelessly at the *Sun* until felled by liver cirrhosis in 1897, Reid, Bennett, and Pulitzer were notably absentee.

Reid was appointed U.S. minister to France in 1888, after which he was essentially "an absentee newspaper owner," investing little time, money, or attention in the *Tribune*. While keeping its appeal to an elite and conservative audience, by 1897 the *Tribune* had entered a sustained period of decline.[20] Bennett of the *Herald* spent most of the late nineteenth century in Paris, tapping his newspaper's profits "to live like royalty," according to Richard Kluger's engaging study of the *New York Herald-Tribune* and its predecessor titles. Bennett, a yachtsman who liked being called "the Commodore," ran the *Herald* by telegraph, for better or worse. "A ranking official was on duty at the paper twenty-four hours a day," Kluger wrote, "to receive any messages that might be sent by the Commodore. ... All the New York papers were sent to him regularly, and he kept the cable humming with instructions and complaints."[21] Bennett's rare and brief visits to New York often were worthy of mention in trade journals and other publications. An example came in late spring 1897, when the Commodore visited New York and, for the first time, saw his newspaper's new building at Herald Square. *Harper's Weekly* said of the visit: "Mr. James Gordon Bennett has been to New York, has viewed the city, and especially the new home of his newspaper in it, and has gone away again. What he thought about it seems not to have [been] divulged, at least no newspaper has printed any authoritative expression of his sentiments."[22]

Pulitzer's gathering blindness and other infirmities forced him to yield in-person management of the *World* in the late 1880s[23] and begin a peripatetic, mostly unsuccessful effort to recover his health. He seldom visited New York after 1890 and, in Bennett's fashion, tried to run his newspaper remotely. From retreats in Maine, Georgia, and Europe, Pulitzer fired off telegrams and dictated an unending stream of letters and memoranda to his senior editorial and business managers. He cajoled, bullied, and overwhelmed them with instructions. To read Pulitzer's 1897 letters these days is to be struck by their churlishness. "You ought to be very unhappy over the bad showing—for the July [financial] report is a very bad showing," Pulitzer said in August 1897, in a letter dictated to John Norris, the *World*'s beleaguered general manager. "Try to work out some scheme or ideas for the fall."[24] He also told Norris: "Please tell Mr. Seitz to lock himself up for a week if necessary, to see whether he cannot think of something striking and effective."[25]

Don C. Seitz, the *World*'s business manager who later wrote one of the several glowing biographies of Pulitzer, was a frequent recipient of his boss's acerbic, long-distance advice. "I wonder if you could go over the Sunday paper once—all the sixty pages—and enumerate how many pages are really wasted; uselessly, overzealously—but really wasted," Pulitzer wrote Seitz in December 1897.[26] A few months before, he asked Seitz to recruit spies inside the newsroom of the *Journal*, the code name for which was "Geranium": "Please find someone in Geranium's office with whom you can connect, to discover exactly who furnishes their ideas, who is dissatisfied and obtainable or available even in the second class of executive rank. We are getting shorter and shorter [on talent] and need recruiting."[27]

The *World*'s decline had become striking by 1897. It was a money-losing shell of its aggressive former self— "beyond redemption," *The Journalist* declared.[28] The *World* was no longer the daring, imaginative newspaper that sent Nellie Bly (Elizabeth Cochrane) on a round-the-world stunt in 1889 or had raised funds for the base of the Statue of Liberty. Pulitzer's abrasive, long-distance hectoring drove away talent[29] and cut short promising careers, weakening the *World* at the very time it confronted challenges from upstarts such as Hearst and Ochs. As historian David Nasaw has written, Pulitzer by the late 1890s "had become an impossible man to work for, a nasty, vituperative, foul-mouthed martinet."[30] *The Journalist* attributed Pulitzer's petulance to his shattered health, saying his physical condition had "made him suspicious and querulous."[31] Whatever the reason, Pulitzer's mean-spirited letters to senior managers do little to support the reputation historians have accorded him, that of a heroic and innovative journalistic icon.

The correspondence, moreover, reveals Pulitzer to have been far more concerned with the *World*'s finances than its news report. Pulitzer repeatedly told his managers to pare expenses and to do so dramatically. As he instructed Norris in May 1897: "I want a radical reduction of expenses from beginning to end of every department, wherever it is reasonable and feasable [sic]. ... Retrenchment should be based upon the idea of absolute necessity. Unless you do something neither morning nor the evening [editions] can pay expenses the next three months. ... There is a lot of deadwood on the payroll anyhow."[32] Three months later, in a letter that referred to editors Bradford Merrill and Arthur Brisbane, Pulitzer told Norris: "Now that you certainly have a tactful and submissive man in Bradford, you must go over the payroll again and see whether you cannot get the expenses down to the bases of [1895] at least, if not lower; ditto for Brisbane and the evening" edition of the *World*.[33]

Ochs, Hearst, and Steffens were all strong-willed. But none of them was anything like the dictatorial Pulitzer. Their relative youthfulness, their significant prior experience, and their hands-on presence represented three of the four crucial variables that explain why the clash of paradigms emerged when it did. The fourth variable was the extraordinarily competitive nature of New York City journalism in the late 1890s. According to U.S. census data, 2,226 daily newspapers were published in *fin-de-siècle* America, fifty-eight of them in New York, the most by far in any American city.[34] To be sure, not all these newspapers were prominent, and not all were English-language dailies. Some, such as Hearst's *Morgen Journal*, were published in German. Even so, the intensity of the competition for readers encouraged experimentation in differing journalistic forms and formulae. As Paul Starr observed in *The Creation of the Media*, the competitive environment was a "prod to ... innovation in journalistic practices."[35]

The three-sided clash of paradigms would require years to play out. But the clash took shape in 1897, with enduring and decisive implications for American journalism.

"WONDERFULLY ABLE & ATTRACTIVE"

As distant and disagreeable as he had become by 1897, Pulitzer was not without moments of keen insight. Invoking "Geranium," his code name for the *Journal*, Pulitzer said in a letter to Seitz as the year neared its close: "I personally think Geranium a wonderfully able & attractive and popular paper, perhaps the ablest in the one vital sense, of managing to be talked about; of attracting attention; of constantly furnishing something which will compel people wherever they meet, whether in the drawing room, or in the poor house, elevated car or dinner table, to talk about something in that paper. That is the sort of brains the World needs. Pardon me for saying also, that with all its faults, which I should not like to copy—though they have been exaggerated—it *is a newspaper*."[36]

It was a remarkable acknowledgment for Pulitzer, who usually was scathing and derisive in his characterizations of the *Journal*. Yet his argument was unassailable. By the end of 1897, Hearst's *Journal* was the country's boldest, most energetic, most-talked-about newspaper. And 1897 was a remarkable year for the *Journal*, during which it proclaimed a new kind of journalism that "does not wait for things to turn up,"[37] but cuts through inertia to "get things done."[38] This was, the *Journal* announced, the "journalism of action," a paradigm of agency and engagement that went beyond simply gathering, printing, and commenting on the news. The "journalism of action" obliged a newspaper to "fitly render any public service within its power," the *Journal* declared.[39] As such, the "journalism of action" represented a clear, new choice for the profession.

The "journalism of action" was not meant to be sporadic or episodic in application. As the *Journal* envisioned it, the "journalism of action" was to be a sustained force, defined by a panoply of activist strategies and fueled by frequent doses of self-promotion and self-congratulation. As we shall see, the *Journal* in 1897 injected itself as a prominent actor in solving crime, extending charity, and thwarting suspected abuses of

Figure 2.2
The *New York Journal* sent a former U.S. senator, John J. Ingalls, to Nevada in March 1897 to cover the heavyweight boxing match between Robert Fitzsimmons and James Corbett. Ingalls' assignment was emblematic of the *Journal's* eagerness to hire well-known personalities and literary figures to report on major events. Ingalls' report was prominently displayed in the *Journal*. (Library of Congress.)

municipal government. For the *Journal*, 1897 was a veritable "calendar of achievements"[40]—a year of activism when, among other exploits, it rescued Evangelina Cisneros, a nineteen-year-old political prisoner from jail in Havana, and organized the New Year's Eve celebration to mark the consolidation of the boroughs of New York City.

The *Journal's* "journalism of action" embraced new practices and techniques in journalism, such as awarding bylines to reporters, experimenting with dramatic page designs, and publishing "extra" editions on Sunday afternoons. Unlike the *Times* and other rival newspapers, the *Journal* was not disinclined to hire talented women to its reporting staff. And the *Journal* was known to celebrate their contributions, such

Figure 2.3 Stephen Crane, author of *The Red Badge of Courage*, covered the brief Greco-Turkish War in 1897 for Hearst's *New York Journal*. One of his dispatches, critical of the commander of the Greek forces, carried the headline, "Blue Badge of Cowardice." Note the revolver at Crane's hip. It was not uncommon for war correspondents in the 1890s to carry firearms. (Syracuse University.)

as Eva McDonald Valesh's interview with President William McKinley in the summer of 1897. The *Journal* touted Valesh's work as a coup —as "the first interview ever given at the White House to a newspaper reporter by the nation's Chief Executive."[41]

The *Journal* also tapped then-new technologies, by bringing typewriters into the newsroom, by splashing pages with color illustrations, and by investing in the latest and most expensive high-speed web perfecting presses. To the envy and, no doubt, the resentment of its rivals, the *Journal* spent money, lots of money, in pursuing its activist vision.[42] It spent lavishly to hire, at least temporarily, some of the most prominent figures in American letters, giving the newspaper unrivaled cachet in 1897. The *Journal* paid $3,000 to Richard Harding Davis for a month-long assignment to Cuba. It sent a former U.S. Senator, John J. Ingalls of Kansas, to Carson City, Nevada, as its lead correspondent covering the heavyweight boxing championship in March 1897 between Robert Fitzsimmons and James Corbett.[43] The *Journal* arranged for no fewer than a dozen correspondents[44]—including two women[45]—to "make the Journal's columns a veritable kinetoscope picture" of the month-long Greco-Turkish War.[46] Most prominent among the *Journal*'s war correspondents was Stephen Crane, author of *The Red Badge of Courage*.[47] Mark Twain, who was then living in London, led the *Journal*'s roster of star correspondents covering Queen Victoria's Silver Jubilee in June 1897.

Even the *Journal* seemed astonished at times by the sums it invested in gathering the news. In describing the team of correspondents it assembled to cover the unfolding gold rush to the subarctic Klondike, the *Journal* declared: "The public at large has no conception of the magnitude of an expedition of this kind. In the first place, the actual and necessary expense is almost beyond belief ..."[48]

While the *Journal* routinely congratulated itself on lining up high-profile writers,[49] it must not have been altogether pleased with the reports they filed. Crane, for example, was not especially comfortable with the demands of daily journalism and preferred to write mostly about what interested him.[50] Although Crane filed several superb dispatches during the Greco-Turkish War,[51] he missed the much of the conflict's key early battle at Velestino in northern Greece, explaining that he had been "rather laid up."[52] After arriving at the battle, he acted strangely under fire. John Bass, another *Journal* correspondent, wrote that Crane, when he arrived at Velestino, "seated himself on an ammunition box amid a shower of shells and casually lighted a cigarette."[53]

Twain's reporting about Victoria's jubilee seemed half-hearted. The spectacle was easily the most regal international event of 1897, and came at a time when the British empire was at or near its height. But Twain found the celebration overwhelming—"a spectacle for the kodak [camera], not the pen."[54] His dispatch also included this strange observation: "I was not dreaming of so stunning a show. All the nations seemed to be filing by. They all seemed to be represented. It was a sort of allegorical suggestion of the Last Day, and some who live to see that day will probably recall this one if they are not too much disturbed in mind at the time."[55]

The association with Twain allowed the *Journal* to puncture rumors about the writer's failing health. The source of the erroneous reports was the *New York Herald*, which in early June 1897 reported Twain "grievously ill and possibly dying. Worse still, we are told that his brilliant intellect is shattered and that he is sorely in need of money."[56] The *Journal* promptly exposed the *Herald*'s report as erroneous, and published Twain famous if often-distorted denial: "The report of my death was an exaggeration."[57]

In its embrace of new techniques and technologies, and in its willingness to spend money, the *Journal* was the archetype and embodiment of the "new journalism" in America—a term borrowed from Britain and replaced, beginning in 1897, by "yellow journalism." The latter term was introduced and vigorously promoted by the *New York Press* as a devastating way of disparaging the *Journal* and its sometimes over-the-top content. The *Journal* did traffic in oddities, in strange and improbable stories that typically appeared in its Sunday supplements. The wacky content—such as "Can Man Breed Men From Monkeys?"[58] and "Is the Sun Preparing to Give Birth to a New World?"[59]—would be seen today only in the gaudy likes of the *National Enquirer, Weekly World News,* and other supermarket tabloids.

It is important to recognize, however, that the oddball stories were largely diversions on Sunday and not mainstays of the *Journal*'s report. What's more, the *Journal* had a fair amount of company in presenting oddball material on Sundays.[60] There was so much of it that *Fourth Estate* objected repeatedly, declaring: "The ordinary Sunday supplement needs revision. It is often indecent and not unusually stupid."[61] It is also important to recognize that the late nineteenth century was a period of great promise and breakthrough in science and technology. The development and application of the X-ray, the prospect of life on Mars, and the sustained efforts to develop heavier-than-air navigation all exerted a powerful hold on popular imaginations in the late 1890s. In their distorted way, the oddball stories in the Sunday supplements reflected and dramatized the broad interest in *fin-de-siècle* marvels.

To be sure, the *Journal* was known to err badly in its daily reporting. A notable example was the inaccurate report from Madrid in January 1897 that the Spanish government had agreed to an American plan to extend political autonomy to Cuba.[62] In such cases, the *Journal* was inclined not to correct its lapses, but to move on and forget they were ever published. Probably more than anything, however, it was the *Journal*'s indulgence in oddball stories in its Sunday supplements that gave rise to the lasting sense that it was a frivolous newspaper, that it blithely trivialized the news, and that it aimed for lowbrow, even semi-literate audiences. Historians typically have focused on the *Journal*'s oddball content as representative of "a shrieking, gaudy, sensation-loving, devil-may-care kind of journalism."[63] They usually have ignored, or dismissed, the newspaper's energetic and imaginative side. Similarly, journalism historians have often cast Hearst in the role of derivative imitator—a wealthy publisher who merely borrowed and cheapened Pulitzer's techniques in the sensational treatment of the news.[64] But such an interpretation is misleading, too. The activist model that Hearst's *Journal* developed and pursued in 1897 was far more sustained and consequential than anything that preceded it. Not even Pulitzer's *World* in the days of Nellie Bly and her round-the-world race against the clock in 1889–90 ever put together the succession of dramatic accomplishments that marked the *Journal*'s crowded and exceptional year of 1897.

The "journalism of action" owed a modest debt of inspiration to the *World* and its participatory "stunt journalism" of the 1880s and early 1890s. But the antecedents of the "journalism of action"—which maintained that a "newspaper, hardly less than a government, is the guardian of the people's rights"[65]—are more clearly found in a mid-1880s theory of "government by journalism."[66] The foremost advocate of "government by journalism" was William T. Stead,[67] a central figure in Britain's "new journalism" movement of the 1880s and founding editor in the 1890s of the *Review of Reviews*.[68]

Stead described his elaborate vision of "government by journalism" in a lengthy essay written in 1885, while serving a three-month prison sentence for abducting a young girl in an investigation to demonstrate the ease of trafficking of minors. His "government by journalism" essay, published in *Contemporary Review* in 1886, was a sweeping and even stunning assertion of powerful media effects, in which the journalist was seen as "the ultimate depository of power in modern democracy."[69]

Central to Stead's vision was the editor's ability to frame and shape public opinion, which he called "the greatest force of politics."[70] Editors, he wrote, "decide what their readers shall know, or what they shall not know. ... He can excite interest, or allay it; he can provoke public impatience, or convince people that no one need worry themselves about the matter." In essence, Stead asserted, an editor, by applying "either a stimulant or a narcotic to the minds of his readers," could bring to bear decisive influence on the important matters of the day.[71] No other voice, he added, is so regular, persistent, or far-reaching than that of the editor. "And it is not in one man's ears, but in his neighbour's and his neighbour's, until the whisper of the printed word seems to fill the very air."[72]

Stead conceded that some issues were beyond an editor's power to influence, writing that "there are some causes as dead as Queen Anne, which all the king's horses and all the king's men could not bring to life again." But he brushed aside that drawback, writing, "other things being equal, or nearly equal, it is the voice of the Press which usually decides which [topic] should be taken first."[73]

Stead urged journalists to dare to aspire, to think grandly of their profession. The journalist, he wrote, was more than "the keeper of a peep-show" of life,[74] more than a missionary or apostle. Rather, Stead insisted on the notion of "the journalist as ruler," acknowledging that such an idea would likely seem absurd to those practitioners "whose one idea of their high office is to grind out so much copy, to be only paid for according to quantity, like sausages or rope-yarn."[75] The more accurate and uplifting way to consider the profession, Stead wrote, was to recognize the editor as "the uncrowned king of an educated democracy. The range of his power is limited only by the extent of his knowledge, the quality rather than the quantity of his circulation, and the faculty and force which he can bring to the work of government."[76]

Stead was certain of such power, noting that in his career as editor of the *Pall Mall Gazette*, he had seen "Cabinets upset, Ministers driven into retirement, laws repealed, great social reforms initiated, Bills transformed, estimates remodeled, programs modified, Acts passed, generals nominated, governors appointed, armies sent hither and thither, war proclaimed and war averted, by the agency of newspapers. There were of course other agencies at work; but the dominant impulse, the original initiative, and the directing spirit in all these cases must be sought in the editorial sanctum rather than in Downing Street."[77]

Stead was keenly aware of the "journalism of action" and in 1897 enthusiastically endorsed the *Journal*'s activist paradigm. Stead specifically welcomed the *Journal*'s "splendid deed of knight-errantry" in organizing the Cisneros jailbreak in Havana. "No more worthy use can be made of the sceptre of modern journalism than this," he declared.[78] In a book published late in 1897, Stead hailed Hearst as "far and away the most promising journalist whom I have yet come across,"[79] and said the *Journal*'s publisher was well-positioned to "make his newspaper the organizing, vivifying, rallying center for all the best forces and influences" of New York City.

Stead suggested in 1897 that the "journalism of action" could be best applied in the form of a permanent tribunal endowed with investigative powers, much like those of a grand jury to compel testimony and recommend prosecution in cases of official misconduct. The tribunal, as Stead envisioned it, would take testimony in public and be empowered to punish perjury.[80] "The enterprise of the American newspaper is great," Stead wrote. "But although it can ... rescue Miss Cisneros, it cannot locate the boodler and prove who it is that levies blackmail."[81] Stead insisted the idea of newspaper-as-tribunal was offered "in all seriousness." But this elaboration of his "government by journalism" was too extreme for Hearst and the *Journal*. The *Journal* gave prominence to Stead's suggestions, publishing excerpts on its first Sunday news page on November 28, 1897.[82] But the *Journal* never went so far as to endorse or even seriously contemplate them.[83]

By that time, the *Journal* had developed a legal tactic that seemed more promising and less cumbersome than Stead's proposed tribunal. That tactic was to secure injunctions to block the suspected "grabs" or "giveaways" in awarding municipal public service contracts, such as those for trolley lines and public utilities franchises. These contracts were often suspect, calling as they did for the tearing up of city streets to install superfluous gas mains and the like.[84] The *Journal* first turned to the injunction in December 1896 to prevent the award of a gas main franchise in Manhattan.[85] It repeatedly invoked the tactic in 1897, in keeping with its self-described obligation of "acting when public service requires; acting in the way to accomplish beneficent results."[86] The *Journal* notably moved against a suspicious $10 million electric lighting contract in Manhattan[87] and gas and electric lighting deals in Brooklyn, which together were worth $5 million.[88] The newspaper organized a public meeting, attended by hundreds of people in early December 1897, to protest a "trolley grab" in Brooklyn.[89]

One of the *Journal*'s noisiest campaigns in 1897 was against what it called "the death loop" trolley terminus at the Manhattan side of the Brooklyn Bridge. The *Journal* claimed the design forced pedestrians to cross four sets of heavily traveled tracks to reach the bridge promenade. Seeking an injunction to block the hazard was, the *Journal* declared, "the legitimate province of a newspaper." It said it was "acting for more than a million readers" and added:

> There are many wrongs and oppressions that stand derelict and abandoned in our civilization because, though they menace all, they are not the special concern of any single citizen. ... All Greater New York realized that a death trap was being set when it was planned to make the bridge crowd [pedestrians] cross four lines of trolley cars to get to the promenade, but the outrage would have been without effective opposition had it not been for the Journal's injunction.[90]

When the *Journal* won a temporary injunction against "the death loop," it congratulated itself in a banner headline that declared: "The Journal Achieves Another Great Victory for the People."[91] But there was more than self-indulgence in the tactic of securing injunctions. In a very real sense, the *Journal* was fulfilling a consumer-protection role at a time when independent advocates were few or fledgling.[92] New York's Consumers Union was, for example, founded in 1897 as a political reform movement.

The *Journal*'s consumer-protection impulse—its big-heartedness[93]—was evident in other ways in 1897. In the immediate aftermath of a heavy snowstorm that swept the city in late January 1897, the *Journal* established a relief effort, saying, "The time has come to help the poor who starve, who freeze. Charity's hand is almost empty."[94]

Consumer protection also was the impulse for the *Journal*'s brief bicyclists-protection campaign. In June 1897, the *Journal* published a flurry of articles calling attention to the recklessness of the drivers of horse-drawn delivery wagons, many of whom detested cyclists and hated sharing the street with them.[95] The *Journal* promised to take up and publicize the cases of cyclists who were injured by the reckless conduct of wagon drivers and it urged victims to "send the particulars to the Journal's attorney for action."[96] The newspaper gave particularly prominent attention to the case of a one-armed bicyclist, Joseph H. Dougherty, who was nearly run down by a horse-drawn milk wagon. The driver had screamed at Dougherty, "Go ride in the park. Bicycles have no business on the streets."[97]

The cyclists-protection campaign quickly faded as the *Journal* threw its resources into solving a sordid and sensational murder mystery that took shape in late June 1897, when a dismembered human body began washing up in the East River.[98] The victim's headless torso was first to be found: it had been wrapped in a red-and-yellow oil cloth and bound with twine. The victim's arms were folded across his chest, which was torn and mutilated, as if a birthmark or tattoo had been cut away.[99]

At first, the New York police seemed stymied by the prospect of identifying the victim, let alone finding the killer. The *Journal* deployed a phalanx of reporters to pursue any number of leads. And it published in color the pattern of the oilcloth in which the torso was wrapped. It may have been "the first time color printing had been used to add impact to a breaking news story," according to historian John Stevens.[100] Reporters for the *Journal* soon found a dry goods store in Queens where yards of the oilcloth had been sold to a stout German woman, an unlicensed midwife named Augusta Nack. Meanwhile, another *Journal* reporter overheard a barroom conversation in which patrons wondered why a strapping Turkish bath masseur named William Guldensuppe had suddenly gone missing. The *Journal* reporter arranged for the patrons to visit the morgue and they immediately identified the remains as those of Guldensuppe, whose chest had borne a prominent tattoo.[101] The *Journal* soon determined that Guldensuppe had lived with Nack in a sometimes-violent *menage-à-trois* on East Ninth Street in Manhattan. The woman was estranged from her husband and had divided her affections between Guldensuppe and a barber named Martin Thorn.

It had taken the *Journal* less than a week to solve the gruesome murder mystery. It was first to report that Guldensuppe was the victim and to link him to Nack,[102] who was soon arrested, with Thorn, and indicted in Guldensuppe's killing. Nack testified against Thorn at trial, saying they had lured Guldensuppe to a cottage on Long Island. There, Thorn shot and stabbed him. He cut the body into five parts, wrapped them in the oilcloth, and tossed them into the East River. The victim's severed head was encased in plaster and dropped into the river.

The *Times* claimed to be appalled by the *Journal*'s "noisy detective work," declaring it in exceeding bad taste. "The grossness and needless explicitness of this kind of news reporting must have a demoralizing influence upon the younger generation," the *Times* declared, adding, "There has been nothing in the development of this case from the beginning that could be read without disgust."[103] To be sure, the *Journal*'s accounts of the Guldensuppe case—"'a murder, most foul, deliberate, mysterious and terrible'"[104]—were replete with gruesome detail. But the significance of the case lay in the *Journal*'s sleuthing, in its highly visible role in solving a murder mystery that had riveted New York City. The newspaper exulted in its accomplishment. "But for the Journal," it said, "the arm of the law would have been palsied. Only the evidence which this newspaper ferreted out compelled an indictment and thereafter forced the confession of the murderers."[105]

For the *Journal*, the Guldensuppe case demonstrated the public-spirited nature of its activist paradigm. "To bring a murderer to justice is to discharge a great public duty," the *Journal* declared, and added: "The new journalism strives to apprehend the criminal, to bring him to the bar of justice and thereafter not convict him but to show him as he is. The coarseness, the vulgarity and the inherent brutality of the Nack woman and her paramour, Thorn, have been brought before the public day by day."[106] Nack was sentenced to nine years in prison for manslaughter. Thorn was convicted of first degree murder and executed at Sing Sing prison in 1898.[107] While rival newspapers such as the *Times* sneered at the *Journal*'s detective work, the *Fourth Estate* declared itself impressed by the speed and ingenuity with which the *Journal* had solved the case. The trade journal wondered whether the newspaper was "not a more terrifying Nemesis to evil-doers than the officers of the law," and asserted: "The marvelous energy that characterized the rise of the Journal continues."[108]

Even more stunning than solving the East River murder mystery—and certainly more ethically dubious—was the *Journal's* "forcible liberation"[109] of Evangelina Cisneros in early October 1897. It was one of the most extraordinary episodes in participatory journalism history and marked the zenith of the "journalism of action." For more than a year, Cisneros had been held at the Casa de Recogidas, Havana's notorious jail for female prisoners. Cisneros was awaiting trial on charges of instigating an uprising against the Spanish military on the Isle of Pines in July 1896. Cisneros was accused of attempting to lure the Spanish commander on the island into a deadly trap. The *Journal*, however, claimed she was defending herself from the officer's unwelcome sexual advances. The newspaper also declared Cisneros' long imprisonment without trial was emblematic of Spain's routine mistreatment of Cuban women.[110]

The Cisneros case, which will be explored in detail in Chapter 4, revealed more than the breathtaking potential of the "journalism of action." The case also demonstrated the wiliness of the *Journal* and its readiness to abandon activist tactics if they were failing. In its campaign to win freedom for Cisneros, the *Journal* organized a petition campaign that urged Spain's queen regent to order the release of "the Cuban girl martyr."[111] Many well-known American women, including the mother of President William McKinley, lent support to the campaign.[112] But the campaign was mostly ignored by Spanish officials who suggested, disingenuously, that the clamor raised by the *Journal* had served only to delay Cisneros' release. When the petition drive stalled, the *Journal* sent Karl Decker to Cuba, ostensibly as the correspondent in the Havana bureau. His secret orders were to rescue Cisneros from the Casa de Recogidas.

Ominously for the "journalism of action," the Cisneros case also illuminated the *Journal's* weakness for hyperbole and exaggeration—a flaw that would ultimately erode the appeal of the activist paradigm. In its first accounts about Cisneros in August 1897, the *Journal* reported that she had been sentenced to twenty years' imprisonment[113] at a Spanish penal colony on Ceuta, off the north coast of Africa. At best it was unclear whether such a sentence had been passed. Spanish authorities insisted Cisneros had not been tried, let alone sentenced.[114]

Moreover, the *Journal* exaggerated the conditions of Cisneros' confinement at the Casa de Recogidas, saying she was forced to scrub

the prison floors[115] and endure other indignities. In another overstated report, the *Journal* said that prolonged imprisonment had left
the young woman "in death's shadow."[116] Such characterizations were
pointedly rejected as "false and stupid" by Fitzhugh Lee, the chief
American diplomat in Havana.[117] Upon arriving in New York in early
September 1897, at the start of an extended leave, Lee told reporters
that Cisneros had "two clean rooms" at the Casa de Recogidas and was
"well-clothed and fed. It is all tommy-rot about her scrubbing floors
and being subjected to cruelties and indignities," he declared.[118] Lee's
denunciation delighted other New York newspapers. They crowed
about the *Journal*'s unreliable reporting. The *Commercial Advertiser*
declared: "At least nine-tenths of the statements about Miss Cisneros
printed in this country seem to have been sheer falsehood."[119]

But when the jailbreak succeeded, many American newspapers
cheered the stunning exploit. For days after Cisneros' arrival in New
York, the *Journal* published excerpts of editorials from scores of newspapers that saluted the exploit.[120] "Few novels have a more stirring
theme," the *Post* newspaper in Pittsburgh said of the rescue, "and no
newspaper enterprise has equaled this feat."[121] The *Philadelphia Press*
called it "one of the brilliant achievements in journalism" and said the
Journal's feat "deserves all the praise it receives."[122] The trade journal
Fourth Estate reported that many U.S. newspaper editors regarded the
Cisneros rescue as the "greatest feat of modern journalism,"[123] suggesting that the *Journal*'s activism had stimulated wide interest and
appeal.[124]

But for the *Times*, the *Journal*'s conduct in freeing Cisneros was
inexcusably lawless. It said "the invasion of Havana by our contemporary's agent was perfectly indefensible" and said the release of Cisneros
"would better have remained for other agencies to accomplish."[125] Significantly, no other New York newspaper was as critical or as indig-
nant in its reaction.[126] But the *Journal* brushed aside the criticism. It
said it was "quite aware of the rank illegality" of the Cisneros jailbreak,
but declared itself "boundlessly glad" to have freed the prisoner.[127] The
Journal acknowledged "a savage satisfaction in striking a smashing
blow at a legal system that has become an organized crime. Spanish
martial law in Cuba is not, thank God, the law of the United States."[128]

In the aftermath of the Cisneros rescue, the *Journal* elaborated on
its vision of the "journalism of action," describing it more fully than
on any previous occasion. It said a newspaper's duty must not be "confined to exhortation." Rather, the *Journal* declared, when "things are
going wrong it should set them right, if possible." The Cisneros case
represented the "brilliant exemplification of this theory."[129]

The *Journal* insisted that "action" was "the distinguishing mark of the new journalism." Activism in journalism, it said, represented "the final state in the evolution of the modern newspaper." Newspapers of the late eighteenth century "printed essays; those of thirty years ago— the 'New journals' of their day—told the news and some of them made great efforts to get it first," the *Journal* said. "The new journal of to-day prints the news, too, but it does more. It does not wait for things to turn up. It turns them up."[130] It was an astonishing theory of journalism—that newspapers had a *duty* to take prominent and participatory roles in public life, to act when no other agency was able or willing. But the "journalism of action" envisioned no checks or restraints on a newspaper's conduct, suggesting that an activist journal was answerable only to itself. If the aims were worthy, even acts of lawbreaking could be morally justified. The "journalism of action" was not only a restless paradigm; it could be reckless, too.

NEW YEAR'S EVE 1897

The *Journal* again filled the void of government inaction as 1897 drew to a close. New York officials had planned no special event to celebrate the political consolidation of the five boroughs of New York City which, after years of planning and controversy, took effect January 1, 1898. William Strong, the city's outgoing mayor and a foe of consolidation, suggested that a mock funeral would be more appropriate than a celebration. Hearst would have none of that. He stepped forward to organize[131] what the *Journal* called a "great carnival,"[132] and what the *Fourth Estate* described as the "most remarkable undertaking ever conceived by any American newspaper."[133]

Weather conditions made for an awful night. Drizzling rain turned to ice and snow in the waning hours of 1897. In the early afternoon of December 31, the *Journal* said the weather was so poor that the festivities would be postponed. An hour or two later, it reversed itself and the celebration was back on.

The *Journal* estimated that 100,000 merrymakers went that night to City Hall park and its environs in lower Manhattan for "volcanoes of fireworks and floods of pulse-quickening music."[134] An enormous parade that included floats and dignitaries made its way down Broadway to City Hall. One enormous float featured a replica of the Brooklyn Bridge, where a wedding of Father Knickerbocker and Mrs. Brooklyn was celebrated "amid much merriment."[135] The parade was not without disruption. A burst of fireworks startled a team of horses who bolted from formation and ploughed through the ranks of the procession.

The animals trampled and injured several members of Francesco Fanciulli's 71st Regiment Band. For a few minutes, the *New York Herald* reported, "the wildest consternation reigned."[136]

As midnight approached, the parade reached City Hall, which was bathed in brilliant lights. When midnight struck, a small white object was seen climbing the flagpole at City Hall. Reaching the top of the staff, the object unfurled and revealed itself as the flag of New York City.[137] With that, "bedlam broke loose," said one reporter.[138] Fireworks burst over lower Manhattan, "sending down ... showers of blazing stars" and a National Guard battery began firing a one-hundred-gun salute.[139] The *Journal* made sure that its sponsorship was inescapable. It indulged in a vivid display of self-promotion. As *Fourth Estate* reported:

> "Read the *Journal*" ads danced up and down the neighboring buildings and on the clouds. Ads of the paper were everywhere and in all the popular places. There was a procession of floats and bands and militia, with their calcium lights. ... Of course there was lots of advertising in this, but it was of a good sort, and we comment upon it for that reason. The *Journal* had pledged itself to do something and it surpassed itself. That is a good way for a newspaper to become popular. ... [I]t carried off its enterprise in a manner that defied horribly adverse weather and delighted a vast multitude. ... We offer our congratulations to William R. Hearst.[140]

As the *Journal* had promised, the celebration was the "luminous starting point from which the history of the expanded New York will be dated."[141] It also was an extravagant and triumphant close to the *Journal*'s exceptional year. Even the usually bitter *New York Sun* complimented the *Journal* for having organized and underwritten the festival.[142] It cost the *Journal* at least $25,000[143] (the contemporary equivalent is about $500,000) to prevent the embarrassment of a consolidated New York City coming into existence "without a salvo of guns or a single public expression of the importance of the occasion."[144] It was a tremendous opportunity for the *Journal* to celebrate its activist ethos.

But the last day of 1897 also brought an unmistakable sign of limitations to the "journalism of action." On December 31, the *Journal*'s temporary injunction blocking construction of the trolley "death loop" was lifted. In the last hour of the year, officials and workmen of one trolley line, the Nassau Electric Railroad, made a symbolic first crossing on tracks spanning the bridge.[145] Within days, laborers had begun building the trolley loops.[146] The *Journal* pursued a series of appeals to halt the work, and urged the newly installed mayor of consolidated New York to intervene. But those efforts failed, leaving the *Journal* not only stunned but uncharacteristically disheartened.

"The Journal can do no more," it conceded during the first week of January 1898. "It has exhausted the resources of the law, and therefore has performed its full duty. No responsibility for the consequences of the construction and operation of the death loops can rest upon this newspaper, which acted while others talked, and acted up to the legal limit."[147] It seemed a shocking realization to the *Journal* that the courts could act independently of its wishes, and that the injunctions it secured were subject to reversal.

It must have galled the *Journal* that by late summer 1898, the Brooklyn trolley cars were carrying 150,000 passengers across the bridge every day.[148] The tracks were often crowded with pedestrians, as the *Journal* had warned. But there were few reports of pedestrians being struck by trolley cars and seriously injured.[149]

The *Journal*'s failure to block the trolley "death loop" was ominous for the "journalism of action." But anyone reviewing the sweep of the *Journal*'s energetic undertakings in 1897 can only be impressed by what an accomplished year it had been. The *Journal* saw it that way, too, declaring: "Never before in the history of journalism has a newspaper made such a record for a year as the New York Journal achieved during the year" just closed.[150] "The year saw the introduction of a new principle in journalism," the *Journal* said, adding:

> Up to the time the Journal showed the way newspapers contented themselves, at the utmost, with pointing out existing evils or giving warning of impending dangers. They constituted themselves [as] sentinels merely. They gave the alarm and whether it was heeded or not was no concern of theirs. The Journal made its business that great volume of wrong-righting which was everybody's business and which therefore was neglected. It went into the courts to fight for the people's rights, and time after time it preserved New York for spoliation. The community is much the [stronger] for the Journal's presence in the field during the past year.[151]

At the close of 1897, the *Journal* undeniably was America's ascendant newspaper. It had repeatedly demonstrated the effectiveness and appeal of its muscular agency as it injected itself conspicuously in civic matters and even in foreign affairs. It had shown that it could bring speedy resolution to untidy matters, as the East River murder mystery, the Cisneros jailing, and the New Year's Eve celebration of an amalgamated New York City had all demonstrated. The *Journal* had won praise even from its most bitter rivals, including Pulitzer and the *New York Sun*. Such recognition signaled that the *Journal's* activism had attracted considerably more than faint or passing interest among journalists by the close of 1897.[152] The "journalism of action" was by no means an idle notion. It was a restless paradigm, and the *Journal* declared the "journalism that does things has come to stay."[153]

During the crowded year of 1897, the *Journal* had no more persistent critic, no more high-minded rival than the *New York Times* of Adolph Ochs. The *Times* lacked the resources of the *Journal* and seldom competed in 1897 with the latter's enterprise in expensive, far-flung newsgathering. But the *Times* did position itself as a sober, moral counterweight to the *Journal's* audacity and excesses. More often than any other New York newspaper, the *Times* challenged the wisdom, ethics, and even the legitimacy of the *Journal's* frequent forays into activism. To the *Times*, the Cisneros rescue was, for example, essentially a matter of the *Journal's* pursuing an independent foreign policy, a development that the *Times* deemed utterly indefensible. The rescue, the *Times* said, "was without the shadow of legal excuse" and warned that "if acts like this are to be committed, international relations become impossible, and war is the only condition in which nations can exist."[154]

On occasion, the *Times'* criticism turned shrill and strained, as when it condemned "the hideous slang and cant terms" appearing in the *Journal's* sports columns.[155] "There is much to be said in favor of a statute punishing with fine and imprisonment the publishing of east side dialect stories and of newspaper reports couched in the English of the prize ring and the gutter," the *Times* declared in an editorial remarkable for its hostility.[156] More often the *Times* rebuked its yellow press rivals as "our esteemed freak contemporaries"[157] and as practitioners of "freak journalism."[158]

The frequent critique of the *Journal* helped define and energize a counteractivist paradigm and served to establish the *Times* as the antithesis of Hearstian activist journalism. The *Times* represented everything the *Journal* was not. It published no front page illustrations, no dramatic or experimental layouts, no color comics, no banner headlines. It seldom opened its news columns to indulgent self-promotion or self-congratulation. It insisted that readers were entitled to have the news presented "with entire impartiality."[159]

The *Times'* effort in 1897 to position itself as a moral and paradigmatic alternative to the *Journal* went well beyond name-calling and sloganeering. There was quality content to be found in the *Times*, and Ochs was innovative to the extent his resources permitted. At a time when the *Journal* and other newspapers were under attack for the pseudoscience and fact-fiction content of their Sunday supplements, the *Times* began publishing on Sundays a serious-minded, illustrated magazine. It was printed on high-quality paper and "stressed current events over the fluff and filler" of the supplements of rival newspapers.[160] The *Fourth Estate* said the *Times'* supplement was "the realization of the newspaper magazine, clean, clever and excellently printed."[161] On July 4, 1897, the *Times* magazine published a striking halftone section that contained thirty-seven official photographs from Queen Victoria's Silver Jubilee. "It is not too much to say," the *Times* declared, "that he who looks over these pictures will really see more of the jubilee than any one visitor could have seen, and more than the Queen herself could possibly have witnessed."[162] It was a pictorial coup for the *Times*. Moreover, the Silver Jubilee photographs signaled that the *Times* was inclined, even eager to embrace new methods and technologies, but on its own terms. Halftones and illustrations had their place—in the Sunday magazine, but not on the *Times'* ever-so-somber front page. Not until 1910 did a photograph appear on page one of the *Times*.[163]

Early in Ochs' first year as publisher, the *Times* launched another serious-minded supplement, a Saturday section devoted to literary news and book reviews. The *Times* also began publishing a Monday financial review. These sections represented a level of sophistication and seriousness of purpose that Hearst's *Journal* did not routinely offer and they helped to set the *Times* apart in New York journalism. The *Times'* coverage of financial and commercial news was exceptional, outstripping that of seven other newspapers examined in a crude but revealing content analysis published in 1897.[164]

Beyond the high-minded content, Ochs during his first months as publisher assiduously courted favorable attention for the *Times*. He sought to project the newspaper as tasteful yet ambitious, as innovative yet honest. He demonstrated what journalist Harrison Salisbury has called "a flair for ... understated public relations,"[165] while cultivating a remarkable amount of flattering commentary in trade publications and out-of-town newspapers. The issues of *Fourth Estate* from 1896 to 1898 are sprinkled with generous comments and observations about Ochs and his stewardship of the *Times*.[166] The tributes likely were solicited, directly or indirectly, by Ochs. In any case, they began soon after he was installed as publisher. "A glance at the New York *Times* since it has been in the hands of Adolph S. Ochs is like a gleam of sunlight on a cloudy day," *Fourth Estate* declared nine days after Ochs completed the acquisition. "The professional sees at once the handiwork of a fellow artist."[167] The trade journal noted that under Ochs, the *Times* had immediately done away with the agate type "that once hurt the eyes," removed the standing announcements from the editorial page, and began spelling datelines in capital letters.[168] The *Fourth Estate* article, which clearly was based on information from Ochs, also speculated the *Times* would soon build the tallest structure in New York, a twenty-nine-story edifice near Newspaper Row in lower Manhattan that would be "an ascension into the clouds."[169] Given Ochs' precarious financial status, such a plan was plainly absurd. But the "ascension into the clouds" story did the *Times* no harm. It certainly contributed to Ochs' efforts to differentiate the newspaper from its rivals, suggesting as it did that the *Times'* new owner was engaged, energetic, and more than a little unconventional. By 1904, Ochs had amassed enough resources to begin building a skyscraper, uptown.[170]

Ochs came in for more praise in November 1896, after the *Times* called attention to an absurd and extravagant city printing contract. Under terms of the contract, the *Times* and five other newspapers were to publish official returns of the 1896 election from all 1,392 precincts in New York. To print the returns in such detail, the *Times* figured, would fill forty pages of newsprint, even if very small type were used. At normal advertising rates, the contract would have cost the city $200,000, of which the *Times'* share would have been more than $33,000. Although Ochs badly needed the money, the *Times* assailed the deal as a "wasteful and extravagant use of the public funds."[171] The embarrassed New York aldermen narrowed the contract's scope to require publication of a less-detailed set of returns, for which no newspaper would receive more than $2,000.[172] The *Fourth Estate* praised the *Times* for its act of self-denial, saying its restraint was reminiscent of the *Times'* rejection, some twenty-five years before, of bribes offered by the corrupt Tweed ring then running City Hall. "Mr. Ochs did well and will get his reward in public confidence that the … spirit of the old *Times* has evidently been revived and retained," *Fourth Estate* declared.[173]

At a time when publishers often were absent or kept a distance from the day-to-day workings of their newspapers, Ochs' highly visible management style drew favorable attention. *The Journalist* described Ochs as quite unlike the "swarm of publishers … who think it beneath their dignity to get out on the street. They sit at their elegant roll-top desks surrounded by telephones, electric buttons, speaking tubes and stenographers and fancy that they are Generals. Mr. Ochs guides and directs his army of subordinates with skill and wisdom and he jumps into the fight himself as well. When a man can combine both kinds of ability, active and executive, he is pretty liable to make a success, and that is what Mr. Ochs does."[174] Meanwhile, Ochs was taking steps to enhance the *Times'* reputation for even-handedness by publishing letters that reflected varying opinions of public controversies, "regardless of whether the writer agreed with the *Times* point of view."[175] In their study of Ochs and his descendants, Susan E. Tifft and Alex S. Jones termed the practice "a revolutionary act in an era of polemical press lords."[176] More generally, the *Times* asserted its commitment to even-handed treatment of the news. As the 1897 New York mayoral election campaign unfolded, the *Times* declared: "We hold that the reader is entitled to have as fully as practicable, and in any case with entire impartiality, the facts as they come out on one side or another of the questions at issue."[177] The *Times* insisted that its editorial views would not taint its news columns.[178]

Such high-minded claims of impartiality were not much of a departure in American journalism. Newspapers in the past had characterized themselves in similar ways. As media historian David Mindich has noted, the elder James Gordon Bennett promised in the inaugural issue of the *New York Herald* in 1835 that the newspaper would "'record facts on every public and proper subject, stripped of verbiage and coloring.'"[179] In the mid-1770s, James (Jemmy) Rivington, a Tory printer in New York, insisted his newspaper was "open and uninfluenced."[180] Nonetheless, the claim of impartiality was a central plank in the *Times'* counteractivist paradigm—a claim that dated to the first days of the newspaper under Ochs' control. Almost immediately upon becoming publisher, Ochs promised "to give the news impartially, without fear or favor, regardless of party or sect, or interests involved."[181]

In the years that followed, Ochs cultivated this notion until it had become an unshakable component of his reputation as the *Times'* "presiding genius."[182] In 1932, for example, *Vanity Fair* said Ochs seemed "to have been the first great journalist to have treated news with consistent objectivity over a long period of years" and had "established a new canon of impartiality and of indifference to politics."[183] Several years after that, William L. Chenery, editor of *Collier's* declared that "Adolph Ochs, in the *New York Times*, introduced a new principle in daily journalism ... of printing all the important news regardless of what the paper felt about its implications. ... This separation of the functions of news gathering and reporting and of the expression of editorial opinion seem[s] to me to be one of the superb achievements of the American press. For what Mr. Ochs did in his own paper became the standard avowed by most publishers even though not all had the courage of Mr. Ochs's convictions."[184]

But not all analysts were so generous. Will Irvin, in his path-breaking analysis of the American press [185] that appeared in *Collier's* in 1911, offered this back-handed compliment to Ochs: "His newspaper is not clever, and it is not especially illuminating. But it comes nearest of any newspaper in New York to presenting a truthful daily picture of life in New York and the world at large."[186] Irwin rightly complained that the *Times* under Ochs demonstrated little interest or taste in exposing corruption. "Believing in no responsibility further than telling the news truthfully and giving an intelligent direction to the opinions of his readers," Irwin wrote, Ochs "does not go out of his way, as he might, to expose the filthy corners of a city which piles up considerable dirt now and then. ... Yet Adolph Ochs, with his New York 'Times,' is the best we may reasonably expect from the commercial [news-as-a-business] attitude toward journalism."[187] Indirectly, Irwin's assessment addressed a central reason for the ascendancy of the *Times'* model: it was the most adept and flexible in accommodating the multiple pressures that were reshaping American journalism. Especially in America's expanding urban centers, journalism was becoming a profession[188] *and* a big business. Its audiences were increasingly literate and educated and, increasingly, college graduates were attracted to its ranks as reporters, editors, and editorial writers.[189]

Irwin also had identified an important flaw in Ochs' counteractivist paradigm. The detached model certainly was incompatible with the sorts of high-profile campaigns and crusades, which the *Journal* had made central components of its "journalism of action."[190] The initiative-taking and exposure-driven qualities of investigative journalism do pose conflicts for a newspaper that is assiduously committed to the detached, impartial, and nonparticipatory treatment of news.

More than anything, what lent character and dimension to the *Times'* counteractivist paradigm was its slogan, "All the News That's Fit to Print." The slogan's assertiveness obscured an inherent ambiguity—that it could be interpreted as justification for censoring or ignoring some types of important stories. Even if it was slightly controversial,[191] the slogan was easily remembered and almost immediately popular. It was a key element in establishing what Tifft and Jones called the *Times'* "mystique"—that "carefully cultivated image of reliability, comprehensiveness, and objectivity,"[192] developed by Ochs and cultivated and respected by his successors. The slogan thus represented a pithy summation of the *Times'* alternate vision for American journalism, a model that stood in apposition to the extravagance and self-promotion of activist journalism.

In historical context, the slogan remains a daily rebuke to—and "a loud and emphatic repudiation of"[193]—the yellow journalism practiced during the late nineteenth century. As *Times* historian Elmer Davis wrote, "All the News That's Fit to Print" was "a war cry, the slogan under which the ... *Times* fought for a footing against the formidable competition of the *Herald*, the *World*, and the *Journal*. What it meant, in essence, was that the *Times* was going to be as good a vehicle of news as any of those papers, and that it would be free from their indecency, eccentricity, distortion or sensationalism."[194] It promised a restrained yet authoritative approach to the news.

Curiously, the slogan's precise derivation is murky. At the *Times*' centenary in 1951, the newspaper's in-house newsletter, *Times Talk*, said the logo was a hybrid, a version that was also cited by Tifft and Jones. According to the *Times Talk* account, Ochs supposedly borrowed the motto of the *Philadelphia Times*, "All the News," and appended "That's Fit to Print."[195] That version is incorrect, however. A thorough search of the issues of the *Philadelphia Times* published in the summer and fall of 1896 reveals that the newspaper never used "All the News" as its slogan or motto. The *Philadelphia Times* used any number of promotional statements, none of them pithy. The nearest approximation to "All the News" was this rambling assertion, placed immediately beneath the newspaper's front page nameplate: "If You Want All the News of Every Description Attractively Presented You Will Read the Times."[196] That statement appeared in the *Philadelphia Times* on August 4, 11, and 17, 1896; Ochs was formally installed as *New York Times* publisher on August 18, 1896.[197] "All the News That's Fit to Print," however, did not appear in the *New York Times* until October 1896. So, it appears that the famous slogan was Ochs' creation, as Harrison Salisbury maintained in his study of the *Times*.[198] It was, however, a slogan that Ochs was willing to toy with, at least a little.

THE MOTTO CONTEST

The motto first appeared on the *Times*' editorial page on October 25, 1896, the day the newspaper announced it would pay $100 to the person who proposed in ten words or fewer "a phrase more expressive of the Times' policy" than "All the News That's Fit to Print."[199] The contest elicited thousands of suggestions. Among the entries sent to the *Times* on postcards were: "Full of meat, clean and neat," "News Without Nastiness," "Pure in Purpose, Diligent in Service," and "Clean, crisp, bright, snappy; read it daily and be happy."[200] Others—such as "All the News Worth Telling," "All the News That Decent People Want," and "The Fit News That's Clean and True"—were unimaginative, clunky, and derivative.[201]

Before the contest ended, the *Times* altered the stakes by making clear it would not abandon "All the News That's Fit to Print." The *Times* attempted to justify this change of heart by saying no phrase entered in the contest was more apt and expressive than "All the News That's Fit to Print." The $100 prize would be awarded to the person adjudged to have submitted the best entry. But the motto would not be changed.[202] The contest thus became something of an abstract exercise. It certainly was an exercise in self-promotion. But the *Times* tried to characterize the contest as an opportunity for high-minded rumination about newspapers and their content. It "set the people of this city to thinking upon the subject of newspaper decency in a more attentive and specific way than has been their custom," the *Times* claimed.[203] The contest also had an important secondary effect, that of emphasizing the *Times'* commitment to decorum in journalism. As Michael Schudson noted in *Discovering the News*, "The *Times'* slogan ... emphasized decency as well as accuracy."[204]

A committee of *Times* staffers winnowed the entries to 150 semi-finalists, which were submitted to Richard Waterson Gilder, editor of *The Century* magazine. Gilder narrowed them to four finalists, which were:

- Always Decent, Never Dull.
- The News of the Day; Not the Rubbish.
- A Decent Newspaper for Decent People.
- All the World's News, But Not a School for Scandal.

Gilder pointed out that the terms of the contest had changed from the original intent of selecting a slogan that "more aptly express the distinguishing characteristics" of the newspaper to the more theoretical task of determining which entry "would come nearest to it in aptness."[205] That entry, Gilder determined, was submitted by D. M. Redfield of New Haven, Connecticut. Redfield's suggestion: "All the World's News, But Not a School for Scandal."[206]

"All the News That's Fit to Print" won for the *Times* no small amount of flattering attention.[207] Favorable references to the slogan often appeared in commentaries and tributes published in newspapers, magazines, and trade journals—tributes that the *Times* was eager to reprint. In reviewing the first year of Ochs' stewardship at the *Times*, the trade journal *Printer's Ink* said: "Trusting to an intelligent public to appreciate high standards, [the *Times*] introduced better paper, better press work, more suitable type, a greater variety and better quality of contents, and above all, strict insistence upon absolutely trustworthy and impartial news reports, and a rigid maintenance of its apt motto, 'All the news that's fit to print.'"[208] In Connecticut, the *Waterbury Republican* said the *Times*' motto was "not only theoretically admirable, but practically successful."[209] In Pennsylvania, the *Scranton Truth* said the slogan "epitomizes genuine journalism."[210] At the end of 1896, the *Independent* magazine declared: "The progress the *New York Times* is making in all directions is encouraging for good journalism. ... We would like to say a good word for a morning paper that stuck to its motto 'all the news that's fit to print.'"[211]

"All the News That's Fit to Print" was not without detractors. The *Boston Advertiser*, while complimenting the *Times* as "in many respects a most excellent newspaper," quarreled with the slogan and said, no newspaper "does or can or ought to 'print all the news'." The proceedings of the courts and of literary and artistic societies, as well as financial and mercantile transactions, were all elements of what the *Advertiser* called the "mass of news which could not possibly be printed, even in the finest and closest newspaper type."[212] The *Times* sniffed in reply that the examples offered by the *Advertiser* were "for the most part, not news."[213]

Far more antagonistic was Pulitzer's *World*, which denounced the *Times* as among the "derelicts of journalism" in New York City.[214] The *World*'s scathing article in March 1897 was aimed primarily at the *Sun*, the most vigorous supporter of the anti-yellow press boycott then spreading in metropolitan New York. The *Times* had given the boycott a fair amount of coverage, and the *World* reacted by calling it the money-losing instrument of trusts, or monopolies. "The shadow of death," the *World* said, "is settling slowly but surely down upon" the *Times*.[215] There was some truth in the *World*'s sneering attack. Although Ochs in 1897 was not taking direction from trusts and monied interests in publishing the *Times*, financiers and insurance executives had been instrumental in his acquiring the newspaper. Although it was then not known to the *World* or other rival newspapers, controlling stock interest in the *Times* was held for several years by the Equitable Life Assurance Society. The founder of Equitable Life, Henry B. Hyde, probably extended Ochs a loan that was vital to completing the *Times* acquisition in 1896. And in 1904, August Belmont, a powerful financier and a director of Equitable Life, was crucial in the city's decision to rename the parcel at Broadway and 42nd Street "Times Square."[216]

Although the *Times* was still losing money by the end of 1897, the "shadow of death" that the *World* had melodramatically identified was not quite so threatening or ominous. The *Times*' circulation and prestige were climbing, and the practical and theoretical elements of its counteractivist paradigm were falling into place. But it would take an entirely unanticipated, even desperate move to ensure the eventual preeminence of the *Times* and its journalistic model. And that was Ochs' abrupt decision in October 1898 to trim the newspaper's daily price from three cents to one penny. The move placed the *Times* with the *Journal* and the *World* in New York's one-cent newspaper market and prompted fears the *Times* would soon indulge in the flamboyance of yellow journalism.[217] But the *Times* insisted otherwise, stating: "It is the price of the paper, not its character, that is changed. ... That statement we make in full sincerity and firm resolution. We wish to make it with all possible emphasis, so that no reader of The Times in the past need scan the column of this morning's issue or of any subsequent issue with the least misgiving or apprehension lest the reduction in price may be concurrent with a lowering of tone and quality."[218]

The *Times* claimed the price cut was motivated by its desire to build circulation rapidly: "Everybody appeared to praise The Times and what everybody praises pretty much everybody ought to have and enjoy. Why not? This reasoning led almost inevitably to the conclusion that the high price of The Times was an obstacle to its rapid increase in circulation."[219] Over the years, the price cut has taken on the aura of having been a daring, hard-stakes gamble and a masterstroke of financial genius.[220] But Tifft and Jones have noted that Ochs was inspired by motives more desperate and tawdry than an eagerness to score rapid gains in circulation. The price cut was in fact a reaction to a disgruntled former bookkeeper and his threats to tell department store advertisers that the *Times*' circulation figures had been substantially inflated. "Revealing the truth about the *Times*' actual circulation would be a catastrophe," wrote Tifft and Jones. "The paper would lose the only advertisers that separated it from insolvency, and, far more important, Adolph would be denounced as a liar."[221] But dropping the daily price to a penny would quickly boost circulation, and thus render innocuous the bookkeeper's threatened disclosures.

Despite its dubious inspiration, Ochs' move was masterful because it had the effect of offering serious-minded journalism at a yellow press price. In retrospect, it seemed an almost-obvious recipe for success. But in the late 1890s, the notion that a respectable, high-quality newspaper would sell for a penny was absurd, and dismissed as a business plan for disaster. Some advocates, such as the *Fourth Estate*, had argued years before the *Times*' price cut that a newspaper could be "both good and cheap."[222] When the *Times* experiment proved successful, *Fourth Estate* declared: "All this goes to show that the people want and will support a clean, enterprising, high-grade newspaper that is sold for one cent and contains 'all the news that's fit to print.'"[223]

If Ochs and the *Times* represented the antithesis of Hearst's activist journalism, then Lincoln Steffens, for a few years beginning in 1897, offered the antithesis of journalistic practice. Steffens became city editor of the venerable but stodgy *New York Commercial Advertiser* in late 1897 after five years at the *New York Evening Post*, where he was an assistant city editor.

Steffens' anti-journalistic literary paradigm—or, as he called it, "our theory of journalism"—held that "anything that interested us would interest our readers and, therefore, would be news if reported interestingly."[224] It was an eccentric if stimulating experiment, and the most narrow of the three paradigms that took shape in 1897. It applied only to the *Commercial Advertiser*'s city news staff, which was under Steffens' supervision. The experiment disintegrated in just a few years, in part because of Steffens' restlessness, in part because of the management's impatience with the experiment.

But as it unfolded, Steffens regarded his experiment with enthusiasm, telling his father: "I have the beginnings of one of the best staff of reporters ever organized in this city. ... Nearly all of those I have brought to the paper with me are writers, educated, thoughtful fellows with character and ambition, who are hand in glove in the conspiracy with me to make a newspaper that shall have literary charm as well as daily information, mood as well as sense, gayety as well as seriousness. We are doing some things that were never done in journalism before."[225]

Steffens placed a premium on young, talented writers while shunning and disparaging veteran journalists. He recruited such emerging talents as Hutchins Hapgood, who later wrote *The Spirit of the Ghetto*, "a classic account of immigrant life,"[226] and Abraham Cahan, a novelist who became the long-serving editor of the *Jewish Forward*. Mostly, though, Steffens brought to his staff recent college graduates, many from Harvard University, who showed talent for writing and let them loose in New York to gather stories and hone their skills. "My reporters," Steffens later wrote, "... were picked men and women, picked for their unusual, literary pose. I hate the professional newspaper man; I had seen him going down and down and dreaded his fate. ... I wanted none of my staff. I wanted young, fresh, enthusiastic writers who would see and make others see the life of the city."[227] He added, "'We' had use for any one who, openly or secretly, hoped to be a poet, a novelist, or an essayist."[228] The neophyte reporters—"the freshmen of Park Row"[229]—were paid just $12 to $20 a week[230] but remuneration came also in encouragement to develop their own writing styles. Steffens vowed that "if any two reporters came to write alike, one of them would have to go."[231]

Not surprisingly, journalists at other New York newspapers sneered at the *Commercial Advertiser*'s experiment, but Steffens professed not to care. As the city's youngest reporting staff, he wrote, "we could outdo their contempt with our pity."[232] The city room of the *Commercial Advertiser* was an electric place where afternoons sometimes were devoted to staff discussions about art, life, and literary styles. "They were delightful talks," Hapgood recalled, "frank, enthusiastic, democratic; full of contrasts due to the differing personalities of the men [on the staff]."[233]

In developing the anti-journalistic literary paradigm, Steffens tapped into a vein of the "new realism" literary movement that had emerged with "epidemic suddenness"[234] in the late 1890s.[235] Steffens' experiment reflected his fascination with New York's Jewish ghetto and the city's immigrant life—subjects that he had explored in articles and character sketches for the *New York Evening Post* and other publications.[236] *Fourth Estate* said Steffens' writings about "the picturesque and pathetic life on the East Side of New York have won for him a place in the foremost ranks of the city's best short story writers."[237] Steffens later wrote that the inspiration for his experiment was, broadly, "a love for New York City, just as it was, and my ambition was to have it reported so that New Yorkers might see, not merely read of it, as it was: rich and poor, wicked and good, ugly but beautiful, growing, great."[238]

A more specific and immediate inspiration for Steffens' eccentric model were the forces of commercialization that had been gathering for years and were, by 1897, redefining journalism. Steffens' article in *Scribner's Magazine* in October 1897 about the *fin-de-siècle* American press was a thoughtful if long-winded assessment drawn from interviews with scores of U.S. newspaper editors and publishers. The article, which attracted considerable notice,[239] called attention to the rise of impersonal, advertising-based "commercial journalism." "Newspaper men," Steffens wrote, "see the drift of their profession into commercial hands. I found editors everywhere who deplored it as a fact, and business managers who rejoiced at it as a hope yet to be fully realized."[240] Steffens' article described not only the vast expenditures and capitalization required of large-city daily newspapers, but explored as well the implications of an elaborate but still-emergent corporate structure that empowered business and circulation executives often at the expense of newsroom managers.[241] "Not one managing editor in a hundred," Steffens wrote, "directs his department to his taste."[242]

Within weeks of the article's publication, Steffens was supervising the city staff at the *Commercial Advertiser*, where he clearly rejected the impersonal nature of "commercial journalism" and sought instead to manage the staff according to his own terms and idiosyncratic interests. His off-beat experiment produced curious if uneven results.

In his autobiography, Steffens recalled assigning Cahan to write about the case of man who killed his wife in "a rather bloody, hacked-up crime."[243] He encouraged Cahan to go beyond relating the crime's sordid details and find out why a man who had "loved someone once well enough to marry her" came to hate her so intensely that he cut her to pieces. "'If you can find out just what happened between that wedding and this murder," Steffens told Cahan, "you will have a novel for yourself and a short story for me.'"[244]

Steffens sometimes assigned his new reporters to write stories about "the difference between Fifth Avenue and Broadway or Thirty-sixth and Thirty-seventh Streets."[245] These offbeat, life-of-the-city reports could be more tedious than edifying, more perplexing than revealing. Sometimes they resembled news or news feature articles only in the vaguest way. For example, the *Commercial Advertiser*'s Saturday edition of December 18, 1897, included articles that described a circus clown's ruminations on the origin of pink lemonade, [246] an Italian poet's recollections of how he met his fiancée, [247] and the after-dinner reminiscences of an aging physician.[248] None of those accounts carried a byline and none was especially newsworthy.[249] And all of them seemed more than a little self-conscious.

But on other occasions, the offbeat reporting in the *Commercial Advertiser* offered thoughtfully crafted and sympathetic accounts about the aggravations and uncertainties that New Yorkers confronted in their growing and crowded city. A telling example was "Wreck on the Elevated," a column-long front page account that described the turmoil created by the derailment in December 1897 of a five-car elevated train near Eighth Avenue and West 147th Street. No one was hurt in the train wreck but the morning rush hour was thrown into utter disarray. "Never has there been a greater jam on the West Side elevated road than that following the accident," the *Commercial Advertiser* reported. Every station platform above West 59th Street was soon jammed with waiting commuters. Trains ran more than thirty minutes late, and railroad managers failed to alert the stations along the line. "As usual," the account said, "no information could be had of the station employees as to the cause of the delay or the time when delayed express trains might be expected to arrive."[250]

At the height of the disrupted rush hour, a *Commercial Advertiser* reporter squeezed aboard a downtown-bound express train at the West 135th Street station, and later wrote:

> Every seat was filled and all the standing room, not only in the cars, but on the platforms, seemed to have been taken. Nevertheless, the two or three hundred persons [at] the station formed rush lines, with end of the wedges directed at the car platforms. The crowds on the car platforms and in the cars were driven back and wedged tighter. ... The passengers were packed so tightly that every lurch of the fast running train threw to one side or the other in one compact mass. The few persons who could get hold of straps could no more prevent tumbling about than if they had been so many straws.[251]

It was not dramatic news, but the article certainly met Steffens' aim of writing newspaper stories "so humanly that the reader will see himself in the other fellow's place."[252] It was very tangible and recognizable reporting, describing as it did the frustrations and capriciousness about which New Yorkers were all too familiar. And it was the kind of story that other newspapers, including Hearst's *Journal* and Ochs' *Times,* did not duplicate, or even contemplate.

Nevertheless, the literary reports produced by Steffens' staff did not dominate the *Commercial Advertiser*'s content. The issues published in late 1897 and early 1898 offered considerable routine coverage of breaking events as well as a good deal of news from Washington, especially as the crisis over Cuba spilled into warfare between the United States and Spain in the spring of 1898. The four-month Spanish-American War was fought in the Caribbean and in the Pacific, making it extraordinarily expensive to cover. The *Commercial Advertiser,* like the *Times* and other cash-strapped newspapers, relied principally on wire service reports for their war coverage. The *Commercial Advertiser* supplemented its war reporting by publishing the lengthy letters from a Marine captain aboard the U.S. warship *Iowa,* which took a prominent role in the war's pivotal naval battle off Santiago de Cuba in early July 1898.[253] Steffens later said the war was "a smoke-screen under which we played around in city news, developing our cubs into reporters. We reported the local preparations for war and the formation of the Rough Riders and other units in the army."[254]

Less than a year after the war, the experiment at the *Commercial Advertiser* began to lose its vigor.[255] Steffens grew tired, "lost his freshness," and "became more interested in his own work than that of his reporters," as Hapgood later recalled.[256] The newspaper's managing editor, H. J. Wright, began to rein in Steffens and the city staff; Hapgood said that Wright "often accused me of 'thinking aloud' in my articles, rather than giving objective pictures of the news."[257] Steffens eventually "took the hint if not the point of view of his chief," Hapgood wrote, "… and began to discourage his reporters whose work in consequence rapidly became conventionalized."[258] The anti-journalistic literary paradigm had all but disintegrated by 1901. By then the *Commercial Advertiser* had become what Hapgood called "a perfectly conventional, dull and commonplace sheet."[259] Steffens soon left daily journalism for *McClure's Magazine* and a spectacular career in muckraking.

Given its brevity and eccentricities, it is tempting to conclude that the Steffens experiment left "little mark on influencing standards in journalism."[260] Such a judgment is probably too harsh. As John Harstock has suggested, the appeal of literary journalism in the 1890s was probably greater than is usually recognized. The work of novelist-journalist Stephen Crane suggested as much, Harstock said. During the 1890s, Crane "published his true-life sketches of local color in [nearly] every major New York newspaper."[261] More significantly, the rule-bending unconventionality of Steffens' experiment anticipated the literary "new journalism" movement of the late 1960s and early 1970s. That movement likewise rejected journalistic conformity and conventional norms, and dabbled in such practices as developing composite characters and offering recreated or imagined dialog.[262]

Traces of the Steffens paradigm also can be found in what nowadays is called mainstream journalism. The emphasis Steffens placed on stories written "so humanly that the reader will see himself in the other fellow's place"[263] has become standard guidance for students of American journalism. "Make me see" was advice notably offered by Eugene Roberts, the executive editor of the *Philadelphia Inquirer* in the 1980s.[264] Steffens' appeal to his staff to find "the charm and beauty and significance of commonplace men and women"[265] remains a challenge to contemporary American journalists.

WHY THE *TIMES* MODEL PREVAILED

Steffens once described Harry Thurston Peck as "one of those geniuses who never have enough to do."[266] Peck was a professor at Columbia University and editor of the monthly *Bookman* magazine. He became literary editor at the *Commercial Advertiser* as well. Peck was also something of a *fin-de-siècle* press critic and in 1897 he wrote a lengthy and searching analysis of American newspapers for *Cosmopolitan* magazine.

Peck's article was published in December 1897, under the headline, "A Great National Newspaper."[267] Peck reviewed familiar failings of American newspapers—their sensationalism, their partisanship, their relentless local focus, and their inclination to indulge in "reckless vituperation."[268] But Peck closed on a hopeful and even prescient note. The time would arrive, Peck predicted, when

> there will be established a journal that shall be national, not local; a journal that shall stand side by side with existing ones, performing faithfully the task which they have failed to undertake. It will be a journal whose pages shall be neither dull on the one hand, nor vulgar on the other. It will be courteous to its opponents, setting forth their arguments strongly and fairly, and answering them rationally, crisply, and convincingly. If it makes mistakes, it will correct them gladly and thus win the confidence of even the men who reject its views. It will have a light touch for lighter themes, but with the fire of earnest conviction glowing through it all; with an American sense of humor and an equally American sense of decency, and propriety, and fair play; and it will in the end possess an influence that shall surpass the influence of Presidents and cabinets, in that it will appeal to right reason and truth and elemental justice. And the exceptional man whose fortune it shall be to edit and direct it, will become in the nation a force for good such as it is seldom granted anyone to wield.[269]

To be sure, no newspaper in 1897 came close to fulfilling that imposing standard. But Peck's article, when read from the distance of more than one hundred years, suggests or hints at the emergence of the *New York Times* as the country's preeminent daily newspaper. The *Times* and its detached, impartial, counteractivist paradigm has come closest to fulfilling Peck's prophesy. For periods in the twentieth century, the *Times* was a journal neither dull nor vulgar, a newspaper that attempted to present the range of arguments in public debates "strongly and fairly," as Peck had written. It earnestly, if not "gladly," corrected its errors. During the latter years of the twentieth century, the *Times* developed "a light touch for lighter themes," and not infrequently displayed a "sense of decency, and propriety, and fair play." Its power and influence never exceeded that of presidents and cabinets, although its critics sometimes thought it did.

When Peck wrote the article in 1897, the *Times'* climb to the top ranks of American journalism seemed improbable. So why did the *Times* and its counteractivist paradigm succeed in becoming the guiding *leitmotif* for American journalism? What factors explain the rise and embrace of detached, authoritative journalism? How did the *Times* over the years come to best approximate the vision Peck described at the end of 1897?

Certainly the price cut in October 1898 was vital in ensuring the *Times'* emergence to superiority. (*Times Talk,* an in-house publication, said in 1951 that the price cut was the "turning point in modern Times history."[270]) The price cut drew thousands of news readers to the *Times.* But perhaps more significantly, the move effectively blocked the *Journal* and *World* from raising their prices to two cents from a penny. Although they remained fierce rivals during and after the Spanish-American War, the *Journal* and *World* periodically discussed a joint price hike to two cents, an arrangement that today would be tantamount to illegal price-fixing. Their talks continued until late 1899, but no agreement was ever reached, in part because they were disinclined to leave the one-cent market to Ochs. The *Times'* price cut had the effect then of locking the *Journal* and *World* into a long-term revenue squeeze. Hearst's "journalism of action" required a large staff and the expenditure of substantial sums of money. It was expensive, and yet the *Journal* was unable to boost revenues by increasing its price. This crucial consequence of the *Times'* price cut has been largely overlooked by historians.[271]

The price cut also differentiated the *Times* from New York City's conservative but more expensive titles, notably the *Herald,* the *Tribune,* and the *Evening Post.* For one cent, New Yorkers could buy a daily newspaper that was both serious and inexpensive, both authoritative and accessible. The combination was unbeatable—and was unmatched by any other conservative daily. The *Times* did not spurn or insult readers of the yellow press in announcing its price cut. It reached out to them by offering itself as an affordable alternative. The *Times* said it believed that thousands of New Yorkers "would like to buy and read a newspaper of character and quality of The Times in preference to, or let us generously suppose, in conjunction with, the papers they have been reading."[272]

The price cut also helped solidify the *Times'* standing as the newspaper best positioned in New York to stand up to the yellow tide—and, more broadly, best positioned to accommodate and absorb the multiple pressures that were turning American journalism into a big business serving audiences that were progressively more urban and educated. The *Times* was decidedly anti-yellow in offering no comics, no front-page illustrations, no big headlines, few bylines, limited self-promotion, and no pseudoscience in its Sunday magazine. Its supplements were well done and serious-minded, demonstrating that somber journalism could be impressive and even appealing. Moreover, Ochs during his first full year as *Times* publisher in 1897 won recognition as a different sort of publisher—earnest, engaged, and successful in courting favorable publicity while obscuring the newspaper's precarious financial status and its ties to financiers and insurance interests.

There was no more regular critic of the *Journal*'s activist ways than the *Times*. In any event, the price cut set the *Times* apart from its rivals, a process that had begun with its frequent critiques of the *Journal*'s activism in 1897. The *Times* was not alone in its attacks on yellow journalism. But the *Times*' critique was unrelenting and pointed. It was also savvy, even cerebral. The *Times* seldom resorted to name-calling or offering ugly insults, as did the *Sun* and the *New York Press*. Rather the *Times*' critique became more nuanced and sophisticated during 1897. It held forth, as no other newspaper did, about the potential international implications of the *Journal*-led jailbreak in Havana. In short, the *Times* went beyond New York's other conservative newspapers in addressing the concerns about how the ferment in the field in 1897 would play out. No other newspaper in New York was better positioned in the late 1890s to counter the appeal of the "journalism of action." The *Sun* was weakened by Dana's irritable ways and his fatal illness. The *Tribune*, while innovative in some respects, was too aristocratic and its owner, Reid, was an absentee proprietor. The *Herald* likewise was run by an absentee publisher, James Gordon Bennett Jr. And the *Press* was too rabid and too partisan and too protectionist in policy. The *Times*, cool and dispassionate, possessed none of those defects.

WHY THE "JOURNALISM OF ACTION" FAILED

Perhaps a more intriguing and revealing way to frame the question of why the *Times*' counteractivist template prevailed is to ask why Hearst's "journalism of action" failed to consolidate the successes and considerable momentum it had achieved in 1897. By the end of the year, the *Journal*, as we have seen, was America's ascendant newspaper. Eighteen-ninety-seven was for the *Journal* a remarkable year of accomplishment and recognition that few newspapers have ever achieved.

Figure 2.4 Charles A. Dana, the brilliant but foul-tempered editor of the *New York Sun*, died in October 1897. Dana had been a force in American journalism for nearly fifty years and his death underscored the transitory character of 1897. Many of Dana's bitter foes, including Hearst and his *New York Journal*, were charitable in recalling Dana's contributions to the field. (Library of Congress.)

As surprising as it may seem today, the "journalism of action" was easily the most promising of the three paradigms that emerged in 1897. More than any other large American newspaper, the *Journal* embraced the "new," the *zeitgeist* of the late 1890s. The *Journal* projected a sense of energy, a robust dynamism, in *fin-de-siècle* urban journalism. Its "journalism of action" was very much in sync with the vigor and the ethos of the times. It was the *Journal*'s vision, and not that of the *Times*, which appeared more likely to prevail, to win acceptance as the model for American journalism in the twentieth century.

Figure 2.5 In his *New York Journal* in 1897, William Randolph Hearst announced the development of a new model of journalism, one infused by a self-activating ethos that sought to "get things done." The *Journal* called it the "journalism of action" and said it represented "the final state in the evolution of the modern newspaper." (Library of Congress.)

Hearst invested in new technologies, such as banks of typewriters, huge presses, and batteries of typesetting machines. He spent heavily on newsgathering,[273] deploying a large number of reporters to cover important stories—a practice that one hundred or so years later would be known at the *New York Times* as "flooding the zone."[274] That was precisely how the *Journal* in 1897 covered the Cuban insurrection, the brief Greco-Turkish War, the Silver Jubilee of Queen Victoria, and the Klondike gold rush.

The *Journal* also took keen interest in major sporting events, such as the Robert Fitzsimmons–James Corbett heavyweight boxing match in March 1897, and arranged for Fitzsimmons to file exclusive reports to the *Journal* about his preparations. Hearst, moreover, was quick to recognize the potential of the early cinema and he teamed the *Journal* with Thomas Edison's fledgling motion picture company to produce several short films in the run-up to the Spanish-American War.[275]

During the war, Hearst engaged in "flooding the zone" to an unprecedented extent. The *Journal* spent $50,000 a week—the equivalent one hundred or so years later of more than $1 million a week—on cable tolls, reporters' salaries, and dispatch boats that ferried correspondents' reports from the front in Cuba for transmission to New York.[276] The financial commitments buttressed the *Journal's* frequent boast— "While the others talk, the Journal acts." Pulitzer had little taste to match Hearst's spendthrift ways. Ochs in the late 1890s couldn't begin to do so; nor, for that matter, could Steffens. The "journalism of action" also promised to be an antidote to the deepening perception that the American press was losing influence in the late 1890s—a troubling notion that seemed confirmed in New York City's mayoral election in 1897, when no major newspaper, other than the *Journal*, backed the winning candidate, Robert Van Wyck.

The *Journal's* panoply of activism exerted no small appeal in American journalism. In a glowing assessment of the newspaper during Hearst's first five years as owner, the trade journal *Fourth Estate* said of the *Journal*: "It does not expend all its energies in talk or in setting forth in type what it proposes to do or what somebody else ought to do. Figuratively speaking, when the Journal sees that something ought to be done it takes off its coat and does it."[277] So what happened? Why did the appeal and muscular agency of the "journalism of action" fail to become the gold standard for the American news media? Why was its promise left undeveloped and unfulfilled? The "journalism of action," after all, was certainly more captivating than the somber, detached paradigm of the *Times*, more broadly appealing than the eccentric literary model of the *Commercial Advertiser*. Unlike Ochs, Hearst ran a newspaper not in financial distress. Unlike Steffens, Hearst owned his newspaper.

Others have identified this conundrum, but have failed to offer satisfactory explanations for the ultimate failure of the "journalism of action." Willis J. Abbot, once a top editor at the *Journal*, wrote in his memoir that Hearst "in the last years of the nineteenth century seemed destined to revolutionize journalistic methods." But no sooner had he discovered "a style and a formula to his liking," Abbot wrote, "than he settled down contentedly to maintain it for the rest of his days."[278]

Just as the "journalism of action" was a complex paradigm, so are the causes of its ultimate repudiation. Several reasons offer themselves, including:

- The exaggerated coverage of the Spanish-American War in 1898. It diminished the appeal of activist journalism and helped to seal Hearst's standing as an unpopular figure in American journalism. The "journalism of action" suffered for his unpopularity.
- The politicizing of the "journalism of action." It became clear during the first years of the twentieth century that the paradigm was effectively a platform for Hearst's lofty and mostly unfulfilled political ambitions.
- The emergence of muckraking and the recognition that investigations and exposés of official wrongdoing were perhaps better suited to long-form magazine formats. Hearst's *Cosmopolitan* magazine in 1906 published one of the landmark series of the muckraking genre.
- The expansion of Hearst's newspaper holdings. Their growth prevented Hearst from honing the "journalism of action" into a widely applicable model. Activist journalism, as practiced by Hearst's *Journal*, was an expensive undertaking and not many newspapers could underwrite such costs. Similarly, it was difficult to sustain the excitement and sense of novelty upon which the "journalism of action" thrived.

Each of these elements will be discussed in turn.

The *Journal*'s activist model was blighted, and perhaps doomed, by its overheated coverage in 1898 of the deadly explosion of the U.S. battleship *Maine* in Havana harbor and the subsequent Spanish-American War. The *Journal* was quick to publish thinly documented claims of Spanish complicity in the destruction of the *Maine*,[279] the cause of which has never been unequivocally determined.[280] The *Journal*'s sister publication, the raunchy *Evening Journal*, was particularly extreme, prominently reporting fanciful stories such as the purported discovery of a torpedo hole in the sunken *Maine*[281] and the "mysterious" Spanish warships that supposedly were nearing the East Coast of the United States.[282]

During the war, the *Journal* made unauthorized use of the *Chicago Record*'s dispatch about the U.S. Navy's destruction of a Spanish squadron in Manila Bay,[283] the most stunning victory of the four-month war. The *Record* condemned the *Journal*'s ethical lapse and the *World*, with unconcealed delight, reprinted the *Record*'s criticism.[284] When a Spanish relief squadron headed for Manila from the Iberian Peninsula, Hearst contemplated scuttling a vessel across the most narrow point of the Suez Canal, to prevent the Spanish vessels from passing en route to the Philippines. Hearst abandoned the outlandish idea when Madrid recalled the warships to protect the Spanish mainland from a prospective U.S. naval attack. [285]

To his credit, Hearst was the only New York newspaper publisher to travel to the cockpit of the war. But he did so absurdly, chartering a refitted fruit company steamer, the *Sylvia*, to travel in luxury to the Caribbean theater. The yacht was equipped with printing presses, darkroom, and "food fit for a king."[286] Cooks, stewards, editors, reporters, and two women whom Hearst had been escorting in New York were also aboard. Hearst's timing was impeccable. The *Sylvia* reached the waters off Santiago-de-Cuba just before U.S. ground forces invaded eastern Cuba. Hearst was there to report the U.S. victory in a battle on the San Juan Heights near Santiago on July 1, 1898. Two days later, he positioned the *Sylvia* amid the action when Spanish warships tried to escape the U.S. naval blockade of Santiago. The fleeing Spanish vessels were all destroyed. As the naval battle ebbed, Hearst brought aboard the *Sylvia* twenty-nine Spanish sailors as his prisoners.[287]

Despite the energy and expense devoted to covering the conflict, Hearst's wartime journalism seemed intemperate and extreme. The *Journal*'s exaggerations about the *Maine* disaster allowed the *Times* to sneer: "The grotesque inventions of the yellow journalist's fancy must still produce tumultuous excitement among stable boys and scullery women, but they now interest intelligent people only by their weird deformity."[288] Edward L. Godkin, editor of the antiwar *New York Evening Post*, sneered that Hearst, "a blackguard boy with several millions of dollars at his disposal," wielded "more influence on the use a great nation may make of its credit, of its army and navy, of its name and traditions, than all the statesmen and philosophers and professors in the country."[289] Godkin's characterizations were preposterous, of course. But they reflected a deepening sense that the *Journal* had fomented an unnecessary war.[290] That Hearst and his newspapers brought on the Spanish-American War remains an attractive though erroneous interpretation—but one that helped to discredit the "journalism of action" and undercut its appeal.

While outlandish, the allegations of war-mongering did little to burnish Hearst's persona. Although the *Editor & Publisher* trade journal, in its inaugural issue in 1901, described him as "the foremost figure in American journalism," Hearst was never very likable or sociable. A columnist for *The Journalist* wrote in 1897 that Hearst was "always pale, always preoccupied, always brooding, always sad-eyed, and always … with a grievance."[291] Hearst never completely shook the reputation of a spoiled rich kid, and the "journalism of action" suffered because of his personality.

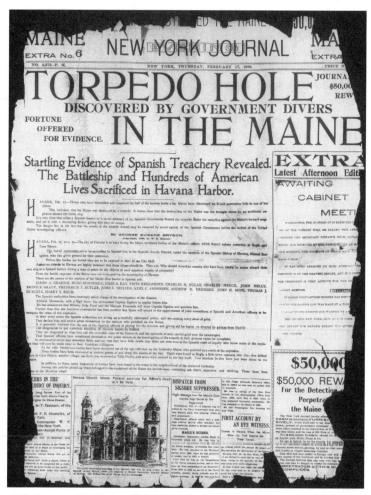

Figure 2.6 The appeal of the *New York Journal*'s activist journalism was diminished by its over-heated reporting of the destruction of the *Maine*, an American warship on a friendly visit to Havana in early 1898. The *Journal*'s sister paper, the *Evening Journal*, went so far as to report, erroneously, that a torpedo was found to have blown an eight-inch hole in the *Maine*. (Library of Congress.)

A measure of how toxic Hearst's persona became is apparent in a detailed study of press-related comments published in leading American magazines from 1890 to 1914. Of nine prominent American journalists of the nineteenth and twentieth centuries included in that portion of the study, only Hearst received more negative than positive appraisals.[292] Hearst often was accused in the magazines "of compelling his correspondents to send fake cable news, of seeking the sordid

Figure 2.7 Although his *Journal* became America's ascendant newspaper in 1897, William Randolph Hearst was not very likable. A columnist for *The Journalist* trade journal wrote that Hearst was "always pale, always preoccupied, always brooding, always sad-eyed." But under the pen of a sympathetic artist, Homer Davenport, Hearst seemed coiled with energy and even a bit fanatical. (Library of Congress.)

and trivial in order to create circulation, and with fomenting discontent and unrest."[293] The vehemence directed at Hearst was extraordinary, and signaled keen distaste for his practices.

By no means did Hearst give up on the "journalism of action." The *Journal* declared, after all, that it had "adopted the policy of action deliberately, and it means to stick to it. … We expect to see great results flow from this work."[294] If anything, Hearst's embrace of the activist paradigm grew stronger in the years immediately after 1897. In 1899, for example, the *Journal* reasserted that it was "the right and duty of a newspaper to do anything whatever that will promote the public interests, and that can be better done by the newspapers than by any other agency."[295] In 1900, the *Journal* characterized the "journalism of action" as a long-sought mechanism "for concentrating public opinion" and introducing "direct responsibility into every branch of public service."[296]

But by the turn of the century, the politicizing of the "journalism of action" was also becoming apparent. As David Nasaw has noted, newspapers of the time "were not just the principal, but practically the only, effective campaign medium."[297] Hearst's newspapers became the vehicles for promoting his lofty political ambitions. In early 1899, Hearst's newspapers published under his name an editorial calling for domestic social and political reforms under the headline "An American Internal Policy."[298] It was a lucid, entirely reasonable domestic reform agenda that called for public ownership of utilities, "destruction of criminal trusts" or monopolies, a graduated federal tax on incomes, direct election of U.S. senators, and improvements to public school systems. But the agenda was also a platform for Hearst. By 1900, editorials appeared in the *Journal* signed by "W.R. Hearst, President of the National Association of Democratic Clubs."[299] Two years later, he was elected to the first of two terms in Congress.

The politicizing of the "journalism of action" was probably inevitable, given Hearst's frequent campaigns for public office: Not only did he twice win election to Congress, he sought but lost the Democratic nomination for president in 1904, lost the New York gubernatorial race in 1906, and twice ran unsuccessfully for New York City mayor. Like Hearst's toxic persona, his political ambitions did little to enhance or sustain the attractiveness of the "journalism of action."

The spirit of activist journalism was perhaps better suited to long-form magazine exposés—notably those that characterized the muckraking movement during the first years of the twentieth century. Exploring and exposing official corruption, indifference, and incompetence in their complexity typically required extended periods of research and writing, which the muckraking journals allowed. Ida Tarbell's famous exposé of Standard Oil was five years in the making. She described Standard Oil's abuses in a series of nineteen articles that was published in *McClure's Magazine* over a two-year period.[300] Hearst, himself, entered the muckraking market in 1905 by acquiring *Cosmopolitan.* Within a year, *Cosmopolitan* had produced one of the most memorable series of the muckraking genre—David Graham Phillips' nine-part series "Treason of the Senate," a withering and unrestrained attack on high-level political corruption among U.S. senators who were selected by state legislatures.

So in important ways, the muckraking movement absorbed, channeled, and refined the aggressive spirit of the "journalism of action."[301] Hearst's acquisition of *Cosmopolitan* suggests another related factor in the decline and failure of the "journalism of action." Hearst became a press lord. His decision to start a newspaper in Chicago in 1900, to support the Democratic presidential ticket that year, not only was an expression of political ambition but a portent of a media empire. By 1925, Hearst was the owner of twenty-five newspapers in seventeen cities. He also had become intrigued by tabloids and their pithy treatment of the news. "If you want to obtain and retain anyone's attention," Hearst said in an interview with *Editor & Publisher*, "you must say something worth while and say it quickly. Hence the tendency of journalism towards the tabloid … in condensation and presentation of the news."[302] Nor were Hearst's leading editors then speaking of the appeal or urgency of activist journalism. Arthur Brisbane, who became editor of the *New York Evening Journal* in 1897 and worked for Hearst longer than any journalist, declared in 1925 that the principal obligation of a newspaper was "to stimulate thought, that's the only really important thing anybody does."[303] There was not even a hint in Brisbane's assessment about the "journalism of action."

While building a chain of newspapers may have heightened perceptions of his influence, the diverse commitments prevented Hearst from honing and refining the "journalism of action." As a press lord, he was too busy to develop a sophisticated approach to activist journalism.[304] Hearst suggested as much in an interview with Lincoln Steffens in 1906. "If I had stuck to one newspaper, I might by personal direction in detail have made a newspaper to suit me exactly," Hearst was quoted as saying. "But I went off starting other newspapers in widely separated places, and, of course, I can supervise all of them only in a general way. I can't give myself to any one."[305] Intentionally or not, Hearst's comment was an allusion to the focused approach of Adolph Ochs. Among the three central figures in the clash of paradigms, only Ochs concentrated on a single newspaper, the *Times*.[306] He briefly considered building a newspaper chain after acquiring two Philadelphia dailies in the early twentieth century. But he soon merged the two newspapers and sold off the combined entity.[307] Ochs' singular focus was essential to the *Times*' emergence from near-bankruptcy to a powerful and profitable enterprise. The success of the *Times* under Ochs led "newspaper publishers all over the country to study his methods," said an article in *Vanity Fair* in 1932. A "large section of the press adopted Ochs' impartiality in news and headlines in the hope that Ochs' prosperity would follow."[308]

Figure 2.8 In 1897 Adolph S. Ochs was in his first full year as publisher of the *New York Times*. Despite the newspaper's desperate financial condition, Ochs began positioning the *Times* as a moral counterweight to the yellow press, which was then dominant in New York City journalism. In February 1897, Ochs moved the slogan, "All the News That's Fit to Print," to a permanent place on page one of the *Times*. (From *Fourth Estate*.)

In the end, it probably was impossible to sustain the excitement and sense of novelty on which the "journalism of action" thrived. As press critic Walter Lippmann observed in 1931 in discussing the decline of yellow journalism: "When everything is dramatic, nothing is dramatic. When everything is highly spiced, nothing after a while has much flavor. When everything is new and startling, the human mind just ceases to be startled."[309] In a sense, then, the "journalism of action" wore out its appeal and anesthetized its audiences with unending doses of self-promotion and self-congratulation. Lippmann also declared, in a reference to the ascendancy of the *New York Times*: "The most impressive event of the last decade in the history of newspapers has been the demonstration that the objective, orderly and comprehensive presentation of news is a far more successful hope of journalism today than the dramatic, disorderly, episodic type."[310]

And even at its most daring and exciting, the "journalism of action" did not always exert lasting influence. Even at its zenith, the paradigm revealed its limitations. In dramatic and unprecedented fashion, the *Journal* rescued Evangelina Cisneros in October 1897. But by the end of the month, the story was off the *Journal*'s front page and mentioned only irregularly afterward. While some historians have argued the jailbreak stirred popular sentiment against Spain and contributed to the outbreak of the Spanish-American War in 1898,[311] such an interpretation is implausible. When the United States and Spain declared war in April 1898, the Cisneros jailbreak—the high-water mark of activist journalism—was scarcely mentioned at all, even by the *Journal*.

3

EXCEPTIONAL JOURNALISM IN JOURNALISM'S EXCEPTIONAL YEAR

The Pulitzer Prize is the most coveted, most desirable award in American journalism. Careers are made on winning a Pulitzer and many American newspapers spend thousands of dollars a year to prepare elaborate contest entries.[1]

But in 1897, it would have been absurd, even insulting, to award a *Pulitzer* prize as a high honor in American journalism. Given the controversies surrounding Joseph Pulitzer's newspapers, given his well-deserved reputation for arbitrariness, pettiness, and downright mean-spiritedness, a Pulitzer prize would have been an empty tribute. Only after his death in 1911—and after he had endowed the Graduate School of Journalism at Columbia University and the prize that bears his name—was Pulitzer's reputation redeemed.

In the late nineteenth century, no prominent profession-wide awards were made in American journalism. The first Pulitzer Prizes in journalism were not awarded until 1917. But if something akin to Pulitzer Prizes had been given in 1897, the winners would have included: The *New York Sun* for best editorial; Richard Harding Davis, for best example of international reporting; and Sylvester (Harry) Scovel of

Figure 3.1 American journalism's most famous editorial—"Is There A Santa Claus?"—was written in 1897 by Francis P. Church of the *New York Sun*. Church was a reticent, retiring man little known beyond a small circle of friends and colleagues. But because of the editorial's timeless appeal, Church is one of the few editorial writers whose name has been known through generations. (The Century Club/Newseum.)

Pulitzer's *New York World* for the most spectacular and audacious succession of assignments.

The *Sun's* editorial was "Is There A Santa Claus?"—a lyrical and timeless tribute to childhood and the Christmas spirit. The editorial, a response to the inquiry of an eight-year-old girl, was written by Francis P. Church, whose authorship was posthumously revealed in April 1906. In time, "Is There A Santa Claus?" became the most famous, most reprinted editorial in American journalism. And Church, a reticent, retiring man little known outside a tight circle of friends and colleagues,[2] would be one of the very few editorial writers whose name has been known through generations.

Davis' article, which appeared in Hearst's *New York Journal* on February 2, 1897, described in compelling detail the firing-squad execution of Adolfo Rodríguez, a twenty-year-old Cuban farm boy who had joined the rebellion against Spanish colonial rule. Rodriguez was captured by the Spanish elite *guardia civile* and executed near Santa Clara, Cuba, at dawn on January 19, 1897. Davis depicted Rodríguez as fearless and unshaken as he faced death. The cigarette Rodríguez held so nonchalantly between his lips was to become an iconic image, one that would appear in innumerable iterations of the condemned man's final moments.

Scovel's assignments for the *World* in 1897 traced the arc of the year's most noteworthy international events—from the rebellion in Cuba (where he crossed paths with Davis), to the brief Greco-Turkish War in southern Europe, to the gateway of the Klondike gold rush, and back to Cuba on the eve of the Spanish-American War of 1898.[3] His succession of coveted assignments, his audacity in filling them, his month-long imprisonment in Cuba in early 1897, and his taste for look-at-me participatory stunts all combined to make Scovel the country's best-known journalist. No reporter in 1897 had a year quite like Sylvester Scovel.[4]

The work of Church, Davis, and Scovel in 1897 was exceptional journalism in journalism's exceptional year and will be examined in separate sections in this chapter. The conceptual bond linking the three sections is the emergence of journalistic identity and reputation in *fin-de-siècle* American journalism. By 1897, the obscurity in which most American journalists labored was beginning to lift, if slowly, and Church, Davis, and Scovel were representative of the ways in which reputations were won or lost. Church cared little for celebrity but became famous anyway. Davis made his reputation in his evocative, descriptive writing, but his journalistic and literary fame did not outlive his death in 1916. Scovel strove relentlessly for fame, only to be best remembered for his angry, fist-swinging encounter with a U.S. army general during the Spanish-American War.

Church, Davis, and Scovel were markedly different men in attitudes, tastes, experience, and abilities. Church, who was fifty-eight when he wrote "Is There A Santa Claus?" spent more than thirty years writing editorials for Charles A. Dana's *Sun*. Church joined the newspaper fulltime in 1878 after the demise of *Galaxy*, a literary magazine he had established with his brother. Like Davis and Scovel, Church was headstrong; his features were said to suggest a "gentlemanly pugnacity" and a "latent aggressiveness."[5] But Church was no self-promoter. He venerated the anonymity of the editorial page and fit in well at the *Sun*, a writer's newspaper that, paradoxically, did little to promote writers' identities.[6]

Davis, who turned thirty-three in 1897, was both gifted and conceited—and not especially well-liked by journalists. He "knew enough to know his own worth," *Fourth Estate* once said of Davis, and he did little to "conceal his knowledge."[7] But Davis undeniably was an accomplished writer, one at home in the respective worlds of newspapers and magazines, and of plays and novels. His father, L. Clark Davis, was a newspaper editor in Philadelphia and his mother, Rebecca Harding Davis, was a writer of some modest fame. Richard was something of a prodigy, having become the managing editor of *Harper's Weekly* before he was thirty. His chiseled good looks, moreover, "helped define masculine beauty" in *fin-de-siècle* America, his biographer wrote.[8] The most popular of Davis' novels—an improbable adventure-romance called *Soldiers of Fortune*—was published in early 1897.

Scovel, the wayward son of an Ohio college president, was emblematic of a notion afoot in *fin-de-siècle* American journalism that if the circumstances were right, one could enter the field at the top. After a few years in college, Scovel had drifted from job to job at ranches in the West before becoming director of the Cleveland Athletic Club. He then decided to enter journalism, as a correspondent in Cuba. From there he wrote dispatches for several newspapers before signing on with the *World*. He spent most of 1896 in Cuba, filing perceptive reports that described the unlikelihood of Spain's restoring authority over the restive island.

A HARD-LUCK FIELD

Church, Davis, and Scovel were in the select company at or near the top of a hierarchy emergent in American journalism.[9] Church traded in ideas and achieved status by dint of the authority of editorials he never signed. Davis was propelled to the top by literary gifts that permitted him *entrée* in the disparate worlds of journalism and literature. Scovel indulged in gritty adventure and won renown through ceaseless scheming and risk-taking. But for the multitude of journalists, the *métier* was just as likely to disappoint as it was to reward. Metropolitan journalism, especially that of New York, had become "overrun"[10] with reporting talent, both real and prospective, in 1897. The late spring of 1897 brought sweeping layoffs to New York newspapers, dismissals that underscored the precarious status for most reporters in the city. "It is not an over-exaggeration to say that several ferryboat loads of reporters [seeking work] have been carried from New York," *Fourth Estate* observed in June 1897. Among "these pencil-pushers," the trade journal said, "were many men of undoubted ability."[11]

Fourth Estate said the spring dismissals represented a triumph of the business side over the newsgathering operation. City editors, *Fourth Estate* said, had grown reckless and had overhired, fearing they might lose exceptional reporting talent to a rival newspaper. "It did not take them very long to learn the [lessons] of extravagance," *Fourth Estate* said. "The natural result was that [the business executives] 'downstairs' … ordered a general clearing out."[12]

The Journalist agreed with *Fourth Estate*: the field *was* overpopulated—with deadwood, not promising talent. Journalism, it said, attracted "just the sort of people who don't belong in it. Men who have failed at everything else; young men, just out of college, who fancy it an easy and fascinating life. Scribblers of every sort and variety, and old fossils who have written themselves out years ago, but who hang on to the outskirts of the profession on the memory of what they have done."[13]

The uncertain nature of employment for journalists was also reflected by an unfavorable pay structure. Many journalists of the late 1890s worked "on space," meaning they were paid by the article or by the column inch.[14] Contracts and long, unbroken service—like Church's many years at the *Sun*—were uncommon. Young newspaper reporters in New York could expect to earn $10 to $15 a week. By the end of the 1890s, *Fourth Estate* said the number of reporters making $15,000 a year in New York "can probably be enumerated on five fingers."[15] A more prestigious posting, to a newspaper bureau in Washington, D.C., would pay on average $40 to $50 a week.[16] Chiefs of bureau in Washington received a little less than $100 a week.[17]

The insecurities helped ensure that most reporters toiled in anonymity. A turn-of-the-century handbook advised journalists new to the field to surrender "the hope of personal fame." As a rule, a reporter was "unknown beyond a very limited circle; the reading public knows nothing of him personally, but only the paper in which his work appears."[18] Instead of fame and celebrity, reporters were more likely to be the recipients of sneers and sweeping insults. James Fullarton Muirhead, a prickly British travel writer, deplored the "slip-shod style and the faulty grammar"[19] of American journalists, whom he characterized as "distinctly inferior" to their counterparts in Britain.[20]

Journalism in *fin-de-siècle* America offered scant job security, paid none too well, and encouraged little individual identity. Such conditions prompted *Fourth Estate*, usually a solicitous friend of journalists, to describe the newspaper world as "heartless as the usurer's collector, pitiless like fate and less merciful than the plague."[21] Young, would-be journalists were given such advice in the 1890s as: "Don't go into journalism unless you have to, unless you would rather live on cold hash once a day as a newspaper man than three square meals in any other line of work."[22] And still, would-be journalists swarmed to the field, many of whom brought college degrees.[23]

Each summer in the mid- and late-1890s, scores of recent college graduates—"fresh, green, sappy," *The Journalist* called them[24]—sought work in journalism. Lincoln Steffens' *New York Commercial Advertiser*, as we have seen, was eager to try out and hire recent college graduates, especially those from Harvard University. Few other newspapers were as eager or welcoming, and the newcomers often became disillusioned. "They all want to be connected with papers either in New York, Chicago or Boston, and they all expect large renumeration for their labors," *The Journalist* said in 1897, "and they pretty generally are disappointed." *The Journalist* figured that of the 500 or so newcomers to journalism, perhaps only one hundred would still be in the field in a year's time. "The remaining one-hundred [will] bravely accept subordinate positions," the trade journal said, "and soon drop into the treadmill routine."[25]

Thus in 1897, few American journalists could only aspire to the job security of Frank Church at the *Sun*. Few journalists could expect to make in a year anything close to the $3,000 that Hearst paid Davis for a month-long trip to Cuba in early 1897. Few journalists could hope for the fame or celebrity the swashbuckling Scovel won on his assignments in 1897.

In terms of pay and job security, the lot of American journalists changed little during 1897. But anonymity was eroding. Perceptive observers of American journalism called attention to the more frequent appearance of the byline, or what was known then as "the signed article." *Fourth Estate* noted "a distinct tendency towards signed articles" in the press.[26] Melville E. Stone, general manager of the Associated Press, wrote that "the signed article in the newspaper is becoming more and more common, and marks another departure in modern journalism; and in so far as it secures better and more careful—that is to say, more responsible—work, it is to be commended."[27] Alfred Balch, a persistent advocate of bylines for journalists, said in 1897: "I have written about signature [the byline] for years, and I am glad to see it is coming to newspaper men very fast. In the seventies it was not allowed even in the magazines. Now, you can see it in the great dailies."[28]

Bylines were not unheard of in American journalism before 1897. It was not uncommon for Civil War correspondents to affix their names, pseudonyms, or initials to their dispatches. And even before the war, bylines were given to journalists on occasion.[29] In France, the signed article was commonplace by the end of the nineteenth century.[30] But as Stone noted in 1897, no lasting success had emerged from periodic efforts in the United States "to adopt the custom of affixing the signature of the writers who contribute to the daily press."[31] To many publishers, the veil of anonymity was essential to projecting a sense of homogeneity and detachment in their newspapers. Florence Finch Kelly, who reviewed books for the *Los Angeles Times* in the late 1890s, recalled years later how she tried to persuade the newspaper's publisher, Harrison Otis, to allow her name to identify her work. Otis refused, she wrote, insisting "on the proposition that the *Times* was a unit, and a unit it must remain, an integral body and force whose power and influence must not be weakened by permitting the work of any of its constituent atoms to be singled out for individual credit."[32] Similarly, Adolph Ochs of the *New York Times* insisted that "the business of the paper must be absolutely impersonal," and rarely permitted bylines in the *Times* in the late nineteenth and early twentieth centuries.[33] Not until the 1940s and 1950s did bylines[34] intrude regularly on the "blank impersonality"[35] of the *Times'* front page.

Another reason that bylines were discouraged was that name-recognition could boost reporters' standing and value. In turn, they could demand more compensation for their work.[36] Advocates of signed articles such as Balch insisted that bylines were fair and appropriate rewards. "Newspaper work demands intellectual as well as physical effort, and therefore the writer's personality is one recompense he has a right to expect," Balch wrote.[37] "To the writer himself," Balch said, the byline "is an unmixed good. He gains the results of his own work exactly as an actor gathers up reputation."[38] Balch also argued that use of bylines would destroy the notion, encouraged by anonymity, that reporters were timorous, afraid to stand behind their work.[39]

Moreover, Balch and other advocates also saw in bylines an important way to promote reliability and accountability among journalists. "When we sign," Balch wrote, "we are more careful both in verification of alleged facts and in our style. It is our work, not that of the paper in which it is printed, and we make it just as true and just as good and just as clever as we can."[40] Signed articles, *Fourth Estate* noted, "carry the weight of personal responsibility with them."[41] As such, bylines promised to be a tool to enhance the quality and credibility of journalism.

But those were not the primary objectives for Hearst's *Journal* and Pulitzer's *World* as they promoted the work of their star correspondents in 1897. As suggested by the prominence given the dispatches of Davis and Scovel, the *Journal* and the *World* used bylines primarily as promotional tools, as means of calling attention to the accomplishments and exploits of their most prominent contributors. The *Journal* and the *World* after all had become fierce rivals and they sought any competitive advantages they could. Developing and trading on a reporter's popularity could bolster a newspaper's circulation.[42] For the *Journal* and the *World*, bylines were used to promote the newspaper's exceptionality and affirm its indispensability. The *Journal* and the *World* not only awarded bylines to their star correspondents: sometimes they placed the correspondents' names in headlines. So eager was the *Journal* to promote Davis' work that it turned to a banner headline to announce his presence in Cuba in mid-January 1897, two weeks before his first dispatch was published.[43]

Whatever their motives, the *Journal* and *World* helped lift the obscurity and second-class status in which newspaper reporters labored in the late nineteenth century—a little-recognized contribution of the yellow press of New York City. Balch specifically credited Hearst, Pulitzer, and Charles Taylor of the *Boston Globe* for promoting the use of signed articles, saying journalists owed "a good deal" to those men.[44] The status accorded Davis and Scovel also demonstrates that treating journalists as celebrities is hardly of recent vintage, and certainly not a consequence of the *Washington Post*'s coverage of the Watergate scandal in the early 1970s.[45] Davis and Scovel were celebrity journalists in 1897, just as globe-trotting Nellie Bly (Elizabeth Cochrane) had been for a time in 1890. Perhaps because they were celebrities, Davis and Scovel felt they could grouse without reserve about inept editors and their muddled guidance. After his trip to Cuba in 1897, Davis vowed never again to work for Hearst, whom he blamed for a succession of missteps and bungled plans that had dogged the assignment. The petulance and frustrations of far-flung correspondents is scarcely new.

The notion of "signed editorials"—that newspapers should identify the authors of their editorial commentaries—also drew some attention in 1897. A measure was placed before Congress that year requiring disclosure of the authors of editorials. The proposal died in obscurity, but not before prompting objections from Balch. He dismissed the measure as absurd. A signed editorial made little sense, he said, because editorials were "the utterances of the paper, not of any one man." While generally true, this did not apply to "Is There A Santa Claus?" The famous editorial was neither the voice nor collective wisdom of the *New York Sun*. It was a singular work by a veteran journalist who had been assigned to address the imploring of an eight-year-old girl named Virginia O'Hanlon. "Some of my little friends say there is no

Santa Claus," the girl had written. "Papa says 'if you see it in the Sun, it's so.' Please tell me the truth; is there a Santa Claus?"[46]

The task of writing a reply went to Church, who took on the assignment grudgingly. Edward P. Mitchell, the *Sun's* editorial page editor, recalled that Church "bristled and pooh-poohed at the subject when I suggested he write a reply to Virginia O'Hanlon; but he took the letter and turned with an air of resignation to his desk" to write.[47] Church drafted his reply quickly, in the course of a day's work, without the faintest hint[48] that his editorial would become a classic in American journalism and ensure him enduring and posthumous fame.

"Virginia, your little friends are wrong," Church wrote. "They have been afflicted by the skepticism of a skeptical age. They do not believe except they see. They think that nothing can be which is not comprehensible by their little minds. All minds, Virginia, whether they be men's or children's, are little." After ruminating a little about the limitations and narrow dimensions of human imagination, Church began a new paragraph and wrote the editorial's most lasting and memorable passages:

"Yes, Virginia, there is a Santa Claus. He exists as certainly as love and generosity and devotion exist, and you know that they abound and give to your life its highest beauty and joy. Alas! how dreary would be the world if there were no Santa Claus. It would be as dreary as if there were no Virginias."

Church closed the editorial with these reassuring lines: "No Santa Claus! Thank God! he lives, and he lives forever. A thousand years from now, Virginia, nay, ten times ten thousand years from now, he will continue to make glad the heart of childhood."[49]

It is curious to note that many of the exceptional moments in journalism in 1897 were so inconspicuous at the time. The first known published reference to "yellow journalism" was on January 31, 1897, in a small, obscure headline near the bottom of the editorial page of the *New York Press*.[50] "Yellow journalism" soon became, and remains, one of the most-invoked epithets in newsgathering. Without explanation or announcement, Ochs placed the *Times'* slogan, "All the News That's Fit to Print," in a box at the upper left corner of the front page on February 10, 1897. The motto has long since become the most famous in American journalism. So it was with the editorial that became an unrivaled classic in American journalism. "Is There A Santa Claus?" appeared inconspicuously in the third of three columns of editorials in the *New York Sun* on September 21, 1987. It was subordinate to seven other commentaries that day, on such matters as "British Ships in American Waters," the ambiguities in Connecticut's election law, and the features of the chainless bicycle anticipated in 1898.[51] Although it

Figure 3.2 Throughout her life, Viriginia O'Hanlon enjoyed the attention that came her way at Christmastime. She would gladly read portions of the Francis P. Church's famous 1897 editorial, which her letter had inspired. Here she poses with young schoolchildren at a Christmastime event. (Courtesy James Temple.)

was published at a time when newspaper editors routinely commented on—and often disparaged—the work and content of their rivals, the oddly timed editorial prompted no comment from the *Sun*'s rivals in New York City.

But readers noted it and found it memorable.[52] In untold numbers over the years, readers asked the *Sun* to reprint the essay. "Every December, as surely as the revolving year brings back the holiday season," the *Sun* noted in 1918, "we receive from our friends many requests to reprint again the Santa Claus editorial article written" by Church.[53] Requests often came from parents of young children, such as the letter-writer identified in the *Sun* only as D. F. C.: "I am an old time reader of the Sun and have a little girl, Anna, who seemingly is doubtful about there being a 'Santa Claus.' I have told her that if she looks in the Sun on Christmas morning she will be convinced by reading the famous reply of one of your staff writers to little Virginia O'Hanlon, which I have oftentimes read with much pleasure. Please do not fail to reprint it in your coming Christmas number."[54]

Over the years, readers found solace, joy, and inspiration in the passages of "Is There A Santa Claus?" "Though I am getting old," said a letter-writer in 1914, the essay's "thoughts and expressions fill my heart with overflowing joy."[55] A letter-writer told the *Sun* in 1926 that "Is There A Santa Claus?" offered "a fine relief from the commercialism and unsentimental greed" of the Christmas season.[56] In 1940, a writer to the *Sun* likened the editorial to "a ray of hope on the path to human understanding in our troubled times."[57] "Is There A Santa Claus?" became a way for parents to answer their children's' inquiries about Santa Claus, and be truthful in doing so.[58] Inevitably perhaps, the essence of "Is There A Santa Claus?" also became prone to exaggeration. At the editorial's centenary in September 1997, Thomas Vinciguerra wrote in the *New York Times* that the timeless appeal of "Is There A Santa Claus?" seemed "to suggest that what most readers of editorial pages care about are ruminations on single subjects like blizzards and the death of a princess. For such observations can constitute a national gathering of sorts, validating emotions that people want to share but can't quite express."[59] A "national gathering of sorts" was no doubt far from what Church and the *Sun* had in mind in 1897. More likely, Church was guided by a contemporaneous view that editorials should strive for boldness. "Better no editorials than dreary ones," a journalists' trade publication advised in 1894. "Audacity is a necessary feature of every good editorial."[60]

Church's authorship of "Is There A Santa Claus?" was revealed soon after his death in April 1906, in what for the *Sun* was eloquent and extraordinary tribute. Perhaps the only other time the *Sun* revealed the authorship of an unsigned editorial[61] was in 1927, when Harold M. Anderson was identified as having written "Lindbergh Flies Alone," a fulsome tribute to Charles A. Lindbergh as he made his trans-Atlantic solo flight. [62]

The *Sun* identified Church as the author of "Is There A Santa Claus" in an editorial note that stated: "At this time, with the sense of personal loss strong upon us, we know of no better or briefer way to make the friends of the Sun feel that they too have lost a friend than to violate custom by indicating him as the author of the beautiful and often republished editorial article affirming the existence of Santa Claus, in reply to the question of a little girl."[63] The *Sun* closed its tribute to Church by publishing the two concluding paragraphs of "Is There A Santa Claus?"

It is unlikely Church would have been much pleased by the *Sun's* revealing his authorship. He was a guarded, reticent man who respected and even cultivated, the anonymity of editorial-writing. According to J. R. Duryee, a friend whose testimonial the *Sun* published in April 1906, "Mr. Church by nature and training was reticent about himself, highly sensitive and retiring. ... Even with intimates he rarely permitted himself to express freely his inner thought.

"I doubt if an editor was ever more consistently loyal in maintaining the privacy of the sources of his journal's statements," Duryee wrote. "In our talks together, I have frequently referred to an editorial my intuition told me was from his pen, but never could induce him to own the writing. ... I have never known a literary man as ingenuous as he in his self-repression."[64] In what he presumed was Church's work, Duryee found the imprint of "gentle humor" and "a simple, chaste style."[65] His work in "a lighter vein," Duryee wrote, possessed "rare charm" and was notable in its delicacy of touch.[66] Duryee did not say so specifically, but he could well have been referring to Church's "Is There A Santa Claus?"

A DIFFIDENT EMBRACE

It is generally believed that Church's editorial was an immediate success and that it was reprinted by the *Sun* at every Christmas season after 1897.[67] But the accepted wisdom about "Is There A Santa Claus?" is incorrect. The famous editorial in fact was reluctantly embraced by the *Sun*, as became clear in a review of the newspaper's year-end issues from 1897 to 1949, or just before the *Sun* went out of business.

After publishing the editorial in September 1897, the *Sun* did not reprint it until December 1902. It did so then with an air of annoyance, stating: "Since its original publication, the Sun has refrained from reprinting the article on Santa Claus which appeared several years ago, but this year requests for its reproduction have been so numerous that we yield." That prefatory comment closed with a gratuitous swipe: "Scrap books seem to be wearing out."[68] The *Sun* did not again publish "Is There A Santa Claus?" until the Christmas of 1906, eight months after Church's death. In reintroducing the editorial that year, the sneering tone that had accompanied republication in 1902 was gone. The *Sun* acknowledged the appeals of its readers, stating in an introductory comment that it was reprinting the editorial "on this Christmas morning at the request of many friends of the Sun, of Santa Claus, of the little Virginias of yesterday and to-day, and of the author of the essay, the late F.P. Church."[69]

In the years immediately after Church's death, the *Sun* was somewhat more inclined to republish "Is There A Santa Claus?" In the ten years from 1898–1907, the editorial was reprinted in the *Sun* at Christmastime only twice. In the ten subsequent years, the editorial was republished in the *Sun* six times. The *Sun*'s reluctance to republish or to say much at all about "Is There A Santa Claus?" gave rise to error in other publications. For example, the *Arizona Republican* published "Is There A Santa Claus?" on December 25, 1897, but mistakenly attributed the editorial to Dana, saying: "One of the best things the late Charles A. Dana ever wrote, and which ought to sanctify children's and all humanity's memory of that great man, was the following editorial reply to an anxious inquiry by a little 8-year-old girl."[70]

Over time, the *Sun* warmed to "Is There A Santa Claus?" In reprinting the editorial in 1916, the *Sun* said: "Perhaps no other editorial article ever written has been republished so often or has been read by so many millions of people who have come to regard it as one of the loveliest utterances of the Christmas sentiment."[71] By then, the sneering references to worn-out scrapbooks were long gone. Instead, the *Sun* was inclined to liken "Is There A Santa Claus?" to momentous works with which readers would be immediately familiar. "Perhaps it is not too much to say that it must be classed with Lincoln's Gettysburg address respecting the number of those who know its phrases and regard affectionately its sentiment and teachings," the *Sun* said in reintroducing the editorial on Christmas 1913.[72] On that occasion, the *Sun* again acknowledged the editorial's profound appeal to readers: "Every Christmas season for the past sixteen years, the Sun has been asked by many of its friends to reprint the editorial article entitled 'Is There A Santa Claus?' ... Sometimes we have complied with the request; sometimes it has seemed better not to do so."[73]

Over the years, readers implored the *Sun* not to fail to reprint the editorial. "It will neither be Christmas nor the Sun without it," declared one reader in 1927.[74] "Every year, as I grow a little older, I find added significance in its profound thoughts," wrote another reader in 1940.[75] Such responses seemed to astonish the *Sun*. At times the newspaper conceded to amazement that the editorial had become so profoundly admired. In 1918, for example, the *Sun* declared that it was reprinting the editorial "with extreme pleasure that the vitality and charm of this famous piece of Christmas literature are unimpaired after a period long enough to make a voter of a new born babe."[76]

Not until the 1920s did the editorial begin appearing prominently and without fail in the *Sun* at Christmastime. The *Sun*'s owner, Frank A. Munsey, ordered "Is There A Santa Claus?" to lead the editorial columns[77] on Christmas Eve in 1924—a move that signaled the *Sun*'s complete recognition of the exceptionality of the editorial it called an "immortal expression of faith."[78] In the years afterward, "Is There A Santa Claus?" was the *Sun*'s lead editorial on December 23 or 24.[79]

It was a triumph for the *Sun*'s readers. Repeatedly over the years, readers asked the *Sun* to reprint "Is There A Santa Claus?" And ultimately, the newspaper gave in—tacitly acknowledging that editors are not always as perceptive as their readers in identifying journalism of significance and lasting value.

The *Sun's* hesitant embrace of the classic editorial represented a measure of restraint at a time in American journalism when self-promotion was pronounced, even routine. In the late 1890s, the *Sun* largely abstained[80] from conspicuous self-promotion, an inclination that helps account for its diffident embrace of "Is There A Santa Claus?" The *Sun* also was disinclined to republish content—or what it called "repetitions from the past." During its vituperative campaign against the yellow press in 1897, the *Sun* noted but rejected a reader's suggestion that it reprint a letter assailing the *World* and Joseph Pulitzer. The letter had appeared six months earlier. "Since then," the *Sun* explained, "the stream of fresh denunciations [against the *World*] is too voluminous" to permit the republication of "repetitions from the past."[81]

In its editorials in 1897, the *Sun* was more inclined to vituperation and personal attack than to evoke the eloquence and lyricism that distinguished "Is There A Santa Claus?" *Fourth Estate* described the *Sun* as never happy unless it was on the attack,[82] a characteristic particularly evident in its assaults on Hearst's *Journal* and Pulitzer's *World*, which the *Sun* excoriated collectively as a "menace … too vile for respectable people to read."[83] The *Journal* brushed aside the *Sun's* criticisms, saying they were motivated solely by the *Journal's* rapid and enviable growth in circulation. The *Journal*, moreover, was charitable in marking Dana's death in October 1897, devoting much of the front page to eulogizing its foe.[84] The *Journal's* generous gesture was not matched by Pulitzer's *World*, which briefly mentioned Dana's death at the top of the obituary column on its back page.[85]

The enmity between Dana and Pulitzer was deep-seated and extreme, even by the standards of the late nineteenth century when many rival editors harbored deep grudges and routinely exchanged insults in their editorial columns. Such resentments sometimes gave rise to fisticuffs[86] and even lawsuits.[87] Dana and Pulitzer had traded taunts and insults since the mid-1880s, when the *World* emerged as New York's largest newspaper, luring many readers away from the *Sun*. Their hostility turned exceptionally ugly with Dana's vicious, anti-Semitic attacks[88] on Pulitzer who, in reply, called Dana a "mendacious blackguard" capable of "any amount of distortion of facts."[89] In 1897, the *World* disparaged Dana's newspaper as among the "derelicts of journalism" in New York.[90] In reply, the *Sun* called the *World* "the shameless exponent in chief" of all that was "indecent and rascally in journalism."[91] Against such venom, the delicate charm of "Is There A Santa Claus?" seemed decidedly out of place.

Figure 3.3 This photograph shows Viriginia O'Hanlon at about the age when she wrote her famous letter to the *New York Sun*, imploring, "Please tell me the truth; is there a Santa Claus?" She recalled years later, "My birthday was in July and, as a child, I just existed from July to December, wondering what Santa Claus would bring me. I think I was a brat." (Courtesy James Temple.)

INCONGRUOUS TIMING

A modest mystery has surrounded the editorial's anomalous timing.[92] Why was a Christmastime editorial published three months before the holiday? No exogenous factors seem to have prompted Virginia O'Hanlon's inquiry. No prominent news reports in August or September 1897 discussed Santa Claus, Christmas, or related topics. A mild controversy percolated late in the year over efforts to discourage children from believing in Santa Claus,[93] because it was simply "wrong to poison the minds of the young with untruths."[94] A kindergarten in Philadelphia, for example, advocated telling children who asked that

Santa Claus did not exist. "As long as [the child] catches the spirit of love and giving that is in the air," the kindergarten's director said, explaining the policy, "it is all we want."[95]

The *Sun* first published "Is There A Santa Claus?" eight days after the school year began in New York City in September 1897,[96] coincidental timing that encouraged speculation that Virginia O'Hanlon and her friends were weighing the existence of Santa Claus as their classes resumed after summer vacation.[97] While it plausibly accounts for the reference in Virginia O'Hanlon's letter to skeptical "little friends," such a scenario is unlikely. Discussing the editorial years later, Virginia O'Hanlon said she addressed her letter to the *Sun*'s question-and-answer column and waited impatiently for the newspaper to publish a response.[98] The *Sun*'s question-and-answer column, usually called "Notes and Queries," was not a daily or even a weekly feature. It appeared irregularly on Sundays, offering pithy and often witty replies to inquiries such as: "What is the derivation of 'bunny,' as used in the term 'bunny rabbit?'"[99] and "Please state the exact method by which 'selling short' in stocks and grain is performed."[100] Given its fact-based character, the "Notes and Queries" column clearly was not best suited to address a question about the existence of Santa Claus.

Years later, Virginia O'Hanlon recalled that the *Sun* did not promptly take up her inquiry. "After writing to the Sun," she told an audience in December 1959, "I looked every day for the simple answer I expected. When it didn't appear, I got disappointed and forgot about it."[101] One of her seven grandchildren, James Temple, said he recalls his grandmother saying that "a long time"—perhaps weeks—had passed before the *Sun*'s editorial appeared.[102] Such recollections indicate that O'Hanlon's letter asking about Santa Claus was sent to the *Sun* well before the start of the school year in mid-September 1897. After arriving at the *Sun*, her letter was probably overlooked or misplaced for an extended period. That there was such a gap seems certain, given both O'Hanlon's recollections about having waited for a reply and the accounts that say Church wrote the famous editorial in "a short time"[103] or "hastily, in the course of the day's work, and without the remotest idea of its destiny of permanent interest and value."[104] The only explanation that reconciles the two accounts—O'Hanlon's extended wait and Church's quickly written response—is that the *Sun* for a time had overlooked or misplaced the letter that inspired American journalism's classic editorial.

The most plausible explanation for the editorial's incongruous timing lies in the excited speculation of a little girl who, after celebrating her birthday in mid-summer, began to wonder about the gifts she would receive at Christmas. "My birthday was in July and, as a child, I just existed from July to December, wondering what Santa Claus would bring me," O'Hanlon told an audience of Connecticut high school students in December 1959. "I think I was a brat."[105]

Virginia O'Hanlon and Francis Church never met, although she once said she knew someone who lived next to Church. She earned master and doctoral degrees and for forty-three years was a teacher or principal in the New York City school system.[106] Her marriage to Edward Douglas was brief and ended with his deserting her shortly before their child, Laura, was born.[107] Virginia O'Hanlon kept the "Douglas" surname, however.

She came to embrace the recognition and modest fame that came with "Is There A Santa Claus?" She occasionally read the editorial at Christmas programs, such as that in 1933 at Hunter College, her alma mater.[108] Virginia O'Hanlon lived to be eighty-one and her death at a nursing home in upstate New York in May 1971 was reported on the front page of the *New York Times*.[109] Her daughter, Laura Temple, was briefly associated with the *Sun*, working at the newspaper's advertising office for two years in the 1930s.[110] "They all knew who I was," Laura Temple was quoted years later as saying about the *Sun* staff. "And we all had the same feeling about the editorial that my mother had—that it was a classic."[111]

ON ASSIGNMENT TO CUBA

New Year's 1897 brought the reaffirmation of traditions in New York and in Washington—traditions that have long since passed. In New York City, revelers blowing tin horns and other noisemakers gathered by the thousands near old Trinity Church on lower Broadway, waiting for the pealing chimes, which for forty-seven years had offered a hearty greeting to the new year. The *New York Times* said the city's welcome to 1897 was exceptional in that "so many women" had shown up at the ceremonies downtown. Many of the female revelers, the *Times* said, "were from the uptown districts and they were not at all backward in cheering and blowing the horns."[112]

Washington on New Year's Day 1897 took on the appearance of a European capital, with a showy presence of army and navy officers dressed in full uniform to pay their calls. New Year's was the one day, said the *Evening Star* of Washington, when officers "burst forth on the admiring populace in the full glory of their gay regimentals, and it is hard to realize that they are the very same men that we pass on the street every day, and without ever giving them the tribute of a second glance."[113] Wherever the officers found a New Year's reception, the *Evening Star* said, "they were pretty sure to have their own way, for feminine fondness for the fine feathers is proverbial."[114] At the White House, President Grover Cleveland welcomed representatives of the diplomatic corps while renewing another New Year's Day tradition—that of shaking hands with several thousand well-wishers; many of them had waited outside for as long as six hours.[115]

New Year's Day 1897 found the novelist-journalist Richard Harding Davis in Key West, Florida, stewing in mind-numbing frustration about a stretch of unexpected idleness. The smug but immensely talented Davis was supposed to have been in Cuba before Christmas. He was to have traveled there with the famous artist, Frederic Remington, aboard William Randolph Hearst's high-speed yacht, the *Vamoose*. The plan was to infiltrate Davis and Remington into rebel-controlled territory of Santa Clara province where they would spend a month with the rag-tag forces of General Máximo Gómez. The Cuban insurgents had waged a guerrilla war against far larger Spanish forces for nearly two years, and had fought them to a standoff.

In Key West, a succession of lapses—including the late arrival of the *Vamoose*, a brief strike by its crew, and two failed attempts to cross the Straits of Florida to Cuba—forced Davis and Remington to wait idly for more than two weeks. Davis did little to conceal his displeasure. Waiting, he complained in a letter to his family, "is all we do and that's my life at Key West. I get up and half dress and take a plunge in the bay and then dress fully and have a greasy breakfast and then light a huge Key West cigar ... and sit on the hotel porch. ... Nothing happens after that except getting one's boots polished."[116] Hearst's *Vamoose*, he complained, "is the fastest thing afloat and the slowest thing to get started I ever saw."[117]

He and Remington contemplated pocketing their $3,000 advances from Hearst and calling off the Cuba trip altogether. But Davis could not bear the embarrassment of turning around, not after having cut short an assignment a couple of years before. He had then set off to cover the Sino-Japanese War but turned around in Ottawa, Canada, after realizing his heart wasn't in that assignment.[118] Davis and Remington finally gave up on the idea of reaching Cuba covertly. They booked passage on a passenger steamer that arrived in Havana harbor on the morning of January 9, 1897.[119]

Davis and Remington didn't stay together for long. They were an ill-matched team and six days after arriving in Cuba, they parted ways. Legend has it that Remington found Cuba much calmer than expected and that he cabled Hearst from Havana, purportedly saying:

"Everything is quiet. There will be no war. I wish to return." Hearst supposedly sent a telegram in reply, telling Remington: "Please remain. You furnish the pictures, and I'll furnish the war."[120] The purported exchange, first reported in 1901, was so succinct and delicious that it has lived on as American journalism's best-known, most-recounted anecdote. It is often cited as exhibit "A" in the dubious argument that Hearst fomented the Spanish-American War of 1898.[121] Nonethless, the anecdote is almost certainly apocryphal; the Remington–Hearst exchange almost surely never took place.

The reasons for challenging the anecdote's authenticity are many and persuasive.[122] Foremost among them are the letters that Davis wrote from Cuba. His correspondence contain no hint that Remington wanted to leave because "everything [was] quiet" in Cuba. Rather, Davis said *he* asked Remington to go, "as it left me freer" to operate in Cuba. "I am as relieved at getting old Remington to go as though I had won $5000," Davis said in a letter to his mother. "He was a splendid fellow but a perfect kid and had to be humored and petted all the time." Davis declared himself "very glad" that Remington left, "for he kept me back all the time and I can do twice as much in half the time." Davis complained that Remington "always wanted to talk it over and that had to be done in the nearest or the most distant cafe, and it always took him fifteen minutes before he got his cocktails to suit him. He always did as I wanted [in] the end but I am not used to giving reasons or traveling in pairs."[123] So Remington left Cuba on the passenger steamer *Seneca,* which reached New York on January 20, 1897.[124]

Davis, meanwhile, stayed on in Cuba. The day after he and Remington parted ways, Davis traveled to Cardenas on Cuba's northern coast. In a letter to his mother, Davis mentioned plans to travel soon to Santa Clara—and offered a glimpse of the pride he took in *Soldiers of Fortune,* the novel he had just completed. The moonlit view from the balcony of his hotel room in Cardenas was, he told his mother, "just like the description in that remarkable novel of mine" where the protagonists Robert Clay and Alice Lagham "sit on the balcony of the restaurant. I have the moonlight and the Cathedral with the open doors and the bronze statue in the middle and the royal palms moving in the breeze straight from the sea and the people around the plaza below," Davis wrote. "If it was in anyway as beautiful as this[,] Clay and Alice would have ended the novel that night."[125]

On January 17, 1897, Davis arrived in Santa Clara. Before dawn two days later, he witnessed the firing-squad execution of Adolfo Rodrí-guez, an event that moved Davis to the highest levels of his descriptive abilities. Over the next couple of days, Davis crafted a 2,550-word

Figure 3.4 The finest work of foreign correspondence in 1897 was Richard Harding Davis' account of the firing-squad execution of a young Cuban captured in the rebellion against Spanish rule. The lean, descriptive power of Davis' 2,550-word dispatch anticipated the style of Ernest Hemingway, critics say. (Library of Congress.)

dispatch that was superb in its narration, in pacing, and in its evocative detail. Davis' dispatch focused on the brave but doomed young Cuban, a powerfully effective technique that suggested the cruelty and the futility of Spain's efforts to quell the island-wide rebellion. Davis made clear his sympathy for Rodríguez and, by extension, his quiet support for the Cuban cause. "I hope it is not impertinent for the writer to introduce himself, so far as to say that he did not go to see this man die through any idle or morbid curiosity," Davis wrote in his dispatch. "The young man's friends could not be present. It was impossible for them to show themselves in that crowd and that place with wisdom or without distress, and I like to think that, although Rodriguez could not know it, there was one person present when he died who felt keenly for him, and who was a sympathetic though unwilling onlooker."[126]

Davis spoke little Spanish and included no dialogue in his dispatch, which the biographer Arthur Lubow has aptly described as unfolding "like a silent movie."[127] Rodríguez, who had been condemned to die by a military court for taking up arms against Spanish rule, was on the day of his execution, forced to march a half-mile outside of Santá Clara. "I expected to find the man, no matter what his strength at other times might be, stumbling and faltering on this cruel journey," Davis wrote, "but as he came near I saw that he led all the others, that the priests on either side of him were taking two steps to his one, and that they were tripping on their gowns and stumbling over the hollows, in their efforts to keep pace with him as he walked erect and soldierly at a quick step in advance of them."[128]

Rodríguez, said Davis, seemed "shockingly young for such a sac-rifice, and looked more like a Neapolitan than a Cuban. You could imagine him sitting on a quay at Naples or Genoa, lolling in the sun and showing his white teeth when he laughed."[129] As the condemned man passed by, Davis noticed with quiet satisfaction "that he held a cigarette between his lips, not arrogantly or with bravado, but with the nonchalance of a man who meets his punishment fearlessly and who will let his enemies see that they can kill him but not frighten him."[130]

From the contingent of three hundred Spanish soldiers who had marched out from Santa Clara, a six-man firing squad was selected. Rodríguez was trussed and turned so that his back faced the firing squad. He let the cigarette fall from his lips as he bent to kiss a cru-cifix, held up to him by one of the priests. As he straightened himself, Davis wrote, Rodríguez "made a picture of such pathetic helplessness, but of such courage and dignity, that he reminded me on the instant of that statue of Nathan Hale which stands in the City Hall Park" in New York.[131] The firing squad was now in position and the order was given to prepare to fire. "And then happened one of the most cruelly refined, though unintentional acts of torture that one can very well imagine," Davis wrote. "As the officer slowly raised his sword, preparatory to giv-ing the signal, one of the mounted officers rode up to him and pointed out silently with his sword what I had already observed with some satisfaction, that the [soldiers of the] firing squad were so placed that when they fired they would shoot" several of their comrades.[132]

Rodríguez had steeled himself for a volley of bullets. Now he was told he had to move. "You would expect that any man who had been snatched back to life in such a fashion would start and tremble at the reprieve, or would break down altogether," Davis wrote, "but this boy turned his head steadily, and followed with his eyes the direction of the officer's sword, then nodded his head gravely, and, with his chin still held in the air and his shoulders squared, took up a new position, straightened his back again, and once more held himself erect."[133]

The firing squad, now repositioned, quickly finished its grim duty. The soldiers fired and Rodríguez slumped to the wet grass, "without a struggle or sound, and did not move again. It was difficult to believe that he meant to lie there, that it could be ended so without a word … or that at least some one would be sorry or say something or run to pick him up," Davis wrote. As the soldiers reassembled and marched back to Santa Clara, Davis saw that the cigarette was still burning, "a tiny ring of living fire, at the place where the figure had first stood."[134] This image of the condemned man's last cigarette has, as Lubow observed, burned on for more than one hundred years in "innumerable reincarnations, in novels and movies."[135]

As he began to walk back to town, Davis turned to look back at the lifeless crumpled form of the young Cuban. It was as if he was "asleep in the wet grass," Davis wrote, "with his motionless arms still tightly bound behind him, with the scapula twisted awry across his face and the blood from his breast sinking into the soil he had tried to free." That was the lone reference to "blood" in Davis' dispatch.

As critics and biographers have noted, the lean, descriptive power with which Davis wrote about Rodríguez anticipated the style of Ernest Hemingway.[136] But Davis' dispatch has also been badly misinterpreted. John Seelye argued in his *War Games: Richard Harding Davis and the New Imperialism* that the article "aroused the sympathies of U.S. readers" for the Cuban rebellion[137] and "contributed to the growing hostility in the United States toward the Spanish presence in Cuba."[138] While Davis certainly described the Spanish soldiers as inept and depicted the Cuban insurgents as stoic and brave, there is no evidence that the article exerted any lasting effect on American public opinion. The insurrection in Cuba—vicious and costly though it was— failed to command the unbroken attention of American newspapers or of American public opinion in 1897. Not until the destruction of the U.S. warship *Maine* in Havana harbor in mid-February 1898—more than a year after the *Journal* published Davis' dispatch about Rodríguez —was the American public consumed by the plight of Spanish-ruled Cuba.

While it had no enduring influence on American attitudes about the Cuban rebellion, Davis' dispatch refuted the notion afoot in the 1890s that U.S. foreign correspondents were dullards incapable of writing well. "They have never been taught to write, or rather they have been taught all too well to write badly," one critic, Cleveland Moffett, had written.[139] Davis in his account of Rodríguez's death certainly demonstrated American correspondents could write vividly and well. Davis was quite proud of the dispatch, polished versions of which were in separate anthologies of his work—*Cuba in War Time* (1897) and *Notes of a War Correspondent* (1910). He called the story "The Death of Rodriguez."

Curiously, however, Davis did not refer to the execution in the many letters he sent to his family from Cuba. He may have been alluding to it in a letter to his mother, dated January 19, 1897, the day Rodríguez was shot. In that letter, Davis said cryptically he had "stories to tell Mr. Hearst but I don't know as I am quite safe in telling them until I see more."[140] Davis probably suspected Spanish authorities were intercepting and reading his letters home, given that he vigorously asserted they were not. "I don't believe the[y] read my letters and that is why I speak so freely and go into such detail," he wrote. "I have nothing to conceal and so I write freely." [141] He may have wanted to mislead the Spanish authorities by encouraging them to think he had nothing to hide. But he kept his "Death of Rodriguez" dispatch hidden away until he was able to send it to the *Journal* surreptitiously, from the southern Cuban port of Trinidad, on 23 January 23, 1897. The dispatch reached Key West on February 1, 1897, where it was telegraphed to New York. It appeared in the *Journal* the next day.[142]

Davis was hardly circumspect in denouncing his employer in his letters home. They bristled with frequent and disparaging references to Hearst and the *Journal*. "All Hearst wants is my name," he complained in one letter. "I am not writing for the *Journal*, the *Journal* is printing what I write ... and all I am getting out of it is a lot of money, very dearly earned, and a greater knowledge of myself. ..."[143] Davis blamed Hearst for "queering," or compromising, Davis' attempts to reach the insurgents by publishing on January 17, 1897, a full-page account that declared: "Richard Harding Davis and Frederic Remington in Cuba for the *Journal*."[144] The publicity, Davis felt, made him a marked man in the eyes of the Spanish, and rendered it impossible for him to slip through Spanish lines and into insurgent-controlled territory. "I fear my usefulness is ended," Davis complained. "My fondest hope is that the authorities will order me out of the island on the strength of the *Journal*'s saying I was with the insurgent army. I could then go home and kick Hearst and sue him for not letting me alone."[145] For Davis, however, the worst turn of his assignment to Cuba was yet to come.

Aboard the passenger steamer *Olivette* on his way back to the United States, Davis met and fell into conversation with Clemencia Arango, a young Cuban woman expelled by the Spanish because of her ties to the insurgents.[146] She told Davis about her ordeal in leaving Cuba. The Spanish, she said, were looking for concealed letters and other documents from the insurgents and they had strip-searched her and her two female companions. The women were searched first at home, then at the Havana custom house, and once again on board the Olivette, which was an American-flagged vessel.[147] Davis was appalled. After arriving at Tampa, Florida, he filed a detailed dispatch to the *Journal* denouncing the Spanish conduct. He claimed, erroneously, that Spanish authorities had violated international law by conducting a search on an American-flagged vessel.[148] And he described Arango as "a well bred, well educated young person who spoke three languages and dressed as you see girls dress on Fifth avenue after church on Sunday."[149] Davis closed his dispatch by predicting "that when the United States punishes Spain it will be for some such indignity to American vessels as the one I have just described."[150]

But as to precisely who had conducted the strip-searches, Davis' account was ambiguous. His dispatch suggested they had been carried out by male Spanish officers, but did not say so explicitly. But that was the interpretation at the *Journal* offices in New York, where Remington drew a lurid sketch that depicted a naked and helpless young woman surrounded by three leering male officers aboard the Olivette. Davis' dispatch was published beneath the headline, "Does Our Flag Shield Women?" It was placed on the lower half of the *Journal*'s front page of February 12, 1897, a prominent but somewhat subordinate position. Remington's provocative illustration appeared on page two. Despite the rather understated presentation, the dispatch and illustration raised howls of indignation and calls for a congressional investigation.[151]

But the *World* soon tracked down Arango, who clarified the ambiguity that Davis had left in his dispatch. The strip-searches, she said, had been conducted by a matron, not by male officers.[152] Davis seethed in anger about the exaggerated illustration in the *Journal*. He wrote to the *World* and pointedly blamed Remington for misinterpreting his dispatch. But as biographer Lubow has noted, "Remington's eye-popping sketch plausibly illustrated Davis's text."[153]

Davis soon again wrote to the *World*, this time to praise a rival correspondent, Sylvester Scovel, who was in jail in Cuba. Scovel was arrested in early February 1897, on charges of crossing Spanish lines without a permit, communicating with the insurgents, traveling without a Spanish military pass, and carrying a fraudulent identity card in the name of "Harry Williams."[154] In his letter to the *World*, Davis said he had encountered Scovel in Cuba and knew him to be strictly a noncombatant—a journalist "in the legitimate pursuit of a legitimate though hazardous calling."[155] Davis closed his letter with a strange and ominous non sequitur: "Scovel may die, but if he does, his death will free Cuba."[156]

SCOVEL THE FEARLESS

Scovel, whose thick, broad-shouldered build resembled that of a football linebacker, was an extrovert who made friends readily. His temper, the *World* said after his arrest, was "as sunny as a child's."[157] Scovel had succeeded where Davis had failed, in crossing Spanish lines to reach the Cuban insurgents. Scovel said in a dispatch to the *World* in early January 1897 that within just twelve hours, he had arrived in Havana, managed to slip out of the city, and had located an insurgent force.[158] "I find that the situation here looks better for the insurgents to-day than when I left ... last August," Scovel wrote. "Even the Spaniards admit that none of the insurgents have surrendered."[159] Scovel's dispatch was thin on detail, but *World* treated it as a remarkable development and declared in an editorial:

> The World had the pleasure of laying before its readers ... the first authentic news of the movements of the Cuban patriot armies that has reached New York in many weeks. This service was due to the unrivaled skill and daring of its correspondent with the patriots, Sylvester Scovel.
>
> Mr. Scovel's work in the field has been unique. He writes of what he sees, not of what he hears. Every moment of every day he is in peril, as he insists upon being where there is activity, because there also is the most important news.
>
> Mr. Scovel has shown that he combines all the great and high qualities of the war correspondent—devotion to duty, accuracy, graphic descriptive power, absolute courage and skill both in getting the news and in sending it through the enemy's lines to his newspaper.[160]

The editorial's references to the dangers Scovel faced were prophetic. On February 5, 1897, while traveling with forged documents in the name of "Harry Williams," Scovel was arrested aboard a train near Sancti Spíritus in mountainous central Cuba. He was en route from the insurgents' camp to the coastal town of Tunas de Zaza, from where he had intended to send dispatches to the *World*.[161] He was jailed in Sancti Spíritus and, in a report smuggled to the *World*, declared himself "a prisoner of war."[162] The *World* reacted with alarm, declaring Scovel to be in "imminent danger of butchery by decree of a drumhead court-martial."[163] The *World* said Scovel was "a prisoner in the hands of bandits who hesitate at nothing. He is held in a remote part of the island, where it has happened that the Spanish guerrillas [irregulars], upon pretense of a rebel raid, have incontinently butchered all their prisoners, and where at other times they have put innocent men to death and reported them as suicides, confident that the military authorities would not inquire closely into the facts."[164]

The *World* blamed Scovel's "helpless and nearly hopeless position" on "the neglect of our State Department to do its duty in any virile way."[165] But in truth, American diplomatic personnel in Cuba intervened earnestly in his case.[166] And the *World*'s hysteria about Scovel's predicament was based on assumptions that were wildly in error. Scovel in jail faced nothing approaching the "imminent danger of butchery." Thanks to the connections and generosity of the American consular agent in Sancti Spíritus, a rotund and cheery man named Rafael Madrigal, Scovel was kept in conditions that were absurdly lavish. Madrigal, who weighed more than three hundred pounds, was "the biggest man in town," Scovel wrote, and "under his watchtull [*sic*] care, I am very comfortable indeed."[167]

Madrigal saw to it that Scovel's cell was furnished with a comfortable bed, rocking chairs, throw rugs, flowers, and a private bath.[168] Scovel dined on bountiful meals prepared and brought to the jail by Madrigal's wife, whom he called "Madame Mad."[169] He received fat bundles of New York City newspapers, which Madrigal brought to the jail.[170] Scovel's many visitors included beautiful Cuban women and Spanish officers—including the lieutenant who arrested Scovel. He reportedly apologized to Scovel for having done so.[171] Other inmates sent Scovel hand-made tokens of their respect, including paper roses and "highly decorated toothpicks."[172] Except for a nightmare in which he dreamt he was shot by a firing squad,[173] the closest Scovel came to danger was the brief visit by Captain-General Valeriano Weyler y Nicolau, the feared commander of Spanish military forces in Cuba. He was reviled in the American press for his policy of "reconcentration," which forced Cuban noncombatants from the countryside into garrison towns, where many died from disease and malnutrition. At the jail in Sancti Spíritus, Weyler scowled when he saw Scovel's luxurious accommodations—and reportedly fired the warden.[174]

Thomas Alvord, a *World* reporter who traveled from his base in Havana to see Scovel in Sancti Spíritus, described Scovel's cell as "like a parlor," a place of "many luxuries and all privileges except liberty."

Alvord wrote that his jailhouse interview with his colleague "was interrupted by the arrival of seven beautiful Cuban girls to see Scovel. They brought flowers, and fairly overwhelmed him by their kindnesses. Then came ten more."[175] The *World*, meanwhile, was pressing Spain to release Scovel. The editors, publishers, and chief executives of most of the largest U.S. newspapers outside of New York endorsed the *World's* petition that called indirectly for Scovel's release.[176] The roster of petition-signers read almost like a "who's who" of *fin-de-siècle* American journalism: Clark Howell of the *Atlanta Constitution*, Charles Taylor of the *Boston Globe*, H. H. Kohlsaat of the *Chicago Times-Herald*, Joseph Medill of the *Chicago Tribune*, John R. McLean of the *Cincinnati Enquirer*, Charles Emory Smith of the *Philadelphia Press*, and Michael H. DeYoung of the *San Francisco Chronicle*.[177] Davis' father, L. Clark Davis, the managing editor of the *Philadelphia Public Ledger*, also was among the signatories.[178] More than a dozen state legislatures adopted resolutions that urged the federal government to press for Scovel's freedom,[179] and members of the American Newspaper Publishers' Association, at their annual convention in New York City, adopted a resolution in support of Scovel that declared, "we make his cause our own."[180]

Given such attention, Scovel in early 1897 was easily America's most famous foreign correspondent. Such prominence may have seemed astonishing and improbable to people familiar with Scovel's background. After all, he had almost no experience in journalism before 1895. Scovel was the son of the president of what is now Wooster College in Ohio. His parents wanted him to train for the Presbyterian ministry, which he rejected. He spent his early adulthood in meandering and unfocused pursuits, such as working on cattle ranches in Colorado, Utah, and Wyoming. He returned to Ohio and entered the hardware business in Cleveland and later became general manager of the Cleveland Athletic Club. He also joined the First Cleveland Troop, an award-winning national guard cavalry unit.[181]

Scovel was twenty-six when the rebellion in Cuba broke out in February 1895 and he soon "made up his mind to visit the island and see the fighting," according to a biographical account in the *World* in 1897. "He made arrangements to furnish letters [or dispatches] to several Western newspapers, and went direct to Havana. Without much difficulty, he made his way out of the city and succeeded in joining Gómez in the eastern provinces."[182] Scovel returned to the United States later in the year and went back to Cuba in January 1896, this time as an accredited correspondent for the *World*[183]—a highly desirable assignment for what then was the country's largest newspaper. Scovel's brief career in foreign correspondence was meteoric—and unimaginable by today's rung-climbing ways. In a very real sense, he had entered journalism at a pinnacle.

As a hard-living, risk-taking correspondent, Scovel had few rivals. He lived and traveled with the insurgents and yet managed to smuggle many dispatches out of Cuba. His presence with the insurgents so angered Spanish authorities that they reportedly offered a $5,000 reward for his arrest.[184] But Scovel was no journalistic hero, although he was portrayed as such in Joyce Milton's *The Yellow Kids*, an engaging look at American foreign correspondents in the late 1890s. To Milton, Scovel was the best of what she called the "yellow kid reporters." But in saying so, she was willing to overlook, or assign the best-possible interpretation to, Scovel's many absurd and implausible ideas.

Scovel's character and assignments offer intriguing avenues for examining the conflicted and unsettled state of *fin-de-siècle* American journalism, the professionalization of which was slowly developing in 1897. Scovel was attracted to journalism as a way of winning attention and becoming rich. To those ends, he schemed constantly,[185] leading to his proposing or undertaking a succession of madcap adventures. He indulged his celebrity and habitually blamed others for his failings. For good reason Joseph Pulitzer considered Scovel to be "somewhat of a sharper."[186] Even so, Scovel accomplished some top-notch reporting in 1897, often at no small risk to his life and freedom. Scovel's scheming certainly suggested a need for standards and professional training in journalism. But his rapid mobility and willingness to travel abroad on very short notice anticipated the practice of "parachute journalism" of the late twentieth century, when correspondents alighted in troubled countries with little notice or preparation.

From the lavish jail cell in Sancti Spíritus, Scovel wrote lengthy articles for the *World* about the Cuba situation. These were discerning analyses that seldom were rivaled for insight and perspective. The many months Scovel spent with the insurgents had turned him into a keen and perceptive analyst of the Cuban rebellion. His dispatches accurately described the obstacles the Spanish faced in putting down the insurgency, not the least of which were the Cubans' elusive, hit-and-run tactics. "The Cuban policy is not to fight," Scovel wrote in a lengthy dispatch published in the *World* on February 20, 1897. "They are winning this war by running away."[187] Such insight challenges a latter-day critique that American correspondents failed to grasp the guerrilla nature of the Cuban insurrection and sought to explain what essentially was "a new war within old and comfortable terms," as Gerald Linderman wrote in *The Mirror of War*.[188] Scovel was keenly aware of the nature and effectiveness of the insurgents' tactics.

Figure 3.5 Frances Cabanné of St. Louis married Sylvester Scovel of the *New York World* in 1897 and traveled with her globe trotting husband on his assignments to Alaska and Cuba. She endured hardships as well as long periods of separation from her husband, but remained loyally devoted to him. (Missouri Historical Society, St. Louis.)

Scovel kept a detailed journal while in jail. In one entry, he wrote that Spain would defeat the insurgency only by dividing its large and ponderous conventional army into small, mobile detachments of no more than three hundred soldiers—adopting in effect "the methods of the insurgents themselves."[189] Such a strategy, if vigorously pursued, might turn the tide and suppress the insurgency, Scovel wrote. Otherwise, the Spanish war effort was hopeless, he said.[190] Scovel's analysis proved largely correct. Spain never adjusted, never consistently adopted "the methods of the insurgents," and never put down the Cuban rebellion.

Finally, after a month, the *World*'s pressure won Scovel's release without trial. "After weeks of hard, trying work, amid scenes of constant danger and thirty-one days of confinement in a Spanish prison,

Figure 3.6 Sylvester Scovel was nothing if not self-promoting. Here his wife, Frances, poses with Klondike gold-seekers at a sign touting Scovel's presence in the boomtown of Skagway, Alaska. During the gold rush, Skagway was a gateway to Canada's Klondike region, some 600 miles to the north. (John H. Walker/Klondike Gold Rush National Park.)

he was glad to get within sight of the Statue of Liberty," the *World* exclaimed in reporting Scovel's homecoming.[191] He returned from Cuba a hero. He was daring, swashbuckling, and now jail-tested. There was no reporter in 1897 quite like Harry Scovel.

Scovel's adventures in Cuba were just the opening chapters in what was for him an exceptional year. Within a month of his return to New York, Scovel was received by President William McKinley, was married to Frances Cabanné in St. Louis, and was sent to Europe—without his bride—to cover the Greco-Turkish War for the *World*. He believed the war coverage would catapult him to the *World*'s coveted London correspondency, which had just come open. But while Scovel took the best assignments in 1897, he did not always fill them with skill or confidence. From a distance, he clashed frequently with the *World*'s management over its penny-pinching ways. The *World* paid Scovel $100 a week—not a meager salary in 1897, but not particularly generous, either. But the newspaper was often reluctant or unable to forward him funds to cover expenses such as telegraph tolls, forcing Scovel to tap his own limited reserves.

Scovel told his bride that he hoped to report "'eye-witness' stuff" in the Greco-Turkish War and thus "make reputations for the [*World*] and for us."[192] But he missed the war's decisive final engagement, when outflanked Greek troops retreated in disorder before a Turkish assault at Domokos, Greece, in May 1897. "It is too bad that I should have

Figure 3.7 Sylvester Scovel of the *New York World* became America's best-known journalist in 1897, owing to his succession of high-profile assigments and the month he spent in jail in Cuba. Scovel was constantly scheming about turning his assignments into avenues for becoming rich and famous. (Missouri Historical Society, St. Louis.)

come out here expressly to see a battle, and then miss the only one likely to happen," he told Frances. But he insisted that missing the battle "was distinctly not my fault." The *World*'s managing editor, Scovel said, had suggested that he seek interviews with the Greek king and the Turkish military leader. "So of course I stayed here [in Athens] and the battle did happen just about the time I would have gotten to it," he complained to Frances.[193]

Although he saw little or none of the hoped-for "'eye-witness' stuff," Scovel had managed to interview Greek cabinet ministers and the country's inept military leader, Crown Prince Constantine. But at best his reporting from Greece was uneven and contributed little to his hope[194]—which the *World* had encouraged[195]—of landing the newspaper's London correspondency. The job instead went to Edward Marshall, the Sunday editor of the *New York Journal.*[196] Scovel learned of Marshall's appointment weeks after it had been announced in New York and was keenly disappointed. He ruminated about quitting newspaper work and returning to Cuba to make money. Scovel told his wife that he felt "able to do better work in other lines than in journalism. I think Cuba has a fortune stowed away somewhere for us."[197]

In Greece, Scovel displayed another tendency, that of complaining vehemently about the *World*'s inability to send him funds to cover telegraph tolls and other expenses. Those expenses included a horse and a chartered boat that he thought would be useful in speeding reports to Athens from the front. He described to his wife how he had asked the *World* to wire 200 British pounds to Athens. Instead, the *World* sent him $200, a lesser sum, by mail, via Rome.[198]

With the odd, month-long war at an end, Scovel returned to the United States by way of Spain. Scovel had hoped he would interview the Spanish premier, Antonio Cánovas del Castillo, and other officials in Madrid. But Spain's conservative newspapers learned of his presence in Madrid—or, as he put it, "that the enemy [was] in their midst"—and they "most beautifully roasted me in large print."[199] The publicity, Scovel told his wife, "closed old Canovas' mouth tighter than a clam's,"[200] and he left Spain without the hoped-for interviews.[201]

TO THE KLONDIKE

No assignment in Scovel's exceptional year was more grandiose or more controversial than his reporting in late summer 1897 from southeastern Alaska, gateway for the Klondike gold rush. In the raw Alaska boomtown of Skagway, Scovel took the lead in a disputed and much-publicized attempt to reopen a narrow, boulder-strewn mountain pass that led gold-seekers into Canada and the Klondike fields far to the north. Scovel also hatched what he called "the greatest newspaper scheme ever"—an improbable plan to deliver the *World* by dog trains running from Skagway to Dawson City in the heart of the Klondike region, during the long, subarctic winter. The *World* turned down Scovel's wild idea and, he said, ordered him to cut short his assignment and return immediately to New York. He did so, only to encounter Pulitzer's wrath when he arrived.

Scovel's Klondike adventure took shape suddenly, with orders from the *World* that were sent by telegraph. Scovel had returned to New York from Europe in early summer and was reunited with his bride. She joined him on his assignment to Pittsburgh in late July, to cover unrest in the western Pennsylvania coalfields. At the end of the month, the *World* ordered him to Alaska. As he later recalled, Scovel was to cover the human dimension of the chaotic unfolding gold rush, to "follow the crowd [and] write of the human debris upon the mountain passes" leading from southeastern Alaska to Canada. And before the subarctic winter took hold in earnest, Scovel was to travel on to Dawson City.[202] The assignment meant many months, possibly even a year, in the hardscrabble Klondike. Within hours of receiving the orders from New York, Scovel was aboard a cross-country train bound for Seattle, the supply depot for the gold-rush stampeders. Unknown to the *World*, Frances Scovel was traveling with him. At first, she had planned to accompany her husband as far as Chicago. But as the express train rolled westward, they decided she would stay with him to Seattle[203] and there await his return from the Klondike sometime in 1898.[204] Scovel needed just a day and a half in Seattle to outfit himself with clothing, hardware, tools, and food for the anticipated year-long stay in the Klondike.

In Seattle, Scovel attracted the fawning attention of a local newspaper[205]—and again encountered the *World*'s money problems. He expected to have access to $1,000 to buy his Klondike outfit and pay for its shipment by boat to Skagway. But the money had not arrived. "I had sent three telegrams and had not received authority to draw a cent. At the last moment" before the ship left Seattle, he wrote, "I was handed a message containing instructions" that he could draw the $1,000. The *World* promised that "an additional $500 would be placed 'where I could get it.'"[206] But as Scovel later pointed out to Pulitzer, Seattle was "the last point north that money could be sent to 'where I could get it.'"[207] Owing to rapid inflation caused by the gold rush, $1,000 was far short of what he needed for the Klondike assignment.[208] By then, the Scovels had decided that Frances would go on to Skagway, too. Years later, she recalled that the trip from Seattle was "delightful.... We made friends with everybody, and as we were all on a kind of a wild mission we became very good friends. We were seven days going up to Skagway," arriving in pouring rain on August 12, 1897. Frances Scovel said her first look at Skagway revealed "nothing but a few little tents and those huge mountains" on all sides. "It seemed," she said, "to be the end of the earth."[209]

From Skagway, gold-rush stampeders faced an arduous trek to the Klondike, some six hundred miles to the north. The route from Skagway was daunting and quickly blocked. Stampeders tried to cut through the mountains and into Canada by following the narrow White Pass Trail. But the crude trail was never meant for the volume of goldseekers and it soon became impassible with boulders and muddy quagmires that sucked in horses up to their tails. Many stampeders abandoned the White Pass for the nearby town of Dyea and the steeper Chilkoot Trail into Canada.[210] But many others waited, stalled in Skagway or strung out along the White Pass. Scovel, in what he said would be a coup for the *World*,[211] decided he would open the White Pass trail. He went to Juneau and brought back hundreds of pounds of explosives, which were used to blast away at boulders and other barriers on the trail. He organized what he called the "World Miners' Committee," which dispatched four hunded stampeders to work repairing the trail.[212] By early September, the trail was passable and the Scovels made a harrowing, seven-day trek across the Canadian border to another tent city on the shores of Lake Bennett.

But weeks later, a darker version of Scovel's exploits in Skagway reached New York. The *Sun* in late November published two reports that impugned Scovel's trail-opening heroics. One report was an excerpt from an interview published in the London periodical *Black and White* with a British military officer, Captain Arthur Lee. He had been sent to the Klondike by the *London Daily Chronicle* and recalled in the interview that we had jokingly suggested to Scovel that someone could "purchase some tons of dynamite, blow up all the obstructions [on the White Pass Trail] and ... so win everlasting renown for himself and his paper. To my amazement, he leaped at the suggestion."[213] The blocked stampeders at first were "enchanted with [the] philanthropic zeal" of Scovel's efforts, Lee said, "but when the rocks began to rain about their tents and pack trains without improving the route in the least, and they realized they were merely assisting in a gigantic advertising scheme [for the *World*], they rejected further newspaper aid and proceeded to grapple single-handed with the task themselves."[214]

The *Sun* also cited reports in two Alaska mining periodicals that said Scovel had covered his expenses in Skagway with hundreds of dollars in bank drafts, which the *World* refused to honor. The *Alaska Mining Record*, according to the *Sun*, declared that the first snowfall of any consequence in Skagway in September 1897 was the "shower of protested drafts on the New York World, drawn by Sylvester Scovel."[215]

The *Sun's* reports ring true, at least in part. The comments of Lee, a British officer, seem particularly credible about the derivation and the limited success of Scovel's trail-opening efforts. His work allowed a limited number of stampeders— Scovel and his wife among them—to cross the White Pass corridor before the trail again became overburdened and impassible. Snow and rains during the second half of September finally reduced the beleaguered trail to mire.[216] The account about the bank drafts that bounced also are credible. Scovel probably covered his expenses with the drafts, believing in good faith that the *World* would honor them. He was chronically strapped for cash while on his assignments for the *World*, so it is plausible that he would resort to passing drafts. His correspondence, however, contains no reference to that controversy. In the end, the *World* quietly made good and honored the drafts.

Soon after reaching Lake Bennett with his wife and their provisions, Scovel went back to Skagway, this time via Dyea, through the Chilkoot Pass. It was to have been a weeklong trip, after which the Scovels were to travel by boat down the Yukon River, reaching Dawson City just before winter set in. But in Skagway, Scovel heard that no more than three mail deliveries likely would be made to Dawson City during the long winter ahead. That nugget of gossip fired a wild brainstorm: Why not fill the gap in mail service to Dawson City by running dog teams from Skagway and make a small fortune selling issues of the *World* and other supplies to the goldseekers holed up there?[217]

Scovel thought it a grand idea, "the greatest newspaper scheme ever inaugurated," in fact.[218] He told Frances that the plan promised to be "a tremendous thing for you and me both in money and in reputation." Scovel figured they could transport from Skagway to Dawson City enough copies of the *World*'s thrice-weekly edition "to clear expenses and take in besides medicines and light articles enough to make thousands of dollars, and we can go in and come out when we want to, comfortably."[219] In *The Yellow Kids,* Milton argued that Scovel's scheme was not without merit.[220] But in fact it was an absurd and imprudent idea. Indeed, it was an invitation to disaster that scarcely recognized the hardships and uncertainties of traversing six hundred or so miles of snow-covered trails and frozen lakes amid unrelenting sub-zero conditions. Experienced travelers in the winter of 1897–98 needed twenty-five to thirty days to travel by dogsled from Dawson City to Skagway or Dyea, and encountered no little hardship in doing so.[221]

Improbable though it was, the dogsled plan was born of the recognition that by going to Dawson City and spending the long winter there, Scovel would have few opportunities to send dispatches to the *World*. Scovel envisioned staying in Dawson City eleven months, until August 1898, during which time he said he "could only hope to get three dispatches out to the World."[222] The assignment to the Klondike would have become an extended honeymoon, he told his wife, "with nothing to do but hunt, fish, prospect for gold and write three batches of correspondence—one for each mail!"[223]

Informing the *World* of "the greatest newspaper scheme ever" was no easy task. The nearest reliable telegraphic connections were in Seattle, about 1,000 miles by steamer from Skagway. With his wife living in a tent on the shores of Lake Bennett and only faintly aware of his plans, Scovel boarded a steamer to Seattle. From there, he cabled the *World*, telling the editors of his audacious plan. He anticipated an early and favorable reply. The *World* took nearly three days to respond,[224] and turned Scovel down flatly. According to his correspondence, the *World* editors ordered him back to New York straightaway.[225] The order presented him with a wrenching choice—either comply and head for New York or ignore the *World*'s summons and return to his wife. "I thought it over and over and I couldn't see anything to do for us both but to obey," Scovel explained in a letter to Frances.[226] He guessed that the urgency of the order to return meant the *World* had another important assignment for him—probably in Cuba.[227] So he boarded a transcontinental train for New York. En route, he wrote to Frances, saying that he almost left the train at its first stop, to return to the coast and take the first steamer to Skagway. He said he had a fight with himself and decided in the end to remain onboard.[228]

Before leaving for New York, Scovel sent word to William Saportas, a parttime newspaper correspondent in Skagway and an associate of the boomtown's underworld boss, Soapy Smith. Scovel asked Saportas to find "the madame" at Bennett, the boomtown bordering Lake Bennett, sell their Klondike gear, escort Frances to Skagway, and place her on a steamer to Seattle. From there she would take a train to New York. As an incentive to Saportas, Scovel promised to "have the World send you full credentials as a special correspondent" in Alaska.[229] Until Saportas reached her in early October, Frances Scovel had heard nothing from her husband in four weeks.[230] "I had nothing to read, nothing to do," she recalled of her time at Bennett, "and no one to talk to but a lot of men, who were as kind as they could be and I got at such a stage that my brain refused to work and after a while I could hardly sleep."[231] She told her mother that she was terribly lonely without Scovel but held no resentment toward him. Any place "is good enough where Harry is," she wrote from Bennett, "but ... it is awful, awful without him and in this hole—it is death."[232]

During his five-day train trip to New York, Scovel took advantage of a layover in Chicago to visit relatives; among them were "various middle-aged aunts" who leveled "severe interrogatory expressions" at him. Finally, Scovel's "Dear Aunt Belle" rebuked him, saying: "Harry, I don't care how much it means to ... you to obey" the *World*'s orders. "You ought never to have left Frances." With that Aunt Belle boxed his ears.[233] Far more serious trouble awaited Scovel in New York. Pulitzer and Bradford Merrill, the *World*'s managing editor, were angry about the aborted Klondike adventure.

Pulitzer was furious about the expenses Scovel had incurred, including all the Klondike gear that had been trekked to Lake Bennett only to be sold at a substantial loss. He accused Scovel of "gross extravagance," a charge that stung, and prompted Scovel to write a fifteen-page memorandum. In it, Scovel accounted for his expenses in great detail and insisted that he had traveled as sparely as he could. He defended taking his wife along to Alaska. She was an asset, Scovel insisted, not a hindrance. She had tapped $700 from her savings to cover expenses.[234] And she had paid for some of the explosives that were used on the White Pass trail.[235]

As was his wont, Scovel blamed someone else—in this case, Merrill—for a mistake in judgment. "You see," Scovel told his wife, "Mr. Merrill now sees he made a mistake in ordering me home while there was still time for us to get … to the Klondyke. … He doesn't wish to shoulder the blame and naturally (if I don't explain matters thoroughly) I am the scapegoat."[236] Scovel's job hung in the balance for a time. Ironically, what may have kept Scovel from being fired were overtures from Hearst's *New York Journal*. The *Journal* had courted Scovel, seeking to add him to a staff already populated by many refugees from the *World*. Pulitzer and Merrill likely recoiled at the prospect of losing to their keenest rival the most famous correspondent in American journalism—even if that correspondent was impetuous, headstrong, and extraordinarily difficult to handle. Scovel's activist, adventurous spirit was probably better suited to Hearst's rambunctious "journalism of action." Even so, Scovel remained at the *World*, acknowledging a sense of loyalty to Pulitzer and the newspaper that "practically made me."[237]

Frances Scovel finally reached New York on October 26, 1897. Saportas had found her at Bennett, escorted her to Skagway, and traveled with her on the steamer *Alki* to Seattle. She then traveled alone across the continent only to wait two days more for a reunion with her husband. The *World* indeed had sent Scovel to Cuba but he was promptly expelled on the orders of Weyler, the captain-general.[238] Weyler, however, was not long for Cuba. He had been recalled to Spain and left on October 31, 1897. After a hurried reunion in New York, the Scovels, boarded a steamer for Havana and arrived there in early November. Their relationship had survived the separation. In Seattle, Frances had retrieved a stack of anguished, lovelorn letters that her husband had sent. Sylvester found that his wife had returned "strong and flushed from her awfully hard but healthy Alaskan experience." To him, she "never looked better."[239] Frances said that if Scovel were ordered back to Alaska, she would not hesitate to go with him.[240]

In Cuba, much had changed since Scovel's release from jail eight months before. Weyler's successor, General Ramón Blanco y Arenas, was keen on developing amiable ties with American correspondents, including Scovel. One morning in November, Blanco and his staff entered the dining room of the Inglaterra, the hotel of choice for American correspondents in Havana. Seeing Scovel and his wife, the general walked across the room, and chatted with the correspondent, holding his hand as they talked.[241] As such cordiality suggested, Blanco's arrival meant fewer restrictions and obstacles for American journalists in Cuba.

Cuba was also the theater of a humanitarian crisis that had only worsened since Scovel's release from jail. Scovel's principal assignment that autumn was to travel from town to town, documenting the ravages of Spain's "reconcentration" policy.[242] On the first leg of their trip, by train from Havana to Matanzas, the Scovels were accompanied by Walter B. Barker, the rough-edged American consul in Sagua la Grande who had just returned from a month-long visit to the United States.[243] The diplomat traveled with them "for safety," Frances Scovel told her father.[244] With Barker present, Scovel was less likely to be harassed or arrested.

In a blunt and unadorned fashion, Frances Scovel's correspondence captured the horror and devastation that crept across Cuba in the closing weeks of 1897. "Right at the edge of Havana there are people dying of hunger," she wrote. "I went to one house with Harry the day after we arrived and I never shall forget those poor people, most all women and children.... The streets are filled with the most ragged, the thinnest people you can imagine. It is awful."[245] As the Scovels and Barker rode the train, they could see the lush Cuban countryside rolling out before them. It was "God's own land," Frances wrote, "so green [with] great rows [of] Royal Palm growing every where." But the countryside was desolate, eerily so. Reconcentration had removed many inhabitants or had sent them into hiding. "We passed through deserted sugar estates, great broad white houses, with their white pillars and trees, gardens, sugar press, and fields of cane, all deserted," Frances wrote.[246] The few Cubans seen tilling fields were so thin and ragged they reminded her of scarecrows.[247]

In Matanzas, east of Havana, the Scovels and Barker were joined by the local American consul, A. C. Brice, and two Cuban-Americans. They went to a band concert at the town square and then to a café for drinks. On leaving the café, they were met by scrawny, malnourished, big-eyed children who begged them for money. The Americans tossed them copper coins, which sent the children scrambling. As they searched for the coins, a burly, well-dressed man approached, snapping a long, menacing whip. He was the local police chief and he began flogging the children, forcing them disperse. "It seemed like a horrid dream," Sylvester Scovel wrote in a dispatch for the *World*. He and his party stood stunned for a moment, not sure just what was happening.[248] Hearing the children scream, they stepped in. The hot-tempered Barker clenched his fist as if to strike the police chief, but thought better of it.[249] "Oh, how I would like to have been a man indeed," Frances said later. "I forgot that I was not and started for him, too, calling him a coward but he didn't understand my English." The episode was shocking, enough to "have made any true American's blood boil," Frances wrote.[250]

From Matanzas, the Scovels went on to Sancti Spíritus and visited the jail where Sylvester had been detained earlier in the year.[251] Their principal reason for visiting Sancti Spíritus was to meet up with Madrigal, the rotund U.S. consular agent. With the permission of Spanish authorities, Madrigal and the Scovels then traveled to the camp of the insurgent leader, Gómez, to collect the effects of Charles E. Crosby. He was an American correspondent killed in May 1897 during a skirmish between the insurgents and Spanish forces.[252] That duty indirectly revealed the celebrity Scovel had become by the end of 1897. When he and his wife were late returning from Gómez's camp, reports circulated that the insurgents had arrested them and sentenced him to death.[253] But soon enough, the Scovels arrived in Havana, alive and well. And Sylvester had a final, year-end scoop to send to the *World*. He had interviewed Gómez on December 23 about Spanish plans to extend a limited measure of home rule to the Cubans, in an attempt to quell the insurgency by political means. Gómez reaffirmed in his interview with Scovel that he wanted no part of Spain's autonomy offer. The insurgents would settle for nothing short of political independence. The interview with Gómez was published on January 2, 1898 beneath a headline that read: "The World Again Makes History for Spain and Cuba."[254] Adjoining Scovel's report was a sketch of the correspondent on horseback, a faint smirk stealing across his face.

CONCLUSION

The work and accomplishments of Church, Davis, and Scovel in 1897 together represent an intriguing case study about the development of journalistic identity and reputation at the end of the nineteenth century. It is remarkable how dissimilar they were and how each of them followed markedly different routes to the top of the journalistic hierarchy in *fin-de-siècle* America.

Church cloaked himself in the anonymity of the editorial page. His reputation, the *New York Times* said in an editorial tribute after his death in 1906, "was merged in that of the institution which he served, and he was scarcely known by name outside of the circles of his own acquaintance and of his own profession. Within those circles he was highly and justly esteemed."[255] The *Times'* tribute was quite unusual. Few journalists of the time—especially those who courted anonymity as assiduously as Church—were ever so singled out. While its editorial contained no specific reference to "Is There A Santa Claus?" the *Times* said Church's treatment of religious or theological topics from a secular point of view often "seemed far too sardonic and cold-blooded. But they showed a determination on the part of the writer ... to be nobody's dupe, not even his own." [256]

Davis made good on his vow never again to work for Hearst, and his career suffered not at all. Davis distinguished himself in reporting from Cuba and Puerto Rico during the Spanish-American War, sealing his reputation as a top-notch correspondent. His articles for the *New York Herald* and, especially, for *Scribner's* magazine were among the best of what was a brief but intensively reported war. His articles in *Scribner's* were so richly detailed that one critic said that Davis deserved "a reputation as one of the most vivid and picturesque of living writers" working in English.[257] Davis' account in *Scribner's* of the American assault of the San Juan Heights near Santiago de Cuba helped establish the warrior reputation of Theodore Roosevelt, who had led the famous charge. Davis' article depicted a triumphant, risk-taking Roosevelt, "mounted high on horseback, and charging the rifle-pits at a gallop and quite alone"—an image, wrote Davis, that "made you feel that you would like to cheer."[258]

Davis burnished his reputation as a gifted and prominent war correspondent in the Boer War and early in the First World War. His account in *Scribner's* describing the occupying German forces as they marched into Brussels in 1914 stands as a legend in war correspondence.[259] "This was a machine," Davis wrote, "endless, tireless, with the delicate organization of a watch and the brute power of a steam-roller. And for three days and three nights through Brussels it roared and rumbled, a cataract of molten lead."[260] The war was Davis' last. He died of heart failure in 1916, just shy of his fifty-second birthday.

The Spanish-American War sealed Scovel's reputation, too, but ultimately in a controversial and humiliating way. He had distinguished himself in reporting from Havana in February 1898 about the destruction of the U.S. warship *Maine*. Scovel's energetic work kept the *World* consistently ahead of the *Journal* and other rivals in the aftermath of the *Maine* disaster and the run-up to the brief war with Spain. But in July 1898, at the surrender of the Spanish garrison at Santiago de Cuba, Scovel's meteoric career suffered a damaging reversal. The centerpiece of the surrender ceremony was raising the American flag above the Governor's Palace, the seat of Spanish authority in Cuba's second-largest city. Scovel had clambered to the palace rooftop to position himself at or near the flagpole, which would ensure that his likeness would appear in photographs of the flag-raising. American officers spotted Scovel and ordered him down from the roof. In a rage, Scovel confronted and exchanged words with Major General Rufus Shafter, commander of the U.S. forces in Santiago. Shafter, an obese and insufferable officer, slapped Scovel, who then took a swing at the general. Scovel's blow grazed Shafter's double chin.[261] "I was a light weight college champion," Scovel later wrote, "... and to strike back was as natural as breathing, I let fly with my right."[262]

It was one of the most bizarre confrontations ever between an American journalist and a senior U.S. military officer. Scovel was promptly arrested, deported, and soon fired by the *World*. He was eventually reinstated, only after writing a lengthy, self-pitying letter to the *World*.[263] But Scovel the swashbuckling journalist-adventurer of 1897 had become Scovel the pariah. He had his defenders, but he never lived down his intemperate encounter with Shafter.

Scovel returned to Cuba for the *World* but soon drifted out of journalism and became the first automobile dealer in Cuba in 1902.[264] He died in 1905 after an operation in Havana for an abscessed liver. A brief obituary in the *New York Times* recalled that Scovel had "attained prominence during the Spanish-American war on account of an altercation with Gen. Shafter."[265] Scovel's widow, Frances, remarried in 1917. Her new husband was William Saportas, the parttime newspaper correspondent in Skagway who had escorted her to Seattle from the shores of Lake Bennett in October 1897.

4

NOT A HOAX

New Evidence in the New York Journal's
Rescue of Evangelina Cisneros

William Randolph Hearst's vision of the "journalism of action" found it most dramatic expression on the moonlit rooftop of the Casa de Recogidas, a wretched jail for women in Havana. During the early hours of October 7, 1897, Karl Decker, a Washington-based reporter for Hearst's *New York Journal,* and two accomplices, used Stilson wrenches to snap a bar of the prison window, allowing the escape of Evangelina Cosío y Cisneros, a petite, nineteen-year-old Cuban accused of plotting against Spanish military authority.

According to the *Journal's* accounts of the jailbreak,[1] Decker and his accomplices led the young woman across a "sagging decrepit ladder"[2] to the roof of a ramshackle house that Decker had rented. They rushed inside, down the stairs, and into the street. Waiting there was a horse-drawn carriage that sped Cisneros[3] to refuge just a few blocks from the Casa de Recogidas, at the home of another accomplice—an affluent, Cuban-American banker named Carlos F. Carbonell.

After nearly three days in hiding, during which time Spanish authorities in Havana conducted a house-to-house search for the fugitive, Cisneros was walked to a pier at the Havana harbor. She was

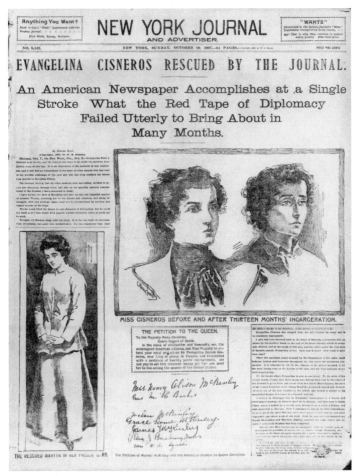

Figure 4.1 In huge deadlines, the *New York Journal* claimed credit for rescuing a Cuban political prisoner, Evangelina Cosío y Cisneros, from a wretched jail in Havana. The exploit was a high-water mark of activist journalism. With typical bravado, the *Journal* declared the jailbreak "the greatest journalistic coup of this age." (Library of Congress.)

disguised as a boy and carried a forged passport in the name of "Juan Sola." While Spanish detectives were distracted by an offer of drinks below decks, Cisneros slipped aboard the *Seneca*, an American-flagged passenger steamer bound for New York City. She reached New York on October 13, 1897, and was lodged by the *Journal* in a palatial room at the Waldorf Hotel.[4]

A few days later, Cisneros was hailed at a thunderous outdoor reception organized by Hearst and the *Journal*. Nearly 75,000 people[5] came

Figure 4.2 Evangelina Cisneros and her rescuer, Karl Decker of the *New York Journal*, were given an enthusiastic welcome at Convention Hall in Washington in late October 1897. While in the capital, they called on President William McKinley, who shook their hands but reportedly said nothing to them. (Library of Congress.)

to Madison Square to welcome the young woman and her rescuer, who had returned to New York aboard a Spanish-flagged vessel. Cisneros was rapturously received not because she was a daring and clever prison escapee, but because she was a frail and wily embodiment of the Cuban struggle for political independence from Spain. A Philadelphia newspaper reporter wrote that the "wild acclamation" for Cisneros in New York revealed that "the American people [were] ready at any and all times to take sides with the oppressed and especially ready now to show that they are not selfish in the freedom they enjoy."[6] It was, the reporter declared, "a great night—great for the heroine, great for the hero, great for the 'Journal,' and greatest of all, for the great liberty-loving American public."[7] The *Journal* declared the turnout "the greatest gathering New York has seen since the close of the war" in 1865.[8]

Decker and Cisneros received a similarly rousing and emotional reception a week later at Convention Hall in Washington, D.C. When Decker and Cisneros arrived at the hall, the *Washington Post* reported, "people arose from their chairs, waved handkerchiefs, threw hats in the air, shouted, cheered, clapped their hands and stamped their feet. … It was several minutes before Mr. Decker could be heard." Outside was "a vast throng that had been unable to crowd into the hall," the *Post* said. "They wanted to at least secure a glimpse of the hero and the heroine. They waited outside throughout the entire programme, to see Mr. Decker and Miss Cisneros, notwithstanding the inclemency of the weather. They were rewarded for their patience, for when the couple descended the stairs the bright glare of an electric light fell full upon them and they were to be plainly seen. 'Hurrah for Karl!' was the shout as they passed down the steps."[9]

Nothing in American journalism in 1897 quite rivaled the Cisneros jailbreak and its aftermath. It was an extraordinary episode. None of Sylvester Scovel's schemes and exploits came close to matching the audacity and brazen lawlessness of what the *Chicago Times-Herald* disparaged as "jail-breaking journalism."[10] Many U.S. newspapers and trade journals cheered the *Journal's* exploit.[11] The *Fourth Estate* congratulated Decker and the *Journal* for an "international triumph" and saluted them for having "smashed journalistic records."[12] The *Journalist* said the case was remarkable and more evocative of "medieval romance than of nineteenth century journalism."[13] For the *Journal*, the Cisneros jailbreak was "epochal,"[14] a "supreme achievement of the journalism of action."[15]

While the Cisneros case demonstrated what the "journalism of action" could accomplish, it also was a demarcation of the paradigm's limits. Decker, who was acting under orders from Hearst and the *Journal*, organized a daring and successful jailbreak and escape. But as this chapter demonstrates, the success of the "journalism of action" in the Cisneros case hinged on—and was made possible only by—the little-known support of a clandestine network that had become adept in smuggling arms, ammunition, and medicine into Cuba and, on occasion, people out.[16] Carbonell, the Cuban-American banker who gave Cisneros refuge, was a central figure in the underground network, from which Decker quietly recruited his accomplices.[17] In addition, U.S. diplomatic personnel based in Cuba took direct and indirect roles in supporting the Cisneros jailbreak and escape. Specifically, a junior member of the U.S. consulate staff in Havana, Donnell Rockwell, provided a file or similarly small instrument with which Cisneros sawed surreptitiously, if futilely, at the bars of her cell. Walter B. Barker, the U.S. consular officer in Sagua la Grande in central Cuba, effectively acted as chaperone in accompanying Cisneros to New York aboard the *Seneca*.

In addition to directing attention to those crucial and heretofore little-known elements of the *Journal*'s rescue of Cisneros, this chapter pursues forensic leads that appear in accounts of the jailbreak written by its principals—notably, Decker and Cisneros. Their accounts include meteorological and lunar-phase details, which even now can be corroborated. The evidentiary record shows, for example, that a waxing moon would have been visible over Havana when the jailbreak occurred, much as Decker and Cisneros described.

The evidence presented in this chapter not only presents new detail about the Cisneros case, it explodes the persistent belief that the jailbreak was a hoax or a "put-up job,"[18] brought about by bribing Spanish authorities in Cuba. The suspicion of bribe-paying has become widely accepted in the literature of the jailbreak, even though the evidentiary record supporting such a claim is extremely thin.

A word of caution is in order here, because to examine the Cisneros affair in any detailed way is to confront a tangle of contradiction, exaggeration, and misdirection. Some details of the case were disputed, even by the principals themselves. This chapter recognizes and pays heed to those complicating factors while pointing nonetheless to the inescapable conclusion that the Cisneros rescue was not a hoax. It was, rather, the successful result of an intricate plot in which Cuba-based operatives and U.S. diplomatic personnel filled vital roles—roles that have remained obscure for more than one hundred years.

Evangelina Cisneros, a Cuban teenager barely five feet tall, would seem an unlikely central figure in American journalism's greatest escape narrative. She was a daughter of respectable though hardly prominent Cuban parents. Her mother died when Evangelina was a child. Evangelina's father, Agustín Cosío, was accused of aiding the rebels in the insurrection against Spanish rule and in May 1896 was deported to the Spanish garrison and penal colony on the Isle of Pines (now Isle of Youth), south of the Cuban mainland. Evangelina and her sister, Carmen, went with their father, to look after him in what was, effectively, minimum-security internment.[19] In July 1896, Lieutenant Colonel José Bérriz, a nephew of Spain's minister of war, was appointed commander of the Spanish military contingent on the Isle of Pines, setting in motion events that would send Evangelina to the Casa de Recogidas in Havana.

According to the *Journal*, the dark-eyed Evangelina soon attracted Bérriz's attention and she became the victim of what today would be recognized as acute sexual harassment. Bérriz was "a beast in uniform," the *Journal* said,[20] who sought sexual favors from the vulnerable teenager. Evangelina "indignantly repulsed" his overtures,[21] but Bérriz was undeterred. He threatened to deport Evangelina's father to a penal colony off the north coast of Africa, where conditions were far more severe than on the Isle of Pines, unless she showed him affection and "gratitude."[22] One night, he visited her quarters, uninvited and in full uniform. Evangelina resisted his advances; he grabbed her by the shoulders and told her he loved her.[23] Evangelina broke away, screaming. Her cries alerted her friends who rushed to her rescue, seizing the officer, and tying him to a chair. "Murder!" Bérriz shouted as he was being bound. A passing Spanish patrol rescued him. Evangelina and her comrades soon were rounded up, and accused of attempting to kill Bérriz.[24]

That, essentially, was the *Journal*'s version: Evangelina was only guilty of "having in her veins the best blood in Cuba"[25] While not implausible, the *Journal*'s account that Evangelina was an innocent victim is impugned by other evidence that describes her as a wily central participant in a scheme to kidnap Bérriz and foment an uprising on the Isle of Pines. This evidence includes a brief statement that Evangelina gave to a U.S. consular officer[26] as well her father's recollections about the case.[27] These accounts agree with the *Journal*'s in that Bérriz was enamored with Evangelina, who rejected his overtures. Bérriz sought to pressure Evangelina by threatening to expel her father to a penal colony.[28] That led Agustín Cosío to devise an improbable and ill-fated plan in which Evangelina lured Bérriz to her house, where he was seized. At the same time, other Cubans attacked the Spanish garrison on the island.[29] That uprising was soon put down. Bérriz was quickly rescued, and the Cuban who had bound and gagged him was executed by firing squad.[30] Evangelina, her sister Carmen, their father, and several other conspirators were rounded up and taken in chains to Havana.[31] Agustín Cosío was imprisoned at the Cabaña fortress in Havana. Carmen was released after a short time at the Casa de Recogidas, but Evangelina was kept there for months, without trial.

Her plight became known to the wife and daughter of Fitzhugh Lee, the U.S. consul-general in Havana. They visited her in prison in early 1897, seeking to "relieve the tedium and distress of her imprisonment."[32] Evangelina recalled Mrs. Lee's visit as akin to "the coming of an angel. She spoke to me as she might to her own daughter. She

Figure 4.3 As the U.S. consul-general from Havana in 1896–1898, Fitzhugh Lee set up an intelligence-gathering network in Cuba and may have encouraged Karl Decker's plans to rescue Evangelina Cisneros from jail. Lee was acquainted with Cisneros and urged the Spanish military leader in Cuba to set her free. Lee was a Confederate cavalry leader during the American Civil War and a nephew of General Robert E. Lee. (Library of Congress.)

promised to do for me a number of little things, that only a woman could do. ..."[33] No doubt encouraged by his wife and daughter, Lee also took exceptional interest in the case, going well beyond his duties as the chief American diplomat in Cuba to urge Spanish authorities to ease the conditions of Cisneros' imprisonment.[34] "Words fail me," Lee later wrote, "in describing the horrors of this place, and the appearance of the dissolute gang of women confined therein."[35]

Lee—a former Confederate cavalry commander, a nephew of Robert E. Lee, and a favorite source for U.S. correspondents covering the Cuban rebellion[36]—first noticed Cisneros while visiting American women who briefly were jailed there. "I succeeded in having the Americans finally released," Lee wrote, "but the picture of this pretty young girl being left behind continued to haunt me." He took up her case with senior Spanish authorities in Havana and less-punishing accommodations were soon built for what Lee called "the better class of prisoners"—Cisneros among them.[37] Those accommodations were completed in February 1897, as an addition built atop the jail's flat roof.[38] It was from that rooftop in October 1897 that Decker and his accomplices broke Cisneros from jail.

The *Journal* disclosed Evangelina's imprisonment in mid-August 1897, in a front-page report headlined, "The Cuban Girl Martyr."[39] The article claimed, incorrectly, that Cisneros had been tried by a martial tribunal and was "in imminent danger" of being sentenced to twenty years' imprisonment at Spain's harsh penal colony on Ceuta, off the north coast of Africa.[40] The article also inaccurately identified her as a niece of Salvador Cisneros y Betancourt, a former leader of a would-be Cuban civilian government.[41]

For the *Journal*, the mistaken details mattered little. Far more important was that the prolonged imprisonment of Cisneros represented a brutish and unambiguous example of Spain's cruel treatment of Cuban women—a topic of not infrequent attention in U.S. newspapers.[42] The *Journal* soon stoked an uproar about the Cisneros case. It enlisted the support of prominent American women, such as Julia Ward Howe, who wrote to Pope Leo XIII, asking him to intercede with Spanish authorities. Varina Davis, the widow of the Confederate president Jefferson Davis, wrote to the Queen Regent of Spain, asking her to spare Evangelina from a sentence to Ceuta and "a fate worse than death." The *Journal* exploited these heartfelt appeals by publishing their contents on the front page.[43] Soon, the *Journal* claimed, more than 10,000 women from all parts of the United States had added their names to petitions calling for Cisneros' release.[44] "The whole United States is aroused," the *Journal* declared. "From all parts of the Union come expressions of horror" about the Cisneros case.[45]

By late August, however, the *Journal*'s petition drive had stalled. Spain was unmoved by the appeals to free Cisneros. Decker was sent to Havana,[46] ostensibly to replace George Eugene Bryson, a *Journal* correspondent expelled because of his reporting about the Cisneros case.[47] While in Havana, Decker acted as the *Journal*'s correspondent and worked from the newspaper's bureau in Casa Nueva, a three-story building at Cuba and Obrapia streets, in the heart of the city. Casa Nueva also housed the U.S. consulate[48] and offices of Hidalgo & Co., the Havana agents of the Ward steamship line, which operated several passenger steamers, including the *Seneca*.[49]

Although he occasionally filed reports to the *Journal*, Decker was in Havana to secure the release of Cisneros. Decker was a hefty six-footer who was born in Staunton, Virginia, and grew up in the Georgetown section of Washington. He was working in the *Journal*'s Washington bureau when summoned to New York and given the task of rescuing Cisneros. He had been to Cuba before, having spent several weeks in late 1896 and early 1897 with the insurgents in Santa Clara province in central Cuba.

Decker was also the principal author of what can be called the *Journal*'s jailbreak narrative. Decker's detailed, first-person accounts about the jailbreak appeared in two installments[50] in the *Journal* soon afterward, and as an expanded version in *The Story of Evangelina Cisneros*, which contained a companion section attributed to Cisneros, who spoke and wrote little English. According to the jailbreak narrative, Decker and two accomplices tried to free Cisneros in the early hours of October 6, 1897, but failed to cut open the bars of Cisneros' rooftop cell. They returned on October 7, 1897, and using the heavy wrenches, quickly broke a window bar, allowing Cisneros to flee. The *Journal* reported the jailbreak in its editions of October 8 and 9 1897—and claimed credit for the rescue on October 10, the day after Cisneros left Havana aboard the *Seneca*. The *Journal*, as was its wont, indulged heartily in self-congratulation. "Evangelina Cosio y Cisneros is at liberty," it declared, "and the Journal can place to its credit the greatest journalistic coup of this age."[51] The "journalism of action" never seemed more robust, or more proud of itself.

Within days of the *Journal*'s self-disclosure, suspicions arose that the rescue was a hoax (or, as one scholar later wrote, a case of "metafiction"[52]). Detractors argued that the rescue would have been impossible without bribing Spanish officials, to keep them quiet and to induce them to look the other way as Cisneros boarded the *Seneca* in leaving Havana. Lee was quoted as telling a State Department official that Spanish authorities "must have winked at" Cisneros' flight from Cuba because she never could have left the island "without their permit."[53] Lee, who was on home leave in the United States at the time of the jailbreak, muddled matters by soon after dismissing the notion of Spanish collusion in the escape. That would have been "absurd," he said, adding: "I have good authority for the statement that [Spanish officials] in Cuba are greatly incensed over the young woman's escape."[54] Lee was quoted in the *Journal* as saying that it "took brave, resolute and fearless men to plan and carry out the scheme."[55]

Lee's contrary statements about the Cisneros case escaped wide notice, however, and the suggestion the jailbreak was a hoax took hold. The *New York Times* referred to Lee's "must-have-winked-at" comment in describing the jailbreak as a "remarkable case of unobstructed rescue."[56] The *Times* also raised doubts about whether Cisneros' cross-dressing disguise would have fooled anyone. "The most adroit and experienced performers on the stage rarely succeed in this effort, and usually they fail to a ludicrous degree," the *Times* stated. "A glance should have told the Spanish detectives [checking identities of passengers as they boarded the *Seneca*] the secret of this amateur masquerader" dressed as a boy.[57]

The *World* was eager to denounce the rescue as fraudulent. "Gold did it," the *World* declared. "The Spanish could not withstand its glitter. It oiled the palms of turnkeys and guards, of officers and civilians. Miss Cisneros's friends had it a-plenty. And so she got out of her cell while her jailers looked the other way."[58] However, the *World* offered no evidence or details to support its accusation. The *Sun*, meanwhile, reported that a "Señor Gil," the Havana police inspector investigating the jailbreak, suspected the "complicity of persons on the inside" at Casa de Recogidas. "It will not be surprising if Señor Gil is right," the *Sun* reported, "inasmuch as money in countries administered by Spain is well known, as the Spanish themselves say, 'to be a force that opens all doors.'"[59] The *Sun* also reported that the jailer, José Quintana, and a guard, Ramon Garcia, had been arrested.[60] The disposition of their cases is not known.

Suspicions that authorities in Havana connived in or "winked at"[61] the escape of Cisneros were not long in reaching Madrid. The Spanish minister of overseas territories, Segismundo Moret, on October 12, 1897, instructed the commander of Spain's forces in Cuba, Governor-General Valeriano Weyler y Nicolau, to provide "the necessary information" to allow the minister "to deny" the "absurd" report of Spanish connivance in the jailbreak.[62] Weyler's reply is not known, but the Spanish cabinet was reported in mid-October 1897 to have discussed his cabled report about the Cisneros escape.[63] The cabinet was also reported to have asked Weyler for more detail.[64] In the end, Madrid did not demand Cisneros' extradition and allowed the matter to drop. It is likely that the government of Premier Práxedes Mateo Sagasta, which had taken office just days before the jailbreak, was relieved to be rid of an irritant in its relations with the United States. Hannis Taylor, the former chief U.S. diplomat to Madrid, said as much a few days after the jailbreak: "Sagasta probably will give a royal decoration to those who have been good enough to rid Spain of this troublesome subject."[65]

It is not hard to understand why the rescue attracted doubters and detractors. Elements of the jailbreak narrative do seem incredible. How could Decker and a handful of accomplices have so thoroughly outwitted authorities in the very seat of Spanish power in Cuba? How could they have smuggled her aboard the *Seneca* when Spanish authorities were combing the city, looking for her? A skeptical account published in 1898 asserted: "It would have been utterly impossible for Miss Cisneros to escape from the Cuban prison, to walk on a vessel in the port of Havana in open day … if the Spanish officials had not been made to understand that it was necessary for them not to recognize her at any time until she had successfully fled from the Island. Neither General Weyler nor any of the Spanish authorities in Cuba dared publicly confess that they actively or passively aided the escape of Miss Cisernos."[66]

NO EVIDENCE OF BRIBERY

Over the years, conventional wisdom has solidified aroud the suspicion that the Cisneros rescue was a fraud, due more to "bribery than bravery."[67] But such claims have never been supported by compelling evidence. No one has identified to whom bribes were paid, how much was paid, by what method, and how the purported payoffs would have secured the enduring silence of the authorities. A conspiracy of silence that included Weyler and other Spanish authorities in Cuba would have been so extensive—so many people would have known—that concealment could not one possibly have lasted for long, certainly not one hundred years and more.

It is exceedingly unlikely that Weyler took bribes or otherwise countenanced the jailbreak.[68] In October 1897, Weyler was in the final days of his controversial tenure in Cuba. Sagasta's liberal government was determined to recall Weyler, who had been given command of Spanish forces in Cuba by a predecessor conservative government in Madrid. It seems implausible that at what was a low point of his military career, Weyler would have risked besmirching his reputation and undermining his standing among conservative political forces in Spain[69] by conniving in or facilitating the Cisneros escape. Weyler was proud of his record in Cuba and, before leaving, described the rebellion as nearly extinguished and his mission largely a success.[70] Neither characterization was true. Nonetheless, it is far-fetched to suggest that Weyler would have participated in a scheme to free Cisneros—a scheme which, if disclosed, would only redound to his disfavor and humiliation.

It is likewise far-fetched that Weyler would have given the *Journal*—which, days before the jailbreak, had called him "the monster of the century"[71]—a publicity bonanza at his expense. Weyler disliked American newspapers[72] and jailed or expelled several U.S. correspondents who covered the Cuban insurrection. Among them was Bryson, the *Journal* correspondent who was ordered to leave Cuba in late August 1897. It would have been more in character for Weyler to have spurned inducements from any newspaper to free Cisneros and instead to have ordered the arrest of anyone making such an overture.

It is important to confront what stands as the most compelling argument that the jailbreak was fraudulent. That argument was presented in

1933 by Willis J. Abbot, a former top editor for Hearst who by then had joined the *Christian Science Monitor*, a newspaper founded expressly to counter the effects of yellow journalism. In his book of reminiscences, *Watching the World Go By*, Abbot dismissed the Cisneros rescue as "a magnificent farce"[73] and "a false bit of cheap sensationalism."[74] Abbot claimed insider's knowledge about the rescue, writing that he was "at the office during the progress of this comedy and in daily contact with Hearst."[75] Abbot asserted that the escape was facilitated by bribes paid to Cisneros' jailers and that the *Journal*'s jailbreak narrative was meant not only to present readers with a riveting tale but "to exonerate" complicit jailers in Havana as well.[76] Abbot did not, however, describe the amounts of the purported bribes or how they were supposedly paid.

Abbot's challenge to the *Journal*'s jailbreak narrative not only was thin on documentation, it was short on logic: It failed notably to explain why the *Journal* would have gone to such lengths, after the escape, to protect the jailers in Havana—and it neglected to mention that they had been arrested shortly after the jailbreak.[77] Abbot also overlooked the official notice, published in Havana and widely reported in the United States,[78] in which the Spanish prosecutor ordered civil and military authorities to search for Cisneros, arrest her, and return her to Havana.[79]

Abbot's claim to have been in close contact with Hearst at the time of the jailbreak—an assertion crucial to the believability of his account—is exaggerated and probably untrue. By early October 1897, Abbot had begun a leave of absence from the *Journal* to lead the campaign committee of Henry George, one of the four major candidates running that fall to become New York mayor.[80] The George campaign began in earnest October 5, 1897—two days before the Cisneros jailbreak—with a rally at Cooper Union, at which Abbot participated as chairman of the resolutions committee.[81] News accounts in early October describe Abbot as working tirelessly to reconcile the fractious elements of George's ill-fated campaign,[82] which ended with the candidate's fatal stroke just five days before election. Given his absence from the *Journal* and his commitments to the George campaign, Abbot's dismissive claims about the Cisneros case simply are not credible. He was too preoccupied with electioneering to have been very familiar with the unfolding plan to free Cisneros and bring her to the United States.

Abbot's account was marred by other inaccuracies. These include his referring to Hearst's *Journal* as the "*American*." The newspaper's name was changed to the *American* in 1902, five years after the jailbreak. In addition, Abbot identifies Carlos Carbonell as a dentist; he was a banker.[83] Despite its flaws, Abbot's version has informed many subsequent accounts of the Cisneros escape—including those appearing in

Kristin Hoganson's *Fighting for American Manhood: How Gender Politics Provoked the Spanish-American and Philippine-American Wars*,[84] Ben Procter's *William Randolph Hearst: The Early Years*,[85] John Stevens' *Sensationalism and the New York Press*,[86] and W. A. Swanberg's *Citizen Hearst*.[87] Joyce Milton in her work about war correspondents in Cuba in the 1890s asserted flatly that the warden and guards at Casa de Recogidas "had all been bribed."[88]

This is not to say that Decker didn't try to pass bribes. He acknowledged in the jailbreak narrative that "a sturdy attempt was made to reach some of the guards or keepers with bribes, but nothing was effected."[89] Upon returning to New York from Havana, Decker told reporters that he had attempted to bribe the jailer, Quintana, "but he wanted $15,000 for the job and assurances that he and his family could get to the United States in safety. That was too rich a proposition for me," Decker was quoted as saying.[90] By failing to follow through on his proposition and rejecting the jailer's demands, Decker quite likely heightened the risks he and his accomplices faced, because his overture may have left the jailer more vigilant about attempts to free Cisneros. In any case, the available record offers no persuasive evidence to support the conventional wisdom that bribes were paid to facilitate the escape.

THE CLANDESTINE ACCOMPLICES

Decker may not have paid bribes in the Cisneros escape, but he had a great deal of help—assistance that he and *Journal* never acknowledged in any detail. That Decker had accomplices was but a minor, subordinate detail.

Vital to the covert operation was Carlos Carbonell, the Cuban-American banker who earned a degree at Rensselaer Polytechnic Institute in 1875.[91] Carbonell was a well-to-do bachelor who turned forty-seven just three days before the jailbreak. He was associated with Hidalgo & Co., the Havana agent for the Ward Line. As such, Carbonell was well-positioned to help make sure Cisneros got aboard the *Seneca* undetected.

Significantly, Carbonell was also a central figure in a shadowy clandestine network which, according to a 1925 study by Francisco M. Duque, smuggled arms, ammunition, and medical supplies into Havana for the Cuban insurgents.[92] The contraband usually was transported on steamers of the Ward Line[93] and off-loaded at the Regla Electric Plant, which was run by a young American named Charles H. Thrall.[94] On occasion, the covert operatives moved people wanted by the Spanish off the island.[95] In one especially risky case, they extricated from Cuba a popular insurgent leader named Baldomero Acosta, two other insurgent officers, and one of their aides.[96]

This was the network Decker tapped in organizing the Cisneros jailbreak. The covert operatives also included William B. MacDonald, an American national and the Havana agent for the Munson steamship line, and Francisco (Paco) De Besche.[97] Both men were with Decker on the moonlit roof of the Casa de Recogidas.

Carbonell's link to the Cisneros escape remained a secret until May 1898, when the *Journal* disclosed that he had been an accomplice, or what it termed "not the least important of Karl Decker's aid[e]s"[98] in the jailbreak. The *Journal*'s report was prompted by news that Carbonell was engaged to be married to Cisneros.[99] The *Journal* reported that he had proposed marriage to Cisneros, who was staying at Lee's house in Richmond.[100] Carbonell joined most American nationals in leaving Cuba in April 1898,[101] shortly before the United States and Spain went to war. Lee and other U.S. diplomatic personnel departed for the United States that month as well.[102]

The *Journal* said that Carbonell had wanted "no public mention" of his engagement to Cisneros. Nonetheless, the *Journal* said, news of the betrothal "spread in that mysterious manner in which such fascinating morsels invariably will, and so the public is talking the matter over and rejoicing with the lovers over their happiness." Given his clandestine activities in Cuba, it is not surprising that Carbonell was wary of publicity. He objected to Evangelina's name appearing in print after their engagement and felt she had received "sufficient publicity."[103]

The extent and decisive character of Carbonell's role in the jailbreak remained unknown until an unpublished manuscript written by Fitzhugh Lee became available to scholars in 2001. Before then, access to a collection of Lee's papers at the University of Virginia at Charlottesville had been highly restricted, under terms of an agreement with the donor.[104] Lee's manuscript describes Carbonell as vital to Cisneros' successful flight from Cuba and offers new details about Cisneros' refuge at Carbonell's house.[105] Her time there was harrowing from the moment she arrived in a horse-drawn carriage that had sped her from the jail. As she left the carriage, two policemen were passing on foot and one of them "had to stop to let the young lady go into Mr. Carbonell's house," Lee wrote. "The servant who was opening the door upon hearing the carriage approach, told Mr. Carbonell just as the girl did when she entered[,] 'What a pity the police have seen us.'"[106] But the suspicions of the policemen were not stirred, Lee wrote, as they did not search the premises.

Once inside, Cisneros was troubled to find that Carbonell had no family. She presumed him a widower, Lee wrote. Carbonell replied that he was a bachelor. Cisneros grew nervous, but Carbonell assured her that "she would be respected in his house as much as his own mother."[107] She was terrified that her hiding place would be found and that she would be arrested. She told Carbonell "that she would not surrender," meaning that "she would kill herself first."[108] According to Lee, Carbonell told her:

> [I]f the police came to search the house, there would be three of them as that was the usual custom, one would stop at the door and the other two would come up stairs. Mr. Carbonell said in that case he would tell the police that she was his friend, and not the lady for whom they were looking; in case they would not believe him, he would try to bribe them. He then asked her what she would do in that case and [she] answered, 'All that we can do is to fight. I know where your revolver is,' upon which Mr. Carbonell sent for another revolver, and there they remained both of them having pistols.[109]

Carbonell took other precautions to prevent Cisneros' recapture, having rented a house next door. "The windows between the two houses were broken so that she could escape [next door] if necessary," Lee wrote.[110] Carbonell had intended to smuggle Cisneros aboard the *Seneca* during the night of October 8, after the steamer's arrival from Mexico. But the *Seneca* was hours late and did not arrive at Havana until October 9. So Carbonell had no choice but to smuggle her aboard in daylight.[111] After the *Seneca* docked, Carbonell sent for the captain, a portly man of florid features named Frank Stevens.[112] Carbonell introduced Stevens to Cisneros, who by then was wearing boy's clothing. Stevens agreed to take her to New York, if she managed to get aboard, Lee wrote.[113]

During the afternoon of October 9, Carbonell told Decker and Mac-Donald that Cisneros would be taken aboard the *Seneca* that evening. MacDonald wanted a photograph of Cisneros dressed as a boy, "but as he had never taken a photograph before, they made a mistake and took all five [exposures] on one plate," Lee wrote.[114] Carbonell and Cisneros, who had an unlighted cigar in her mouth, then walked the two blocks from her refuge to the wharf and boarded a launch to the *Seneca*. The launch was piloted by José García González, another operative in the clandestine network.[115] While Cisneros waited in the launch, Lee wrote, Carbonell and *Seneca*'s purser persuaded the police detectives onboard to go with him to the dining room for a drink. Stevens then sent the *Seneca*'s quartermaster to fetch Cisneros from the launch.[116] She was hidden in an overheated stateroom. The stuffiness of the room and the taste of the cigar combined to make her quite nauseated, Lee wrote. But the *Seneca* was soon to leave. After its departure, Carbonell informed Decker that "everything was all right."[117]

Lee's papers make clear that he and Carbonell were well-acquainted before the jailbreak[118] and, if anything, their association deepened afterward. The consul-general came to regard Carbonell as "an excellent man," who was as "conscientious and honest as he can be."[119] Carbonell recommended the manservant whom Lee hired in late 1897.[120] More significantly, Carbonell was a vital source of information for the consul-general. Several weeks after the Cisneros escape, he took Lee to visit a hospital in Havana where Cuban doctors treated Cuban women and children. Many patients were *reconcentrados*—victims of Spain's policy of *reconcentración*, or "reconcentration," in which Cuban noncombatants were ordered into garrison towns. The policy was intended to deprive the Cuban insurgents of popular support in the countryside. But in practice, reconcentration led to vast suffering and the deaths of tens of thousands of Cubans. Lee told his wife about visiting the hospital with Carbonell, describing a malnourished "baby child of a *reconcentrado*—6 months old and only a foot long."[121]

With the onset of the Spanish-American War in April 1898, Lee was assigned to command the U.S. Army Seventh Corps. He appointed Carbonell to his staff, with the rank of lieutenant. The Seventh Corps remained in the United States during the war but afterward was sent to Cuba.[122] Shortly before the Seventh Corps was deployed there, Carbonell traveled to Havana. He was under instructions from Lee "to quietly make investigation in reference to certain properties that I know must largely increase in value the very instant the Corps reaches Havana, and proves by its presence that the United States proposes to see that law and order is maintained, and human life and property protected."[123] Lee envisioned buying land for a trolley line in Havana and solicited the financial backing of Daniel Lamont, a former U.S. secretary of war. "If a few of us can pick these properties up now, and build the trolley line, there are real millions in it," Lee wrote to Lamont.[124]

Carbonell reported from Havana that he had completed his investigation and told Lee "that the sooner we buy the land and houses will be the better. You might write to your friends and try to have them come when you do it, as it will be a matter that should be decided right off as the longer it is delayed, the more it will cost."[125] Carbonell also told Lee: "Everybody is anxious to see you arrive to welcome you. ... All

Cubans look at you as the salvation of the country."[126] The investment plans apparently never went forward. But Carbonell's quiet inquiry was significant because it underscored his attachment to Lee and his continuing eagerness to engage in intrigue in Havana many months after the Cisneros jailbreak.[127]

Given Lee's interest in Cisneros, his close association with the clever Carbonell, and his popularity among American journalists in Cuba, it is likely that Lee, too, had a hand in the Cisneros jailbreak. The available evidentiary record does not, however, unequivocally tie him to the plot. (There is certainly no evidence to suggest that senior State Department officials in Washington—including John Sherman, the secretary of state, or William R. Day, the first assistant secretary of state—encouraged, countenanced, or even knew about the conspiracy.[128]) Cora Older, in her hagiographic study of Hearst, asserted that Decker, in recruiting accomplices in Havana, "obtained the assistance of Lee," who made available the services of Donnell Rockwell, a consular clerk.[129] As intriguing as those claims are, Older's account must be treated with caution because it contains several errors. Among those lapses is Older's mistaken reference to the jailbreak as having occurred in November 1897.[130]

But it is inconceivable that Lee was unaware of or uninformed about the plot to free Cisneros, especially in light of the keen interest in Cisneros' well-being that Lee, his wife, and daughter had shown. Lee's unpublished manuscript about the Cisneros case[131] offers insights and detail that are not to be found in other sources—notably the description of Carbonell's vital role in Cisneros' escape. Such insights suggest that Lee had more than superficial familiarity about the plot.

As consul-general, moreover, Lee clearly relished scheming, intrigue, and intelligence-gathering. His official correspondence shows that Lee believed his duties included the pursuit of "delicate [and] important secret functions."[132] With the State Department's consent, Lee in 1896 set up a $1,200 fund to pay for what he called a "secret service"[133] or "a secret detective system" that he believed allowed him to be "accurately informed of all that goes on in the city [of Havana] and some other parts of the Island."[134] Although his correspondence offers little detail about the identities or workings of his "secret service" personnel, the intelligence-gathering operation was intended to warn Lee about emergent crises and deteriorating conditions in Cuba.[135] His correspondence suggests that while Lee sought no guidance from Washington in conducting his intelligence-gathering operation in Havana, he often informed the State Department about the reports from sources he called his "scouts"[136] in Cuba.[137] The "secret service" network placed Lee in an exceptional position to know whether the Cisneros rescue was a hoax. Assuredly, Lee would not have described the escape as genuine had he known it to be spurious. As such, his unpublished manuscript represents further persuasive testimony that the rescue was no hoax.

As we have seen, Lee went well beyond the duties of an American diplomat in urging Spanish authorities to ease the harsh conditions of Cisneros' detention. In mid-August 1897, soon after the *Journal*'s disclosures about Cisneros' imprisonment, Lee went to the extraordinary length of writing a personal letter to Weyler. In the letter, Lee invoked his wife and daughter in asking for Cisneros' release.[138] In his reply, Weyler rejected Lee's overture and alluded to the *Journal*'s noisy campaign to press Spain to release Cisneros. Weyler told Lee: "I cannot conceal that the propaganda which is going on in the United States [would make] my action rather difficult, but I trust that this will disappear and that when the time comes I may be able to see if I can find a way of acceding to Mrs. and Miss Lee's request."[139]

Weyler's letter—which ruled out a timely release—was written August 28, 1897, the day, coincidentally, when Decker arrived in Havana to begin plotting the jailbreak.[140] A week later, Lee left Cuba on home leave.[141] While in the United States, Lee lost his billfold to a pickpocket in Richmond, while on his way to attend Buffalo Bill's Wild West Show. The billfold was soon recovered. But missing were $20 cash and a letter from Cisneros that Lee had tucked inside his wallet. What Cisneros said in the letter is not known.[142]

Although Lee's manuscript and official correspondence make clear the Cisneros case was far more important to U.S. diplomatic officials in Cuba than previously understood, the nature of his role in the plot remains imprecise. He was in the United States when the jailbreak took place, and his absence from Havana grants him at least a measure of plausible deniability. But it is important to recognize that when Lee left Cuba in early September 1897, he was not certain whether he would return to the post—his first and only diplomatic assignment.[143] Lee was a Democrat, a holdover from the administration of President Grover Cleveland.[144] In June 1897, the McKinley administration had promised the Havana consul-generalship to James Franklin Aldrich,[145] a Republican former congressman. Although Aldrich was preparing to take up the post, the press of events kept Lee in Havana throughout the summer. It was only after Lee had conferred in Washington with McKinley and State Department officials that his return to Havana was assured[146]—much to Aldrich's surprise, consternation,[147] and lasting bitterness.[148]

Given the uncertainty surrounding his assignment in Havana, it is quite conceivable that Lee, before taking home leave, was told about and endorsed the plot to free Cisneros. Lee was in Havana for a week after Decker arrived. He and Decker were Virginians and they were acquainted.[149] The U.S. consulate, the *Journal's* Havana bureau, and the offices of the Ward Line's local agents were all in the same building, allowing Lee, Decker, and Carbonell ample opportunity to confer without arousing suspicion or attracting attention.

Moreover, there was good reason for U.S. diplomatic personnel and their associates to conceal or deflect attention from their roles in the plot, given the lawlessness inherent in the Cisneros jailbreak. Likewise, there was ample reason for Hearst and Decker to have minimized or ignored the contributions of others. The *Journal*—ever inclined to self-promotion—characterized the jailbreak as almost entirely the result of the shrewdness and skill of its correspondent, Decker. In the jailbreak narrative, Decker assigned pseudonyms to De Besche and MacDonald, the men who accompanied him to the rooftop near the Casa de Recogidas. Decker called them "Hernandon" and "Mallory." But the jailbreak narrative does not describe how Decker recruited his accomplices beyond vaguely stating that "everything depended upon finding the right men, and in this I was most fortunate. I needed men who spoke Spanish as a native tongue and were familiar with Havana."[150]

In his manuscript, Lee wrote that the "idea of releasing from prison Evangelina seems first to have entered the brain" of Donnell Rockwell, the consular clerk. Rockwell had spoken with her several times on visits to the jail. According to Lee, Rockwell mentioned the idea of a jailbreak to Decker who cleared it with Hearst and editors at the *Journal*. That account of course is at odds with the more common and more likely version that after the failure of the *Journal's* petition drive, Hearst dispatched Decker to Cuba to free Cisneros.[151] But it is probable that Rockwell had contemplated a jailbreak and Lee's manuscript identifies him as having taken an active role in the plot.

Specifically, Rockwell smuggled into the jail "an instrument," probably a small file, and gave it to Cisneros. She used it to saw at the bars of her cell before her rescue.[152] But she did not accomplish much because she "did not understand the management of the instrument Mr. Rockwell gave her," according to Lee's manuscript.[153] Lee also wrote that Rockwell gave Cisneros "some sweet meats that had opium mixed with them," which were to induce the deep sleep of her cellmates before the jailbreak.[154]

The manuscript does not say that Lee knew in advance about Rockwell's contributions to the plot. But it is highly unlikely the consular clerk would have acted unilaterally, especially because Rockwell effectively was on probation. In early 1897, a senior State Department official named William Rockhill asked Lee about rumors that Rockwell had been "drinking as hard as ever."[155] In reply, Lee confirmed that Rockwell had "on several occasions been unfit for duty from drink. He has also been temporarily indisposed from slight illnesses and been in hospital for several days."[156] Lee further reported that he had suspended Rockwell in March 1897, "when again he was somewhat under the influence of liquor." Lee also wrote: "After two or three days of suspension and repentance and the most solemn promises that I should not have occasion to find fault with him again, I reinstated him in his duties with the warning and with the understanding that any further offense would be reported to the Department."[157]

The chastened Rockwell eventually sought a transfer "to some other post."[158] But after his suspension, he worked earnestly to stay in Lee's good graces. He completed an unofficial, fact-finding assignment for Lee in late July 1897, while on a visit to friends in Artemisa, a town in Pinar del Rio, Cuba's westernmost province. Lee had asked Rockwell to inquire about the plight of *reconcentrados* in Artemisa. On his return, Rockwell wrote a vivid and detailed report that described dreadful conditions in what he called a "doomed settlement." Deaths from starvation in Artemisa, Rockwell wrote, reached as many as twenty-five to thirty-five a day. "The death cart makes its rounds several times daily, and into it the corpses are thrown without ceremony, and taken to the cemetary[sic] where they are interred in a long ditch," Rockwell stated. "A thin layer of earth is then cast on the remains, and the next day the operation is repeated till the ditch is full."[159] He also wrote: "This state of affairs now to be seen in Artemisa is but a repetition of what is taking place in all the towns of reconcentration on the Island."[160]

Lee sent Rockwell's report to the State Department with an accompanying cover letter that stated: "I can assure the Department that there is no exaggeration in the reports of the overwhelming misery, sufferings, and death of the Cuban *reconcentrados*." Lee in the letter vouched for Rockwell as "a very conscientious and truthful man."[161] Margin notes on Lee's cover letter indicate that Rockwell's report was shown to President McKinley. Rockwell's report is revealing of not only of the plight of the *reconcentrados* but of Lee's willingness to call upon consular staff to collect information unofficially. It also suggests Rockwell's sympathies for the Cubans and his earnestness in courting Lee's favor.

The suspicion of Spanish authorities in Havana fell on Rockwell soon after the Cisneros jailbreak. On October 12, 1897, they questioned him "closely as to his knowledge of Miss Cisneros's rescue," the *Journal* reported. "Finally he was able to refute all the accusations of his connivance in the affair. As a friend of the prisoner he frequently visited the Casa [de] Recogidas and was thus suspected by the authorities of assisting in her flight."[162] Soon after the interrogation, Rockwell went to Joseph Springer, the consulate's senior officer during Lee's absence, and asked for a thirty-day leave to go to the United States. Springer promptly approved Rockwell's request and sent it to the State Department, citing "ill health" as justification.[163] The request was quickly approved in Washington.

It is not clear when Rockwell left Cuba or when he returned. Lee's correspondence indicates that Rockwell overstayed his thirty-day leave but that he was still expected back in Havana in late November 1897.[164] In any event, Rockwell's contributing role in the jailbreak represents evidence of an unequivocal link between the U.S. consulate in Havana and the plot to free Cisneros.

BARKER: THE "FIGHTING CONSUL"

While Rockwell was under interrogation in Havana, Cisneros was aboard the *Seneca*, bound for New York City. Also on board was Walter B. Barker, the U.S. consul in Sagua la Grande in central Cuba. Barker was a veteran of the Confederate army whom Lee had once described as "worthy of the highest credence."[165] Barker also was a rough-edged bachelor, prone to hyperbole and known to flout protocol. Once, in response to rumors that his consulate was about to be overrun by a pro-Spanish mob, Barker declared that he had "great faith in God and [my] repeating rifle."[166] Decker told a pro-Cuba rally in Washington, D.C., in May 1897 that Barker five months earlier had deterred demonstrators from moving on the consulate by making clear he would confront them with his Winchester rifle.[167] In 1898, the *Journal* praised Barker as "a fighting consul."[168] In the escape of Cisneros, Barker quite likely was a shadowy, well-placed accomplice.

Barker's presence aboard the steamer taking Cisneros to New York in October 1897 was the culmination of his urgent—and highly unusual—request for a leave of absence. At the end of September, Barker sent a telegram to the State Department, requesting leave. "Unless my presence here next thirty days [is] essential," Barker's cable said, "my health requires asking [that I] visit New York. Kindly wire answer."[169] Requesting leave in such a manner represented a departure from procedure—and suggested a very urgent motivation. The next day, Barker properly requested leave by sending a letter to the State Department, through the Havana consulate. He said in the letter that he hoped "the Department will pardon me for the liberty of conveying my request through a telegram."[170]

Barker's letter did not explain the urgency of his request, beyond stating: "During the entire summer I have suffered from impaired health; my physician states, that, if nothing more, a round trip would benefit me. ... Should leave be given me, I will visit New York and Washington only."[171] Barker's application for leave was approved on October 2, 1897, by Springer, the acting consul-general in Havana,[172] and by the State Department on October 4, 1897.[173] Given the urgency of his request, it is curious that Barker failed to travel to New York as speedily as possible. Swifter passage to New York was available to him on the *Concho*, a Ward Line steamer that left Havana on October 7, 1897, two days before the *Seneca*. The *Concho* and twenty-five passengers arrived in New York on October 11, 1897.[174]

Barker left Sagua for Havana on October 8, 1897, the day after the jailbreak. The *Seneca* left Havana on October 9, 1897. Upon arrival in New York, Barker told a reporter for the *Journal* that he had not seen Cisneros until the second day out and did not know how she had slipped aboard. He was also quoted by the *Journal* as saying: "Of course my position forbids my discussing her case."[175] The *New York World*—the *Journal*'s keenest rival and, as such, the newspaper most likely to probe for gaps and inconsistencies in the *Journal*'s version of the jailbreak or of any exclusive report—offered a different and more detailed account about the passage to New York. The *World* reported that Cisneros spent much of her time aboard in the company of Barker and the ship's purser. The *World*'s source was Stevens, the *Seneca*'s captain, who was quoted as saying:

> After supper the first night out, [Cisneros] took a promenade on the deck and met some of the passengers. Among them was Walter B. Barker, United States Consul at Sagua. She addressed him in Spanish with an air which seemed to me as if she had met him before. The purser, too, seemed to recall her as an old acquaintance. All the way she spent much of her time in his office. I didn't see her again till Sunday [October 10, 1897]. Monday and Tuesday she spent most of her time with Mr. Barker and the purser. She was seasick some of the time, but kept on deck.[176]

Barker's presence on the *Seneca*, acting in effect as Cisneros' chaperone, may have been coincidental. Lee did inform the State Department in August 1897 that the U.S. consuls in Cuba were "all more or less sick" and that they would benefit from leaves of absence.[177] But the urgency with which Barker sought his leave, the timing of his request, and his choice of passenger steamer to New York all combine to make such a coincidence quite extraordinary.[178] Those elements point instead to Barker's having a vital supporting role in the plot to free Cisneros. His presence aboard the *Seneca* likely represented a precautionary component of the plot: had Spanish authorities challenged the departure of the *Seneca*, a vessel owned by an American company, who better to have aboard than a tough-minded, Spanish-speaking U.S. diplomat who was not reluctant to bend the rules? The possibility that Spanish authorities might interfere with the vessel's departure was hardly far-fetched. A little more than a year earlier, authorities had forcibly removed Samuel S. Tolon, a naturalized American citizen, from the decks of the *Seneca* as the steamer prepared to leave Havana.[179] Tolon was jailed for three weeks in Havana on suspicion of aiding the Cuban rebellion.[180]

That Barker was inclined to flout protocol is clear. State Department records reveal that Ramon Williams, Lee's predecessor as consul-general in Havana, had reprimanded Barker in 1896 for ignoring diplomatic practice by attempting to forward three private letters through the consulate in Havana. The letters—written by Cubans and addressed to Tómas Estrada Palma, leader of the pro-independence Cuban *junta* in New York—were intercepted by Williams, who rebuked Barker and pointedly reminded him of the regulations governing the conduct of diplomatic personnel.[181] Williams also reported Barker's indiscretion to the State Department.[182]

Barker was not chastened, however, and he seldom shrank from clashing with Spanish authorities in Sagua la Grande. They frequently complained in 1896 and 1897 that Barker had exceeded his authority in "assuming the character of Consul of the United States at Sagua, as he calls himself."[183] The Spanish insisted that he was authorized only to act as a U.S. commercial agent, the position for which he had been accredited in 1894. Barker had been designated U.S. consul in Sagua in August 1896, but Spanish authorities were slow or reluctant to confirm the appointment.[184] In the meantime, they complained that he was a meddlesome irritant. In a letter to Lee, Weyler protested that Barker "frequently addresses communications, sometimes in not very correct form, inquiring with respect to the standing of military proceedings" to which American citizens were parties.[185] In addition, Spain's chief diplomat in the United States, Enrique Dupuy de Lôme, suspected that Barker was an agent of the Cuban insurgents.[186]

Barker's reports to the State Department show that he was appalled by the ruin caused by both sides in the rebellion, saying the Spanish forces and Cuban insurgents were "vying with each other in the devastation of the country."[187] His correspondence was replete with hyperbole. "Anarchy not only reigns," he reported in spring 1896, "but is daily on the increase."[188] By mid-summer 1897, Barker said the insurrection was "no longer a semblance of war, but extermination of the inhabitants, with destruction of all property."[189] His reports were perceptive in asserting that Spain had little hope of quelling the insurrection. Barker, moreover, evinced little respect for Spanish military forces, describing their conduct as amounting to "general inactivity" while "continuing to occupy altogether a defensive position." He also wrote that "the Cuban is rare, of whatever station in life, who is not in arms or in sympathy with the revolt." [190] His correspondence makes clear that Barker's sympathies ran decidedly to the Cubans.

Like Lee, Barker was a favorite source of American journalists in Cuba. Richard Harding Davis had been a guest of Barker's at Sagua la Grande in early 1897.[191] Barker frequently corresponded with his friend, Sylvester Scovel of the *World*. As we have seen, Barker acted as chaperone to Scovel and his wife on the first leg of their travels in Cuba in November 1897. When Scovel's career disintegrated following a fist-swinging encounter with General Rufus Shafter in 1898, Barker sent the disgraced war correspondent a letter of support, saying: "I always regard my friends right—in all they do[,] therefore you were right in your recent little affair in Cuba & I am yours to count on."[192] And when Washington journalists feted Decker at a testimonial dinner in late October 1897, the guest list included one "Walter B. Barker."[193]

TESTING THE INTERNAL EVIDENCE

While the Cisneros case has attracted periodic attention from scholars,[194] the literature reveals that no attempt has been made to scrutinize the forensic leads contained in the *Journal*'s jailbreak narrative and test their precision. The narrative contains several observations and descriptions which, more than one hundred years later, can be tested independently. Should the internal evidence of the jailbreak narrative fail to withstand scrutiny, then the doubts surrounding the case certainly would be reinforced; the believability of the narrative would be cast in doubt. On the other hand, corroborating the internal evidence would enhance the credibility and plausibility of the jailbreak narrative. Moreover, examining and evaluating the narrative's internal evidence is a more valuable and instructive exercise than merely to speculate about the case or dismiss it blithely as a "magnificent farce."

In the jailbreak narrative, Decker made reference to "the great round, white moon"[195] that cast a distracting, "strong white light" [196] on the nights of the jailbreak. Similarly, Cisneros' companion account said the "moon was shining very bright; oh! so big and round and white."[197] These references can be checked against the lunar-phase data kept by the U.S. Naval Observatory in Washington, D.C. Those data show that, in the early hours of October 6 and 7, 1897, the moon was waxing: It was 81 percent of full on October 6, and 88 percent of full on October 7.[198] In that phase, known as a waxing Gibbous, the moon would have shown brightly over what was one of Havana's poorest neighborhoods.[199]

But would the moon have been visible in the early hours of October 6 and 7 1897? That is, were the sky conditions such that the moon could have been seen at those times? October, after all, is usually at the end of Cuba's five-month rainy season.[200] Decker, himself, had mentioned in a dispatch filed from Havana on October 1, 1897, that "heavy and continuous rains" had caused "terrible suffering … in the interior" of Cuba during the closing week of September 1897.[201] The available evidence indicates that the moon would not have been obscured by inclement weather conditions in Havana during the hours of the jailbreak. No rain fell in Havana on October 7, 1897, the day Cisneros escaped the Casa de Recogidas.[202] Moreover, Havana newspapers of 1897 say that meteorological data were collected three times daily— at 8 a.m., noon, and 4 p.m.—at a reading station at the city's marina, and once a day—at 8 a.m.—at the Real Collegio de Belén, which was less than ten blocks from the Casa de Recogidas. None of the readings corresponds precisely to the overnight hours when Decker and his accomplices undertook the jailbreak. The readings nearest to those hours were taken at 8 a.m.; as such, they are the most pertinent meteorological data available in testing the jailbreak narrative.

The respective readings for 8 a.m., as reported in *La Union Constitucional*, a leading Havana newspaper of the time, were as follows:

Date	Marina observations	Real Collegio observations
6 October[203]	Cubierto en parte (partly cloudy)	Despejado (clear)
7 October[204]	Cubierto en parte (partly cloudy)	Cubierto en parte (partly cloudy)

Although the 8 a.m. readings for October 6, 1897, are in mild conflict, they nonetheless suggest the sky was not overcast at the times nearest the jailbreak. Supplemental data are available in the U.S. Weather Bureau observations taken shortly after 7:30 a.m. on those days at Key West, Florida, some ninety miles to the north. They show that the sky over Key West was reported "clear" on the mornings of October 6 and 7, 1897.[205] No rain fell at Key West on either day.[206] While the Key West readings are not a match for those of Havana, they nonetheless indicate that a strong, fair weather pattern prevailed in that part of the Caribbean in early October 1897. Further evidence of such a pattern is contained in a brief report published October 8, 1897, in the Havana newspaper *El Pais*. The report, written October 4, 1897, by the director of a meteorological observatory at Santa Clara, Cuba, discussed the effects of an *anticiclon*—a high pressure system that had brought a favorable weather, north-to-northeast winds, and unusually high barometric pressure to the western Atlantic during the first days of October.[207] The available evidentiary record, then, includes no data that directly impugns or contradicts the claims about the moon's visibility on the nights of the jailbreak.

The Cisneros case unfolded amid political change in Madrid and a huge protest in Havana. Those events—which offer another set of forensic leads in evaluating the jailbreak narrative—were set in motion by the collapse in late September 1897 of a fragile, interim government in Madrid. The government had appointed in August 1897, following the assassination of the conservative Spanish premier, Antonio Cánovas del Castillo.[208] The interim regime's fall brought to power a liberal government led by Práxedes Sagasta and signaled the end of Madrid's support for Weyler,[209] who for twenty months had been commander of the Spanish forces in Cuba. During that time, Weyler had developed his reconcentration policy in a failed attempt to crush the insurrection.[210] As we have seen, reconcentration caused enormous suffering among Cuba's noncombatants and became the target of unrelenting criticism in the United States and, to a lesser extent, in Spain. The *Journal* and many other U.S. newspapers referred to Weyler as wanton in his cruelty.[211] "Butcher" Weyler became a common epithet.[212]

As it took power in early October 1897, Sagasta's government was preparing to order Weyler's recall.[213] In an effort to thwart, complicate, or delay that move,[214] Weyler on October 6, 1897, permitted his supporters to stage a mass demonstration at the Plaza de Armas in central Havana. References to the charged atmosphere that day appear in the jailbreak narrative. Decker wrote that "Spaniards, [N]egroes and Chinese ... discussed volubly and with many gestures the stirring topics of the day, the recall of Weyler and the demonstration in the Plaza de Armas, and the possible war with the United States."[215] His references to the general's recall and the rally were accurate reflections of events in Havana in the hours before the jailbreak. War between Spain and the United States cannot be said to have been imminent, though; the Sagasta government in Madrid was committed to measures it believed would at least address American demands for speedy resolution of the Cuban insurgency.[216]

Nonetheless, anti-American sentiment was pronounced among the demonstrators in Havana on October 6, 1897. The *New York Sun*, which was hostile to Weyler, described Havana as "in a state of terror" that day and said that 20,000 Spanish loyalists marched through the streets, crying: "'Death to the United States! Long live Spain! Long live Weyler!'"[217] The *Sun* also said that "excitement against the United States" was so intense than an attack on Americans in the city was feared.[218] The demonstrators gathered at the governor-general's palace overlooking the Plaza de Armas, the *Sun* reported, and Weyler twice appeared on the balcony "to thank the multitude which frantically acclaimed him."[219] The demonstrations, however, failed to alter Madrid's decision to bring Weyler home. His recall was announced three days later[220] and he left Cuba for Spain at the end of October 1897, just hours after the arrival of his successor, General Ramón Blanco y Arenas.[221]

FROM HIDING TO THE *SENECA*

The jailbreak narrative contains almost no detail about Cisneros' time in hiding. It does not specify where she was hidden, saying only that her refuge was in Havana but "far away" from the jail.[222] When she left her hiding place on October 9, 1897, Decker and his accomplices—all of whom were armed—followed her to the wharf.[223] She was dressed in a blue shirt, flowing tie, and a large slouch hat, Decker wrote, adding: "Her hair was plastered under the hat with cosmetics. As she stepped out into the street a swift swirl of wind caught the hat and whirled it from her head. For a moment our hearts ceased to beat. Every man gripped his gun and waited."[224] Cisneros quickly retrieved the hat, placed it on her head, "and started off jauntily and nonchalantly down the street," Decker wrote. "All the way down Obispo street we followed her, guns swinging loose and ready at hand, a carriage following, for emergencies. ... Fortunately nothing happened."[225]

Decker's reference to Obispo Street[226] suggests that Cisneros found refuge in hiding in central Havana because Obispo was the city's principal commercial avenue, running east and west from the Parque Central to the Plaza de Armas. But it is quite unlikely she took such a route to the *Seneca*. To have done so soon after the jailbreak would have been to invite recognition and recapture. On this point, moreover, Lee's unpublished manuscript contradicts the jailbreak narrative. Lee wrote that Carbonell lived at 4 Paula Street, only a few blocks from the Casa de Recogidas and not, as Decker stated, "far away" from the prison.

Lee also wrote that late in the afternoon on October 9, 1897, Carbonell and William MacDonald escorted Cisneros the "two intervening blocks" from Carbonell's house to the pier.[227] En route, according to Lee's account, Cisneros lost her hat and Carbonell retrieved it, telling two passersby, "This little boy is always dropping his hat."[228] In walking from Paula Street to the wharf, Cisneros and Carbonell would have gone nowhere near Obispo Street. Lee's account, being more detailed, must be regarded as more plausible and credible than Decker's version of the route to the *Seneca*. Decker's erroneous reference to the route to the *Seneca* probably was intentional, and meant to deflect attention from Carbonell, Decker's most important accomplice.

Beyond that instance of misdirection, the jailbreak narrative contains a few claims that are nothing short of mystifying. Particularly puzzling is Decker's description of his sawing the bars of the jail during the first attempt to free Cisneros, on October 6, 1897. "It was impossible to use the saw quickly," Decker wrote, "as the bars were not set firmly in the frame, and rattled and rang like a fire alarm every time the saw passed across the iron."[229] Why such a din aroused no one at the jail or in the houses nearby defies understanding. Cisneros also raised this point in her account, stating: "The saw made a terrible noise. I do not see how the women in the cell could sleep through it,"[230] even though she claimed to have slipped a narcotic painkiller, laudanum, into their coffee to induce deep sleep.[231] Decker wrote that breaking the bar of the prison window made "a clear, ringing sound that we feared must have been heard at the [captain-general's] palace."[232] That such a noise attracted no attention in the small hours of a quiet, moonlit night is almost beyond belief.

However, it is not inconceivable that those details were embellishments injected into the jailbreak narrative to heighten its dramatic effect and to ridicule Spanish authorities in Havana as incompetent. While no doubt exaggerated, those perplexing claims, alone are not enough to discredit or dismiss the jailbreak narrative—or to declare the Cisneros escape a hoax or "magnificent farce."[233] Indeed, where the jailbreak narrative's most important forensic leads can be tested for accuracy, they mostly check out.

Beyond the forensic clues, another ignored aspect of the Cisneros case—a component that provides revealing insight as whether the rescue was a hoax—is the reaction of Spanish authorities in Havana after the jailbreak. The aftermath of the Cisneros escape, which heretofore has been given no attention by scholars, revealed lingering Spanish hostility toward the *Journal*. During the closing months of 1897 and the first weeks of 1898, the newspaper was not infrequently the target of harassment and reprisals. Such a reaction is scarcely surprising: The Cisneros escape clearly stung and the *Journal*, in its self-congratulatory publicity, could only have deepened the humiliation felt by Spanish authorities in Havana.

In the weeks and months following the jailbreak, George Clark Musgrave, a Briton who reported for the *Journal* in Havana, was "constantly shadowed" by the secret police.[234] The offices of Hidalgo & Co., the Ward Line agents in Havana, were searched and its officials questioned by authorities seeking evidence in the Cisneros escape.[235] The Hidalgo offices were on the floor above the *Journal*'s bureau in the Casa Nueva building. On separate occasions in late 1897, a suspected parcel bomb was planted at the entrance to Casa Nueva, near the *Journal*'s bureau.[236] Neither device exploded, and doubts arose whether one of the parcels contained a bomb.[237] The *Journal* nonetheless declared the suspicious packages clear evidence of "Spanish hostility to the Journal for its humanitarian efforts on behalf of Miss Cisneros."[238] Near the end of the year, the *Journal* was evicted from Casa Nueva, ostensibly because of the suspected explosive devices. But the *Journal* said it was evicted because resentful Spanish authorities were intent on settling scores.[239]

The clearest evidence of harassment by Spanish authorities came in early February 1898, when they briefly seized Hearst's yacht, the *Buccaneer*, in Havana harbor.[240] The *Journal* called the vessel's seizure "the Spanish-Journal War."[241] The confrontation may have been provoked by an erroneous report that Hearst's yacht had ferried Decker back to Cuba and landed him near an insurgent camp.[242] In fact, the *Buccaneer* brought to Havana another *Journal* correspondent, Julian Hawthorne, who was assigned to write about the misery of the Cuban *reconcentrados*.

The *Buccaneer* episode caused a mild diplomatic dispute, which Lee worked to resolve. The Spanish authorities claimed the vessel had not cleared Spanish customs and illegally carried "a rapid fire gun." Moreover, they said, because Hearst was the *Buccaneer*'s owner, "it would not be rash to suppose that it intends by fraud and cunning to violate ... the laws in order to favor the enemies of Spain."[243] Lee insisted in his reply to authorities in Havana that private yachts were exempt from customs requirements and that the *Buccaneer* carried a small gun "for saluting purposes."[244] At Hearst's request, Lee submitted, under protest, Hearst's payment of a $500 fine.[245] The petulant reaction of Spanish authorities in Havana suggests lingering anger, resentment, and a desire to exact even a small measure of revenge on the *Journal* in the jailbreak's aftermath.

DISCUSSION AND CONCLUSION

The variety of evidence presented and assessed in this chapter decisively punctures the conventional view that the Cisneros rescue was a hoax or "put-up job" facilitated by the *Journal*'s bribing Spanish authorities. The allegations or suspicions of bribery rest more on assertion—and newspaper rivals' contempt for the *Journal*—than on specific, persuasive documentation. They are supported more by argument than evidence.

It is illogical to believe that Weyler and his officers would have participated in a scheme that produced an enormous publicity bonanza for the *Journal*—a publicity bonanza in which they were cast as dupes and villains. Officers loyal to Weyler's successor, General Blanco, certainly would have had no reason to maintain a conspiracy of silence about the Cisneros escape. They likely would have exposed such a scheme, had it existed, to discredit Weyler and distance themselves from his controversial policies.

The recollections contained in Lee's unpublished manuscript represent the single most persuasive piece of evidence that the Cisneros rescue was no hoax. Lee was in a position to know whether the rescue was a sham, and it is inconceivable that he would have written about it in such detail had the case been fraudulent. Likewise, it is implausible that Carbonell and Decker's other accomplices would have taken the risks they took had the rescue been a farce or sham. Indeed, the evidence presented here makes clear that the Cisneros case was far more complex, and far more important to U.S. diplomatic officials in Cuba, than previously understood.

Also telling is the participation by operatives of the clandestine smuggling network in Havana, including Carbonell, MacDonald, and De Besche. All of them were Decker's accomplices in the Cisneros case. Although the jailbreak narrative minimizes the contributions of Decker's accomplices, tapping and relying on operatives of the clandestine network simplified Decker's tasks considerably.

Further, it is interesting to consider how the claims of fraud and hoax took hold. They were inspired by envy of, and hostility toward, Hearst and the *Journal*, and by the eagerness of the *Journal*'s rivals to degrade and diminish the exploit. It is far easier to dismiss the case as another example of Hearst's madcap ways, and scholarly and popular accounts routinely have done just that. Allegations that bribes were paid have become widely accepted, without regard for Decker's denial or, more important, without acknowledging that the supporting record for such claims is quite meager. The literature also shows that until now no attempt ever has been made to assess the internal evidence of the Cisneros case. Where it can be tested for accuracy, the internal evidence for the most part can be corroborated. The jailbreak narrative is not without its flaws. It does contain exaggeration and misdirection. But the evidentiary record does not reveal the narrative to be replete with error—a finding that would suggest the jailbreak was "a false bit of cheap sensationalism."[246] But it was not that. It was instead a well-planned covert operation that succeeded stunningly. It was truly the high-water mark of the "journalism of action."

So why does it matter whether or not the Cisneros was a hoax? Why it is important to assess the evidentiary record of a case more than one hundred years old? Several reasons suggest themselves. For one, it matters because the Cisneros jailbreak was an episode unique in American journalism. On that basis, alone, the case demands as much clarity and resolution as possible. It is intrinsically worthy and useful to correct or clarify the historical record. Doing so demonstrates that the Cisneros escape was hardly "a masterpiece of manufactured news,"[247] but a remarkable episode in activist journalism. The jailbreak and escape demonstrated what the full-blown "journalism of action" could accomplish.

Setting straight the historical record also matters because the Cisneros case, in recent years, has become overgrown with imprecision and improbable conjecture. Milton in her *Yellow Kids*, for example, said the *World* sent Sylvester Scovel to Havana in early October 1897 on a secret plan "to steal the *Journal*'s thunder by getting Evangelina Cisneros out of prison before Karl Decker did."[248] This speculation was reiterated by Denis Brian in his study, *Pulitzer: A Life.*[249] Such claims, however, are sheer fancy, unsupported by the evidentiary record. They are in fact refuted by Scovel's own correspondence, which places him in New York City as late as October 6, 1897.[250] Had Scovel that day taken a steamer for Havana, he would not have arrived before October 11 or 12. By that time Cisneros was out of prison and on her way to New York.[251]

Another misconception about the Cisneros rescue was that it had the effect of "inflaming American public opinion and precipitating the Spanish-American War," as the *Guardian* newspaper in London asserted in 1989.[252] Another, more recent account claimed the United States went to war with Spain "in part to rescue Evangelina Cisneros, a young woman who—according to the Hearst newspapers, at least—was being raped and tortured in a Havana jail."[253]

In truth, the Cisneros case was rarely mentioned in the American press, or by American political figures, as war loomed in the spring of 1898. The jailbreak and escape had no influence whatsoever on the decision to go to war. The conflict was the result of a three-sided diplomatic standoff between the Cubans, Spain, and United States. The Cuban insurgents would accept nothing short of political independence.[254] Spain, for reasons of domestic stability,[255] could not and would not grant Cuban independence. For political and economic reasons, the United States "could no longer tolerate the chronic turmoil"[256] of the rebellion in Cuba. Those were the fundamental factors that gave rise to the Spanish-American War.[257] Had war-mongering been the *Journal*'s principal aim in publicizing the imprisonment of Cisneros, she would have been more useful in prison, a female martyr for Cuban independence. By freeing Cisneros, the *Journal* removed not only an irritant in U.S.-Spanish relations but took away the stimulus for an ongoing story.[258] The enduring hallmark of the Cisneros rescue was not that the case helped bring on a war but that it effectively marked the limits of activist journalism. Not even the *Journal* would come close to matching the exploit of "jail-breaking journalism."

EPILOGUE

Decker supposedly was generously rewarded by Hearst for the successful jailbreak. "It is said," *Fourth Estate* reported in November 1897, that Decker "has received a sum of money that assures him of a comfortable income for life."[259] But Decker never wrote or spoke much about the Cisneros rescue, beyond a few articles for the *Journal* and an account in *The Story of Evangelina Cisneros*. Still, whenever Decker was in the news, his association with the Cisneros jailbreak usually was noted prominently.[260]

Decker returned to Cuba from time to time in the years after the Spanish-American War. He went to Santiago de Cuba in 1899, as a representative of the Washington-based Cuban Land and Trading Company.[261] Decker covered political turmoil in Cuba in 1933 for Hearst's International News Service.[262] He was seventy-three when he died of a heart ailment in New York in December 1941.[263] The obituary in Hearst's *New York Journal-American* called the Cisneros rescue one of Decker's "most brilliant achievements."[264]

Cisneros and Carbonell were married in June 1898, in Baltimore. They had planned to be wed in Washington, D.C., but local laws required foreign nationals to obtain the consent of their governments before marrying. Gaining such approval from Spanish authorities ruling Cuba was out of the question for Cisneros, so she and Carbonell—a naturalized American citizen twenty-three years her senior—traveled to Baltimore for a small, midday ceremony at the Hotel Rennert.[265] Mary A. Logan, Cisneros' legal guardian, and Logan's daughter were the only guests.[266] The newlyweds then traveled south to Florida, where Carbonell rejoined the U.S. Seventh Army Corps, commanded by Fitzhugh Lee. Carbonell, a lieutenant, was on Lee's staff.

Carbonell and Cisneros returned to Havana after the Spanish-American War and lived prosperously, if in relative obscurity. The *Journal* reported the birth of their daughter in 1899.[267] Carbonell died in 1916; Evangelina outlived him by many years. She remarried in Havana and bore two daughters. Near the end of her life, Cisneros found herself acclaimed as a revolutionary hero by the regime of Fidel Castro, which appropriated the 1896 uprising on the Isle of Pines as a notable act of revolution. Cisneros died in May 1970 and was buried in Havana with military honors.[268]

Donnell Rockwell, the troubled consular clerk in Havana, took an assignment in 1900 at the U.S. consulate in Paris.[269] He eventually left the U.S. diplomatic service and found work in the Brooklyn advertising department of Hearst's *New York American*, a successor title of the *Journal*. Rockwell died in Brooklyn in 1915. His wife and their two children were traveling in Switzerland at the time of his death.[270]

Walter B. Barker, the "fighting consul" of Sagua la Grande, became a captain and assistant quartermaster in the U.S. volunteer army after the Spanish-American War and returned to Cuba in that capacity. He was killed in 1906 in Japan, where he was an army depot quartermaster. Barker was traveling to a spa for treatment for sciatica when a typhoon swept his train from its tracks, sending it tumbling forty feet down an embankment.[271]

Fitzhugh Lee's Seventh Corps was never deployed outside the United States during the Spanish-American War, but Lee made a triumphal return to Cuba in 1899, as a top officer in the American military occupation of the island. He commanded the military district that included Havana. Lee retired from the Army in 1902 and died of a stroke in 1905.[272] Fifty-thousand mourners paid tribute to the old general, lining the streets of Richmond as Lee's funeral procession wound its way to Hollywood Cemetery. Lee, whom newspapers described as "Virginia's greatest cavalryman," was buried next to the grave of Jefferson Davis.[273] Evangelina Cisneros was among the many people who wired their condolences to Lee's family.[274] At the time of his death, Lee was head of the organization preparing the celebration of the 400th anniversary of the founding of Jamestown, Virginia, the first English settlement in North America.

In 1940, eleven years before his death, Hearst recalled the Cisneros case in a column of reminiscences about the Spanish-American War period. "Your columnist was an active young journalist at that time," Hearst wrote, "and had not only a finger on the public pulse, but a finger in the Cuban pie." Hearst referred to Decker as "our most daring and brilliant young reporter" and called Cisneros "Cuba's Joan of Arc." Even then, forty-three years after the rescue, Hearst seemed more than a little awestruck by the exploit. It was, he wrote, a "Herculean task [that] Decker amazingly succeeded in accomplishing."[275]

An intriguing footnote to the Cisneros case appeared fifty years after the jailbreak, in a four-paragraph obituary published by the *New York Times*. The brief notice announced the death in Havana of Harry I. Skilton, an eighty-three-year-old American national who ran Compania Importadora Skilton, S.A., an import-export business in Cuba. The obituary included this tantalizing passage about Skilton: "In 1897 he aided Karl Decker, Hearst correspondent, to escape after Decker had rescued Evangelina Cisneros from a Spanish prison."[276] What that meant was left unclear. Other New York newspapers either ignored Skilton's death[277] or carried a similarly vague reference to Skilton's having helped Decker leave Cuba.[278]

In the jailbreak narrative Decker said he forged the signature of a Spanish official on the visa that enabled him to leave Cuba.[279] But the narrative made no reference to Skilton. Likewise, an enormous collection of Skilton family papers at Cornell University offers no clues about Harry Skilton's supporting role in Decker's departure. The Cornell collection shows that Skilton traveled to Havana in mid-September 1897, to negotiate an electric lighting contract, and that he returned to New York in early November, about three weeks after Decker's arrival.[280] That Skilton had any role at all in the Cisneros case represents additional, if modest, evidence that the jailbreak was no hoax. Had it been a fraud, there certainly would have been no reason for an American businessman on his first visit to Cuba to have participated in what probably was some sort of a ruse to help Decker leave the island. It is tempting to speculate that Skilton allowed Decker to make use of his identity papers, or that he concocted an alibi that permitted Decker's departure. But the evidentiary record contains no substantive clue as to what Skilton did to help Decker. Skilton's role in the Cisneros case thus remains a small but not unimportant mystery.

While it now safely can be said that the Cisneros rescue was neither hoax nor fraud, it is fitting indeed that this remarkable case of activist journalism refuses to surrender all its mysteries.

CONCLUSION

How 1897 Lives on

Even his most strenuous critics conceded that William Randolph Hearst for a time brought energy, vigor, and excitement to daily American journalism. H. L. Mencken was no admirer of Hearst but granted that Hearst's activist journalism "shook up old bones and gave the blush of life to pale cheeks."[1] Those contributions were never more apparent than during the crowded year of 1897 when Hearst—and Ochs and Steffens—were developing rival models for the future of American journalism. Their clash of paradigms energized American journalism and gave definition to the wider ferment in the field at the end of the nineteenth century.

The fervor that characterized the journalism of 1897 in some ways seems alien these days. The ambition, the risk-taking, the brickbats that editors exchanged in print, the swashbuckling high jinks are largely absent.[2] American journalism of the early twenty-first century surely could use some of the dash and vitality that characterized the field in 1897. But beneath the troubled, even depressing facade of contemporary journalism, there are telling reminders of 1897 and its exceptionality. The year in multiple ways reverberates still in American journalism.

The epithet "yellow journalism" has been in unending use since 1897 to condemn sensationalism and cases of purported misconduct in journalism in the United States and, more broadly, English-speaking countries around the world.[3] "Yellow journalism" is the idiom of rebuke that letter-writers in America most often turn to in criticizing the content and judgment of their newspapers.

The most entertaining if misleading anecdote about the wayward power of the press is Hearst's supposed vow to "furnish the war" with Spain. Hearst supposedly made the pledge in mid-January 1897 in a telegram sent to the artist Frederic Remington, who was then on assignment in Cuba. Although the evidence is overwhelming that the anecdote is apocryphal, the story is simply too tidy and too delicious ever to die away.[4]

Modern photojournalism at big city daily newspapers can be traced to 1897[5] and Stephen Horgan's successful application of halftone technology on the high-speed presses of the *New York Tribune*. Horgan's breakthrough, while no doubt inevitable, was crucial to the rise of the image in American journalism.

No artifact of journalism in 1897 lives on like Francis P. Church's "Is There A Santa Claus?" Indeed, no single work in American journalism is so often celebrated and so often republished. But beyond its regular, late December reappearance in innumerable newspapers and magazines, "Is There A Santa Claus?" lives on as enduring inspiration in American journalism.

To its many admirers in journalism, "Is There A Santa Claus?" offers timeless lessons. At the editorial's centenary in 1997, Eric Newton, then of the Freedom Forum's Newseum, wrote: "Newspapers today need Church's poetry on their editorial pages." In their writing, Newton said, journalists too often "climb upon stacks of facts and fall asleep."[6] Geo Beach, writing in *Editor & Publisher* in December 1997, said of the editorial: "It was brave writing. Love, hope, belief—all have a place on the editorial page."[7] That "Is There A Santa Claus?" appeared in September 1897 and was not held for publication at Christmastime suggested the important lesson, Beach wrote, of "never holding anything back for imagined future work."[8]

Less reverently, Rick Horowitz wrote in 1997: "For a century now, readers have loved what Church created—but no more than journalists do. They're ecstatic that they don't have to crank out another Christmas essay of their own every year; they can just slap Francis Church's 'Yes, Virginia,' up there on the page and go straight to the office party."[9] The editorial even stirred criticism and protest, long after it was written. In 1951, for example, participants at an anti-Santa Claus demonstration in Lynden, Washington, complained that the editorial had the effect of encouraging little Virginia O'Hanlon to think of her skeptical friends as liars.[10]

Not all journalists are comfortable with the sleight of hand that Church achieved in writing the editorial. In 1997, a columnist for the *Chicago Sun-Times* declared: "Fie on Francis P. Church! Fooey to Virginia O'Hanlon! One hundred years ago, those two got together and cooked up what is America's best-known editorial. ... It's not that I don't hold stock in Church's sermon. But allow me to add a little known but highly pertinent fact to the story: Francis Pharcellus Church had no children. If he had, he would have written something like, 'Ginny, talk to your father.' Then, he would have jotted down a note to the dad: 'Nice try, pop. But reconciling lies is your job.'"[11]

In the final analysis, the editorial has succeeded in engaging the emotions and the memories of generations of Americans. "Is There A Santa Claus" may be elliptical in places but it is altogether stylish, whimsical, and charming—elements that seldom typify contemporary newspaper editorials. With wit and insight, "Is There A Santa Claus?" affirmed the impossible in a sparkling way, and that's why it has lived on since 1897.

The journalism of 1897 lives on in other, less direct ways, too. The periodic laments in the early twenty-first century about investigative reporting's limited impact[12] brings to mind the taunts that appeared in Hearst's *New York Journal*. The "complaints and denunciations" appearing in other newspapers were feeble, the *Journal* said, "as idle as the breeze from a lady's fan."[13] Moreover, the temptation of activism has never been entirely excised from American journalism. Like a mild malarial fever, the allure returns episodically—unpredictably but often with intensity.

There was no better recent example of American journalism's activist fever than the experiments in "public" (or "civic") journalism of the mid- and late-1990s. Public journalism envisioned the news media as an active, problem-solving force that would stimulate citizen participation in public life. It anticipated helping to bring about consensus on vital local issues and making sure that elected officials responded accordingly.[14] According to one grand but improbable vision, newspapers practicing public journalism would, "story by story ... knit together a fractured community and repair the idea of the common good."[15]

The rhetoric of the most militant advocates of public journalism echoed Hearst's rationalization of the "journalism of action." Both models were impatient with the passive and aloof character of most newspapers. Both envisioned harnessing the presumed power of the press for such therapeutic or remedial ends as forcing governments to function more effectively and responsively. Arthur Charity wrote in 1995 that practitioners of public journalism "could well argue that the mainstream's rule of noninvolvement is the one that realistically threatens the public. ... Which form of journalism is really more flawed and dangerous in a free society: the one that sits passively by while people grow divided, or the one that finds ways of bringing them together?"[16] Charity's justification for activism more than faintly evoked the *Journal*'s rhetorical flourishes in 1897. "May a newspaper properly do things, or are its legitimate functions confined to talking about them?" the *Journal* asked. "It may criticise corruption and maladministration in office, but has it a right to protect the public interest by deeds as well as words?"[17] Of course it did, the *Journal* declared. It was duty-bound to "render any public service within its power."[18]

For reasons described in detail in Chapter 2, Hearst's vision of the "journalism of action" eventually faded. Similarly, after the 1990s public journalism receded for a number of reasons, including the limited success of newspapers that developed and pursued strategies to stimulate popular participation in civic life. Public journalism also ran headlong into the reflexive and well-developed loathing in American journalism to participate in making the news. The normative paradigm of detached, impartial treatment of the news, which the *New York Times* came to represent in 1897, remains the defining principle of mainstream American journalism. The *Times*' rebuff of public journalism helped shove the movement into eclipse.

Even so, the *New York Times* has not been immune to the fever of activism. In the first years of the twenty-first century, the *Times* veered away on occasion from its traditional, Ochsian ideal of impartial treatment of the news. It indulged in crusading that was at least faintly reminiscent of Hearst's activist journalism. In editorials and in several front-page articles, the *Times* campaigned strenuously in 2002 and 2003 to open the private Augusta National Country Club in Georgia to membership for women. Media critics puzzled over the prominence and intensity devoted to what one of them called "some kind of bizarre crusade that the *New York Times* was on."[19] The Augusta National crusade was far disproportionate to the issue's importance. "Every newspaper, but especially the *New York Times*, has a finite amount of capital," the historian Susan Tifft was quoted as saying. "I'm not sure I would use my capital trying to admit wealthy women, probably mostly white, to a golf club. I might save my fire for something more important."[20]

Other evidence emerged in the first years of the twenty-first century that the *Times* was straying from the paradigm of detached impartiality. In 2004, the newspaper's public editor, or in-house critic, declared that an "implicit advocacy" had come to characterize the newspaper's coverage of social issues such as gay rights, gun control, and environment regulation. "And if you think The Times plays it down the middle on any of them," the public editor, Daniel Okrent, wrote, "you've been reading the paper with your eyes closed."[21] For readers whose views and values are not oriented to the left of center, Okrent added, "a walk through this paper can make you feel you're traveling in a strange and forbidding world."[22] In response to such criticism, the *Times*' executives said in 2005 said that they planned to enhance viewpoint diversity at the newspaper by seeking to reach "beyond our predominantly urban, culturally liberal orientation, to cover the full range of our national conversation." The *Times* pledged "an extra effort" to recruit staff members from varied religious backgrounds and military experience, and from differing regions and classes in the country.[23]

The critiques that roiled the *Times* in the early years of the twenty-first century were largely but not entirely in response to disclosures that one of the newspaper's energetic young reporters, Jayson Blair, had invented and plagiarized key scenes and passages in at least three dozen articles written in late 2002 and early 2003. The *Times*, in a detailed published report, called the serial fabrications "a profound betrayal of trust and a low point in the … history of the newspaper."[24]

While Blair acted without the knowledge or connivance of his superiors, the newspaper's executive and managing editors were ousted in the scandal. And the *Times* stood guilty of having published faked stories—the kind of "grotesque inventions"[25] for which it used to flay the *New York Journal*. And that was a small cruel twist to a newspaper scandal that had few precedents.

Despite the Blair scandal and other lapses, the *Times*' self-view remained undimmed early in the twenty-first century. The *Times* still saw itself as the country's finest, most authoritative newspaper—a self-appraisal that had been in place since the first years of Ochs' ownership. Even after his ouster as executive editor in the Blair scandal, Howell Raines described the *Times* as "the indispensable newsletter of the United States' political, diplomatic, governmental, academic, and professional communities, and the main link between those communities and their counterparts around the world."[26] At the height of its self-promoting ways, the *New York Journal* would have been hard-pressed to match such a claim of profound self-importance.

Nevertheless, the bouts of activism that periodically roil contemporary American journalism represent no serious challenge to the dominant paradigm. The *Journal*'s 1897 vision that a newspaper could and should "render any public service within its power"[27] is far from the orthodoxy of mainstream journalism. Cases of undercover journalism—in which reporters expose corrupt practices by setting themselves up as the prey of unscrupulous public officials—enjoyed a surge of popularity in the 1970s and 1980s but have since retreated to the fringes of acceptable journalistic practice. American war correspondents who dare carry firearms for protection—which was common in the 1890s—open themselves to withering rebukes for compromising their status as a "neutral observer."[28] The central planks of the *Times*' counteractivist model still guide American journalism and are effectively enforced by ethicists such as the Poynter Institute's Bob Steele. "Journalists can hold personal views and even strong opinions," Steele has intoned. "But they must recognize that acting on those beliefs can undermine their ability to accomplish their professional duty."[29] So ingrained is the paradigm of detachment and impartiality, so essential is the imperative of keeping a professional distance, that it is newsworthy when American journalists drop the appearance of detachment to let their emotions show—as network television correspondents did in reporting the floods and devastation that a powerful hurricane brought to New Orleans late in the summer of 2005.[30]

There is another and most important way in which 1897 lives on in American journalism, and that is in offering a measure of reassuring context. Journalists are notoriously ahistoric, and there is little immediate reason for them to recall the challenges and pressures of 1897, when new devices and technologies were pressing on a wary profession, when big-city newspaper staffs were being sharply cut, when complaints about the partisanship of the press were reflexively raised. The turmoil of that year can serve as a general guide to thinking contextually about the multiple forces now buffeting contemporary journalism—the forces of technological innovation, employment uncertainty, and popular skepticism about journalism and their impartiality. As we have seen, American journalism faced the riptide of profound change in the late nineteenth century, and emerged the stronger for it. The turbulence of 1897 helped give rise to a newsgathering model that has served American journalism well for more than 100 years.

To read the lessons of 1897, therefore, is to take encouragement. The angst and despair so commonplace in journalism today are quite likely misplaced. The story of 1897 suggests as much.

NOTES

Preface

1. David G. McCullough, *1776* (New York: Simon & Schuster, 2005).
2. William A. Klingaman, *1929: The Year of the Great Crash* (New York: Harper & Row, 1989).
3. Louis P. Masur, *1831, Year of Eclipse* (New York: Hill and Wang, 2001).
4. Kenneth M. Stampp, *America in 1857: A Nation on the Brink* (New York: Oxford University Press, 1990).
5. Tom Lutz, *American Nervousness, 1903: An Anecdotal History* (Ithaca, NY: Cornell University Press, 1991).
6. See, for example, Mike Jay and Michael Neve, eds. *1900: A Fin-de-Siècle Reader* (London: Penguin, 1999), and Judy Crichton, *America 1900: The Turning Point* (New York: Henry Holt & Co., 1998).
7. Margaret Olwen Macmillan, *Paris 1919: Six Months That Changed the World* (New York: Random House, 2002).
8. See Michael Massing, "The Press: The Enemy Within," *New York Review of Books* (December 15, 2005): 36. Massing wrote that the "fear of bias, and of appearing unbalanced, acts as a powerful sedative on American journalists."
9. See W. Joseph Campbell, *Yellow Journalism: Puncturing the Myths, Defining the Legacies* (Westport, CT: Praeger Publishers, 2001), 71–95.
10. See, among others, W. A. Swanberg, *Citizen Hearst: A Biography of William Randolph Hearst* (New York: Charles Scribner's Sons, 1961), 144. "Above all," Swanberg wrote of the Spanish-American War of 1898, "it was Hearst's war."

Introduction

1. "Bulletin 408A," American Newspaper Publishers' Association (New York: January 18, 1897): 9.
2. This is not to say that the Publishers' Association concerned itself only with trivial issues at its meeting in 1897. The agenda included questions of incorporating the association and exploring ways of ascertaining claims about newspaper circulation. Other agenda items were: "What benefits if any come from the publishing of special editions, like 'Christmas Number,' 'Fourth of July Number,' 'Bicycle Number,' etc.?" "What is the present status in reference to colored supplements, books, pictures, music, art and fashion supplements, and all other circulation schemes?" See "Bulletin 408A," American Newspaper Publishers' Association (January 18, 1897).
3. "The Problem of the Hour," *Fourth Estate* (February 25, 1897): 6.
4. See, among others, Robert Taft, *Photography and the American Scene: A Social History, 1839–1889* (New York: Dover Publications, 1964), 446.
5. For a discussion about the emergence and diffusion of the term "yellow journalism" in early 1897, see W. Joseph Campbell, *Yellow Journalism: Puncturing the Myths, Defining the Legacies* (Westport, CT: Praeger Publishers, 2001), 25–49.
6. See, for example, Jeffrey A. Dvorkin, "When Those Pesky Blogs Undermine NPR News," npr.org, posted May 3, 2005 (accessed August 1, 2005). Dvorkin described the blogosphere—the vast array of Web logs— as "an amoral place with few rules. ... It is a place where the philosophy of 'who posts first, wins' predominates."
7. So described by the *Chicago Times-Herald*. See "Jail-breaking Journalism," *Chicago Times Herald* (October 12, 1897): 6.
8. Charles Duval [Karl Decker], "Evangelina Cisneros Rescued by the Journal," *New York Journal* (October 10, 1897): 45.
9. For such characterizations of the editorial see, for example, Geo Beach, "Shop Talk at Thirty: 'Yes, Virginia,' 100 Years Later, Provides Enduring Reminder of Print's Power," *Editor & Publisher* (December 20, 1997): 48.
10. "Is There A Santa Claus?," *New York Sun* (September 21, 1897): 6.
11. See "Socialistic Papers: The 'East Side' Journals of New York City," *Fourth Estate* (June 3, 1897): 5.
12. Charles Musser, *The Emergence of Cinema: The American Screen to 1907* (New York Scribner's, 1990), 107. Musser identified cinema's "novelty year" as the period from late April 1896 to May 1897.
13. Musser, *The Emergence of Cinema*, 198–200. Musser wrote [200]: "The fact that the Corbett-Fitzsimmons fight was an 'illustration' of a fight rather than a fight itself made the attraction not only legally but socially acceptable viewing material." Fitzsimmons won the bout with a

crushing blow to Corbett's midsection in the thirteenth round. See also, "The Veriscope Shows the Fight," *New York Tribune* (May 23, 1897): 8. The *Tribune* article said that an "excellent idea of the fight was to be obtained, however, by watching the screen closely. ..." An account in the *New York Journal* said the fight footage "was so shadowy—yet real, vividly, dreadfully real." See Winifred Black, "Does Modern Photography Incite Women to Brutality?" *New York Journal* (May 30, 1897) 17.

14. Nathan A. Haverstock, *Fifty Years at the Front: The Life of War Correspondent Frederick Palmer* (Washington, DC: Brassey's, 1996), 36. See also, Michael S. Sweeney, *From the Front: The Story of War* (Washington, DC: National Geographic, 2003), 101.

15. Susan J. Douglas, *Inventing American Broadcasting, 1899–1922* (Baltimore, MD: Johns Hopkins University Press, 1987).

16. See Burton St. John III, "Public Relations as Community-building, Then and Now," *Public Relations Quarterly* 43, 1 (Spring 1998): 34.

17. See Stephen Ponder, "The President Makes News: William McKinley and the First Presidential Press Corps, 1897–1901," *Presidential Studies Quarterly* 24, 4 (Fall 1994): 823–36.

18. See "Note and Comment," *Fourth Estate* (June 24, 1897): 6. See also, Stephen Ponder, *Managing the Press: Origins of the Media Presidency, 1897–1933* (New York: St. Martin's Press, 1999), 5–6. Ponder noted (6) that late in 1897 "McKinley formally invited the correspondents and their wives to one of his official holiday receptions. To be on the President's social list ... was regarded by the correspondents as a flattering indicator of acceptance."

19. See "A People's Paper," *Fourth Estate* (January 13, 1898): 2.

20. See Ray Boston, "W.T. Stead and Democracy by Journalism," in Joel H. Weiner, ed., *Papers for the Millions: The New Journalism in Britain, 1850s to 1914* (New York: Greenwood Press, 1998): 97. See also, "Endow in the Klondike," *Fourth Estate* (November 18, 1897): 6. For more on "endowed journalism," see Edward F. Adams, "Newspaper Work: Limitations of Truth-Telling," *Arena* 20, 3 (September 1898): 611, and Marion Tuttle Marzolf, *Civilizing Voices: American Press Criticism 1880–1950* (New York: Longman, 1991), 17–18.

21. See "Not Room Enough for All," *Fourth Estate* (June 10, 1897): 6.

22. See Hartley Davis, "The Journalism of New York." *Munsey's Magazine* 24, 2 (November 1900): 217. Davis said Park Row, the home of New York's leading newspapers in the late nineteenth century, "is to the newspaper world what Wall Street is to finance."

23. "The Journalism that Does Things," *New York Journal* (October 13, 1897): 8.

24. "The Development of a New Idea in Journalism," *New York Journal* (October 3, 1897): 39.

25. See Susan E. Tifft and Alex S. Jones, "Adolph S. Ochs," *Editor & Publisher* (October 30, 1999): 14.

26. Lincoln Steffens, letter to his father (March 23, 1898), Steffens papers, Series II, Box 55, uncatalogued correspondence; Butler Library, Columbia University, New York, NY.

27. Justin Kaplan, *Lincoln Steffens: A Biography* (New York: Simon and Schuster, 1974), 82.

28. John Higham invoked this phrase to describe the dynamism that characterized the American political and social culture in the 1890s. See Higham, "The Reorientation of American Culture in the 1890's," in John Weiss, ed., *The Origins of Modern Consciousness* (Detroit: Wayne State University, 1965): 40.

29. Henry D. Traill, *The New Fiction and Other Essays on Literary Subjects* (Port Washington, NY, Kennikat Press: 1970, reprint of 1897 ed.), 1.

30. See "Profession or Trade?" *Fourth Estate* (October 28, 1897): 4.

31. J. Lincoln Steffens, "The Business of a Newspaper," *Scribner's* 22, 4 (October 1897): 448. The Linotype was invented in 1886 by Ottmar Mergenthaler.

32. See, for example, "The Sorrows of Freak Journalism," *New York Times* (December 25, 1896): 4.

33. See "The Derelicts of Journalism," *New York World* (March 28, 1897): 10–11.

34. "Intimidating the Press," *Fourth Estate* (July 5, 1894): 4.

35. "The Power of the Press," *The Journalist* (July 3, 1897): 84. See also, "Power of the Press," *Fourth Estate* (May 24, 1894): 4. The *Fourth Estate*'s editorial declared: "The power of the press is something that is quite generally overrated."

36. Ted Curtis Smythe, "The Diffusion of the Urban Daily, 1850–1900," *Journalism History* 28, 2 (Summer 2002): 80–81.

37. Smythe, "The Diffusion of the Urban Daily," 81. See also, "Below Two Cents: The Tremendous Drop in the Cost of News Paper," *Fourth Estate* (October 8, 1896): 1. Cheaper newsprint in the 1890s contributed not only to lower per-copy prices but encouraged fatter newspapers, especially Sunday editions.

38. [Price Collier,] *America and the Americans: From A French Point of View* (New York: Charles Scribner's Sons, 1897), 268. See also, Willis J. Abbot, *Watching the World Go By* (Boston: Little, Brown, 1933), 210. Abbot, formerly an editor at the *New York Journal*, offered additional testimony about the centrality of newspapers in *fin-de-siècle* American life, writing: "New York took more interest in the papers and their eternal ballyhoo [in the late 1890s] than it does in the more staid and dignified methods of to-day."

39. The centrality of newspapers in *fin-de-siècle* American life is also addressed in Gunther Barth, *City People: The Rise of Modern City Culture in Nineteenth-Century America* (New York: Oxford University Press, 1980), 59–63.

40. The jubilee issue featured sketches in brilliant colors depicting moments in Chicago's history and a poem that James Whitcomb Riley had written to commemorate the anniversary. See Lloyd Wendt, *Chicago Tribune: The Rise of a Great American Newspaper* (Chicago: Rand McNally & Co., 1979), 341.

41. "Join the Jubilee: All Chicagoans Help 'The Tribune' in Celebrating," *Chicago Tribune* (June 11, 1897): 1.

42. "Join the Jubilee," *Chicago Tribune* (June 11, 1897).

43. "Tribune's Golden Jubilee," *Chicago Tribune* (June 10, 1897): 18.

44. The self-congratulatory impulse has not been completely excised from American journalism—as suggested by the *Washington Post*'s coverage of the disclosure in 2005 of the famous and elusive "Deep Throat" source in the Watergate scandal of the early 1970s. The newspaper devoted columns of newsprint to the revelations, prompting one Internet blogger to declare: "Maybe it's a generational thing but this Deep Throat orgy, er, extravaganza is supremely uninteresting. The Washington Post's wall-to-wall treatment smacks of self love and journalistic hero-worship." Gregory Scoblete, cited in Johanna Neuman, "Watergate-era Players Weigh In on Felt's Role," *Los Angeles Times* (June 2, 2005): A25.

45. "Tribune's Golden Jubilee," *Chicago Tribune* (June 10, 1897). The newspaper also said "the span of the Tribune's life is immeasurable. There is no place for gloom in the vista of years which stretches out full of glorious promise for the future." The commentary proved prophetic. The *Tribune* marked its 150th anniversary in 1997 and, into the twenty-first century, remained one of the ten largest-circulation newspapers in the United States.

46. See "The Santa Claus Press," *Fourth Estate* (December 23, 1897): 12.

47. "The Santa Claus Press," *Fourth Estate* (December 23, 1897).

48. See "Aid the Cold and Hungry; Journal Hears the Cry and Opens a Relief Fund," *New York Journal* (January 27, 1897): 1

49. "What We Want," *The Journalist* (May 1, 1897): 12.

50. "What We Want," *The Journalist* (May 1, 1897).

51. James Fullarton Muirhead, *The Land of Contrasts: A Briton's View of his American Kin* (Boston: Lamson, Wolffe and Co., 1898), 145. See also, Larzer Ziff, *The American 1890s: Life and Times of a Lost Generation* (Lincoln: University of Nebraska Press, 1966): 4–5.

52. Muirhead, *The Land of Contrasts*, 146. Muirhead wrote (146–147) that he found the Sunday issues of large American newspapers especially confusing, filled as they were with "aimless congeries of reading

material, good, bad, and indifferent." Muirhead also wrote that "he who knows where to look for it will generally find some edible morsel in the hog-trough" of American newspapers.

53. See "Must Sell in Silence," *Washington Post* (January 1, 1897): 10. The ban amended a little-enforced statute that barred newsboys from crying out on Sundays from 7 a.m. to 10:30 a.m. See "The Crying of Sunday Papers," *Washington Evening Star* (January 4, 1897): 6.

54. "Crusade a Pretext," *Washington Post* (January 11, 1897): 4.

55. Cited in "Big Ado About Little," *Washington Post* (January 11, 1897): 4.

56. "Newsboys Silenced on Sundays," *Washington Post* (February 18, 1897): 10.

57. See "Stops the Crying of Sunday Papers," *Washington Post* (February 28, 1897): 3; "Newsboys Fined for Crying Papers," *Washington Post* (October 26, 1897): 10, and "Judge Lets the Boys Go," *Washington Post* (June 6, 1899): 10.

58. See "Sabbath at Capital," *Washington Post* (January 7, 1898): 8.

59. See, for example, John Livingston Wright, "Reporters and Oversupply," *Arena* 20, 3 (September 1898): 615. Wright wrote that "an eager, ambitious crowd" of reporters was "constantly heading for New York, Chicago, Philadelphia, Baltimore, and Boston; New York always being the eventually hoped-for goal."

60. "Not Room Enough for All," *Fourth Estate* (June 10, 1897). For further discussion about the centrality of New York City to American journalism of the late nineteenth century, see Fred Fedler, *Lessons from the Past: Journalists' Lives and Work, 1850–1950* (Prospect Heights, IL: Waveland Press, 2000), 216–217, and Hy B. Turner, *When Giants Ruled: The Story of Park Row, New York's Great Newspaper Street* (New York: Fordham University Press, 1999), 139.

61. See "Tribune Ex-Aides Are Arrested Over False-Circulation Scams," *Wall Street Journal* (June 16, 2005): B7. The *Wall Street Journal* report said that "circulation misstatements have incited skepticism about the veracity of circulation figures across the newspaper industry, analysts say, making it more difficult for many newspapers to raise rates for advertising."

62. "Proving Circulations," *Fourth Estate* (July 11, 1895): 6.

63. See Tifft and Jones, *The Trust*, 54–55.

64. See "Acquitted Both Men," *Washington Post* (June 19, 1897): 2, and "Shriver Next at the Bar," *Washington Post* (June 6, 1897): 10.

65. "The Washington Decision," *Fourth Estate* (June 24, 1897): 6.

66. See, for example, Joe Hagan and Anne Marie Squeo, "In Source Case, One Reporter Will Testify, One Goes to Jail," *Wall Street Journal* (July 7, 2005): B1. Judith Miller of the *New York Times* was sent to jail by a federal judge after she refused to identify confidential sources to a grand jury.

67. Harry Thurston Peck, "A Great National Newspaper," *Cosmopolitan* (December 1897): 218.
68. Muirhead, *The Land of Contrasts*, 151–152.
69. See, for example, Philip Meyer, *The Vanishing Newspaper: Saving Journalism in the Information Age* (Columbia: University of Missouri Press, 2004).
70. "The Decay of American Journalism," *The Dial*, reprinted in *The Journalist* (May 1, 1897): 14–15.
71. John Trevor, "The Tendency of New Journalism," *The Journalist* (June 12, 1897): 59.
72. "On the Down Grade," *The Journalist* (October 9, 1897): 196.
73. See "The Linotype," *Fourth Estate* (July 29, 1897): 2.
74. "The Linotype," *Fourth Estate* (July 29, 1897).
75. "The Typewriter Question," *The Journalist* (June 12, 1897). See also, "Bye-the-Bye," *The Journalist* (May 29, 1897): 45.
76. "Bye-the-Bye," *The Journalist* (May 29, 1897).
77. "Bye-the-Bye," *The Journalist* (May 29, 1897).
78. "Bye-the-Bye," *The Journalist* (May 29, 1897).
79. See, for one notable example, Clifford Stoll, "The Internet? Bah!" *Newsweek* (February 27, 1995): 41. Stoll wrote that the Internet was little more than "a wasteland of unfiltered data," and added: "While the Internet beckons brightly, seductively flashing an icon of knowledge-as-power, this nonplace lures us to surrender our time on earth. A poor substitute it is, this virtual reality where frustration is legion and where—in the holy names of Education and Progress—important aspects of human interactions are relentlessly devalued."
80. Cited in "In Olden Times," *Times Talk* 4, 5 (January 1951): 6
81. "The Typewriter Question," *The Journalist* (June 12, 1897).
82. "The Typewriter," *Fourth Estate* (July 29, 1897): 6.
83. "The Typewriter," *Fourth Estate* (July 29, 1897).
84. See Hartley Davis, "The Journalism of New York." *Munsey's Magazine* 24, 2 (November 1900): 221.
85. See "The Twentieth Century," *Fourth Estate* (January 5, 1901): 8.
86. "The Typewriter," *Fourth Estate* (July 29, 1897).
87. "The Typewriter," *Fourth Estate* (July 29, 1897). The *Fourth Estate* account also described the typewriter "as positively necessary" in most newsrooms.
88. See "Fearless But Never Armed," *New York World* (February 7, 1897): 2.
89. "The Typewriter," *Fourth Estate* (July 29, 1897). By early 1895, the *Boston Globe* had declared its preference for typewritten copy and the *Indianapolis News* had purchased for its staff a half-dozen Daugherty typewriters, which featured long, front-striking keybars that allowed copy to be read as it was being typed. See "Typewritten Copy," *Fourth Estate* (January 10, 1895): 4. Hearst bought for the *Journal* staff in late

1896 a large number of Remington typewriters, models notably popular among journalists of the time. See "Remingtons By the Dozen,"
Fourth Estate (October 8, 1896): 5. Allan Forman, editor of *The Journalist*, wrote favorably in 1897 about the Blickensderfer models, which
featured revolving type and became known as "Blicks." See "The Typewriter Question," *The Journalist* (June 12, 1897). See also, Annie Groer,
"True to Type," *Washington Post* (May 3, 2001): H1.

90. A persuasive explanation for this gap in journalism studies was suggested in the former *Media Studies Journal* which, in an issue devoted
to "defining moments" in American journalism, noted: "Looking back
is not something that comes naturally to journalists, immersed as they
are in breaking events and relentless deadlines." See "Defining Moments
in Journalism," *Media Studies Journal* 11, 2 (Spring 1997): xv.

91. Margaret A. Blanchard, "The Ossification of Journalism History: A
Challenge for the Twenty-first Century," *Journalism History* 25, 3
(Autumn 1999): 110. Blanchard also cited a "need to broaden our hori-
zons as to what research approach will yield the most accurate pictures
of our mediated world."

92. Blanchard, "The Ossification of Journalism History," 111. Blanchard's
appeal renewed and extended a critique that dates at least to 1974 and
James W. Carey's "The Problem of Journalism History," *Journalism History* 1, 1 (Spring 1974): 3–5, 27. Carey said (3) that the "study of journalism history remains something of an embarrassment" and argued that
scholars in the field "have defined our craft both too narrowly and too
modestly and, therefore, constricted the range of problems we study and
the claims we make for our knowledge." For a somewhat more optimistic assessment, see Donald Lewis Shaw and Sylvia L. Zack, "Rethinking
Journalism History: How Some Recent Studies Support One Approach,"
Journalism History 14, 4 (Winter 1987): 111–17. The authors concluded
(116): "If our field once was an embarrassment to some, it no longer is."

93. See Richard Landes, Andrew Gow, and David Van Meter, eds., *The
Apocalyptic Year 1000* (New York: Oxford University Press, 2003).

94. See Danny Danziger and John Gillingham, *1215: The Year of Magna
Carta* (New York: Simon & Schuster, 2004).

95. See Frank McLynn, *1759: The Year Britain Became Master of the World*
(New York: Atlantic Monthly Press, 2005).

96. See David G. McCullough, *1776* (New York: Simon & Schuster, 2005).

97. See Glenn F. Williams, *Year of the Hangman: George Washington's War
Against the Iroquois* (Yardley, PA: Westholme Publishing, 2005).

98. See James Chace, *1912: Wilson, Roosevelt, Taft & Debs—The Election
That Changed the Country* (New York: Simon & Schuster, 2004).

99. See Margaret MacMillan, *Paris 1919: Six Months That Changed the
World* (New York: Random House, 2002).

100. See Mark Kurlansky, *1968: The Year That Rocked the World* (New York: Ballantine, 2004).

101. See, for example, Jay Winik, *April 1865: The Month That Saved America* (New York: Harper Collins, 2001) and David Halberstam, *October 1964* (New York: Villard Books, 1994),

102. See, for example, Cornelius Ryan, *The Longest Day: June 6, 1944* (New York: Simon & Schuster, 1959).

103. Michael North, "Virtual Histories: The Year as Literary Period," *Modern Language Quarterly* 62, 4 (2001): 408.

104. Michael North, *Reading 1922: A Return to the Scene of the Modern* (New York: Oxford University Press, 1999).

105. North, "Virtual Histories: The Year as Literary Period," 407.

106. John E. Wills, *1688: A Global History* (New York: Norton, 2001).

107. Louis P. Masur, *1831: Year of Eclipse* (New York: Hill and Wang, 2001) and Kenneth M. Stamp, *America in 1857: A Nation on the Brink* (New York: Oxford University Press, 1990).

108. See David Traxel, *1898: The Birth of the American Century* (New York: Knopf, 1998).

109. Peter Arnett, "Vietnam and War Reporting," *Media Studies Journal* 11, 2 (Spring 1997): 33–38.

110. Ellen Hume, "The Weight of Watergate," *Media Studies Journal* 11, 2 (Spring 1997): 77–82.

111. Judy Woodruff, "Covering Politics—Is There a Female Difference?" *Media Studies Journal* 11, 2 (Spring 1997): 155–58.

112. See, for example: Charles H. Brown, *The Correspondents' War: Journalists in the Spanish-American War,* (New York: Scribner's, 1967) and Joyce Milton, *The Yellow Kids: Foreign Correspondents in the Heyday of Yellow Journalism* (New York: Harper and Row, 1989).

113. See, for example, Joseph E. Wisan, *The Cuban Crisis as Reflected in the New York Press (1895–1898),* (New York: Octagon Books, 1965 reprint of 1934 ed.); Gene Wiggins, "Sensationally Yellow!" in Lloyd Chiasson Jr., ed., *Three Centuries of American Media* (Englewood, CO: Morton Publishing Company, 1999): 155, and Philip Seib, *Headline Diplomacy: How News Coverage Affects Foreign Policy* (Westport, CT: Praeger Publishers, 1997), 1–13.

114. Easily the most unforgiving of Hearst's biographers was Ferdinand Lundberg, who wrote *Imperial Hearst: A Social Biography* (New York: Equinox Cooperative Press, 1936).

115. See, for example, Denis Brian, *Pulitzer: A Life* (New York: John Wiley & Sons, 2001).

116. W. A. Swanberg, *Citizen Hearst: A Biography of William Randolph Hearst* (New York: Charles Scribner's Sons, 1961), 162.

117. David Nasaw, *The Chief: The Life of William Randolph Hearst* (Boston, Houghton Mifflin: 2000), 102.

118. John D. Stevens, *Sensationalism and the New York Press* (New York: Columbia University Press, 1991), 98.

119. Stevens, *Sensationalism and the New York Press*, 99–100.

120. Alva Johnson, "Twilight of the Ink-Stained Gods," *Vanity Fair* (February 1932): 36, 70.

121. Johnson, "Twilight of the Ink-Stained Gods," 36.

122. Michael Schudson, *Discovering the News: A Social History of American Newspapers* (New York: Basic Books, 1978), 106.

123. Schudson, *Discovering the News*, 88–120.

124. Schudson, *Discovering the News*, 90–91. Schudson also wrote (116): "Most people read the *Times* because the elite read it."

125. Schudson, *Discovering the News*, 90.

126. Stevens, *Sensationalism and the New York Press*, 98. See also, Campbell, *Yellow Journalism*, 51–70.

127. John J. Pauly rightly declared the dichotomy as "intellectually feeble." See Pauly, "Rupert Murdoch and the Demonology of Professional Journalism," in James W. Carey, ed., *Media, Myths, and Narratives: Television and the Press* (Newbury Park, CA: Sage Publications, 1988): 252.

128. "A Question and the Answer," *The Journalist* (February 12, 1898): 176.

129. Scovel's assignments in 1897 are recounted in Joyce Milton, *The Yellow Kids: Foreign Correspondents in the Heyday of Yellow Journalism* (New York: Harper and Row, 1989), esp. 70–71, 144–49, 162–66, 173–184, 186. As impressive as Scovel's globe-trotting was in 1897, the *World* often found it difficult to keep pace with the *Journal*, which in 1897 spent liberally on newsgathering and recruiting staff. Scovel's assignments, while revealing, tend to obscure the fact that retrenchment was afoot at the *World* in mid-1897. Pulitzer ordered staff cuts to rid the newspaper of what he called its considerable deadwood. Pulitzer's correspondence, moreover, reveals that he devoted much attention in 1897 to the declining financial condition of the *World*, deploring the losses which stemmed in part from his ill-considered decision in 1896 to trim the newspaper's price to one cent, to compete with Hearst. The staff retrenchment and other cost-cutting measures in 1897 were Pulitzer's attempt to stop the *World*'s flood of red ink.

130. See untitled notes of the *World*'s news staff meeting, November 28, 1898, in Joseph Pulitzer papers, Library of Congress, Manuscript Division, Washington, DC.

131. Tifft and Jones, *The Trust*, 45.

132. Tifft and Jones, *The Trust*, 46.

133. Gerald F. Linderman, *The Mirror of War: American Society and the Spanish-American War* (Ann Arbor: University of Michigan Press, 1974), 161–162.

134. "The Journalism of Action," *New York Journal* (October 5, 1897): 6.

135. "A Newspaper's Duty to the Public," *New York Journal* (November 15, 1897): 6.

136. Traxel, *1898*, 317.

137. Traxel, *1898*, 83.

138. Traxel, *1898*, 83.

139. Frank Luther Mott, *American Journalism, A History: 1690–1960*, 3rd ed. (New York: Macmillan, 1962), 149. Although the Alien and Sedition Acts were allowed to lapse in 1801, journalists still faced the threat of criminal libel, the prosecution of which fell to the states. See Norman L. Rosenberg, "The Law of Political Libel and Freedom of the Press in Nineteenth Century America: An Interpretation," *American Journal of Legal History*, 17 (1973): 337.

140. The notion that the penny press emerged in 1833 and reshaped American journalism has been debunked by historians, notably John Nerone in "The Mythology of the Penny Press," *Critical Studies in Mass Communication* 4 (1987): 376–404. Nerone wrote (377): "The penny press is properly understood as a mutation in one class or species of newspaper, rather than as a revolution in editorial policy and business strategy. The innovations associated with the penny press are functions of forces external to the papers themselves rather than the results of unique personal initiative."

141. Some analysts have rejected the decidedly media-centric view that the *Washington Post*'s reporting brought down the Nixon administration. The roles of Congress and the federal courts in compelling testimony and the production of evidence were far more decisive to that outcome. See, for example, Edward J. Epstein, *Between Fact and Fiction: The Problem of Journalism* (New York: Vintage, 1975), 19–32.

142. See Chris Cobb, "1995: The Year the World Logged On," *Ottawa Citizen* (December 30, 1995): B1. Cobb wrote: "This was the year everyone heard or read about the Internet." See also, Steven Levy, "The Year of the Internet: This Changes ... Everything," *Newsweek* (December 25, 1995): 26. Levy wrote that "in 1995, the Internet ruled."

143. Scott Heller, "What a Difference a Year Makes," *Chronicle of Higher Education* (January 5, 2001): A17.

144. Henry A. Crittenden, "Mr. Hearst and the New Journalism," *The Journalist* (December 4, 1897): 34.

145. Crittenden, "Mr. Hearst and the New Journalism," 34.

146. The *Journal*'s anticorruption campaigns in years immediately after 1897 won similarly high praise. Disclosures about the corrupt Ice Trust

in 1900 prompted the editor of New York's *Town Talk* gossip sheet to write: "'The *Journal*'s exposure and pursuit of the criminal officials who betrayed the people in the interest of the Ice Trust will stand for many years as one of the most splendid and useful achievements of the modern newspaper.'" Quoted in Nasaw, *The Chief*, 151. For a brief discussion about the Ice Trust scandal of 1900, see Campbell, *Yellow Journalism*, 3–4.

147. See Edward P. Mitchell, *Memoirs of an Editor: Fifty Years of American Journalism* (New York: Scribner's Sons, 1924), 112.

148. See "The Development of Illustration," *Wilson's Photographic Magazine* 37 (May 1900): 232. However, more recent research has suggested that newspapers' adoption of the halftone process was delayed by "art and hand-engraving staffs [which] waged a successful propaganda campaign. Their convincing arguments that the readers wanted *art* and not the realism of a cheap mechanized medium like photography appear to have been accepted without serious question." See R. Smith Schuneman, "Art or Photography: A Question for Newspaper Editors of the 1890s," *Journalism Quarterly* 42, 1 (Winter 1965): 52. See also, Michael Carlebach, *American Photojournalism Comes of Age* (Washington, DC: Smithsonian Institutions Press, 1997), 28. Carlebach wrote: "During the 1880s and 1890s, halftone process work was slowed chiefly by the vigorous objections of those employed as sketch and graphic artists."

149. See Schuneman, "Art or Photography," 50. As Schuneman's characterization suggests, Horgan's breakthrough is widely recognized as such in the literature of photojournalism. However, two newspapers in Minnesota claimed in letters to *Fourth Estate* in 1897 that they had introduced halftones in their daily editions before the *New York Tribune*. See "Who Holds the Half-Tone Record on Fast Presses?" *Fourth Estate* (February 11, 1897): 7. The newspapers were the *Minneapolis Tribune* and the *St. Paul Pioneer Press*. As Carlebach usefully noted, "Photojournalism did not appear in America as if by magic … ; nor is it merely a byproduct of Horgan's halftone process. Press photography evolved in America." See Carlebach, *American Photojournalism Comes of Age*, 165.

150. See "Platt Elected Senator," *New York Tribune* (January 21, 1897): 1.

151. "Half-tones for Perfecting Presses," *Fourth Estate* (January 28, 1897): 6.

152. "Half-tone pictures," *New York Tribune* (March 31, 1897): 6. A "web" is a roll of newsprint; "perfecting" is to print on both sides of the web of newsprint as it passes through the press.

153. Untitled Editorial Comment, *Fourth Estate* (March 11, 1897): 7.

154. See Harry W. Baehr Jr., *The New York Tribune Since the Civil War* (New York: Octagon 1972 reprint ed.), 235. See also: Taft, *Photography and the American Scene*, 446; "Twenty-Years Progress in Half-Tone Work," *Fourth Estate* (May 30, 1903): 5; "Halftones 50 Years Old," *New York*

Times (March 4, 1930): 3, and Lida Rose McCabe, *The Beginnings of Halftone: From the Note Books of Stephen H. Horgan, "Dean of American Photoengravers,"* (Chicago: Inland Printer, 1924).

155. "Half-Tone Pictures," *New York Tribune* (March 31, 1897).

156. See "Horgan, Inventor of Halftone, Dies," *New York Times* (August 31, 1941): 23, and Carlebach, *American Photojournalism Comes of Age*, 162.

157. "Stephen H. Horgan, "Photography for the Newspapers," *Philadelphia Photographer* 23 (1886): 142.

158. See, among others, Carlebach, *American Photojournalism Comes of Age*, 161–62.

159. See, among others, Sidney Kobre, *The Yellow Press and Gilded Age Journalism* (Tallahassee: Florida State University Press, 1964), 41.

160. The *New York Tribune* described the halftone as "a perfect reproduction of a photograph, and thus avoids the possible distortion of features or inaccurate conception of a given scene through the necessary haste of the daily newspaper artist." See "Half-Tone Pictures," *New York Tribune*, March 31, 1897.

161 156. "The Development of Illustration," *Wilson's Photographic Magazine* (May 1900): 232.

162. Taft, *Photography and the American Scene*, 446. He also wrote: "The welcome with which [halftone] illustrations were received by readers is said to have been a distinct surprise to the publishers" of many newspapers.

163. "Causes of the Decline of Reporting," *Fourth Estate* (June 1, 1899): 4. The trade journal blamed "pictures and big type display" headlines for having "cut down the space formerly given to the publication of news." *Fourth Estate* added: "The best news stories printed today appear in the papers that do not make a feature of illustrations and freak spread-heads."

164. See also, Kevin G. Barnhurst and John C. Nerone, "Design Trends in U.S. Front Pages, 1885–1985," *Journalism Quarterly* 68, 4 (Winter 1991): 799. The authors described a steady reduction in the number of articles, illustrations, and advertisements in three sample newspapers examined at ten-year intervals from 1885 to 1985.

165. A. B. [Arthur Brisbane], "Hon. Charles Anderson Dana," *The Journalist* (May 15, 1897): 26. Brisbane wrote: "If the newspaper business were religious, which it isn't, Mr. Dana would be the pope … ."

166. See "A Veteran's Words," *Fourth Estate* (September 9, 1897): 3, and Brisbane, "Hon. Charles Anderson Dana," *The Journalist* (May 15, 1897).

167. See "Hon. Charles Anderson Dana," *The Journalist* (October 23, 1897): 2.

168. See "Paul Dana Steps In," *Chicago Tribune* (October 19, 1897): 4.

169. Will Irwin, "The New York Sun," *American Magazine* 67 (January 1909): 304.

170. "The Death of Editor Dana," *San Francisco Chronicle* (October 18, 1897): 4. Similarly, the *Philadelphia Inquirer* said of Dana's significance to American journalism: "His place will not be filled because the school to which he belonged has passed away. But he will be missed by thousands of newspapermen who have taken inspiration from him and his newspaper." See "Death of Charles A. Dana," *Philadelphia Inquirer* (October 18, 1897): 6.

171. Put another way: "The personality of a newspaper is the personality of the man who is running that paper, and the men he calls in to assist him." See Addison Archer, introduction to *American Journalism From the Practical Side* (New York: Holmes Publishing, 1897), 6.

172. "Editorials and Their Value," *Fourth Estate* (September 9, 1897): 4.

173. By 1900, aggregate advertising revenues for newspapers in America exceeded revenues from subscriptions and sales. Before then, subscriptions and sales had raised more funds for newspapers. See "Table 5—Comparative Summary of Newspapers and Periodicals, 1880 to 1900," *Twelfth Census of the United States, Taken in the Year 1900: Manufacturers, Part III* (Washington, DC: United States Census Office, 1902), 1042.

174. See "Table 56—Summary of Receipts and Expenditures of the Philadelphia Record, with Income Per Column from Advertising: 1893 to 1900," *Twelfth Census of the United States*, 1090. The table showed that the *Philadelphia Record* in 1897 reported revenues of $855,934, including $594,337 from advertising.

175. Charles A. Dana, "The Making of a Newspaper Man," lecture at Cornell University, January 11, 1894, reprinted in Dana, *The Art of Newspaper Making: Three Lectures* (New York: Appleton, 1895), 98. He said of illustrations in newspapers: "I don't believe so many pictures are going to be required for any great portion of the next century."

176. Dana, "The Making of a Newspaper Man," 74. Despite his reservations, Dana was well-versed in the innovations and developments in newspaper technology of the 1890s, a period he referred to as "the age of experiment." See Dana, "The Making of a Newspaper Man," 96.

177. "Profession or Trade?" *Fourth Estate* (October 28, 1897). Another critic, writing in the journal *Self Culture*, said of Dana: "Even his animosities, cruel as they sometimes were, were part of the man, as well as of the journal he so ably conducted; yet in spite of them, and of certain erratic moods and antagonistic qualities, he was a power on the press of this country." See "The Late Henry George and C.A. Dana," *Self Culture* 6, 3 (December 1897): 246.

178. "A Great Editor," *Los Angeles Times* (October 19, 1897): 6. The editorial also said of Dana: "If there was a head in sight that deserved to be hit, he hit it, and not with a feather, either."

179. Richard Allen Schwarzlose, *The American Wire Services: A Study of Their Development as a Social Institution* (New York: Arno Press, 1979), 67–68.
180. Schwarzlose, *The American Wire Services*, 67–68.
181. "The United Press Assigns: Associated Press Triumphs in the Long and Costly War of News Associations," *Fourth Estate* (April 1, 1897): 1.
182. "The United Press Assigns," *Fourth Estate* (April 1, 1897).
183. "A Correction," *New York Sun* (April 17, 1897): 6.
184. "Sun Apologizes," *Fourth Estate* (April 22, 1897): 1.
185. "The Work of Rascals," *New York Sun* (February 22, 1895): 6.
186. "A Correction," *New York Sun* (April 17, 1897).
187. "Leprous New Journalism," *New York Sun* (February 27, 1897): 7
188. "Leprous New Journalism," *New York Sun* (February 27, 1897).
189. "Leprous New Journalism," *New York Sun* (February 27, 1897). See also, "Freak Journals Reprobated," *New York Times* (March 3, 1897): 10.
190. "Yellow Journalism Denounced Everywhere," *New York Press* (May 3, 1897): 5
191. These and other, similar decisions were routinely reported on the *Sun*'s front page in March 1897. See, for example, "World and Journal Put Out," *New York Sun* (March 7, 1897): 1; "World and Journal Cast Out," *New York Sun* (March 9, 1897): 1; "World and Journal Cast Out," *New York Sun* (March 11, 1897): 1; "World and Journal Kicked Out," *New York Sun* (March 14, 1897): 1, and "World and Journal Shut Out," *New York Sun* (March 17, 1897): 1.
192. "'New Journalism' at Yale," *New York Times* (March 15, 1897): 1.
193. See "New Journalism Rebuked," *New York Times* (March 18, 1897): 1.
194. In Portland, the local library association banished from its reading room Hearst's California newspaper, the *San Francisco Examiner*. See "Current Notes," *New York Times* (March 10, 1897): 6
195. See "The Protest of Decency," *New York Sun* (March 21, 1897): sect. 2, p. 1.
196. "Newspaper Advertising," *New York Times* (March 10, 1897): 6.
197. See "A Work of Moral Sanitation," *New York Times* (March 4, 1897): 6. The *Times* also declared: "To make the reading of the new journals … a social offense punishable by scorn and contempt would be a salutary and sufficient measure of reform."
198. See, among others, Turner, *When Giants Ruled*, 128.
199. See "A Work of Moral Sanitation," *New York Times* (March 4, 1897).
200. As John D. Stevens perceptively has noted: "Accusations of sensationalism have been more frequent than definitions." See Stevens, "Sensationalism in Perspective," *Journalism History* 12, 3–4 (Autumn-Winter 1985): 78.

201. Cited in "Sunday Newspapers," *Los Angeles Times* (December 23, 1896): 6.
202. See "A Work of Moral Sanitation," *New York Times* (March 4, 1897).
203. Cited in "New Journalism and Vice," *New York Times* (March 3, 1897): 2. Faunce was speaking at a reception marking the twenty-fifth anniversary of the New York Society for the Suppression of Vice, which was founded by Anthony Comstock.
204. John D. Stevens suggested that a source of popular disapproval of the sensational treatment of the news "is that most adults realize they are morbidly fascinated by sex and violence and wish they were not. They have not resolved their ambiguous attitudes, and they dislike the media for forcing them to confront their own uncertainties." Stevens was speaking about twentieth century audiences, but his description may well have applied to readers in metropolitan New York at the end of the nineteenth century. See Stevens, "Sensationalism in Perspective," *Journalism History* 12, 3–4 (Autumn-Winter 1985): 79.
205. "The Past Year: Crusade of the Clubs," *Fourth Estate* (January 6, 1898): 3.
206. A columnist for the New York City gossip sheet *Town Topics* said, tongue in cheek, that sterner penalties should have been proposed. "I hope [the bill] will be amended as to make the first offense punishable by ten years' imprisonment, and the second by electrocution." See "The Saunterer," *Town Topics* 37, 9 (March 4, 1897): 13.
207. See "Ellsworth in Grim Earnest," *New York Tribune* (February 25, 1897): 3. "All sorts of enactments have poured from his fertile brain since, many years ago, he became a member of the Senate," the *Tribune* said of Ellsworth, "but none had attracted the slightest attention until yesterday, when he introduced the bill making it a misdemeanor to print a man's or a woman's portrait in a newspaper or magazine without his or her consent. Then, at one bound, Mr. Ellsworth fastened upon himself the eyes of the State."
208. See "Down on Cartoons," *Troy Press* (February 25, 1897): 4.
209. See, for example, "Gossip: About T.E. Ellsworth's Successor," *Lockport [NY] Union-Sun* (February 11, 1904): 1. The *Union-Sun* article stated: "His friends say that he introduced the bill through friendship for Platt and stuck to it through the worst storm of newspaper criticism that was ever heaped upon a legislator." Ellsworth died in 1904. Platt sent his condolences but did not attend Ellsworth's funeral.
210. "Platt at Work Against Cartoons," *New York Herald* (April 8, 1897): 7. The *Herald's* account speculated that Platt's support of the anti-cartoon measure "was enlisted by a certain New York newspaper which does not publish cartoons," a likely reference to the *Sun*.

211. "Wants the Press Muzzled," *New York Herald* (April 7, 1897): 5. The state senate's vote in favor of the Anti-Cartoon Bill was 35–14.

212. "Danger is Over," *Fourth Estate* (April 29, 1897): 3. In 1898, Ellsworth proposed another measure intended to restrain the press. His "Newspaper Bill" called for a year-long prison term and a $1,000 fine for anyone who "conducts or engages in the business of editing, publishing, printing, selling, distributing, or circulating any licentious, indecent, corrupt or depraved paper." See "New York Legislature," *New York Times* (March 2, 1898): 4. The 1898 measure died without a vote in the legislature. See "Newspaper Bill Dropped," *New York Times* (March 9, 1898): 4. Editors of the state's Republican-oriented newspapers told Republican legislators that supporting the measure would be "suicidal from a party standpoint," especially in an election year. See "Ellsworth Bill is Killed," *Fourth Estate* (March 10, 1898): 3.

213. James Fullarton Muirhead, the hard-to-please Briton who wrote *The Land of Contrasts* after visiting America in the late 1890s, disparaged illustrations in the U.S. press, saying, "In nine cases out of ten, the wood-cuts in an American paper are an insult to one's good taste and sense of propriety, and, indeed, form one of the chief reasons for classing the American daily press as distinctly lower than that of England." See Muirhead, *The Land of Contrasts*, 155.

214. "Facts Are the Best Argument," *New York Journal* (March 12, 1897): 6.

215. See "The Ellsworth Bill," *The Journalist* (April 24, 1897): 6–7.

216. "One Hundred Million Dollars Worth of Babies Coming This Winter," *New York Journal* (October 4, 1896): 43.

217. "Pass the Ellsworth Bill," *New York World* (March 10, 1897): 6.

218. Untitled editorial comment, *New York Sun* (April 9, 1897): 6.

219. "A Bill to Suppress Outrage," *New York Sun* (February 27, 1897): 6.

220. "If it is within the power of the Legislature this year to dictate to the press what pictures may or may not be published," the *Journal* declared, "what is to prevent the Legislature next year from assuming the right to decree what shall or shall not be written and printed in the newspapers?" See "Gov. Black and the Ellsworth Bill," *New York Journal* (April 22, 1897): 6.

221. Untitled editorial comment, *New York Times* (April 7, 1897): 6.

222. "The Public Wants Newspaper Pictures—Good Ones," *New York Herald* (March 8, 1897): 6.

223. See "The Ellsworth Bill," *The Journalist* (April 24, 1897): 6–7.

224. "Dreams of the Unthinking," *Fourth Estate* (March 11, 1897): 6

225. "Hasty Legislation Is Probably Checked," *Fourth Estate* (April 15, 1897): 6. The measure, the trade journal said, was "an effort on the part of certain … 'I-am-holier-than-thou' people to make a hue and cry amounting to self-exultation."

226. "Legislative Damphoolobia," *Fourth Estate* (March 4, 1897): 6

227. "Facts Are the Best Argument," *New York Journal* (March 12, 1897).

228. As Holbrook Jackson wrote, "Young bloods of the period delighted to *épater le bourgeois*, as the phrase went, and with experience a new kind of art came into vogue: the art of the shocking." See Jackson, *The Eighteen Nineties: A Review of Art and Ideas at the Close of the Nineteenth Century* (St. Clair Shores, MI: Scholarly Press, 1972; reprint of 1922 ed.), 126.

229. "The Past Year," *Fourth Estate* (January 6, 1898): 2.

230. This point was articulated quite well in a year-in-review sermon delivered by the Rev. Carleton F. Brown, a Unitarian minister in Helena, MT. He declared: "It is presumptuous for us to imagine we can write the record of 1897 as it will appear in the light of future history. For aught we know new eras of progress may date from that very year, whose significance has not dawned upon us." See "Year's Record," *Helena Daily Herald* (January 3, 1898): 4.

231. "The New Journalism," *The Journalist* (June 5, 1897): 51.

232. See "The Year's Scientific Progress," *New York Tribune* (December 31, 1897): 6.

Chapter 1

1. See Sherwin Cody, "America To-day—Some Signs of the Times," *Self Culture* 6, 1 (April 1897): 15. See also, "Moody Wants a Bonfire Here," *New York Herald* (January 11, 1897): 13. The *Herald* quoted the evangelist Dwight L. Moody as saying: "What a blaze we could have right here on Fifth Avenue if all the lewd books and newspapers with lewd illustrations, and works of so-called art, pictures of lewd women, were in the heap. I tell you the nation is decaying ... and what we want to do is to burn up the Sunday newspapers, and the art works and everything else vile."

2. "The American People Not Extravagant," *New York Sun* (August 20, 1897): 6.

3. See Caleb Clark, "American Extravagance," *Self Culture* 6, 4 (January 1898): 330.

4. A letter to the *New York Herald* in mid-August 1897, signed by "A Working Girl," prompted a revealing and spirited weeklong debate in the newspaper's letters column about the state of matrimony in America. The "Working Girl" wrote: "How many happy marriages are there? Few, very few; probably one in every hundred. Who is to blame? The woman, in most cases. ... Imagine being tied for life to a scolding wife and spoiled, cross children. Change all this, then I'll wager there will be fewer unmarried men—and women." See "Why Do Not Men Marry?" *New York Herald* (August 17, 1897): 5. Among the many replies was one penned by "Defender," who wrote: "But how about the fault finding

husband—he who comes home ... and growls at everything; who meets his wife at the door (where she has run to meet him) with a scowl and pays no attention to her face upturned for a welcoming kiss; growls at dinner and fails to appreciate any little loving attention paid him by his painstaking and devoted wife; neglects utterly to pay her the slightest compliments when she has taken especial pains to please him, either in her personal appearance or by adding to his comfort or pleasure, and conveys all his wishes to her in the form of a peremptory command?" See "Some Reasons Bachelors Exist: One Kind of Husband," *New York Herald* (August 19, 1897): 11. Easily the most pitiable letter came from "A Grief Stricken Wife," who wrote: "If men only knew the torture they inflict on their wives I am sure they would be more careful in their treatment of them. I have made such a hard struggle for my husband's approval in all things, but I have failed. I married my husband because I loved him, and wanted his companionship, kindness and affection. Oh! the bitter disappointment in this! My life with my husband has been one of harsh discipline. And at last he has deserted me and I find myself now in a cheap boarding house, completely crushed with my grief." See "More Reasons for Bachelors," *New York Herald* (August 23, 1897): 12. A streak of independent-mindedness emerged in some letters, notably the one signed by "Bruette Vaughn." She wrote: "I do not agree with 'A Working Girl' that it is the fault of married women that we have so many bachelors. Has it ever occurred to her that the fault may lie (and does) with women in general who are not married, and that it is she who objects to marrying these bachelors, owing to the fact that she is able to support herself? We women, although we cannot entirely reverse the laws made by man, ... can retain our womanliness, our modesty and our independence, although we are so-called 'new women,' and therefore we are not obliged, as heretofore, to marry for a home, for position, for protection, and can afford to wait until we meet a man who is up to our standard." See "Why Bachelors Are," *New York Herald* (August 22, 1897), sect. 3, p. 3.

5. See "Are We Unclean?" *Washington Evening Star* (August 28, 1897): 21.
6. See, for example, William Dean Howells, "The Modern American Mood," *Harper's* (July 1897), reprinted in Susan Harris Smith and Melanie Dawson, eds., *The American 1890s: A Cultural Reader* (Durham, NC: Duke University Press, 2000): 79. Howells wrote that "our present danger is not that we shall praise ourselves too much, but that we shall accuse ourselves too much and blame ourselves for effects from conditions that are the conditions of the whole world."
7. See John Henderson Garnsey, "The Demand for Sensational Journals." *Arena* (November 1897): 681–86.
8. E. S. Martin, "This Busy World," *Harper's Weekly* (March 13, 1897): 247.

9. "The Year's Scientific Progress," *New York Tribune* (December 31, 1897): 6. A year-end review published in the *Cincinnati Enquirer* noted: "Horseless carriages have ceased to be the butt of the cartoonist's pencil and the joke writer's pen. In three great cities of the world—London, Paris and New York—motor carriages have become such a familiar sight as to be an object of curiosity to none but country visitors." See "Retrospective: View of the Dying Year," *Cincinnati Enquirer* (December 26, 1897): 10.

10. "The Automobile," *New York Times* (August 23, 1897): 4.

11. "The Horseless Carriage," *Los Angeles Times* (October 4, 1897): 4.

12. "Aerial Navigation at Last," *New York Journal* (June 4, 1897): 8.

13. Edward Marshall, "Marvelous Invention of Mere Boy," *New York World* report republished in *Chicago Tribune* (August 8, 1897): 1. See also, "X Ray of Electricity is Discovered," *Chicago Tribune* (March 7, 1897): 33. The *New York Tribune* was far less sanguine about Marconi's work, predicting at the end of 1897: "Marconi's methods are not likely to come into extensive use." See "The Year's Scientific Progress," *New York Tribune* (December 31, 1897): 6. Marconi's first wireless demonstrations in London were conducted in 1896 and he received his first wireless patent in 1897. He and associates established the Wireless Telegraph and Signal Company Ltd. in London in July 1897. See Susan J. Douglas, *Inventing American Broadcasting, 1899–1922* (Baltimore: Johns Hopkins University Press, 1987), 17.

14. "Telephone Mania," *New York Tribune* (April 4, 1897), sect. 2, p. 10.

15. "Is the Age Growing Frivolous," *Boston Globe* (October 11, 1897): 6.

16. See Hartley Davis, "The Journalism of New York," *Munsey's Magazine* 24, 2 (November 1900): 217. Davis also declared (217): "The making of a metropolitan daily is the fiercest, bitterest, most exhausting struggle in the world."

17. See "The Noise Nuisance," *New York Journal* (May 22, 1897): 22.

18. "Concerning Leisure," *New York Tribune* (November 21, 1897): 6.

19. "Concerning Leisure," *New York Tribune* (November 21, 1897).

20. [Price Collier], *America and the Americans: From a French Point of View* (New York: Charles Scribner's Sons, 1897), 274.

21. [Collier], *America and the Americans*, 87.

22. "The Year and the World," *New York Tribune* (December 31, 1897): 6.

23. David Traxel, *1898: The Birth of the American Century* (New York: Vintage Books, 1998), 317.

24. See "Big Subway Is Open," *Chicago Tribune* (September 2, 1897): 7. "There was no formal opening," the *Tribune* reported. "The first car came along and was switched in, and went down the incline in the most commonplace, ordinary manner."

25. "First Car Off the Earth," *Boston Globe* extra edition (September 1, 1897): 1.
26. See John L. Wright, "Boston's Useful Subway," *New York Times* (October 10, 1897): 21.
27. Passengers and visitors whose frame of reference was the dark and smoke-choked London underground were surprised by what they did not find in the Boston subway. "No dark, ill-smelling subterranean terror is discovered," announced a writer for the *New York Times*, calling that difference "a surprising contrast to those in Europe." The Boston subway, he wrote, was equipped with "a complete system of electric lighting whereby the passenger upon the trolley car can see to read fine print." See Wright, "Boston's Useful Subway," *New York Times* (October 10, 1897). See also, "Topics of the Times," *New York Times* (September 10, 1897): 6. The *Times* commentary stated: "Boston's new subway ... has given convincing proof that the undoubted horrors of London's old underground railways need not be duplicated by similar enterprises in America."
28. "Boston's Subway Finished," *New York Times* (August 15, 1897): 10.
29. Cited in "The Library of Congress," *Washington Post* (November 4, 1897): 6.
30. Ambrose Bierce, "Prattle," *San Francisco Examiner* (August 26, 1894): 6. See also, Lawrence I. Berkove, ed., *Skepticism and Dissent: Selected Journalism from 1898–1901 by Ambrose Bierce:* (Ann Arbor, MI: UMI Research Press, 1986), iv.
31. Bierce, "Prattle," *San Francisco Examiner* (August 26, 1894). Bierce also wrote in the column, "Madness and suicide are advancing 'by leaps and bounds,' and wars were never so gigantic and reasonless as now."
32. Bierce, "Prattle," *San Francisco Examiner* (August 26, 1894).
33. See Ray Ginger, *Age of Excess: The United States From 1877 to 1914* (New York: Macmillan, 1965), 164–65.
34. See Joseph A. Fry, "Phases of Empire: Late Nineteenth-Century U.S. Foreign Relations," in Charles W. Calhoun, ed., *The Gilded Age: Essays on the Origins of Modern America* (Wilmington, DE: Scholarly Resources, 1996): 272.
35. Ginger, *Age of Excess*, 164.
36. Ginger, *Age of Excess*, 165.
37. "A Happy New Year to the New City and Its People," *New York Herald* (January 1, 1898): 8.
38. See Ginger, *Age of Excess*, 196–98.
39. "Lots of Hoe Presses," *Fourth Estate* (December 23, 1897): 8.
40. "1897 in St. Paul," *St. Paul Pioneer Press* (January 1, 1898): 4.
41. See "Retrospective," *Cincinnati Enquirer* (December 26, 1897).

42. See Richard Harmond, "Progress and Flight: An Interpretation of the American Cycle Craze of the 1890s," *Journal of Social History* 5, 2 (Winter 1971–72): 241–42.

43. E. S. Martin, the *Harper's Weekly* columnist, noted correctly that Andrée's expedition "seems to depend on forces beyond his control, and not to be estimated before hand. He may get a big story in a short time [by crossing the pole and landing safely on the other side]; he may take immense trouble and get only a little story; and he may have a valuable and astonishing experience and not succeed in getting home to share it with mankind." See Martin, "This Busy World," *Harper's Weekly* (July 17, 1897): 707.

44. Edward Adams-Ray, tr., *Andrée's Story: The Complete Record of His Polar Flight, 1897* (New York: Viking Press, 1930), 57–58.

45. Adams-Ray, *Andrée's Story*, 81, 228–32. See also, "Confirm Details of Finding Andree," *New York Times* (August 26, 1930): 6.

46. "Splendors of the Ballroom," *New York Times* (February 11, 1897): 1. The *Washington Post* also invoked the fairyland analogy, writing: "Tiny electric lights and mirrors were used in a bewildering and artistic manner all combining to transform the already beautiful hotel into an enchanting fairy house more beautiful than was ever dreamed of in fairyland." See "Her Social Triumph," *Washington Post* (February 11, 1897): 1.

47. "Her Social Triumph," *Washington Post* (February 11, 1897). See also, "Splendor at the Bradley Martin Ball," *Chicago Tribune* (February 11, 1897): 1.

48. "Mrs. Bradley Martin's Costume," *New York Times* (February 11, 1897): 2.

49. See "Splendor at the Bradley Martin Ball," *Chicago Tribune* (February 11, 1897). The *New York Times* was considerably more reserved in its judgment, stating: "Gossip has not yet brought a complete verdict on the affair, but there is a general impression that the ball, great as it was, did not equal expectations." See "Echoes of the Big Ball," *New York Times* (February 12, 1897): 3. E. S. Martin, the *Harper's Weekly* columnist, likewise was less than enthusiastic about the event, writing: "The ball was a great ball, an astonishing ball, but it was not really a great event. ... The people who went to it are handsome, lively people, but not, as a rule, people of exceptional distinction or importance." See Martin, "This Busy World," *Harper's Weekly* (February 20, 1897): 175.

50. "Decries the Big Ball," *Chicago Tribune* (January 24, 1897): 17.

51. Untitled editorial comment, *New York World* (February 16, 1897): 6.

52. Editors' comments cited in "A Sign of the Times – The Bradley Martin Ball," *New York World* (February 16, 1897): 4.

53. See "Cold Everywhere Except in Florida," *Chicago Tribune* (January 26, 1897): 1.

54. "Zero Weather," *Washington Evening Star* (January 26, 1897): 4.
55. See "Poor People Suffering From the Intense Cold," *Brooklyn Daily Eagle* (January 26, 1897): 16.
56. "Cold Everywhere Except in Florida," *Chicago Tribune* (January 26, 1897). The *Tribune* said, the "spine of the cold wave is … as rigid as an iceberg."
57. "Fires in Mid-Winter," *Washington Evening Star* (January 29, 1897): 6.
58. E. S. Martin, "This Busy World," *Harper's Weekly* (March 13, 1897): 247.
59. In Washington, D.C., the record low temperature for June 2—43 degrees—was set in 1897. See "Official Weather Data," *Washington Post* (June 3, 2003): B8.
60. See "Snow and Ice in June," *New York Journal* (June 2, 1897): 1, and "The Snowflakes of June," *New York Journal* (June 9, 1897): 16.
61. See Willis L. Moore, "No Known Cause," letter to the *New York Journal* (June 9, 1897): 16.
62. "Many Deaths in Chicago," *New York Times* (July 6, 1897): 1.
63. "Thirty-Six Die in Cincinnati," *New York Times* (July 7, 1897): 3.
64. See "More Than Fifty Horses Perish," *Chicago Tribune* (July 5, 1897): 2.
65. See "Parks Tell of the Heat's Torture," *Chicago Tribune* (July 5, 1897): 2.
66. "Parks Tell of the Heat's Torture," *Chicago Tribune* (July 5, 1897).
67. See Holbrook Jackson, *The Eighteen Nineties: A Review of Art and Ideas at the Close of the Nineteenth Century* (St. Clair Shores, MI: Scholarly Press, 1972; reprint of 1922 ed.), 22–23, and Asa Briggs and Daniel Snowman, eds. *Fins de Siècle: How Centuries End, 1400–2000* (New Haven, CT: Yale University Press, 1996), 175.
68. Jackson, *The Eighteen Nineties*, 22–23.
69. Briggs and Snowman, eds. *Fins de Siècle*, 175.
70. Cited in "The New Replies to the Old," *Fourth Estate* (December 31, 1896): 9.
71. Cited in "The Advance of Woman," *New York Sun* (February 7, 1897): sect. 3, p. 5.
72. "The Advance of Woman," *New York Sun* (February 7, 1897).
73. Susan B. Anthony, "The Status of Woman, Past, Present, and Future," *Arena* 17 (May 1897), reprinted in Susan Harris Smith and Melanie Dawson, eds., *The American 1890s: A Cultural Reader* (Durham, NC: Duke University Press, 2000), 137.
74. "Divorce in the United States," *Public Opinion* 23, 6 (October 14, 1897): 493. The article noted a weakening of the social prejudice against divorce in southern states, adding: "But there is a movement throughout the south toward independent thinking and the reorganizing of the individual life, when necessary for happiness."
75. "Divorce in the United States," *Public Opinion* 23, 6 (October 14, 1897).

76. "Divorce in the United States," *Public Opinion* 23, 6 (October 14, 1897): 494.

77. "The Lot of the Old Maid," *New York Sun* (December 5, 1897): sect. 2, p. 5.

78. Anthony, "The Status of Woman," in Smith and Dawson, eds., *The American 1890s*, 138.

79. Anthony, "The Status of Woman," in Smith and Dawson, eds., *The American 1890s*, 138.

80. "She Runs for Congress," *New York Sun* (November 28, 1897): sect. 3, p. 5.

81. "She Runs for Congress," *New York Sun* (November 28, 1897). Ricker also said: "The average woman would not wabble politically so much as the average man does."

82. See Harmond, "Progress and Flight," 240.

83. Ellen Maury Slayden, *Washington Wife: Journal of Ellen Maury Slayden from 1897–1919* (New York: Harper & Row, 1963), 7.

84. Harmond, "Progress and Flight," 237.

85. See "Big Drop in Cycle Prices," *New York Journal* (June 30, 1897): 3. The *Journal* reported that the country's largest bicycle maker, Pope Manufacturing, had cut the price of its $100 model by 25 percent.

86. See Harmond, "Progress and Flight," 236.

87. "Putting Aside the Wheels," *New York Sun* (December 21, 1897): 6.

88. See "The Bicycle and Its Changes," *Philadelphia Evening Bulletin* (April 10, 1897): 28. The *Evening Bulletin* elaborated on the marvel of cycling, stating: "Just think of what it means, what a wonder it is to put at the service of men, women, boys and girls a … mechanism that is at once as strong as a horse (figuratively); as light as a feather (comparatively), as swift as a bird (almost) and as comfortable as a carriage or a rocking chair."

89. "The Wheel Annihilates Distance," *Philadelphia Item* (May 11, 1897): 4.

90. "The Age of Wheeling," *New York Tribune* (August 8, 1897): 6.

91. See, for example, "Putting Aside the Wheels," *New York Sun* (December 21, 1897). See also, Henry Collins Brown, *In the Nineties* (Hastings-on-Hudson, NY: Valentine's Manual, 1928), 54.

92. "A Smashing of Records," *Philadelphia Item* (October 11, 1897): 4.

93. "The Bicycle," *New York Herald* (March 5, 1897): 8. The *Herald's* commentary was prescient in suggesting that "there is something better than the bicycle in the future; possibly a horseless carriage which will convert us all into globe trotters in companies of ten, or possibly a balloon or flying machine will enable us to loaf among the stars. We are grateful for what we have, but, like Oliver Twist, we should like a little more."

94. "The Value of Bicycles to Newspaper Men," *Fourth Estate* (January 10, 1895): 4.

95. "The Bicycle Not For Sunday Use," *New York Journal* (April 16, 1897): 1.
96. See "Washington News Notes: Bicycling and Beer," *New York Tribune* (August 5, 1897): 7.
97. See "Note and Comment," *Fourth Estate* (May 23, 1895): 6.
98. E.S. Martin, "This Busy World," *Harper's Weekly* (June 12, 1897): 583.
99. See "Hard Times: Some Causes and Alleviations," *Self Culture* 4, 1 (October 1896): 9.
100. "The End of the Bicycle Race," *New York Journal* (December 13, 1897): 6.
101. See "The Bicycle Race," *Literary Digest* 15, 34 (December 18, 1897): 998. The *Washington Post* called the marathon "an exhibition of unadulterated brutality [that] has no parallel. Football is pampered luxury compared with it." See "Six-day Bicycle Races," *Washington Post* (December 12, 1897): 6.
102. Century runs still exert a measure of appeal for cyclists. See Rita Zeidner, "Get Out: Ride A Century," *Washington Post* (September 11, 2005): M4. The *Post* article noted that "no century is a walk in the park. To be safe, any rider should have built up a fitness base over time and logged at least several hundred miles in the weeks leading up to the event."
103. "The Wheel Annihilates Distance," *Philadelphia Item* (May 11, 1897).
104. "Double Century for Manhattans," *New York Herald* (July 12, 1897): 11.
105. "She Is a Century Rider," *New York Sun* (January 17, 1897): 8.
106. "Women and the Bicycle," *New York Herald* (October 5, 1897): 10.
107. See, for example, Marguerite Merington, "Woman and the Bicycle," *Scribner's* 17 (June 1895), reprinted in Smith and Dawson, eds., *The American 1890s: A Cultural Reader*, 290. Merington wrote: "The occasional denunciation of the pastime as unwomanly is fortunately lost in the general approval that a new and wholesome recreation has been found, whose pursuit adds joy and vigor to the dowry of the race."
108. Harmond, "Progress and Flight," 244.
109. Automobiles were noticeably more common in Europe, particularly in France and Germany, in 1897, owing to the greater expanse of paved and improved roadways. See "Topics of the Times," *New York Times* (May 6, 1897): 6. See also, See "Horseless Carriages," *New York Sun* (July 11, 1897): sect. 1, p. 3.
110. One of the oldest names in American car manufacturing, Oldsmobile, dates to 1897 and the company R. E. Olds founded in Michigan. Oldsmobiles were manufactured until 2004. In Britain, the predecessor of the Royal Automobile Club was founded in 1897.
111. See "Horseless Carriages," *New York Sun* (July 11, 1897). The *Sun* also noted that the emergence of the automobile would mean the "noise of

horses' iron-clad hoofs would be abolished and the greatest source of fouling the streets would be removed."

112. See "Motor Carriage Here," *Washington Post* (April 3, 1897): 3.
113. See "Without Horses: Gasoline Carriage Invented in Los Angeles," *Los Angeles Times* (May 31, 1897): 3.
114. "Without Horses," *Los Angeles Times* (31 May 1897). The *Times* speculated that it probably would "not be long before a factory is established in Los Angeles for the manufacture of motor wagons."
115. Without Horses," *Los Angeles Times* (May 31, 1897).
116. Without Horses," *Los Angeles Times* (May 31, 1897).
117. "Horseless Wagons Tabooed," *Washington Post* (August 13, 1897): 10.
118. "Horseless Wagons Tabooed," *Washington Post* (August 13, 1897).
119. But not everyone of course was persuaded the horse was doomed. The columnist E. S. Martin declared in *Harper's Weekly* in May 1897: "A good deal of nonsense is written and printed about the prospective elimination of the horse from the landscape of cities. ... If a new species of animal could be invented that was better suited than the horse for hauling carriages on asphalt, the horse might be crowded out. But there is no prospect of the discovery of such a beast. ... Very likely the steam or electric carriage will have some vogue, but it is an ugly vehicle, and probably never can compete in style with the carriage that is hauled by horses." See Martin, "This Busy World," *Harper's Weekly* (May 1, 1897): 434.
120. "Horseless Carriages," *New York Sun* (July 11, 1897).
121. "Horseless Carriages," *New York Sun* (July 11, 1897).
122. "The Automobile," *New York Times* (August 23, 1897).
123. "The Automobile," *New York Times* (August 23, 1897).
124. See "Topics of the Times," *New York Times* (May 6, 1897).
125. See E. S. Martin, "This Busy World," *Harper's Weekly* (April 24, 1897): 410.
126. See S. P. Langley, "The 'Flying-Machine,'" *McClure's* 9, 2 (June 1897): 659.
127. Langley, "The 'Flying-Machine,'" 659.
128. See, among others, Seth Shulman, *Unlocking the Sky: Glenn Hammond Curtiss and the Race to Invent the Airplane* (New York: Perennial, 2003), 8.
129. Cited in Langley, "The 'Flying-Machine,'" 659.
130. Langley, "The 'Flying-Machine,'" 660.
131. Langley, "The 'Flying-Machine.'"
132. "Aerial Navigation at Last," *New York Journal* (June 4, 1897): 8.
133. Martin, "This Busy World," *Harper's Weekly* (June 12, 1897).
134. See "Flying Machine Tried and Fails," *Chicago Tribune* (December 9, 1903): 1, and Shulman, *Unlocking the Sky*, 14.
135. See Shulman, *Unlocking the Sky*, 16–17.

136. Cited in "A Flyer With Langley," *Washington Post* (December 17, 1903): 6.
137. Cited in "A Flyer With Langley," *Washington Post* (December 17, 1903).
138. "Prof. Langley's Ill-Luck," *Chicago Tribune* (December 10, 1903): 6.
139. See "Hundreds See Airship at Omaha," *Chicago Tribune* (April 7, 1897): 1.
140. E. S. Martin, "This Busy World," *Harper's Weekly* (April 17, 1897): 383.
141. Martin, "This Busy World," *Harper's Weekly* (April 24, 1897).
142. "Live Topics of Today," *Chicago Tribune* (April 13, 1897): 6.
143. "Live Topics of Today," *Chicago Tribune* (April 13, 1897). "Aeronaut" was the term commonly applied in 1897 to scientists and others experimenting in aerial navigation.
144. "Edison Scoffs at the Airship," *Chicago Tribune* (April 20, 1897): 4.
145. See Rene Bache, "Light on the Airships," *Washington Post* (May 2, 1897): 28.
146. See Percival Lowell, *Mars and Its Canals* (New York: Macmillan, 1907), 173. Lowell wrote that the "discovery" of Martian canals was "so unprecedented ... that the scientific world was at first loath to accept it. Only persistent corroboration has finally broken down distrust."
147. See David Y. Hughes, "*The War of the Worlds* in the Yellow Press," *Journalism Quarterly* 43, 4 (Winter 1966): 645. As Hughes noted, the *Boston Post* also published localized excerpts of *War of the Worlds*.
148. "Gold Strikes in Alaska," *New York Times* (July 17, 1897): 2.
149. "Gold Fields of Yukon: Klondike Diggings the Mecca of the Placer Miners," *Washington Post* (May 23, 1897): 27.
150. See "The Alaska Gold Fields," *New York Tribune* (January 24, 1897): 6. The *Tribune* said the U.S. Geological Survey report confirmed "the stories of the last few years about rich gold fields along the Yukon River." See also, "The Alaska Gold Mines," *New York Times* (January 31, 1897): 13.
151. See "Swarming After Gold," *New York Sun* (April 25, 1897), sect. 3, p. 6.
152. See "Big Gold Strikes in Alaska," *New York Times* (July 15, 1897): 1.
153. "More Gold From Klondike Mines," *New York Herald* (July 18, 1897), sect. 1, p. 5.
154. "Ton and One-Half of Gold," *New York Sun* (July 18, 1897): sect. 1, p. 1.
155. Pierre Berton, *The Klondike Fever: The Life and Death of the Last Great Gold Rush* (New York: Knopf, 1958), 100.
156. Berton, *Klondike Fever*, 102.
157. See Frederick Palmer, *In the Klondyke: Including an Account of a Winter's Journey to Dawson* (New York: Scribner's Sons, 1899), 199.
158. "More Gold From Klondike Mines," *New York Herald* (July 18, 1897).
159. "Off For the Gold Fields," *New York Herald* (July 19, 1897): 4.
160. "Off For the Gold Fields," *New York Herald* (July 19, 1897).
161. Berton, *Klondike Fever*, 108.

162. "Talks with the Miners," *New York Times* (July 19, 1897): 2. Some prospectors in the Klondike believed Berry's comments encouraged "an unreasonable stampede of tenderfeet" to the region. See "Wealth from the Klondyke," *New York Times* (September 16, 1897): 3. A report from Seattle in mid-September said: "It is asserted that if Clarence Berry were in Dawson City to-day he would be lynched, for the miners … blame him for the foolhardy stampede of scantily supplied people to the district, imperiling the lives of all, on account of the food famine that has already begun." See "News from the Klondike," *New York Times* (September 13, 1897): 3.

163. Ken Coates, "Introduction," in Tappan Adney, *The Klondike Stampede* (Vancouver: UBC Press, 1994; reprint of 1899 ed.): xvii.

164. See "Klondyke Gold Discoveries," *Literary Digest* 15, 14 (July 31, 1897): 397.

165 "Talks with the Miners," *New York Times* (July 19, 1897). In keeping with the contradictory character of the early coverage of the gold rush, the *Times* report then quoted Berry as saying: "But then grit, perseverance, and pluck will probably reward the hard worker with a comfortable income for life."

166. See "Klondyke Miners Tell How They Made Fortunes in the Land of Ice," *New York Journal* (August 22, 1897): 36–37.

167. See, for example, "Dare Death for Glittering Gold," *New York Herald* (August 30, 1897): 3. The *Herald* report warned that stampeders "will find themselves battling for life against hunger and cold, cut off from all chance of relief from the outside world." See also, "Hungry Men at Dawson," *New York Sun* (November 29, 1897): 1, and "Dawson's Food Scarcity," *New York Commercial Advertiser* (December 27, 1897): 1.

168. See, for example, "Leaving the Klondike," *New York Sun* (October 25, 1897):1, and "Back From Dawson City: 97 Men and One Woman Brave The Wintry Weather," *New York Sun* (December 29, 1897): 5.

169. See, for example, "Gold," *New York Times* (July 19, 1897): 4. The *Times'* editorial stated: "The conditions of mining in the whole Yukon region are terribly severe. The season of warm weather is short, and the gravel, except at the surface, is frozen the year round. The journey to the Klondike is long and trying, and food and supplies cost more money than at any other place in the civilized world."

170. "Gold Seekers Throng Steamers," *New York Herald* (July 21, 1897): 5.

171. "Klondyke and the Gold Fever," *Self Culture* 5, 6 (September 1897): 543.

172. "The Alaska Gold-Hunters," *Harper's Weekly* (July 31, 1897): 750.

173. Berton, *Klondike Fever*, 431.

174. "The Heirs of the Klondike," in "American Survey," *Economist* (February 15, 1997): 25.

175. "Heirs of the Klondike," *Economist* (February 15, 1997).
176. "Heirs of the Klondike," *Economist* (February 15, 1997).
177. "Airships for the Klondike," *Philadelphia Inquirer* (November 26, 1897): 1.
178. See Berton, *Klondike Fever*, 131. See also, "To the Gold Fields by Balloon," *New York Times* (July 23, 1897): 2.
179. See, for example, "To the Klondike by Bicycle," *Boston Globe* (September 6, 1897): 5.
180. See "Reminiscences of Mrs. Scovel," n.d. typescript; Sylvester Scovel papers, Missouri Historical Society Archives, St. Louis, MO.
181. Adney, *Klondike Stampede*, 124.
182. Berton, *Klondike Fever*, 154.
183. Adney, *Klondike Stampede*, 125.
184. Adney, *Klondike Stampede*, 124. No one knows how many horses and other pack animals died on the White Pass Trail, but fatalities were certainly in the thousands. See Julie Johnson, *A Wild Discouraging Mess: The History of the White Pass Unit of the Klondike Gold Rush National Historical Park* (Anchorage: U.S. Department of the Interior, 2003), 83.
185. Jack London, *The God of His Fathers and Other Stories* (Freeport, NY: Books for Libraries Press, 1969; reprint of 1901 ed.), 79.
186. See William J. Jones, "Very Rich Strikes," *Los Angeles Times* (January 16, 1898): B1.
187. "Glistens With Gold: Klondiker's Christmas Tree," *Chicago Times-Herald* (December 25, 1897).
188. See Ivan Musicant, *Empire by Default: The Spanish-American War and the Dawn of the American Century* (New York: Henry Holt and Co., 1998), 50, 70–71.
189. Lewis L. Gould, *The Spanish-American War and President McKinley* (Lawrence: University of Kansas Press, 1980), 31.
190. "All Hail to the Year '98! The Newcomer Rich in Promise," *New York Herald* (January 2, 1898): sect. 5, p. 2.
191. "All Hail to the Year '98!" *New York Herald* (January 2, 1898).
192. Bennett Burleigh, "The Greco-Turkish War As Seen By an Eye-Witness," *Self Culture* 5, 6 (September 1897): 514.
193. Stephen Crane, "Greeks Waiting at Themopylae," *New York Journal* (24 May 1897), reprinted in R. W. Stallman and E. R. Hagemann, *The War Dispatches of Stephen Crane* (New York: New York University Press, 1964), 48.
194. See, for example, "All Islam to be Roused," *New York Sun* (April 24, 1897): 1.
195. "The Revival of Islam," *New York Times* (June 13, 1897): 18.

196. "Lynchings in 1897," *Chicago Tribune* (January 1, 1898): 20. The following table presents the *Tribune*'s data on lynchings during the 1890s.

Lynchings in the United States: 1891–1900

Year	Number	Year	Number
1891	192	1896	131
1892	235	1897	166
1893	200	1898	127
1894	190	1899	107
1895	171	1900	115

Source: From "Lychings, Hangings, and Embezzlements of the Year," *Chicago Tribune* (January 1, 1901): 23.

197. "Hangings in 1897," *Chicago Tribune* (January 1, 1898): 20.
198. "Lynchings in 1897," *Chicago Tribune* (January 1, 1898). Ida B. Wells, an African American journalist who campaigned internationally to bring attention to lynchings in the South, claimed that white women often charged rape or sexual assault to conceal clandestine liaisons with black men. See Stewart E. Tolnay and E. M. Beck, *A Festival of Violence: An Analysis of Southern Lynchings, 1882–1930* (Urbana: University of Illinois Press, 1995), 207. Not all black leaders at the end of the nineteenth century were inclined to endorse Wells' activism, however. See Christopher Waldrep, *The Many Faces of Judge Lynch: Extralegal Violence and Punishment in America* (New York: Palgrave Macmillan, 2002), 124. Alexander Manly, editor of the Wilmington, NC, *Record* made a similar charge in 1898—and whites retaliated by destroying his newspaper office in a rampage that drove many blacks from the city. Cited in Jeffrey J. Crow, "Cracking the Solid South: Populism and the Fusionist Interlude," in Lindley S. Butler and Alan D. Watson, eds., *The North Carolina Experience: An Interpretative and Documentary History* (Chapel Hill: University of North Carolina Press, 1984): 349.
199. That lynchings were sometimes carried out to punish trivial crimes is also noted in Tolnay and Beck, *A Festival of Violence*, 19.
200. "Lynched for Mule Stealing," *New York Sun* (November 26, 1897): 1. The *Sun*'s report stated: "Why lynching should have been resorted to under the circumstances [of stealing a mule] is a mystery."
201. "Lynchings in 1897," *Chicago Tribune* (January 1, 1898).
202. "Lynchings in 1897," *Chicago Tribune* (January 1, 1898).
203. "Innocent Man Lynched by a Virginia Mob," *New York Herald* (September 8, 1897): 16.
204. See "Lynching in the South," *New York Herald* (August 23, 1897): 8. The *Herald*'s editorial decried the spread of lynchings in southern states, stating: "The most serious aspect of it is that the lawlessness flourishes and spreads with impunity. There is no attempt to punish the rioters guilty of it."
205. "Lynchings in 1897," *Chicago Tribune* (January 1, 1898).

206. "Lynchings in 1897," *Chicago Tribune* (January 1, 1898).
207. According to data compiled by the Tuskegee Institute, 4,743 people were killed by lynching in forty-five states, from 1882 to 1968. Seventy-three percent of the victims (N = 3,446) were black and twenty-seven percent (N = 1,297) were white. One-third of all lynching victims were killed in Mississippi, Georgia, and Texas. Data cited in "Mob Injustice," *Washington Post* (June 19, 2005): B4. See also, Tolnay and Beck, *A Festival of Violence*, 17.
208. "What Lynching Accomplishes," *Philadelphia Inquirer* (November 19, 1897): 6.
209. "The Lynching Fever," *New York Times* (June 11, 1897): 6.
210. See Tolnay and Beck, *A Festival of Violence*, 19.
211. Tolnay and Beck asserted that blacks were less likely to be lynching victims following enactment of measures across the South that effectively disfranchised black men. See Tolnay and Beck, *A Festival of Violence*, 184. For a discussion of the role of a prominent North Carolina newspaper editor in that state's disfranchisement campaigns in 1898 and 1900, see W. Joseph Campbell, "'One of the Fine Figures in American Journalism': A Closer Look at Josephus Daniels of the *Raleigh News & Observer*," *American Journalism* 16, 4 (Fall 1999): 37–56.
212. See Tolnay and Beck, *A Festival of Violence*, 18.
213. Cited in "Mrs. Felton Favors Lynching," *New York Sun* (August 12, 1897): 1. The *Sun's* report said Mrs. Felton's audience enthusiastically welcomed her advocacy of lynching, "shouting themselves hoarse and almost delirious," and refusing "to let the speaker go on for several minutes."
214. "Is Lynching Ever Justified? Governor Taylor Defends the South," *New York Journal* (June 6, 1897): 58.
215. The *New York Times* did note: "It may be admitted that in regions where the blacks equal or outnumber the whites there is occasion for some very special terror of the law to restrain the blacks from a kind of crime to which they are especially prone." See "Civilization in Ohio," *New York Times* (June 9, 1897): 6.
216. "Lynch Law Again," *Philadelphia Item* (June 10, 1897): 4.
217. "The Lynching Fever," *New York Times* (June 11, 1897).
218. "The Lesson of Lynching," *New York Journal* (June 5, 1897): 8. The *Washington Post* declared: "Until Legislatures provide penalties which public opinion accepts as adequate, and until the courts convince the people that they can be relied upon to dispense speedy and unerring justice, communities will continue to protect themselves by punishing, with their own hands, the one crime which is unspeakable and unendurable." The *Post* was referring to black-on-white sexual assault. See "Human Nature in Ohio," *Washington Post* (June 6, 1897): 6.
219. "Civilization in Ohio," *New York Times* (June 9, 1897).
220. "'Hang the Brute,'" *Los Angeles Times* (June 3, 1897): 2.

221. "Ohio Roused By A Negro Lynching: Mob Law Besmirches That State's Abolition Fame," *New York Journal* (June 5, 1897): 1, 4.

222. The use of sledgehammers to batter down jailhouse doors and break cell locks was not uncommon among lynch mobs. See Waldrep, *The Many Faces of Judge Lynch*, 94.

223. "Ohio Roused By A Negro Lynching," *New York Journal* (June 5, 1897): 4. See also "Fired on the Lynchers," *New York Tribune* (June 5, 1897): 1.

224. The *Journal*'s report said the mayor ordered the reinforcements to leave after learning that the mob had gathered a large amount of explosives and was planning to blow up the jail, Mitchell, and his defenders. See Ohio Roused By A Negro Lynching," *New York Journal* (June 5, 1897): 4.

225. "Ohio Roused By A Negro Lynching," *New York Journal* (June 5, 1897).

226. "Ohio Roused By A Negro Lynching," *New York Journal* (June 5, 1897).

227. "Ohio Roused By A Negro Lynching," *New York Journal* (June 5, 1897).

228. See "Mob Eager for Relics," *Chicago Tribune* (June 5, 1897): 2.

229. "Ohio Roused By A Negro Lynching," *New York Journal* (June 5, 1897): 4.

230. "Ohio Roused By A Negro Lynching," *New York Journal* (June 5, 1897): 4.

231. "Fired on the Lynchers," *New York Tribune* (June 5, 1897).

232. "A Disgraceful Outbreak," *New York Tribune* (June 5, 1897): 6.

233. See "The Urbana Lynching," *Los Angeles Times* (June 5, 1897): 6. The *Times* also said: "The militia were justified in firing upon the mob. They were acting as agents and defenders of law, while the 'citizens' composing the mob were seeking to commit murder."

234. Cited in "Topics of the Day: Lynch-Law in Ohio—and Elsewhere," *Literary Digest* 15, 8 (June 19, 1897): 212.

235. "Martin Not Guilty," *Chicago Tribune* (March 10, 1898): 8.

236. "The Football Season," *Chicago Times-Herald* (October 23, 1897): 8.

237. "Football Season's Climax," *New York Times* (November 20, 1897): 4. The *Times* reported the next day that a section of one hundred or so seats was unoccupied during the Yale–Princeton game, "a monument to the thwarted purposes of speculators, who were left with dearly purchased tickets on their hands." See "How the Game Was Played," *New York Times* (November 21, 1897): 2.

238. Yale played two tie games in 1897. Its overall record was nine victories and two ties. See Tom Perrin, *Football: A College History* (Jefferson, NC: McFarland & Co., 1987), 30.

239. See "Summary of Football," *New York Sun* (November 28, 1897): sect. 1, p. 11.

240. See "Hard Fight for the Quakers: Forced to Play Furiously to Defeat Cornell," *New York Sun* (November 26, 1897): 1. In 1897, a touchdown counted four points and an after-goal try counted two points. Field goals counted five points.

241. The injuries often suffered by collegiate football players in the early twenty-first century evoked the hazards of the game at the turn of the twentieth century. See "The Brutal Truth About College Sports," *Wall Street Journal* (September 15, 2005): D7. The article reported that perhaps half of the players at the level of collegiate football would suffer injuries requiring surgery at some point during their collegiate careers.

242. See "Eight Players Killed," *Chicago Tribune* (November 25, 1897): 6.

243. "Wild Over Football," *Chicago Tribune* (November 29, 1896): 13.

244. Perrin, *Football: A College History*, 27.

245. "A Law to Make Football a Crime," *New York Journal* (November 7, 1897).

246. "Fatal Tackle: Football Player Died From Injury," *Boston Globe* (November 1, 1897): 2.

247. "Blow to Football," *New York Herald* (November 9, 1897): 14. The *Herald* said the proposed ban on football was essentially a way for rural Georgia legislators to attack and embarrass the university, which they believed had become too aristocratic and inhospitable to would-be students from the state's farming regions.

248. "Anti-Football Bill Vetoed," *New York Times* (December 8, 1897): 2.

249. "Harvard Favors the Sport," *New York Herald* (November 9, 1897): 14. The *Herald* account indirectly quoted Oliver Wendell Holmes, then a judge on the Massachusetts Supreme Court, as saying that a few broken bones and an occasional death could be excused because football helped developed such qualities as courage and perseverance.

250. "Princeton Likes the Game," *New York Herald* (November 9, 1897): 14. The *Herald*'s account noted: "It is true that at one time in the early stage of Princeton's athletic development the faculty did not want the game played, but all such thoughts have been abandoned even by the most pessimistic members of the corps of instructors. ... Rain or shine, wet or dry, there is always a large percentage of the faculty members at practice, and the large games are attended by them in full force."

251. "Ministers Openly Denounce the Game of Football," *Chicago Times-Herald* (October 12, 1897): 1.

252. Untitled editorial comment, *Chicago Tribune* (October 25, 1897).

253. Perrin, *Football: A College History*, 54–55.

254. See Bill James, *The New Bill James Historical Baseball Abstract* (New York: Free Press, 2001), 66.

255. See T. H. Murnane, "Nervy Nick: 30,000 Persons See Him Pitch Great Ball," *Boston Globe* (September 28, 1897): 1, 5. Murnane reported (5) that about 5,000 other spectators watched the game for free, from rooftops near the Baltimore park.

256. Murnane, "Nervy Nick," *Boston Globe* (September 28, 1897).

257. Murnane, "Nervy Nick," *Boston Globe* (September 28, 1897).

258. Murnane, "Nervy Nick," *Boston Globe* (September 28, 1897). Both teams committed four errors, which was not especially unusual in the 1890s. Not counting error-related unearned runs, the score was 9–5 in Boston's favor.
259. "Echoes of the Game," *Boston Globe* (September 28, 1897): 5.
260. "Disgraceful Fight on the Boston Baseball Grounds," *Boston Post* (August 7, 1897): 1.
261. "Disgraceful Fight," *Boston Post* (August 7, 1897).
262. "Disgraceful Fight," *Boston Post* (August 7, 1897). Baseball umpires in the late nineteenth century were empowered to impose fines immediately, and often did so when their authority was challenged.
263. "Disgraceful Fight," *Boston Post* (August 7, 1897): 3.
264. "Disgraceful Fight," *Boston Post* (August 7, 1897): 3.
265. "Are the Days of Professional Baseball Numbered?" *New York Herald* (July 18, 1897): sect. 1, p. 8. The *Herald*'s editorial declared: "Baseball as a livelihood for professional players will be a thing of the past if there is not better discipline preserved on the field both among teams and the umpires."
266. See, for example, "Baseball Endangered," *New York Sun* (August 11, 1897): 6, and "Baseball Endangered," *New York Sun* (August 15, 1897): 6.
267. "Rowydism in Base Ball," *Philadelphia Times* (September 26, 1897): 4.
268. John B. Foster, "Kick Themselves Out of Victory," *New York Journal* (June 2, 1897): 11. The *Journal* account described a game forfeited by Pittsburgh to New York because its players argued incessantly with the umpire's call.
269. See "Kickers on the Diamond," *New York Sun* (August 8, 1897), sect. 2, p. 6.
270. "Kickers on the Diamond," *New York Sun* (August 8, 1897).
271. "Umpire Hurst Arrested," *Washington Post* (August 5, 1897): 8.
272. "Tim Hurst Fined $100," *Washington Post* (August 12, 1897): 8.
273. [Collier,] *America and the Americans*, 76.
274. See "Record Time: J.J. McDermott Wins the 'Marathon' Race," *Boston Globe* (April 20, 1897): 1, 7.
275. "Beat the Greeks," *Boston Post* (April 20, 1897): 1.
276. "Record Time," *Boston Globe* (April 20, 1897): 1.
277. The crowd estimate appeared in "Beat the Greeks," *Boston Post* (April 20, 1897): 8.
278. "Record Time," *Boston Globe* (April 20, 1897): 7.
279. See "Table 15—Number and Circulation of Newspapers and Periodicals, Classified According to Period of Issue, 1850 to 1900," *Twelfth Census of the United States, Taken in the Year 1900: Manufacturers, Part III* (Washington, DC: United States Census Office, 1902), 1046.
280. See "Table 29—Statistics Relating to Daily Publications in 50 Cities, 1900," *Twelfth Census of the United States, Taken in the Year 1900: Manufacturers, Part III* (Washington, DC: United States Census Office, 1902), 1051.

Chapter 2

1. "The Best 'Ad' in the City," *New York Times* (4 October 1896): 8.
2. "The Best 'Ad' in the City," *New York Times* (4 October 1896).
3. See, "Advertising Mediums: New York Times," *Fourth Estate* (October 15, 1896): 9.
4. No newspaper has won more Pulitzer Prizes than the *New York Times*. Through 2005, the *Times* had received ninety-one Pulitzers, the most coveted award in print journalism in the United States.
5. Richard F. Shepard, *The Paper's Papers: A Reporter's Journey Through the Archives of the New York Times* (New York: Times Books, 1996), 44.
6. Gerald W. Johnson, *An Honorable Titan: A Biographical Study of Adolph S. Ochs* (Westport, CT: Greenwood Press, 1970), 156–57,
7. See "The New Spirit," *New York Times* (September 25, 1901): 8.
8. Tunku Varadarajan, "Hooray for the Lowbrow Media," *Wall Street Journal* (July 17, 2001): A18.
9. "The Development of a New Idea in Journalism," *New York Journal* (October 3, 1897): 38–39.
10. "The Journalism that Does Things," *New York Journal* (October 13, 1897): 6.
11. Lincoln Steffens, *The Autobiography of Lincoln Steffens* (New York: Harcourt, Brace and Co., 1931), 313–14.
12. Steffens, *The Autobiography of Lincoln Steffens*, 314.
13. Steffens, *The Autobiography of Lincoln Steffens*, 340.
14. See David Nasaw, *The Chief: The Life of William Randolph Hearst* (Boston, Houghton Mifflin: 2000), 40.
15. Nasaw, *The Chief*, 63.
16. "Journalistic Mercenaries," *Fourth Estate* (July 11, 1895): 6.
17. "Journalistic Mercenaries," *Fourth Estate* (July 11, 1895).
18. "The advent of young Hearst is an event of the greatest importance, for he means what he says, says what he means and states that he is here to stay," *Fourth Estate* declared in October 1895. "Hearst is young and ambitious. He is worth watching. He wants to prove that he has more than his millions to back him. He is in New York to hustle and not to buy gold bricks. If he can, as he intends to, push the *Journal* into the first rank, he will have proved the power of his purpose and achieved his ambitions." See "W. R. Hearst Here," *Fourth Estate* (October 10, 1895): 1
19. Richard Kluger, *The Paper: The Life and Death of the* New York Herald Tribune (New York: Knopf, 1986), 160.
20. Kluger, *The Paper*, 160–61.
21. Kluger, *The Paper*, 144–45.
22. The *Harper's Weekly* item was reprinted in *The Journalist* as "Americans We Are Interested In," *The Journalist* (June 12, 1897). The article also said:

"Mr. Bennett is one of two American citizens whose preference for living abroad excites a good deal of interest in the minds of their countrymen. The other one is Mr. William Waldorf Astor. … There seems to be so much to interest and retain them in this country that the average American is surprised at the continuousness of their preference to live elsewhere."

23. See, for example, "Mr. Pulitzer's Retirement," *Washington Post* (October 16, 1890): 4. See also, "Mr. Pulitzer Nearly Blind," *Washington Post* (June 17, 1888): 1.
24. Joseph Pulitzer, letter to John Norris, August 4, 1897, Pulitzer papers, Library of Congress, Washington, DC.
25. Pulitzer to Norris, August 4, 1897, Pulitzer papers.
26. Pulitzer, letter to Don C. Seitz, December 23, 1897, Pulitzer papers, Library of Congress, Washington, DC.
27. Pulitzer, letter to Seitz, August 25, 1897, Pulitzer papers, Library of Congress, Washington, DC.
28. "A Question and the Answer," *The Journalist* (February 12, 1898): 176.
29. Even the celebrated Nellie Bly (Elizabeth Cochrane) left the *World*, claiming Pulitzer had not rewarded her as he had promised, following her exploit of traveling around the world in seventy-two days, eclipsing the fictional record of the hero of Jules Verne's *Around the World in Eighty Days*. See Denis Brian, *Pulitzer: A Life* (New York: John Wiley & Sons, 2001), 161.
30. Nasaw, *The Chief*, 105.
31. See "A Question and the Answer," *The Journalist* (February 12, 1898). *The Journalist*'s commentary also said Pulitzer "drove away his best and most loyal friends, and, by his system of espionage and tale-bearing [imposed at the *World*], … made it impossible for a self respecting man to remain on his paper."
32. Pulitzer, letter to Norris, May 21, 1897, Pulitzer papers, Library of Congress, Washington, DC.
33. Pulitzer, letter to Norris, August 21, 1897, Pulitzer papers, Library of Congress, Washington, DC.
34. See "Table 15—Number and Circulation of Newspapers and Periodicals, Classified According to Period of Issue, 1850 to 1900," and "Table 29—Statistics Relating to Daily Publications in 50 Cities, 1900," *Twelfth Census of the United States, Taken in the Year 1900: Manufacturers, Part III* (Washington, DC: United States Census Office, 1902), 1046, 1051.
35. Paul Starr, *The Creation of the Media: Political Origins of Modern Communications* (New York: Basic Books, 2004), 254.
36. Pulitzer, letter to Seitz, December 23, 1897, Pulitzer papers, Library of Congress. Emphasis in the original.
37. "The Journalism that Does Things," *New York Journal* (October 13, 1897).

38. See "The Development of a New Idea in Journalism," *New York Journal* (October 3, 1897).

39. "The Journalism of Action," *New York Journal* (October 5, 1897): 6.

40. "The Journal's Record," *New York Journal* (January 2, 1898): 45.

41. See Eva McDonald Valesh, "A Woman Interviews the President for the Journal," *New York Journal* (July 4, 1897): 28. The assignment of interviewing McKinley was presented to Valesh essentially as an impossible-sounding prerequisite for landing a job at the *Journal*, according to her biographer, Elizabeth Faue. Valesh arranged the interview through a U.S. senator from Minnesota, where she had worked before joining the *Journal*'s staff. Valesh became something of a star at the *Journal*, covering labor strife in New England and the run-up to the Spanish-American War. See Faue, *Writing the Wrongs: Eva Valesh and the Rise of Labor Journalism* (Ithaca, NY: Cornell University Press, 2002), 128–40. Valesh conducted another interview with McKinley in early 1898 which the *Journal* reported prominently, complete with sketch of Valesh. See "M'Kinley Talks to the Journal About the Great Strike," *New York Journal* (January 23, 1898): 45.

42. The *Journal* declared that its willingness to underwrite far-flung enterprise in newsgathering stirred the envy and intense displeasure of conservative rivals, whom it dismissed as representative of the "old journalism." The *Journal* said in February 1897: "The reason the old journalism doesn't like the Journal is that the Journal gets the news, no matter what it costs. The Sun and its kind cannot afford to spend money since the Journal has taken their readers away from them, and the probability is they would not do so if they could afford it." See "'Truth' About Old Journalism," *New York Journal* (February 2, 1897): 6.

43. See John J. Ingalls, "The Great Fight Described by Ingalls," *New York Journal* (March 18, 1897): 1.

44. See "The Journal's War Correspondence," *New York Journal* (April 30, 1897): 8. Some correspondents were local residents who filed only occasionally. In any event, the lengths to which the *Journal* covered the Greece-Turkey conflict anticipated the intensity of its reporting from Cuba during the Spanish-American War in 1898.

45. One of the female correspondents was Stephen Crane's companion, Cora Howorth Stewart, who wrote under the byline "Imogene Carter." See Michael Robertson, *Stephen Crane, Journalism, and the Making of Modern American Literature* (New York: Columbia University Press, 1997), 142.

46. "The Journal's War Correspondence," *New York Journal* (April 30, 1897).

47. One of Crane's reports for the *Journal* was published under the headline, "The Blue Badge of Cowardice." The dispatch assailed as incom-

petent the generalship of the Greek army. Crane's opening paragraph read: "Back fell the Greek army, wrathful, sullen, fierce as any victorious army would be when commanded to retreat before the enemy it had defeated." See Crane, "The Blue Badge of Cowardice," *New York Journal* (May 12, 1897): 3.

48. "How the Journal Goes to Klondyke," *New York Journal* (August 22, 1897): 38.

49. For example, the *Journal* said of its reporters covering the Greco-Turkish War: "Such an array of alert, experienced and courageous correspondents in the service of one newspaper is unparalleled in the history of journalism, not only in the United States but in the world." See "The Journal's War Correspondence," *New York Journal* (April 30, 1897).

50. See R. W. Stallman and E. R. Hagemann, *The War Dispatches of Stephen Crane* (New York: New York University Press, 1964), 107.

51. See, for example, Stephen Crane, "Crane at Velestino," *New York Journal* (May 11, 1897): 1. His dispatch included this evocative passage: "The roll of musketry was tremendous. From a distance it was like tearing a cloth; nearer, it sounded like rain on a tin roof and close up it was just a long crash after crash. It was a beautiful sound—beautiful as I had never dreamed. It was more impressive than the roar of Niagara and fine than thunder or avalanche—because it had the wonder of human tragedy in it. It was the most beautiful sound of my experience, barring no symphony. The crash of it was ideal."

52. Crane, "Crane at Velestino," *New York Journal* (May 11, 1897).

53. John Bass, "How Novelist Crane Acts On the Battlefield," *New York Journal* (May 23, 1897), reprinted in Stallman and Hagemann, *The War Dispatches of Stephen Crane*, 42–43.

54. Mark Twain, "The Great Jubilee As Described by the Journal's Special Writers: Mark Twain's Pen Picture of the Great Pageant in Honor of Victoria's Sixtieth Anniversary," *New York Journal* (June 23, 1897): 1.

55. Twain, "The Great Jubilee," *New York Journal* (June 23, 1897).

56. See "Mark Twain Is Ill in London," *New York Herald* (June 1, 1897): 9.

57. Frank Marshall White, "Mark Twain Amused," *New York Journal* (June 2, 1897): 1. E. S. Martin, a columnist for *Harper's Weekly*, said the erroneous report about Twain's health apparently stemmed from confusing the writer with one of his cousins, J. R. Clemens, who suffered a serious illness while in London in 1897. See E. S. Martin, "This Busy World," *Harper's Weekly* (June 19, 1897): 606.

58. "Can Scientists Breed Men from Monkeys?" *New York Journal* (August 22, 1897): 13.

59. "Is the Sun Preparing to Give Birth to a New World?" *New York Journal* (September 12, 1897): 20–21.

60. See, for example, "Is the Air Vanishing?" *New York Herald* (March 28, 1897): sect. 5, p. 2.
61. "Sunday Supplements and Science," *Fourth Estate* (September 23, 1897): 6.
62. See "Premier Canovas Agrees to Olney's Plan for Autonomy," *New York Journal* (January 12, 1897): 1.
63. See Michael Emery and Edwin Emery with Nancy L. Roberts, *The Press and America: An Interpretative History of the Mass Media*, 8th ed. (Boston: Allyn and Bacon, 1996), 194.
64. See, for example, Ferdinand Lundberg, *Imperial Hearst: A Social Biography* (New York: Equinox Cooperative Press, 1936), 51, 54. Lundberg dismissed Hearst (51) as "Always the imitator."
65. "A Newspaper's Duty to the Public," *New York Journal* (November 15, 1897): 6.
66. W. T. Stead, "Government by Journalism," *Contemporary Review* 49 (May 1886): 653–74.
67. A biographer of Stead wrote that "Government By Journalism" and "The Future of Journalism," a subsequent article Stead wrote for *Contemporary Review*, "did not receive the widespread attention he probably thought [they] would and should." See Raymond L. Schults, *Crusader in Babylon: W.T. Stead and the Pall Mall Gazette* (Lincoln: University of Nebraska Press, 1972), 209.
68. See Ray Boston, "W. T. Stead and Democracy by Journalism," in Joel H. Weiner, ed., *Papers for the Millions: The New Journalism in Britain, 1850s to 1914* (New York: Greenwood, 1988), 91–106.
69. W. T. Stead, *Satan's Invisible World Displayed, or Despairing Democracy* (New York: R.F. Fenno & Co., 1897), 227.
70. Stead, "Government By Journalism," 661.
71. Stead, "Government By Journalism," 662.
72. Stead, "Government By Journalism," 662.
73. Stead, "Government By Journalism," 663.
74. Stead, "Government By Journalism," 664.
75. Stead, "Government By Journalism," 664.
76. Stead, "Government By Journalism," 664.
77. Stead, "Government By Journalism," 664.
78. "Editor Stead Hails It with Joy," *New York Journal* (October 13, 1897): 3.
79. Stead, *Satan's Invisible World Displayed*, 233.
80. Stead, *Satan's Invisible World Displayed*, 244–46.
81. Stead, *Satan's Invisible World Displayed*, 245.
82. "Tammany Through the Eyes of Stead," *New York Journal* (November 28, 1897): 45.

83. The *Journal's* editorial about Stead's book was silent about the recommendation of a press tribunal. See "The Safeguard of Democracy," *New York Journal* (November 30, 1897): 8.

84. See Nasaw, *The Chief*, 121.

85. Nasaw, *The Chief*, 121.

86. "The Journal Stops," *New York Journal* (December 3, 1897): 1.

87. "The Journal Stops," *New York Journal* (December 3, 1897).

88. "Gas Steal Stopped, Electric Grab Checked by the Journal," *New York Journal* (December 2, 1897): 1.

89. "Citizens Denounce Trolley Grab," *New York Journal* (December 5, 1897): 1.

90. "A Newspaper's Duty to the Public," *New York Journal* (November 15, 1897): 6.

91. "The Journal Achieves Another Great Victory for the People," *New York Journal* (November 25, 1897): 1.

92. In her tribute to the yellow press in 1905, Lydia Kingsmill Commander suggested that the *Journal* and the *World* filled a gap in offering aid and assistance to the poor. "Those who suffer injustices and report their grievances to either of the yellow journals find a prompt and powerful friend," she wrote. "This is realized by the poor, who endure a thousand petty but bitter wrongs." See Commander, "The Significance of Yellow Journalism," *Arena* 34 (August 1905): 154.

93. "The yellow journals are full of sympathy," Commander wrote. "They are like human beings, with big, kind hearts. Whenever and wherever there is trouble they spring to the rescue." See Commander, "The Significance of Yellow Journalism," 153.

94. See "Aid the Cold and Hungry: Journal Hears the Cry and Opens a Relief Fund," *New York Journal* January 24, 1897): 1. The *Journal's* charity was dismissed by the *Times* as unnecessary grandstanding and by the *Sun* as offering haven to criminals and ne'er-do-wells. See "Relief Fund Criticised," *New York Times* (February 12, 1897): 12, and "Almsgiving Gone Daft," *New York Sun* (February 7, 1897): 2.

95. "The Journal to Fight for 'Cyclists' Rights," *New York Journal* (June 13, 1897): 43.

96. "Cyclists' Lives to be Made Safe," *New York Journal* (June 23, 1897): 16.

97. "The Journal to Fight for 'Cyclists' Rights," *New York Journal* (June 13, 1897).

98. "Beheaded, Cast into the River," *New York Journal* (June 27, 1897): 51; "More of the Headless Body Is Found," *New York Journal* (June 28, 1897): 1, and "Strange Murder Mystery Deepens," *New York Herald* (June 28, 1897): 1.

99. See "Beheaded, Cast into the River," *New York Journal* (June 27, 1897).

100. John D. Stevens, *Sensationalism and the New York Press* (New York: Columbia University Press, 1991), 92.

101. Stevens, *Sensationalism and the New York Press*, 92.

102. "Discovered by the Journal," *New York Journal*, June 30, 1897. See also, Gerald Gross, ed., *Masterpieces of Murder* (New York: Avon, 1966), 236–7.

103. "The Noisy Detectives' Work," *New York Times*, July 1, 1897. The *Times* speculated that "the grossness and needless explicitness of this kind of news reporting must have a demoralizing influence upon the younger generation." In rejecting the *Times'* criticism, E. S. Martin of *Harper's Weekly* identified an intellectual dimension to the murder mystery, writing: "The interest in ordinary merely brutal murders is somewhat perverse, but when an unknown man's disjointed members are found here and there in the waters that wash a metropolis, and are assembled, and being identified without the recovery of the head, lead to the detection and arrest of the apparent murderers, the interest which attaches to such a sequence of developments and the progressive deduction of theories is intellectual, and no intelligent reader of newspapers or student of life need be ashamed of it." See E. S. Martin, "This Busy World," *Harper's Weekly* (July 17, 1897).

104. Cited in "More of the Headless Body Is Found," *New York Journal* (June 28, 1897). The comment was attributed to Philip O'Hanlon, a coroner's physician. Later in the summer of 1897, O'Hanlon's daughter, Virginia, wrote the famous letter to the *New York Sun* asking, "Is There A Santa Claus?" See chapter 3.

105. "The Journal and the Nack Case," *New York Journal* (November 11, 1897): 8.

106. "The Journal and the Nack Case," *New York Journal* (November 11, 1897).

107. Stevens, *Sensationalism and the New York Press*, 93–94, and Gross, *Masterpieces of Murder*, 238.

108. "Enterprise Means Success," *Fourth Estate* (July 15, 1897): 4.

109. Evangelina Cisneros and Karl Decker, *The Story of Evangelina Cisneros Told by Herself, Her Rescue by Karl Decker* (New York: Continental Publishing Co., 1898), 59.

110. See "The War on Women," *New York Journal* (August 18, 1897): 6

111. Marion Kendrick, "The Cuban Girl Martyr," *New York Journal* (August 17, 1897): 1.

112. Julius Chambers, "Women's Noble Appeal for Miss Cisneros," *New York Journal* (August 19, 1897): 1, and James Creelman, "American Womanhood Roused," *New York Journal* (August 20, 1897): 3.

113. See "The Martyrdom of Evangelina Cisneros," *New York Journal* (August 19, 1897): 6.

114. Enrique Dupuy de Lôme, letter to Varina Davis (August 24, 1897), cited in "Senorita Cisneros's Case," *New York Times* (August 26, 1897): 2.

115. See "Scrubbing the Floors in Casa de Recojidas," *New York Journal* (August 25, 1897): 2.

116. "Miss Cisneros In Death's Shadow," *New York Journal* (August 23, 1897): 1.

117. "Gen. Lee Back from Cuba," *New York Commercial Advertiser* (September 8, 1897): 1.

118. "Gen. Lee Back from Cuba," *New York Commercial Advertiser* (September 8, 1897).

119. "Distress in Cuba," *New York Commercial Advertiser* (September 9, 1897): 4.

120. See, for example, "Editors on the Journal's Rescue of Miss Cisneros," *New York Journal* (October 12, 1897): 6

121. Cited in "Señorita Cisneros and the 'New Journalism,'" *Literary Digest* 15, 27 (October 30, 1897): 786.

122. Untitled editorial comment, *Philadelphia Press* (October 13, 1897): 6.

123. "Newspaper Men's Daring," *Fourth Estate* (October 14, 1897): 5.

124. Even harsh critics of the *Journal* lauded the newspaper for freeing Cisneros. George Bronson Rea, for example, excoriated the *Journal* for having "willfully exaggerated" details about Cisneros' imprisonment but praised the jailbreak. "Although the act in itself was a gross violation of law," Rea wrote, "the nerve and daring displayed by Mr. Karl Decker ... appeals strongly to the hearts of a people who appreciate a courageous action." See Rea, *Facts and Fakes About Cuba* (New York: Munro's Sons, 1897), 234. Rea was a correspondent in Cuba for the *New York Herald* and his book described how some U.S. journalists had exaggerated reports about the Cuban insurrection.

125. "Personal," *New York Times* (October 12, 1897): 6.

126. Most New York newspapers avoided editorial comment about the *Journal*'s exploit.

127. "The Journal's Rescue of Evangelina Cisneros," *New York Journal* (October 11, 1897): 6.

128. "Beyond Weyler's Reach," *New York Journal* (October 12, 1897): 6.

129. "Beyond Weyler's Reach," *New York Journal* (October 12, 1897).

130. "The Journalism that Does Things," October 13, 1897.

131. See Edwin G. Burrows and Mike Wallace, *Gotham: A History of New York City to 1898* (New York: Oxford, 1999), 1219.

132. "Every One Calls the Carnival Superb," *New York Journal*, January 2, 1898: 60.

133. Untitled editorial comment, *Fourth Estate*, December 30, 1897: 5.

134. "New York's Celebration," *New York Journal* (December 19, 1897): 66.

135. "New York is the World's Second City," *San Francisco Chronicle* (January 1, 1898): 1

136. "Horses Trample a Band," *New York Sun* (January 1, 1898): 1.

137. The flag-raising was activated when the mayor of San Francisco pushed a button in California that sent an electric current across the country to New York's City Hall. The mayor was enlisted after President William McKinley declined the *Journal*'s invitation "to touch the button that will raise the flag of Greater New York." See W. R. Hearst, telegram to William McKinley (December 28, 1897), William McKinley papers, manuscript division, Library of Congress, Washington, DC.

138. "New York is the World's Second City," *San Francisco Chronicle* (January 1, 1898).

139. "New York is the World's Second City," *San Francisco Chronicle* (January 1, 1898).

140. "Pyrotechnical Journalism," *Fourth Estate* (January 6, 1898): 6.

141. "The Event of the New Year," *New York Journal* (December 20, 1897): 6.

142. "Creditable Newspaper Enterprise," *New York Sun* (December 23, 1897): 6.

143. Cited in "Pyrotechnical Journalism," *Fourth Estate* (January 6, 1898).

144. "The Greater New York Carnival," *New York Journal* (January 1, 1898): 6.

145. "Trolley Cars on the Bridge," *New York Times* (January 1, 1898): 4.

146. "Work on Bridge Loops," *New York Times* (January 6, 1898): 14.

147. "Is the Bridge Surrendered?" *New York Journal* (January 6, 1898): 8.

148. "Bridge Trolley Problems," *New York Journal* (August 12, 1898): 12.

149. The *New York Times* reported that a twelve-year-old girl lost her right leg in August 1898 after a trolley car struck her at the New York end of the Brooklyn Bridge. See "Run Down by a Trolley Car," *New York Times* (August 8, 1898): 6.

150. "The Journal's Record," *New York Journal* (January 2, 1898).

151. "The Journal's Record," *New York Journal* (January 2, 1898).

152. For example, the *Augusta Chronicle* in Georgia described the *Journal* as "a pioneer in progressive journalism. Its radical departures cause criticisms, but the Journal goes on conquering and to conquer." The *Journal* reprinted the commentary on its editorial page. See "'A Pioneer in Progressive Journalism,'" *New York Journal* (July 21, 1897): 8.

153. "The Journalism of Action," *New York Journal* (October 5, 1897).

154. "Personal," *New York Times* (October 12, 1897): 6.

155. "Corrupters of English," *New York Times* (July 21, 1897): 4.

156. "Corrupters of English," *New York Times* (July 21, 1897).

157. Untitled editorial comment, *New York Times* (November 9, 1897): 6.

158. "Freak Journalism and the Ball," *New York Times* (February 12, 1897): 6.

159. See "The Times's Political News," *New York Times* (October 20, 1897): 6.

160. Susan E. Tifft and Alex S. Jones, *The Trust: The Private and Powerful Family Behind the* New York Times (Boston: Little, Brown, 1999), 44.

161. "Note and Comment," *Fourth Estate* (November 19, 1896): 6.

162. "Panorama of the Jubilee," *New York Times* (July 2, 1897): 7.

163. See Peter Galassi and Susan Kismaric, eds., *Pictures of the Times: A Century of Photography from the New York Times* (New York: Museum of Modern Art, 1996), 180. The photograph, published May 30, 1910, showed aviator Glenn Curtiss leaving on the first nonstop aircraft flight from Albany to New York City.

164. See "Analysis of the Contents of Eight Daily Newspapers," in [Price Collier,] *America and the Americans: From a French Point of View* (New York: Charles Scribner's Sons, 1897), 271. The content analysis was apparently limited to a single issue of the *Times* and these newspapers: *New York Evening Post, New York World, Chicago Tribune, Kansas City Times, Minneapolis Tribune, New Orleans Times-Picayune,* and *Le Figaro* in Paris. The analysis not only showed the *Times* far ahead in financial and commercial news, but indicated that it printed more news about drama and music than any of the other newspapers examined.

165. Harrison E. Salisbury, *Without Fear or Favor: The New York Times and Its Times* (New York: Times Books, 1980), 26.

166. Hearst, too, was the beneficiary of much favorable comment in *Fourth Estate*. In the case of Ochs, it is quite possible the trade journal felt obliged to the *Times* publisher after misidentifying him as "Colonel Adolph Ochs" in reports about his visits to New York in early 1896 to scout for newspaper properties. See "The Mercury Sale," *Fourth Estate* (April 2, 1896): 2, and "Will Ochs Get It?" *Fourth Estate* (April 23, 1896): 1.

167. "New Sky Scraper," *Fourth Estate* (August 27, 1896): 1.

168. "New Sky Scraper," *Fourth Estate* (August 27, 1896): 1–2.

169. "New Sky Scraper," *Fourth Estate* (August 27, 1896): 1.

170. See Tifft and Jones, *The Trust*, 70–71.

171. See "A Waste of Public Money," *New York Times* (November 12, 1896): 4.

172. "Money Saved to the City," *New York Times* (November 22, 1896): 3.

173. "Reward Not Only in Heaven," *Fourth Estate* (November 19, 1896): 6.

174. "He is Both Kinds," *The Journalist* (June 12, 1897): 59.

175. Tifft and Jones, *The Trust*, 45. See also, Kalman Seigel, ed., *Talking Back to The New York Times: Letters to the Editor, 1851–1971* (New York: Quadrangle Books, 1972), 7.

176. Tifft and Jones, *The Trust*, 45.

177. "The Times's Political News," *New York Times* (October 20, 1897): 6.

178. "The Times's Political News," *New York Times* (October 20, 1897). "There is no doubt in the minds of our readers what our opinions are in this campaign," the *Times*' editorial stated. "They are expressed without reserve or qualification in the proper place. We undertake to form them from a careful consideration of all available facts; in the news columns we seek to give our readers these facts, that they may form their opinions in a like manner."

179. Cited in David T. Z. Mindich, *Just the Facts: How 'Objectivity' Came to Define American Journalism* (New York: New York University Press, 1998), 5.

180. Cited in Wm. David Sloan, *The Media in America: A History, 6th ed.* (Northport, AL: Vision Press,) 58.

181. Ochs' statement of principles was published in the *Times* on August 18, 1896, and reprinted one hundred years later. See Adolph S. Ochs, "Without Fear or Favor," *New York Times* (August 19, 1996): A12. An accompanying note said the passage, "to give the news impartially, without fear or favor, regardless of party or sect, or interests involved," had held "a place of honor at the Times" since 1896.

182. At the *Times*' seventy-fifth anniversary in 1926, the trade journal *Editor & Publisher* described Ochs as the *Times*' "presiding genius." See "New York Times: 75 Years Young Today!" *Editor & Publisher* (September 18, 1926): 34.

183. Alva Johnston, "Twilight of the Ink-Stained Gods," *Vanity Fair* (February 1932): 70, 36.

184. William L. Chenery, "Unafraid and Free," in Harold L. Ickes, ed., *Freedom of the Press Today: A Clinical Examination by 28 Specialists* (New York: Vanguard Press, 1941): 77–78.

185. See Robert V. Hudson, "Will Irwin's Pioneering Criticism of the Press," *Journalism Quarterly* 47, 2 (Summer 1970): 263–71.

186. Will Irwin, "The American Newspaper: Part VI—The Editor and the News" [1911]: 18, reprinted in Irwin, *The American Newspaper* (Ames: Iowa State University Press, 1969).

187. Irwin, "The American Newspaper: Part VI—The Editor and the News," [1911]: 19, reprinted in Irwin, *The American Newspaper*.

188. See "Journalism as a Profession," *Fourth Estate* (2 June 1900): 6.

189. See T. B. Connery, "Great Business Operations—The Collection of News," *Cosmopolitan* 23, 21 (1897): 32. See also, "Journalism as a Profession," *Fourth Estate* (2 June 1900).

190. Hy B. Turner wrote in his study of New York City journalism: "The Times was a business, not a battlefield for reform." See Turner, *When Giants Ruled: The Story of Park Row, New York's Great Newspaper Street* (New York: Fordham University Press, 1999), 147.

191. Shepard in *The Paper's Papers* described "All the News That's Fit to Print" as "overweening" and "a slogan that promises the impossible." See Shepard, *The Paper's Papers*, 44.
192. Tifft and Jones, *The Trust*, 64.
193. Johnson, *Honorable Titan*, 157.
194. Elmer Davis, *History of the New York Times, 1851–1921* (New York: Greenwood Press, 1969 reprint of 1921 edition), 199–200.
195. "In Olden Times," *Times Talk* 4, 5 (January 1951): 7. See also, Tifft and Jones, *The Trust*, 799.
196. "If You Want All the News of Every Description Attractively Presented You Will Read the Times," *Philadelphia Times* (August 4, 1896): 1.
197. Tifft and Jones, *The Trust*, 42.
198. Harrison Salisbury, citing an Ochs manuscript in the *Times* archives, wrote that "Ochs invented the slogan himself." See Salisbury, *Without Fear or Favor*, 26.
199. "$100 for 10 Words," *New York Times* (October 26, 1896): 7.
200. "For the Times's Motto," *New York Times* (October 26, 1896): 8.
201. "To Award Motto Prize," *New York Times* (November 15, 1896): 15.
202. "To Award Motto Prize," *New York Times* (November 15, 1896).
203. "The Motto Competition," *New York Times* (November 15, 1896): 12.
204. Michael Schudson, *Discovering the News: A Social History of American Newspapers* (New York: Basic Books, 1978), 112.
205. "The Prize Motto Selected," *New York Times* (November 22, 1896): 4.
206. "The Prize Motto Selected," *New York Times* (November 22, 1896).
207. Of course, newspaper mottos commanded more interest and notice in American journalism of the 1890s than they do today. The *Fourth Estate* in 1897 was inclined to comment on such matters, noting that "All the News, All the Time" had been selected as the slogan of the *Morning Post*, a new title in Joliet, IL. See "New Papers Announced During the Week," *Fourth Estate* (July 25, 1895): 11. Additionally, the *Fourth Estate* puzzled over the slogan, "Steer clear," that was adopted by a newspaper called *Ice Berg* in Winterville, GA. Steer clear, *Fourth Estate* said, "is awkward. The paper ought to explain its motto." See "Note and Comment," *Fourth Estate* (December 2, 1897): 6. In September 1897, the *New York Sun* dropped the slogan, "If You See It in the Sun, It's So," from its front page, and *Fourth Estate* called attention to the motto's sudden disappearance. See Untitled editorial comment, *Fourth Estate* September 30, 1897): 6.
208. Cited in "'A Progressive Newspaper,'" *New York Times* (October 8, 1897): 6.
209. Cited in "The Times's Supplements," *New York Times* (January 4, 1897): 4.
210. Cited in "For Clean Journalism," *New York Times* (May 27, 1901): 6.

211. Untitled editorial comment, *The Independent* (December 17, 1896): 25.

212. Cited in "'All the News,'" *New York Times* (November 14, 1896): 4.

213. "All the News," *New York Times* (November 14, 1896).

214. "Derelicts of Journalism," *New York World* (March 28, 1897): 10–11.

215. "Derelicts of Journalism," *New York World* (March 28, 1897).

216. These details, which Ochs effectively concealed, are described by Tifft and Jones in *The Trust*, 36–40, 71–72. The parcel was previously called Long Acre Square.

217. Meyer Berger, *The Story of the New York Times* (New York: Simon and Schuster, 1951), 125.

218. "The New York Times One Cent!" *New York Times* (October 10, 1898): 6.

219. "The New York Times One Cent!" *New York Times* (October 10, 1898).

220. See, for example, Berger, *The Story of the New York Times*, 124; Turner, *When Giants Ruled*, 146, and Kluger, *The Paper*, 166.

221. Tifft and Jones, *The Trust*, 54–55.

222. "A Newspaper May Be Both Good and Cheap," *Fourth Estate* (December 21, 1899): 8.

223. "A Newspaper May Be Both Good and Cheap," *Fourth Estate* (December 21, 1899).

224. Lincoln Steffens, *The Autobiography of Lincoln Steffens* (New York: Harcourt, Brace and Co., 1931), 312–13.

225. Lincoln Steffens, letter to his father (23 March 1898), Steffens papers, series II, Box 55, uncatalogued correspondence; Butler Library, Columbia University, New York, NY.

226. Justin Kaplan, *Lincoln Steffens: A Biography* (New York: Simon and Schuster, 1974), 83.

227. Steffens, *Autobiography of Lincoln Steffens*, 312–13.

228. Steffens, *Autobiography of Lincoln Steffens*, 314.

229. Steffens, *Autobiography of Lincoln Steffens*, 316–17.

230. Steffens, *Autobiography of Lincoln Steffens*, 317.

231. Steffens, *Autobiography of Lincoln Steffens*, 315.

232. Steffens, *Autobiography of Lincoln Steffens*, 339.

233. Hutchins Hapgood, *Types From City Streets* (New York: Garrett Press, 1970), 109.

234. So described by Holbrook Jackson in *The Eighteen Nineties: A Review of Art and Ideas at the Close of the Nineteenth Century* (New York: Knopf, 1972 reprint ed.), 216. Jackson wrote: "With epidemic suddenness writers of all kinds began to be realistic in their fiction." He also noted (217) that while "the more daring realists aroused a new interest in the art of the novel, there were still more critics to denounce than uphold the new method."

235. See Mary Margaret Cronin, "Profits, Legitimacy and Public Service: The Development of Ethics and Standards in New York City's Newspapers, 1870–1920," unpublished Ph.D. dissertation; University of Michigan, 1992, 103.

236. Kaplan, *Lincoln Steffens*, 85, 88. Among those publications was *Chap-Book*, which Kaplan (88) notes was a "champion of realism and *art nouveau*."

237. "Commercial Advertiser Gets Good Men," *Fourth Estate* (December 23, 1897): 5.

238. Steffens, *Autobiography of Lincoln Steffens*, 311–12.

239. "Commercial Advertiser Gets Good Men," *Fourth Estate* (December 23, 1897).

240. J. Lincoln Steffens, "The Business of a Newspaper," *Scribner's* 22, 4 (October 1897): 448.

241. Steffens, "The Business of a Newspaper," 463. "The circulation manager of to-day is so new that not much is known about him," Steffens wrote.

242. Steffens, "The Business of a Newspaper," 462.

243. Steffens, *Autobiography of Lincoln Steffens*, 317.

244. Steffens, *Autobiography of Lincoln Steffens*, 317.

245. Steffens, *Autobiography of Lincoln Steffens*, 321.

246. "Origin of Pink Lemonade," *New York Commercial Advertiser* (December 18, 1897): 11.

247. "Tales by a Physician," *New York Commercial Advertiser* (December 18, 1897): 11.

248. "An East Side Romance," *New York Commercial Advertiser* (December 18, 1897): 11

249. To Steffens, such material was entirely acceptable. "I was a newspaper man, temporarily," he later wrote of his time at the *Commercial Advertiser*, "but my staff were writers, getting the news as material for poetry, plans, or fictions, and writing is as news for practice." See Steffens, *Autobiography of Lincoln Steffens*, 339.

250. "Wreck on the Elevated," *New York Commercial Advertiser* (December 17, 1897): 1

251. "Wreck on the Elevated," *New York Commercial Advertiser* (December 17, 1897).

252. Steffens, *Autobiography of Lincoln Steffens*, 317.

253. See Ivan Musicant, *Empire by Default: The Spanish-American War and the Dawn of the American Century* (New York: Henry Holt and Co, 1998), 444–45.

254. Steffens, *Autobiography of Lincoln Steffens*, 339.

255. Hapgood, *Types From City Streets*, 110.

256. Hapgood, *Types From City Streets*, 111.

257. Hutchins Hapgood, *A Victorian in the Modern World* (Seattle: University of Washington Press, 1972), 172.

258. Hapgood, *Types From City Streets*, 111.

259. Hapgood, *Types From City Streets*, 110–11

260. See Cronin, "Profits, Legitimacy and Public Service," 106.

261. John C. Harstock, *A History of American Literary Journalism: The Emergence of a Modern Narrative Form* (Amherst: University of Massachusetts Press, 2000), 33–34.

262. See W. Stewart Pinkerton Jr., "'New Journalism': Believe It or Not," in A. Kent McDougall, ed., *The Press: A Critical Look From the Inside* (Princeton, NJ: Dow Jones Books, 1972): 157–64.

263. Steffens, *Autobiography of Lincoln Steffens*, 317.

264. See Christopher Scanlan, *Reporting and Writing: Basics for the 21st Century* (Fort Worth, TX: Harcourt College Publishers, 2000), 91.

265. Hapgood, *Types From City Streets*, 112.

266. Steffens, *Autobiography of Lincoln Steffens*, 317.

267. Harry Thurston Peck, "A Great National Newspaper," *Cosmopolitan* 24 (December 1897): 209–20.

268. Peck, "A Great National Newspaper," 219.

269. Peck, "A Great National Newspaper," 220.

270. Untitled editorial comment, *Times Talk*, 5, 1 (August-September 1951): 13.

271. One of the few studies of the *Times* to emphasize this vital aspect of Ochs' price cut was Gay Talese's *The Kingdom and the Power: The Study of the Men Who Influence the Institution That Influences the World.* Talese described the dilemma that confronted the *Journal* and the *World* in the wake of the *Times*' price cut this way: "Had they gone up to two cents in spite of Ochs, he might have followed them, but perhaps he would not have gone up until he had cut deeply into the penny market. So Pulitzer and Hearst had to hold on, and they were forced to do so for twenty years, until the coverage of World War I proved so expensive that all three publishers were obliged to charge two cents. But by that time, Ochs's paper was preeminent." See Talese, *Kingdom and the Power* (Cleveland, OH: New American Library, 1969), 164.

272. "The New York Times: One Cent!" *New York Times* (October 10, 1898).

273. Hartley Davis, in his detailed and notably even-handed assessment of *fin-de-siècle* journalism in New York City, noted that "the 'yellow journals' ... spend the largest sums to get the latest and best news and to present it most attractively and forcefully." See Davis, "The Journalism of New York." *Munsey's Magazine* 24, 2 (November 1900): 233.

274. See Janny Scott and David Carr, "Changes at the Times," *New York Times* (June 6, 2003): B8.

275. See Nasaw, *The Chief*, 133.

276. "The Year's Record," *Fourth Estate* (January 12, 1899): 2.

277. "Enterprise Tells: The New York Journal's Notable Achievements," *Fourth Estate* (October 27, 1900): 12.

278. Willis J. Abbot, *Watching the World Go By* (Boston: Little, Brown, 1933), 149.

279. See, for example, "Destruction of the War Ship Maine Was the Work of an Enemy," *New York Journal* (February 17, 1898): 1, and "Journal Here Presents, Formally, Proof of a Submarine Mine," *New York Journal* (February 20, 1898): 1.

280. The most recent study of the *Maine*'s destruction, released in 1998 at the centenary of the Spanish-American War, indicated that an underwater mine likely caused the disaster. See Thomas B. Allen, ed., "A Special Report: What Really Sank the *Maine*?" *Naval History* (March-April 1998): 30–39.

281. "Torpedo Hole Discovered by Government Divers in the Maine," *New York Evening Journal* (February 17, 1898): 1.

282. "Spanish Ships on Our Coast!" *New York Evening Journal* (May 12, 1898): 1.

283. The *Chicago Record* permitted the *New York Journal* to publish the account of the U.S. naval victory in Manila, with the understanding that the *Journal* would wait until the report had first appeared in the *Record*, on Monday, May 9, 1898. The *Record* did not publish Sunday editions. The *Journal*—which did not have a correspondent with the naval squadron—broke the embargo by publishing on Sunday, May 8, 1898, a lengthy report based loosely on the *Record*'s dispatch. See Charles H. Brown, *Correspondents' War: Journalists in the Spanish-American War* (New York: Scribner's, 1967), 200.

284. See "Journal Faked Its Manila Bay Story," *New York World* (May 10, 1898): 5.

285. William Randolph Hearst, letter to James Creelman, May 26, 1898, James Creelman Papers, Ohio State University, Columbus. Biographer David Nasaw noted that Hearst began developing the Suez Canal plans without consulting officials in Washington. Nasaw added: "The plan was sheer madness and probably impossible to pull off. But it was no more daring than the rescue of Evangelina Cisneros—and that had succeeded." See Nasaw, *The Chief*, 136.

286. See Nasaw, *The Chief*, 137.

287. Nasaw, *The Chief*, 137.

288. "Spanish Alliances," *New York Times* (March 1, 1898): 6.

289. "The New Political Force," *New York Evening Post* (April 30, 1898): 4.

290. For an early statement of this enduring but grossly misleading argument, see Brooke Fisher, "The Newspaper Industry," *Atlantic Monthly* 89 (June 1902): 751.

291. "A New-Comer," *The Journalist* (December 18, 1897): 113.
292. George Howard Phillips, "An Analysis of 835 Articles in the Leading American Periodicals for the Period 1890–1914 to Determine What Was Said About American Daily Newspapers," unpublished Ph.D. diss., Iowa State University (August 1962): table 4, p. 160. The other journalists in this portion of Phillips' study were: James Gordon Bennett Sr., James Gordon Bennett Jr., Arthur Brisbane, Charles A. Dana, Richard Harding Davis, Edwin L. Godkin, Horace Greeley, and Joseph Pulitzer.
293. Phillips, "An Analysis of 835 Articles," 199.
294. See "The Journal's Settled Policy," *New York Journal* (December 3, 1897): 6.
295. "The Right Arm of Justice," *New York Journal* (January 28, 1899): 6.
296. "The Journalism of Action," *New York Journal* (May 29, 1900): 8.
297. Nasaw, *The Chief*, 152.
298. W.R. Hearst, "An American Internal Policy," *New York Journal* (February 5, 1899): 24.
299. See, for example, "The Paramount Issue," *New York Journal*, (November 2, 1900).
300. Ellen F. Fitzpatrick, "Introduction," in *Muckraking: Three Landmark Articles* (Boston: Bedford Books, 1994), 24.
301. Sidney Kobre made a similar point in *The Yellow Press and Gilded Age Journalism* (Tallahassee, Florida State University Press, 1964), 78.
302. See "W.R. Hearst Notes Tendency Toward Tabloid Presentation of News," *Editor & Publisher* (October 23, 1926): 5. Hearst in the interview also gave this definition: "News is what the public wants to know about."
303. Samuel Crowther, typescript of article, "A Talk with Arthur Brisbane," p. 7; Arthur Brisbane papers, Box 2; Syracuse University, Syracuse, NY.
304 A similar point was made by Stevens in *Sensationalism and the New York Press*, 132.
305. Lincoln Steffens, "Hearst, The Man of Mystery," *The American Magazine* (November 1906): 12.
306. "Ochs," one media critic noted in the early twenty-first century, "was intensely dedicated to two things in his life: his family and *The New York Times*. He passed on those values to three successive generations...." See Seth Mnookin, *Hard News: The Scandals at* The New York Times *and Their Meaning for American Media* (New York: Random House, 2004), 8.
307. See Tifft and Jones, *The Trust*, 88.
308. Johnston, "Twilight of the Ink-Stained Gods," 36.
309. "Lippmann Sees End of 'Yellow Press,'" *New York Times* (January 13, 1931): 35. Similarly, the historian Mitchell Stephens has observed that the successful American newspaper "tends of necessity to be a temperate if not a conservative medium"—a formula the *New York Journal* cer-

tainly did not embrace. See Stephens, *A History of News* (Fort Worth, TX: Harcourt Brace, 1997), 169.

310. "Lippmann Sees End of 'Yellow Press,'" *New York Times* (January 13, 1931).

311. See, for example, Lundberg, *Imperial Hearst*, 71.

Chapter 3

1. See Alicia Shepard, "Journalism's Prize Culture," *American Journalism Review* (April 2000): 22.

2. See "Francis P. Church," *New York Times* (April 13, 1906): 10.

3. The sole major international event of 1897 that Scovel did not cover was Queen Victoria's Silver Jubilee in London. Davis, after his assignment to Cuba in early 1897, reported on the Greco-Turkish War and Victoria's jubilee. He spent the rest of the year working on a book and a full-length play. See Arthur Lubow, *The Reporter Who Would Be King: A Biography of Richard Harding Davis* (New York: Charles Scribner's Sons, 1992), 160.

4. Ralph D. Paine, a fellow correspondent for the *World*, said of the irrepressible Scovel: "For him life was one superb and compelling gesture after another." See Paine, *Roads of Adventure* (Boston: Houghton Mifflin, 1922), 197.

5. See Edward P. Mitchell, *Memoirs of an Editor: Fifty Years of American Journalism* (New York: Charles Scribner's Son, 1924), 112.

6. See A. B. [Arthur Brisbane], "Hon. Charles Anderson Dana," *Journalist* (May 15, 1897): 26. Brisbane's article stated: "There is no aristocracy in the *Sun* building. The editor is the boss, and every other fellow is whatever his work can make him. There are no such things as 'inferiors.'"

7. See "Three Bright Newspaper Men," *Fourth Estate* (May 9, 1895): 3.

8. Arthur Lubow, *The Reporter Who Would Be King: A Biography of Richard Harding Davis* (New York: Charles Scribner's Sons, 1992), 2.

9. Gunther Barth, *City People: The Rise of Modern City Culture in Nineteenth-Century America* (New York: Oxford University Press, 1980), 102.

10. John Livingston Wright, "Reporters and Oversupply," *Arena* 20, 3 (September 1898): 615.

11. "Not Room Enough for All," *Fourth Estate* (June 10, 1897): 6.

12. "Not Room Enough for All," *Fourth Estate* (June 10, 1897).

13. "Is the Profession Overcrowded?" *The Journalist* (October 30, 1897): 12.

14. See Ted Curtis Smythe, "The Reporter, 1880–1900: Working Conditions and Their Influence on the News," *Journalism History* 7, 1 (Spring 1980): 2–3.

15. "Journalism as a Profession," *Fourth Estate* (June 2, 1900): 6.

16. Cited in "Washington Pay," *Fourth Estate* (July 29, 1897): 11. *Fourth Estate* attributed the salary ranges to a report published in the Louisville (KY) *Commercial*.
17. "Washington Pay," *Fourth Estate* (July 29, 1897).
18. Charles Hemstreet, *Reporting for the Newspapers* (New York: A. Wessels Co., 1901), 12.
19. James Fullarton Muirhead, *The Land of Contrasts: A Briton's View of His American Kin* (Boston: Lamson, Wolffe and Co., 1898), 157.
20. Muirhead, *The Land of Contrasts*, 156.
21. "Gray Hairs and Usefulness," *Fourth Estate* (October 7, 1897).
22. Cited in "The New Crop," *The Journalist* (July 24, 1897): 108.
23. See T. B. Connery, "Great Business Operations—The Collection of News," *Cosmopolitan* 23, 21 (1897): 32.
24. "The New Crop," *The Journalist* (July 24, 1897).
25. "The New Crop," *The Journalist* (July 24, 1897).
26. "Personal Journalism," *Fourth Estate* (September 26, 1897): 6.
27. Melville E. Stone, "Newspapers in the United States: Their Functions, Interior Economy, and Management," *Self Culture* 5, 3 (June 1897): 305.
28. Alfred Balch, "Signed Editorials," *The Journalist* (May 22, 1897): 34.
29. In the 1850s, Jane Cunningham's articles about fashion appeared in the *New York Herald* under the byline "Jennie June." See William David Sloan, *The Media in America*, 6th ed. (Northport, AL: Vision Press, 2005), 131.
30. Balch, "Signed Editorials," *The Journalist* (May 22, 1897).
31. Stone, "Newspapers in the United States," 305.
32. Florence Finch Kelly, *Flowing Stream: The Story of Fifty-Six Years in American Newspaper Life* (New York: E. P. Dutton & Co., 1939), 324.
33. See Susan E. Tifft and Alex S. Jones, *The Trust: The Private and Powerful Family Behind the* New York Times (Boston: Little, Brown, 1999), 67.
34. Christine Ogan, et. al., "The Changing Front Page of the New York Times, 1900–1970," *Journalism Quarterly* 52, 2 (Summer 1975): Table 2, p. 342.
35. Tifft and Jones, *The Trust*, 82.
36. See Alfred Balch, "Signature in Newspapers," *Lippincott's Magazine* 62 (1898): 857.
37. See Balch, "Signature in Newspapers," 858.
38. Balch, "Signed Editorials," 34.
39. Balch, "Signed Editorials," 34.
40. Balch, "Signed Editorials," 34.
41. "Personal Journalism," *Fourth Estate* (September 26, 1897).
42. Balch recognized this prospect, writing in 1898 that "the shrewdest newspaper proprietors have at last understood that ... far from a writer's popularity decreasing that of the paper, the reverse is true. These

men now see that just as it pays the proprietor of a theatre to engage actors and actresses who are known and liked, so it pays a newspaper to have known names appear in its columns." See Balch, "Signature in Newspapers," 857.

43. See "Richard Harding Davis and Frederic Remington in Cuba for the Journal," *New York Journal* (January 17, 1897): 1.

44. See Balch, "Signed Editorials," 34.

45. The Watergate scandal of the early 1970s supposedly launched "the era of the journalist as celebrity." See Alicia C. Shepard, "Celebrity Journalists," *American Journalism Review* (September 1997): 26.

46. "Is There A Santa Claus?" *New York Sun* (September 21, 1897): 6.

47. Mitchell, *Memoirs of an Editor*, 112.

48. "Is There A Santa Claus?" *New York Sun* (December 25, 1913): 8.

49. "Is There A Santa Claus?" *New York Sun* (September 21, 1897).

50. "Victory for the Yellow Journalism," *New York Press* (January 31, 1897): 6.

51. "British Ships in American Waters," "The English Language in Connecticut," "The Chainless Bicycle," *New York Sun* (September 21, 1897): 6.

52. Readers of the *Sun* were known to invoke the editorial in discussing controversies about whether children should be discouraged from belief in Santa Claus. For example, a letter-writer to the *Sun* said in December 1898: "A year ago, in a very beautiful editorial, the Sun answered a little girl's question as to the existence of Santa Claus. The interest of your paper in this subject prompts me to call your attention to the outrageous presumption of certain teachers in the public schools in New York and Brooklyn" who had told schoolchildren that Santa Claus did not exist. See "Santa Claus," *New York Sun* (December 22, 1898): 6.

53. "'Is There A Santa Claus?'" *New York Sun* (December 25, 1918): 6.

54. Untitled letter to the editor, *New York Sun* (December 25, 1918): 6.

55. C. Al. Rhines, "Good Old Santa Claus," letter to the editor, *New York Sun* (December 28, 1914): 6.

56. Quoted in "A Classic and Its Author," *New York Sun* (December 23, 1926): 16.

57. Mario Canevaro, "In Appreciation," letter to the editor, *New York Sun* (December 27, 1940): 16.

58. See, for, example, Mrs. G. C. Jefferis, "Santa Claus," letter to the editor, *New York Sun* (October 12, 1897): 6.

59. Thomas Vinciguerra, "Yes, Virginia, a Thousand Times Yes," *New York Times* (September 2, 1997): WK2.

60. The advice about boldness in editorial-writing appeared in the *Missouri Editor* and was reprinted in "The Value of Editorials," *Fourth Estate* (November 29, 1894): 5.

61. Five days after Dana's death in 1897, the *Sun* published a signed editorial comment eulogizing the editor. See Mayo W. Hazeltine, "Charles Anderson Dana—A Personal Tribute," *New York Sun* (October 22, 1897): 6. Hazeltine was the *Sun*'s literary editor.

62. See "H. M'd. Anderson, Editorial Writer," *New York Times* (December 27, 1940): 27, and "Brilliant Names Dot Sun's History," *New York Times* (January 5, 1950). Anderson's editorial said in part: "Alone? Is he alone at whose right side rides Courage, with Skill within the cockpit and Faith upon the left? Does solitude surround the brave when Adventure leads the way and Ambition reads the dials? Is there no company with him, for whom the air is cleft by Daring and the darkness made light by Enterprise?"

63. Untitled editorial comment, *New York Sun* (April 12, 1906): 8.

64. "A Clergyman's Tribute to Francis P. Church," *New York Sun* (April 15, 1906): 6.

65. "A Clergyman's Tribute to Francis P. Church," *New York Sun* (April 15, 1906).

66. "A Clergyman's Tribute to Francis P. Church," *New York Sun* (April 15, 1906).

67. The many accounts that have said the *Sun* routinely reprinted the editorial after 1897 include: "Girl Who Asked Sun of Santa Won't Tell If She Found One," *Washington Post* (December 25, 1934), 14; Murray Illson, "Prompted Santa Claus Editorial," *New York Times* (May 14, 1971): 44; "Haynes Johnson, "One Gift of Words That Turned Into a Christmas Treasure," *Washington Post* (December 25, 1983): A3; Frederic D. Schwarz, "The Big Question," *American Heritage* (September 1997); Mark Neuzil, "In Newspapers We Don't Trust Anymore, Virginia," *Star Tribune* [Minneapolis] (December 18, 1997): 32A; "How Famed Editorial Came to Be," Allentown [PA] *Morning Call* (December 25, 1998): A36; Chris Rovzar, "Sun Shines at Lord & Taylor Display," *New York Sun* (November 14, 2003): 13; "A Look Back: Yes, Virginia, There Is A Santa Claus," Duluth [MN] *News Tribune* (December 25, 2003), and "Yes, Virginia," Syracuse [NY] *Post-Standard* (December 24, 2004): A10.

68. "Santa Claus," *New York Sun* (December 25, 1902).

69. "Is There A Santa Claus?" *New York Sun* (December 25, 1906): 6. In addition, the editorial was the first entry in a collection, published in 1905, of cheery essays and commentaries that had appeared in the *Sun*. See *Casual Essays of the Sun* (New York: Robert Grier Cooke, 1905), 1–3.

70. "There Is A Santa Claus," *Arizona Republican* (December 25, 1897): 7. The newspaper was renamed *Arizona Republic* in 1930. In addition, the *Literary Digest* printed Virginia O'Hanlon's letter and the *Sun*'s editorial reply in its issue dated December 25, 1897. See "Topics of the Day:

Some Christmas Reflections," *Literary Digest* 14, 35 (December 25, 1897): 1021.

71. "'Is There A Santa Claus?'" *New York Sun* (December 25, 1916): 10.

72. "Is There A Santa Claus?" *New York Sun* (December 25, 1913).

73. "Is There A Santa Claus?" *New York Sun* (December 25, 1913).

74. Charles H. Clark, "To-morrow on This Page," letter to the editor, *New York Sun* (December 23, 1927): 16.

75. Canevaro, "In Appreciation," *New York Sun* (December 27, 1940).

76. "'Is There A Santa Claus?'" *New York Sun* (December 25, 1918).

77. See untitled editorial comment, *New York Sun* (December 24, 1925): 10.

78. Untitled editorial comment, *New York Sun* (December 24, 1925).

79. The editorial also figured in an ill-considered Depression era gesture by the *Sun*'s management. According to Haynes Johnson, a *Washington Post* columnist, the *Sun* in the 1930s gave employees framed reprints of "Is There A Santa Claus?" Johnson wrote: "In all the years my father worked as a reporter on the Sun, in time bringing honor to himself and his paper, that was the only Christmas bonus he ever received. Every Christmas that I can remember he would retell, [with] fury and relish, that story of holiday insensitivity in a time of great personal suffering. [The story] became part of our family Christmas tradition, one that still makes me smile so long after whenever I think of it." See Haynes Johnson, "The Old Wisdom May, After All, Offer a New Sense of Serenity," *Washington Post* (December 21, 1980): A3.

80. For a rare exception, see the brief article, "Praise for the Sun," *New York Sun* (December 9, 1897): 1. The article quoted William Lyon Phelps, a literature professor at Yale University, as saying: "The Sun has the best accounts of current events of any newspaper in America."

81. "A Steady Revolt," *New York Sun*. The *Sun* did reprint a brief passage from the letter which the reader had asked the *Sun* to "kindly reproduce."

82. See "The Sun Shows Spite Again," *Fourth Estate* (June 17, 1897): 1. The article noted that the *Sun* in the aftermath of the United Press bankruptcy had assailed Whitelaw Reid of the *New York Tribune* "as a defaulter and in other terms more forcible than elegant. Mr. Reid treated the attack with silent contempt, as most victims of the *Sun*'s malice are in the habit of doing."

83. "Leprous New Journalism," *New York Sun* (February 27, 1897): 7

84. "Charles A. Dana, The Famous Editor, Is Dead," *New York Journal* (October 18, 1897): 1.

85. "Profession or Trade?" *Fourth Estate* (October 28, 1897): 4.

86. See, for example, "Editors Use Their Fists," *Fourth Estate* (October 27, 1898): 7. The *Fourth Estate*'s report said "mutual expressions of editorial

dislike" had given rise to the fisticuffs between two editors in Springfield, IL.

87. See also, "Ohio Editors at War," *Fourth Estate* (June 10, 1897): 3. The article recounted the arrest on criminal libel charges of Port Fullmer, editor of the *Homes News* in West Jefferson, OH. The charges were brought by a rival editor in London, OH, whom Fullmer's newspaper had assailed in large headlines as "The Noted London Crook."

88. See Denis Brian, *Pulitzer: A Life* (New York: John Wiley & Sons, 2001), 127–31. See also, Janet Steele, *The Sun Shines for All: Journalism and Ideology in the Life of Charles A. Dana* (Syracuse, NY: Syracuse University Press, 1993), 144. Pulitzer was born a Jew but converted to Christianity. Steele wrote: "Dana's attacks on Pulitzer as the 'Jew who does not want to be a Jew' were particularly offensive from one who had unfailingly championed religious toleration and diversity."

89. Cited in Brian, *Pulitzer*, 128.

90. "The Derelicts of Journalism," *New York World* (March 28, 1897): 11.

91. "A Steady Revolt," *New York Sun* (April 10, 1897): 6.

92. The editorial's unusual timing tripped up at least one scholar. In her study of Charles Dana, Janet Steele mistakenly wrote that the editorial reply to Virginia O'Hanlon was "published on Christmas Day 1897." See Steele, *The Sun Shines for All*, 109.

93. Such efforts were criticized by the *New York Journal* among other newspapers. The *Journal* declared: "Let us keep Santa Claus despite the outcry of the people who think that no deception can be amiable. There never was a child worse for belief in him." See "Christmas, and Santa Claus," *New York Journal* (December 25, 1897): 6.

94. Cited in "Must Santa Claus Be Banished?" *Philadelphia Evening Bulletin* (December 23, 1897): 8.

95. Cited in "Santa Claus to be Banished," *Philadelphia Press* (December 22, 1897): 8. The *Press* noted in an editorial condemning the policy: "The arguments against the myth if carried out logically would rule out all fairyland from a child's life, would suppress the habit of the game of 'pretending' and make of children not imaginative human beings but wretched prigs to whom a large part of the literature of all ages would be a closed book." See "The Tilt at Santa Claus," *Philadelphia Press* (December 23, 1897): 6.

96. "Public Schools Open To-Day," *New York Sun* (September 13, 1897): 4.

97. See Vinciguerra, "Yes, Virginia, a Thousand Times Yes," *New York Times* (September 21, 1997).

98. Cited in Illson, "Prompted Santa Claus Editorial," *New York Times* (May 14, 1971).

99. "Notes and Queries," *New York Sun* (September 12, 1897), sect. 2, p. 3. The *Sun*'s reply: "Bun is provincial English for rabbit; bunny is a diminutive. Bunny-rabbit is pleonastic."

100. "Notes and Queries," *New York Sun* (October 10, 1897): sect. 2, p. 3.

101. Cited in "Writer of Famed 'Santa' Letter Has Heightened Christmas Spirit," newspaper clipping from December 1959 (publication data missing), in possession of James Temple, North Chatham, NY.

102. James Temple, telephone interviews with author, November 7, 2003, and April 19, 2004.

103. Edward P. Mitchell, *Memoirs of an Editor: Fifty Years of American Journalism* (New York: Scribner's, 1924), 112. Mitchell's account says "Church bristled and pooh-poohed at the subject when I suggested he write a reply to Virginia O'Hanlon; but he took the letter and turned with an air of resignation to his desk" to write.

104. "Is There A Santa Claus?" *New York Sun* (December 25, 1913).

105. Cited in "Writer of Famed 'Santa' Letter Has Heightened Christmas Spirit." See also, Fred Kaplan, "A Child's Query Echoes Across the Ages," *Boston Globe* (December 22, 1997): A3.

106. See, "Virginia, Now 70, Quits As Teacher," *New York Times* (June 12, 1959): 18.

107. See Kaplan, "A Child's Query," *Boston Globe* (December 22, 1997).

108. See "Santa Editorial to be Read Today," *New York Times* (December 20, 1933): 23.

109. "Virginia O'Hanlon, Santa's Friend, Dies," *New York Times* (May 14, 1971): 1.

110. James Temple, telephone interview with author, April 19, 2004.

111. Cited in John O'Mahony, "Yes, Virginia, It Is a Classic Tale; Kin of Santa-Letter Girl Recall Touching Story," *New York Post* (December 14, 1997): 8.

112. See "A New Year Ushered In," *New York Times* (January 1, 1897): 1.

113. "Quiet New Year Day," *Washington Evening Star* (January 1, 1897): 1.

114. "Quiet New Year Day," *Washington Evening Star* (January 1, 1897).

115. "The New Year: Annual Reception at the White House," *Los Angeles Times* (January 2, 1897): 1.

116. Richard Harding Davis, letter to his family (January 2, 1897); Richard Harding Davis Collection, Alderman Library of American Literature, University of Virginia, Charlottesville.

117. Davis, letter to his family (December 25, 1896); Davis Collection, Alderman Library, University of Virginia.

118. See Lubow, *The Reporter Who Would Be King*, 115–116.

119. Davis, letter to Rebecca Harding Davis (January 9, 1897); Davis Collection, Alderman Library, University of Virginia.

120. The original source for the purported Remington–Hearst exchange was James Creelman in his book of reminiscences, *On the Great Highway: The Wanderings and Adventures of a Special Correspondent* (Boston: Lothrop Publishing, 1901), 177–78.

121. See, among others, Upton Sinclair, *The Brass Check: A Study of American Journalism* (self-published, 1920), 254; John Tebbel, *The Compact History of the American Newspaper* (New York: Hawthorn Books, 1963), 202, and Hiley H. Ward, *Mainstreams of American Media History: A Narrative and Intellectual History* (Boston: Allyn and Bacon, 1997), 279.

122. For a detailed discussion debunking the purported Remington–Hearst exchange, see W. Joseph Campbell, *Yellow Journalism: Puncturing the Myths, Defining the Legacies* (Westport, CT: Praeger Publishers, 2001), 71–95.

123. Davis, letter to Rebecca Harding Davis (January 15, 1897); Davis Collection, Alderman Library, University of Virginia.

124. See "Shipping News," *New York Tribune* (January 21, 1897): 14.

125. Davis, letter to Rebecca Harding Davis (January 16, 1897); Davis Collection, Alderman Library, University of Virginia.

126. Richard Harding Davis, "Davis and Remington Tell of Spanish Cruelty," *New York Journal* (February 2, 1897): 1.

127. Lubow, *The Reporter Who Would Be King*, 141.

128. Davis, "Davis and Remington Tell of Spanish Cruelty," *New York Journal* (February 2, 1897).

129. Davis, "Davis and Remington Tell of Spanish Cruelty," *New York Journal* (February 2, 1897).

130. Davis, "Davis and Remington Tell of Spanish Cruelty," *New York Journal* (February 2, 1897).

131. Davis, "Davis and Remington Tell of Spanish Cruelty," *New York Journal* (February 2, 1897).

132. Davis, "Davis and Remington Tell of Spanish Cruelty," *New York Journal* (February 2, 1897).

133. Davis, "Davis and Remington Tell of Spanish Cruelty," *New York Journal* (February 2, 1897).

134. Davis, "Davis and Remington Tell of Spanish Cruelty," *New York Journal* (February 2, 1897).

135. Lubow, *The Reporter Who Would Be King*, 141–42.

136. See, for example, John Seelye, *War Games: Richard Harding Davis and the New Imperialism* (Amherst: University of Massachusetts Press, 2003), 240. See also, Lubow, *The Reporter Who Would Be King*, 141.

137. Seelye, *War Games*, 239.

138. Seelye, *War Games*, 242.

139. Cited in "War Correspondents," *Fourth Estate* (January 17, 1895): 15. The *Fourth Estate* said Moffett's article was published in *Illustrated American* under the title, "The Failure of the American War Correspondent."

140. Davis, letter to his mother (January 19, 1897); Davis Collection, Alderman Library, University of Virginia.

141. Richard Harding Davis, letter to his mother (January 24, 1897); Davis Collection, Alderman Library, University of Virginia.

142. The dates and venues were cited in the dateline of Davis' dispatch to the *Journal*.

143. Davis, letter to his mother (January 20, 1897); Davis Collection, Alderman Library, University of Virginia.

144. "Richard Harding Davis and Frederic Remington in Cuba for the Journal," *New York Journal* (January 17, 1897). As the *Journal* prepared to publish the story, Remington was about to leave Cuba.

145. Davis, letter to his mother (January 24, 1897); Davis Collection, Alderman Library, University of Virginia.

146. Her brother was an insurgent leader near Havana. See Richard Harding Davis, "Does Our Flag Shield Women?" *New York Journal* (February 12, 1897): 1–2.

147. Davis, "Does Our Flag Shield Women?" *New York Journal* (February 12, 1897): 1.

148. As Spain's chief diplomatic representative to the United States, Enrique Dupuy de Lôme, told the *Journal*, Spanish authorities in Havana had "a perfect right to board an American steamer, or any other kind of vessel, and search persons, be they men or women, whom they suspect. A request to the steamer officials is not necessary." See "Minister De Lome's Retort," *New York Journal* (February 13, 1897): 1.

149. Davis, "Does Our Flag Shield Women?" *New York Journal* (February 12, 1897), 1.

150. Davis, "Does Our Flag Shield Women?" *New York Journal*, (February 12, 1897), 2.

151. Lubow, *The Reporter Who Would Be King*, 143. Davis "intended the article to cause a sensation," Lubow wrote, "and it did."

152. "Tale of a Fair Exile: Senorita Arango's Own Story of the Olivette 'Search Outrage,'" *New York World* (February 15, 1897): 1.

153. Lubow, *The Reporter Who Would Be King*, 144.

154. The four charges against Scovel were cited in Thomas G. Alvord, Jr., "How Scovel Fares," *New York World* (February 20, 1897): 2.

155. "Richard Harding Davis Writes of the World's Correspondent," *New York World* (February 18, 1897): 1.

156. "Richard Harding Davis Writes of the World's Correspondent," *New York World* (February 18, 1897).

157. See "Fearless But Never Armed," *New York World* (February 7, 1897): 2.

158. Sylvester Scovel, "Rebels Never More Hopeful, Scovel Cables to the World," *New York World* (January 7, 1897): 1.
159. Scovel, "Rebels Never More Hopeful," *New York World* (January 7, 1897).
160. "A Brave Correspondent," *New York World* (January 8, 1897): 6.
161. Alvord, "How Scovel Fares," *New York World* (February 20, 1897).
162. Sylvester Scovel, "Cable Dispatch from Scovel Written in the Cuban Prison," *New York World* (February 18, 1897): 1.
163. "The Scovel Case," *New York World* (February 8, 1897): 6. The *World's* editorial also stated: "He has done nothing and is accused of nothing that any American citizen has not an indisputable right to do."
164. "Scovel's Perilous Situation," *New York World* (February 15, 1897): 6.
165. "Scovel's Perilous Situation," *New York World* (February 15, 1897). Richard Harding Davis, in his letter to the *World*, took up the criticism of the U.S. State Department, writing: "If through the incomprehensible indifference of the State Department Scovel is permitted to die of disease in jail, or if they shoot him and say he was trying to escape, which they are quite capable of doing, his fate will be due to a most treacherous and cruel desertion of a spirited and brave gentleman by his own government. But the people may remember him." See "Richard Harding Davis Writes of the World's Correspondent," *New York World* (February 18, 1897).
166. After his release in March 1897, Scovel praised the U.S. consul-general in Havana, Fitzhugh Lee, as well as the two American consular officials in Cuba, Rafael Madrigal in Sancti Spíritus and Walter Barker in Sagua la Grande. Madrigal and Barker, he said, "look out for American interests instead of American dollars." See "Scovel Home Again!" *New York World* (March 24, 1897): 3. Donnell Rockwell, the U.S. consular clerk in Havana who was to figure in the jailbreak of Evangelina Cisneros in October 1897, was a friend of Scovel. Rockwell wrote to Scovel soon after the correspondent's arrest, saying: "There was no one, old man, that learned of your arrest with more sorrow than myself, but with the rest of your many friends[,] I rejoice that you are so far comfortable and well-treated." See Rockwell, letter to Sylvester Scovel (February 17, 1897); Sylvester Scovel papers, Missouri Historical Society Archives, St. Louis, MO. In another letter, Rockwell assured Scovel: "All your friends here are watching your case with interest, and I hope it will not be too long before you are free again." Rockwell, letter to Scovel (February 25, 1897); Scovel papers, Missouri Historical Society Archives, St. Louis.
167. See Scovel's Prison Diary (March 1, 1897); Scovel papers, Missouri Historical Society Archives, St. Louis.
168. Thomas G. Alvord, Jr., "Weyler Scowls at Scovel's Cell," *New York World* (February 27, 1897): 1.

169. Cited in Scovel's Prison Diary (February 26, 1897); Scovel papers, Missouri Historical Society Archives, St. Louis.

170. See Scovel's Prison Diary (February 27, 1897); Scovel papers, Missouri Historical Society Archives, St. Louis.

171. Alvord, "Weyler Scowls at Scovel's Cell," *New York World* (February 27, 1897).

172. Alvord, "Weyler Scowls at Scovel's Cell," *New York World* (February 27, 1897).

173. The bad dream was mentioned in Scovel's Prison Diary (February 26, 1897); Scovel papers, Missouri Historical Society Archives, St. Louis.

174. Alvord, "Weyler Scowls at Scovel's Cell," *New York World* (February 27, 1897).

175. Alvord, "Weyler Scowls at Scovel's Cell," *New York World* (February 27, 1897).

176. The petition was rather vague in wording. It urged Spanish authorities in Cuba to extend to Scovel "every consideration which the universal amenities of war accord to conscientious correspondents in the field." See "The World's War Correspondent to be Released Without Trial," *New York World* (March 10, 1897): 1. The *World* nonetheless said of the petition: "So remarkable a tribute was probably never before paid to a war correspondent in the field."

177. See "The World's War Correspondent to be Released," *New York World* (March 10, 1897). See also, "Potentiality of President and the Press," *Fourth Estate* (March 18, 1897): 7.

178. See "Potentiality of President and the Press," *Fourth Estate* (March 18, 1897).

179. See, for example, "Three More States in Line for Scovel," *New York World* (February 20, 1897): 2. See also, Joyce Milton, *The Yellow Kids: Foreign Correspondents in the Heyday of Yellow Journalism* (New York: Harper & Row, 1989), 147. Milton said seventeen state legislatures adopted resolutions supporting Scovel.

180. Cited in "Make Scovel's Cause Their Own," *New York World* (February 20, 1897): 2.

181. Biographic details about Scovel are from "Fearless But Never Armed," *New York World* (February 7, 1897): 1–2.

182. See "Fearless But Never Armed," *New York World* (February 7, 1897).

183. "Fearless But Never Armed," *New York World* (February 7, 1897).

184. "Fearless But Never Armed," *New York World* (February 7, 1897).

185. See, for example, Scovel, letter to Frances Scovel, (n.d., but April 1897); Scovel papers, Missouri Historical Society Archives, St. Louis. In the letter, Scovel complimented his wife for having been "'brave enough to stay at home'" while he went "forward on our path to possible fame and

fortune" by accepting the assignment to cover the Greco-Turkish War in the spring of 1897.

186. Joseph Pulitzer, cablegram to John Norris (August 7, 1897), W. A. Swanberg papers, Butler Library, Columbia University, New York, NY.

187. Sylvester Scovel, "All Cuba Aflame, Scovel Says," *New York World* (February 20, 1897): 1–2.

188. Gerald Linderman, *The Mirror of War: American Society and the Spanish-American War.* (Ann Arbor, MI: University of Michigan Press, 1974), 133–34. Linderman also wrote (133): "It was far easier to pretend to the waging of a familiar war than to explain a new one, especially when the reality was unromantic, unregulated, expensive of noncombatant life and American-owned property."

189. Scovel, Prison Diary (February 18, 1897); Scovel papers, Missouri Historical Society Archives, St. Louis.

190. Scovel, Prison Diary (February 18, 1897); Scovel papers, Missouri Historical Society Archives, St. Louis.

191. "Scovel Home Again!" *New York World* (March 24, 1897).

192. Sylvester Scovel, letter to Frances Scovel (May 7, 1897); Scovel papers, Missouri Historical Society Archives, St. Louis. Emphasis in the original.

193. Scovel, letter to Frances Scovel (May 19, 1897); Scovel papers, Missouri Historical Society Archives, St. Louis.

194. Scovel, letter to Frances Scovel (May 7, 1897); Scovel papers, Missouri Historical Society Archives, St. Louis. See also, Scovel, letter to Frances Scovel (May 25, 1897); Scovel papers, Missouri Historical Society Archives, St. Louis.

195. See, Scovel, letter to Frances Scovel (May 1, 1897); Scovel papers, Missouri Historical Society Archives, St. Louis. Scovel wrote that the *World*'s London correspondent, Ballard Smith, had raised the matter of Scovel's "taking the London office." According to the letter, Smith said he had recommended that Pulitzer assign Scovel to the London correspondency.

196. See "Interesting News of the World," Fourth Estate (May 27, 1897): 3. Marshall returned to the *Journal* as a correspondent in the Spanish-American War, and was shot and severely wounded in Cuba.

197. Scovel, letter to Frances Scovel (June 17, 1897); Scovel papers, Missouri Historical Society Archives, St. Louis.

198. See Scovel, letter to Frances Scovel (May 19, 1897); Scovel papers, Missouri Historical Society Archives, St. Louis.

199. Scovel, letter to Frances Scovel (June 8, 1897); Scovel papers, Missouri Historical Society Archives, St. Louis.

200. Scovel, letter to Frances Scovel (June 15, 1897); Scovel papers, Missouri Historical Society Archives, St. Louis. He also wrote that "the whole

lot of" Spanish officials "know they are beaten [in Cuba] and naturally don't care to say so."

201. Scovel, letter to Frances Scovel (June 17, 1897); Scovel papers, Missouri Historical Society Archives, St. Louis.

202. Scovel, memorandum to Joseph Pulitzer (October 2, 1897); Scovel papers, Missouri Historical Society Archives, St. Louis.

203. "Reminiscences of Mrs. Scovel," n.d.; Scovel papers Missouri Historical Society Archives, St. Louis.

204. Scovel, memorandum to Pulitzer (October 2, 1897); Scovel papers, Missouri Historical Society Archives, St. Louis.

205. See "A Famous Correspondent," *Seattle Post-Intelligencer* (August 6, 1897), Scovel file, Klondike Gold Rush National Historical Park, Skagway, AK. The article described Scovel as "a wonderfully energetic young man. ... He has always been called upon to fill hard 'assignments' and he has got so accustomed to such things that he rather enjoys it."

206. Scovel, memorandum to Pulitzer (October 2, 1897); Scovel papers, Missouri Historical Society Archives, St. Louis.

207. Scovel, memorandum to Pulitzer (October 2, 1897); Scovel papers, Missouri Historical Society Archives, St. Louis.

208. Scovel, memorandum to Pulitzer (October 2, 1897); Scovel papers, Missouri Historical Society Archives, St. Louis.

209. "Reminiscences of Mrs. Scovel," n.d.; Scovel papers Missouri Historical Society Archives, St. Louis.

210. See "Landslide on the Dyea Trail," *New York World* (September 25, 1897): 1.

211. Scovel, memorandum to Pulitzer (October 2, 1897); Scovel papers, Missouri Historical Society Archives, St. Louis.

212. Sylvester Scovel, "Gold-Hunters Cheer for the World on the Skaguay Trail," *New York World* (September 6, 1897): 3.

213. Quoted in "World's Klondike Farce," *New York Sun* (November 22, 1897): 6.

214. "World's Klondike Farce," *New York Sun* (November 22, 1897).

215. Quoted in "Buncoed by the World: Its Work at Skagway," *New York Sun* (November 20, 1897): 2.

216. See "Snow-Balled: Skaguay Pass Too Stuck Up for Use," *Los Angeles Times* (September 20, 1897): 1.

217. Scovel, memorandum to Pulitzer (October 2, 1897); Scovel papers, Missouri Historical Society Archives, St. Louis.

218. Scovel, letter to Frances Scovel (September 12, 1897); Scovel papers, Missouri Historical Society Archives, St. Louis.

219. Scovel, letter to Frances Scovel (September 12, 1897); Scovel papers, Missouri Historical Society Archives, St. Louis.

220. Milton, *The Yellow Kids*, 179. She wrote: "The stranded prospectors in Dawson City had plenty of money, and the situation was ripe for an entrepreneur with the capital and daring to supply their needs."

221. See E. Hazard Wells, *Magnificence and Misery: A Firsthand Account of the 1897 Klondike Gold Rush*, Randall M. Dodd, ed. (Garden City, NY: Doubleday & Co., 1984), 201.

222. Scovel to Pulitzer (October 2, 1897); Scovel papers, Missouri Historical Society Archives, St. Louis.

223. Scovel, letter to Frances Scovel (October 1,, 1897); Scovel papers, Missouri Historical Society Archives, St. Louis.

224. Scovel, letter to Frances Scovel (September 21, 1897); Scovel papers, Missouri Historical Society Archives, St. Louis.

225. Scovel, letter to Frances Scovel (September 22, 1897); Scovel papers, Missouri Historical Society Archives, St. Louis.

226. Scovel, letter to Frances Scovel (September 22, 1897); Scovel papers, Missouri Historical Society Archives, St. Louis. He reasoned that if Frances had been aware of the circumstances, she would have endorsed his decision to go on to New York. See Scovel, letter to his parents (October 6, 1897); Scovel papers, Missouri Historical Society Archives, St. Louis.

227. See Scovel, telegram to William Saportas (n.d, but September 22, 1897); copy in Sylvester Scovel file, Klondike Gold Rush National Historical Park, Skagway, AK.

228. Scovel, letter to Frances Scovel (September 22, 1897); Scovel papers, Missouri Historical Society Archives, St. Louis.

229. Scovel, telegram to Saportas (n.d, but September 22, 1897); Scovel file, Klondike Gold Rush National Historical Park, Skagway, AK.

230. "Reminiscences of Mrs. Scovel," n.d.; Scovel papers Missouri Historical Society Archives, St. Louis.

231. "Reminiscences of Mrs. Scovel," n.d.; Scovel papers Missouri Historical Society Archives, St. Louis.

232. Frances Scovel, letter to her mother (September 26, 1897); Scovel papers, Missouri Historical Society Archives, St. Louis.

233. Scovel, letter to Frances Scovel (September 26, 1897); Scovel papers, Missouri Historical Society Archives, St. Louis.

234. Scovel, letter to Frances Scovel (October 1, 1897); Scovel papers, Missouri Historical Society Archives, St. Louis.

235. Scovel, memorandum to Pulitzer (October 2, 1897); Scovel papers, Missouri Historical Society Archives, St. Louis.

236. Scovel, letter to Frances Scovel (October 1, 1897); Scovel papers, Missouri Historical Society Archives, St. Louis.

237. Scovel, letter to Frances Scovel (October 1, 1897); Scovel papers, Missouri Historical Society Archives, St. Louis.

238. See Frances Scovel, letter to her father (November 12, 1897); Scovel papers, Missouri Historical Society Archives, St. Louis.

239. Scovel, letter to his father (misdated October 4, 1897, probably November 4, 1897); Scovel papers, Missouri Historical Society Archives, St. Louis.

240. Frances Scovel, letter to her father (November 12, 1897); Scovel papers, Missouri Historical Society Archives, St. Louis.

241. Frances Scovel, letter to her mother (November 9, 1897); Scovel papers, Missouri Historical Society Archives, St. Louis.

242. Frances Scovel, letter to her father (November 15, 1897); Scovel papers, Missouri Historical Society Archives, St. Louis.

243. Barker returned to Cuba on November 14, 1897 and resumed his consular duties on November 17, 1897. See Sylvester Scovel, "Gen. Lee in Havana Again," *New York World* (November 15, 1897): 2, and Walter B. Barker to William R. Day (November 17, 1897), Record Group 59, Sagua la Grande Consular Dispatches, National Archives, College Park, MD.

244. Frances Scovel, letter to her father (November 15, 1897); Scovel papers, Missouri Historical Society Archives, St. Louis.

245. Frances Scovel, letter to her father (November 15, 1897); Scovel papers, Missouri Historical Society Archives, St. Louis.

246. Frances Scovel, letter to her father (November 15, 1897); Scovel papers, Missouri Historical Society Archives, St. Louis.

247. Frances Scovel, letter to her father (November 15, 1897); Scovel papers, Missouri Historical Society Archives, St. Louis.

248. [Sylvester Scovel], "Flogged Starving Cuban Children," *New York World* (November 26, 1897): 7.

249. Frances Scovel, letter to her father (November 15, 1897); Scovel papers, Missouri Historical Society Archives, St. Louis.

250. Frances Scovel, letter to her father (November 15, 1897); Scovel papers, Missouri Historical Society Archives, St. Louis.

251. Frances Scovel, letter to her parents (n.d., but December 1897); Scovel papers, Missouri Historical Society Archives, St. Louis.

252. See "Scovel to Return to Cuba," *New York Times* (December 25, 1897): 7.

253. See "Americans Visit Gomez," *New York Times* (December 30, 1897): 5.

254. Sylvester Scovel, "The World Again Makes History for Spain and Cuba," *New York World* (January 2, 1898): 2.

255. "Francis P. Church," *New York Times* (April 13, 1906).

256. "Francis P. Church," *New York Times* (April 13, 1906).

257. Cited in "Newspaper Men in the War," *Literary Digest* (October 15, 1898): 457.

258. Richard Harding Davis, "The Battle of San Juan," *Scribner's Magazine* 24, 4 (October 1898): 402.

259. Lubow, *The Reporter Who Would Be King*, 291.
260. Cited in Lubow, *The Reporter Who Would Be King*, 293.
261. Ralph Paine, a Spanish-American war correspondent, wrote in his memoirs that "Scovel's fist glanced off the general's double chin," leaving a red scratch that remained visible for several days. Paine said the Scovel–Shafter encounter was "an incident of war without precedent." See Paine, *Roads of Adventure*, 266.
262. "Giving the Devil His Due," *Fourth Estate* (August 4, 1898): 5.
263. Sylvester Scovel, letter to the editor, "Gen. Shafter and Sylvester Scovel," *New York World* (August 10, 1898): 4. Scovel wrote: "Gen. Shafter struck me in the face. The blow was stinging, quick, and absolutely unlooked for. I answered it."
264. Milton, *The Yellow Kids*, 366.
265. "Sylvester Scovel Dead," *New York Times* (February 13, 1905): 2.

Chapter 4

1. See, notably, Charles Duval [Karl Decker], "Evangelina Cisneros Rescued by the Journal," *New York Journal* (October 10, 1897): 1, and Karl Decker, "How Decker Hid Evangelina," *New York Journal* (October 16, 1897): 1.
2. Evangelina Cisneros and Karl Decker, *The Story of Evangelina Cisneros Told by Herself, Her Rescue by Karl Decker* (New York: Continental Publishing Co., 1898), 78.
3. The *Journal* and other newspapers referred to her, incorrectly, as "Cisneros." The proper second reference would be "Cosío y Cisneros." However, "Cisneros" will be used here, given that the case is commonly known by that name.
4. See "Evangelina Cisneros Reaches the Land of Liberty," *New York Journal* (October 14, 1897): 1. The *Journal*'s report began this way: "Evangelina Cisneros, one week ago a prisoner among the outcast wretches in the hideous Havana prison, is a guest at the Waldorf Hotel. Surrounded by all the luxury and elegance that hostelry can furnish, she is alternately laughing and crying over the events of one short week."
5. See "Ovation to Miss Cisneros," *New York Times* (October 17, 1897): 5.
6. "Reception to Miss Cisneros," *Philadelphia Press* (October 17, 1897): 1.
7. "Reception to Miss Cisneros," *Philadelphia Press* (October 17, 1897).
8. "The People's Welcome to Evangelina Cisneros," *New York Journal* (October 18, 1897): 6.
9. "Ten Thousand Cheers," *Washington Post* (October 24, 1897): 3.
10. "Jail-Breaking Journalism," *Chicago Times-Herald* (October 12, 1897): 6.

11. See, for example, "Editors on the Journal's Rescue of Miss Cisneros," *New York Journal* (October 12, 1897): 6 and "Newspaper Men's Daring," *Fourth Estate* (October 14, 1897): 5.
12. "New York Newspaper's International Triumph," *Fourth Estate* (October 21, 1897): 6.
13. "Modern Journalism and One of Its Most Remarkable Achievements," *The Journalist* (November 13, 1897): 1. Among the perceptive post-escape commentaries was that of the *Washington Post*, which said of the rescue: "Nothing more out of time with this prosaic age could be imagined." The *Post* added: "No one here has ever been able to understand why the young woman was not publicly tried a year ago; why, if guilty, she was not punished according to her deserts, and why, if innocent, she has been for … months confined in a prison with the lowest criminals of Havana." See "A Chapter Out of Romance," *Washington Post* (October 11, 1897): 6.
14. Duval [Decker], "Evangelina Cisneros Rescued by the Journal," *New York Journal* (October 10, 1897).
15. See "The Journalism that Does Things," *New York Journal* (October 13, 1897): 8.
16. The clandestine network is described in Francisco M. Duque, *Historia de Regla: Descripcion Politica, Economica y Social, Desde su Fundacion Hasta el Dia* (Havana: Rambla, Bouza y Ca., 1925), 172–77.
17. Duque, *Historia de Regla*, 172, 175–177.
18. "Some Probabilities," *Richmond Dispatch* (October 15, 1897): 4.
19. See Cisneros and Decker, *The Story of Evangelina Cisneros*, 150–52.
20. "The Martyrdom of Evangelina Cisneros," *New York Journal* (August 19, 1897): 6.
21. "The Martyrdom of Evangelina Cisneros," *New York Journal* (August 19, 1897).
22. Cisneros and Decker, *The Story of Evangelina Cisneros*, 164.
23. Cisneros and Decker, *The Story of Evangelina Cisneros*, 171–72.
24. Cisneros and Decker, *The Story of Evangelina Cisneros*, 176.
25. Kendrick, "The Cuban Girl Martyr," *New York Journal* (August 17, 1897).
26. "Evangelina Cossio's brief statement about the Rising in the Isle of Pines" [n.d], Fitzhugh Lee papers, Alderman Library, University of Virginia, Charlottesville.
27. See Agustín Cosio, "Concise Statement of what Happened in the Isle of Pines," unpublished typescript, [n.d], Fitzhugh Lee papers, University of Virginia, Charlottesville.
28. "Evangelina Cossio's brief statement," Fitzhugh Lee papers, Alderman Library, University of Virginia, Charlottesville

29. Cosio, "Concise Statement of what Happened," Fitzhugh Lee papers, University of Virginia, Charlottesville.
30. "Evangelina Cossio's brief statement," Fitzhugh Lee papers, Alderman Library, University of Virginia, Charlottesville
31. Cosio, "Concise Statement of what Happened," Fitzhugh Lee papers, University of Virginia, Charlottesville. Spanish officials claimed that Evangelina had used her charms to lure Bérriz into what would have been a deadly trap as part of a wider uprising on the Isle of Pines. See "Gen. Weyler to the World," *New York World* (August 21, 1897): 1, and Enrique Dupuy de Lôme, letter to Varina Davis (August 24, 1897), cited in "Senorita Cisneros's Case," *New York Times* (August 26, 1897): 2.
32. "Journal Will Take Care of Her," *New York Evening Journal* (August 11, 1897).
33. See Cisneros and Decker, *The Story of Evangelina Cisneros*, 189.
34. See Fitzhugh Lee, "Rescue of Miss Cisneros," unpublished manuscript [1898], Fitzhugh Lee papers, University of Virginia.
35. Lee, "Rescue of Miss Cisneros," Fitzhugh Lee papers, University of Virginia.
36. Richard Harding Davis, for example, wrote in early 1897 that there was "no better informed American on Cuban matters than [Lee], nor one who sees the course our government should pursue more clearly. Through the Consuls all over the island, he is in touch with every part of it, and in daily touch." See Richard Harding Davis, "Cuba's Problem an Urgent One," *New York Journal* (February 25, 1897): 41.
37. Lee, "Rescue of Miss Cisneros," Fitzhugh Lee papers, University of Virginia.
38. Lee, "Rescue of Miss Cisneros," Fitzhugh Lee papers, University of Virginia, 6. Lee wrote that until he intervened, Cisneros was confined with other prisoners at Casa de Recogidas. He said he suggested that Spanish civil authorities inspect the jail and they did. "I suppose their report endorsed what I had said," Lee wrote, "because a few days thereafter orders were issued for rooms to be built upon the flat roof of the prison in which the better class of prisoners could be confined and detached from the remaining prisoners, and it was not long afterwards before Evangelina and some others were transferred to these new rooms. I little knew or suspected at the time that I was securing for her a place from which she could afterwards escape." See also, "Asks to See Weyler," *Chicago Tribune* (September 3, 1897): 3. The *Tribune* article, which was reprinted from the *New York World*, said that from July 1896 to February 1897, when the second floor quarters were built, Cisneros was kept "with all the low women and criminals. ... It is a disgrace to any community and to any people to allow so vile a place to be used for women prisoners, no matter what their crimes may have been. ... It is a further

wrong to keep a girl thirteen months without trial." See also, Cisneros and Decker, *The Story of Evangelina Cisneros*, 190. Cisneros said the conditions of her confinement improved dramatically with completion of the cell for political prisoners. "We were allowed to cook our own food and we had books to read," she wrote.

39. See Marion Kendrick, "The Cuban Girl Martyr," *New York Journal* (August 17, 1897): 1.

40. Kendrick, "The Cuban Girl Martyr," *New York Journal* (August 17, 1897). A few days later, the *World* quoted Weyler as saying Cisneros had neither been tried nor sentenced. Her case, Weyler said, was "in the preliminary stages." See "Gen. Weyler to the World," *New York World* (August 21, 1897).

41. Kendrick, "The Cuban Girl Martyr," *New York Journal* (August 17, 1897).

42. See, for example, George Eugene Bryson, "Weyler Throws Nuns Into Prison: Butcher Wages Brutal Warfare on Helpless Women," *New York Journal* (January 17, 1897): 1; "Persecutes Women Now: Beast Weyler, Baffled by Men, Attacks Patriots' Wives, Sisters, Mothers," *New York World* (February 8, 1897): 7, and "Weyler's Women Victims," *New York Sun* (August 22, 1897): 8.

43. Julia Ward Howe, "An Appeal to His Holiness the Pope," *New York Journal* (August 19, 1897): 1, and Varina Jefferson Davis, "Interceding with Maria Christain,"[sic] *New York Journal* (August 19, 1897): 1.

44. "The Whole Country Rising to the Rescue," *New York Journal* (August 23, 1897): 1.

45. "The Whole Country Rising to the Rescue," *New York Journal* (August 23, 1897).

46. Cisneros and Decker, *The Story of Evangelina Cisneros*, 61–62, 65.

47. See "Weyler Resents the Journal's Cisneros Appeal by Expelling Bryson," *New York Journal* (August 21, 1897): 1. Also expelled at that time was Eduardo Garcia, a correspondent for the *New York Sun* who had been jailed since May 1897. See Charles H. Brown, *The Correspondents' War: Journalists in the Spanish-American War* (New York: Charles Scribner's Sons, 1967), 95.

48. See Cisneros and Decker, *The Story of Evangelina Cisneros*, 68.

49. An article in the *Journal* in November 1897 identified the occupants of Casa Nueva, stating: "On the ground floor of the house is the Journal bureau and the inspecting rooms of the Marine Hospital Service of the United States, Lloyd's Shipping Agency and some brokers' offices. The second floor is occupied by Hidalgo & Co., agents of the Ward Steamship Line, and the top floor is the United States consulate." See George Clarke Musgrave, "Tried To Wreck Our Consulate in Havana," *New York Journal* (November 25, 1897): 5.

50. See Duval [Decker], "Evangelina Cisneros Rescued by the Journal," *New York Journal* (October 10, 1897), and Decker, "How Decker Hid Evangelina," *New York Journal* (October 16, 1897). Decker used a pseudonym over his October 10 article because he filed the dispatch via Key West, FL, before leaving Cuba. The *Washington Post* reported that the pseudonym was taken from Decker's given names, "Charles Duval Decker." The *Post* said Decker seldom used his full name but "his intimate friends knew of it." See "Decker Her Rescuer," *Washington Post* (October 14, 1897): 7. See also, "Cisneros Rescue Told by Its Hero," *New York World* (October 15, 1897): 12. The *World*'s account referred to Decker as "Charles Duval Decker."

51. See Duval [Decker], "Evangelina Cisneros Rescued by the Journal," *New York Journal* (October 10, 1897): 45.

52. Karen Roggenkamp, "The Evangelina Cisneros Romance, Medievalist Fiction, and the Journalism that Acts," *Journal of American & Comparative Cultures* 23, 2 (Summer 2000): 25.

53. See "Miss Cisneros's Escape," *New York Sun* (October 14, 1897): 5.

54. "Lee for Senate," *Richmond Dispatch* (October 16, 1897): 1. The report further quoted Lee as saying: "I have good authority for the statement that [Spanish officials] in Cuba are greatly incensed over the young woman's escape, but I am confident that the affair will lead to no complications, so far as this country is concerned."

55. "Lee's Tribute to Miss Cisneros," *New York Journal* (October 16, 1897): 2.

56. "Rescue Made Easy," *New York Times* (October 17, 1897): 12.

57. "Personal," *New York Times* (October 18, 1897): 6. Interestingly, authorities were thoroughly fooled in mid-July 1897 by the case of a woman dressed as a man who arrived in New York from Havana aboard the steamer *Seguranca*. "The passenger looked like a sturdy youth," the *New York Herald* reported, "but the voice was that of a young woman." See "She Hates Her Sex: Supposed Man Passengers on the Seguranca Was Discovered to be a Woman," *New York Herald* (July 16, 1897): 4. Like the *Seneca*, the *Seguranca* was owned by the Ward Line of New York.

58. "Miss Cisneros on Free Soil," *New York World* (October 14, 1897): 14.

59. "Miss Cisneros's Escape," *New York Sun* (October 13, 1897): 5.

60. "Miss Cisneros's Escape," *New York Sun* (October 13, 1897).

61. See "Spain Gets a Chance," *Chicago Times-Herald* (October 12, 1897): 1.

62. "Telegrama Oficial," Minister of Overseas Territories to Weyler (October 12, 1897); Archivo Histórico Nacional, Madrid, Spain.

63. "Telegramas Nacionales; Evangelina Cossio," *La Union Constitucional* [Havana, Cuba] (October 16, 1897): 1.

64. Frank Marshall White, "Details Asked of Weyler," *New York Journal* (October 15, 1897): 1. White's article said Weyler's version differed markedly from reports of the jailbreak published in U.S. newspapers. White's article, which was based upon an official account about the Madrid cabinet meeting, did not describe the differences, however.

65. "Glad to be Rid of Her," *New York World* (October 12, 1897): 7. Similar sentiments were expressed by John G. Carlisle, a former U.S. treasury secretary and a lawyer with ties to the Spanish diplomatic mission in Washington. In an account published in the *Journal*, Carlisle wrote: "My impression is … that Spain will take no stand [on seeking to extradite Cisneros] and that, in fact, she will be only too glad to have Miss Cisneros quietly removed and thus do away with further trouble on this score." John G. Carlisle, "Carlisle Would Give Her Up," *New York Journal* (October 11, 1897): 2.

66. See de Quesada and Northrup, *Cuba's Great Struggle for Freedom*, 608.

67. John D. Stevens, *Sensationalism and the New York Press* (New York: Columbia University Press, 1991), 96.

68. Rumors that Weyler, himself, accepted bribes in the Cisneros case appeared in the U.S. press. For example, a columnist for the *Chicago Times-Herald* wrote: "Among the interesting but probably base rumors in circulation in Washington is one to the effect that the New York newspaper which effected the release of Signorita Cisneros bribes Capitan General Weyler himself into shutting one eye and winking the other while the [escape] was being worked." See Walter Wellman, "Bicycle Court in White House," *Chicago Times-Herald* (October 13, 1897): 6.

69. For a brief discussion about Weyler's standing in Spain after his recall from Cuba, see John L. Offner, *An Unwanted War: The Diplomacy of the United States and Spain Over Cuba, 1895–1898* (Chapel Hill: University of North Carolina Press, 1992), 71–72. See also, "General Weyler Aspires to be a Political Boss; Will Become One of the Leaders of the Conservative Machine," *New York Journal* (October 30, 1897): 9.

70. See "Weyler Issues His Farewell," *New York Times* (October 31, 1897): 1. The dispatch quoted a proclamation Weyler issued before leaving Cuba which said in part: "You all know the state of the island when I arrived, and you are convinced that shortly peace will be re-established in the island. … The sugar estates are preparing for grinding. The railroads are in good condition for passengers and merchandise, and the country can be traveled without ambuscades, while incendiarism has stopped. … I leave the rebellion so reduced as to guarantee Spanish sovereignty, and only by artful means and by a complicity unworthy of Spaniards will the enemies of Spain be able to imperil it!" See also, "Weyler in His Own Defense," *New York Herald* (October 25, 1897): 9.

71. "The Monster of the Century," *New York Journal* (October 3, 1897): 50. The editorial declared: "Hanging for his innumerable murders would be Weyler's just fate." A few days later, the *Journal* called Weyler "the most depraved criminal of the century." See "Spain and the Butcher," *New York Journal* (October 8, 1897): 8.

72. See Halstead, "General Weyler Face to Face," *New York Herald* (November 28, 1897).

73. Willis J. Abbot, *Watching the World Go By* (Boston: Little, Brown, and Company, 1933), 215.

74. Abbot, *Watching the World Go By*, 216.

75. Abbot, *Watching the World Go By*, 216.

76. Abbot, *Watching the World Go By*, 215.

77. See, among other accounts, "Miss Cisneros's Escape," *New York Sun* (October 13, 1897): 5.

78. See, for example, "Miss Cisneros Happy in Freedom; Laughs Heartily on Reading Weyler's Official Notice of Her Escape; It Calls Upon Spanish Officials to Capture the Refugee and Convey Her to Havana," *New York Evening Journal* (October 14, 1897): 1. See also, "Evangelina Ordered Back," *New York World* (October 14, 1897): 14, and "Called on to Give Herself Up," *Florida Times-Union and Citizen* (October 14, 1897): 1.

79. "Administracion de justicia: Juzgados militaires: Habana," *Gaceta de la Habana* [Cuba] (October 13, 1897): 721. The official notice indicates that Spanish authorities in Havana regarded the jailbreak as a serious matter. A contrary interpretation is that the official notice "was simply playing for the galleries." See Gonzalo de Quesada and Henry Davenport Northrop, *Cuba's Great Struggle for Freedom* (n.p., 1898), 608. Their argument is implausible, however. Accepting that version means accepting that numerous Spanish authorities participated in a broad-based conspiracy of silence—and that they kept their silence during a time of instability and upheaval in the military leadership in Cuba.

80. Abbot, *Watching the World Go By*, 195–96. Abbot wrote: "It is perhaps illustrative of Hearst's methods with his employes, and his invariable willingness to concede personal liberty of political action to them, that he gave me a leave of absence, with full salary, to conduct this campaign, although the paper was supporting the regular Democratic ticket."

81. See "George Begins His Fight," *New York Tribune* (October 6, 1897): 1.

82. "George Factions Mixed," *New York Times* (October 7, 1897): 1.

83. See *Watching the World Go By*, 213, 216–17.

84. Kristin L. Hoganson, *Fighting for American Manhood: How Gender Politics Provoked the Spanish-American and Philippine-American Wars* (New Haven, CT: Yale University Press, 1998), 60. Hoganson flatly declared: "Decker bribed the prison guards to let her escape and then

fabricated an elaborate rescue plan to exonerate the guards and furnish newspaper material."

85. Ben Procter, *William Randolph Hearst: The Early Years, 1863–1910* (New York: Oxford University Press, 1998), 108–9. The index to Procter's book includes an entry titled "Cisneros hoax." In addition, David Nasaw included in his fine biography of Hearst a passing reference to "well-placed bribes" that supposedly facilitated the Cisneros jailbreak. Nasaw offered no supporting evidence for the claim, however. See Nasaw, *The Chief: The Life of William Randolph Hearst* (Boston: Houghton Mifflin, 2000), 129.

86. Stevens, *Sensationalism and the New York Press*, 96.

87. W. A. Swanberg, *Citizen Hearst: A Biography of William Randolph Hearst* (New York: Charles Scribner's Son, 1961), 125. Swanberg wrote that the "thrilling artifices" in the *Journal*'s account of the Cisneros escape "were necessary only for the purpose of making a good story and protecting the guards at the prison. The guards had been bribed in advance with Hearst's money and were conscientiously looking the other way."

88. Joyce Milton, *The Yellow Kids: Foreign Correspondents in the Heyday of Yellow Journalism* (New York: Harper & Row, 1989), 199.

89. Cisneros and Decker, *The Story of Evangelina Cisneros*, 73.

90. "Cisneros Rescue Told By Its Hero," *New York World* (October 15, 1897): 12. See also, "Miss Cisneros's Rescuer Here," *New York Times* (October 15, 1897): 7, and "Decker's Close Call," *Washington Post* (October 15, 1897): 1.

91. See Henry B. Nason, ed., *Biographical Record of the Officers and Candidates of the Rensselaer Polytechnic Institute, 1824–1886* (Troy, NY: William H. Young, 1887), 449–50. The volume's entry for Carbonell says he went to preparatory school in Philadelphia and matriculated at Rensselaer in 1872.

92. Duque, *Historia de Regla*, 172–77.

93. Duque, *Historia de Regla*, 174, 176.

94. Duque, *Historia de Regla*, 172.

95. Duque, *Historia de Regla*, 176.

96. Duque, *Historia de Regla*, 173. While the Cisneros jailbreak was a major coup, it was not the only time a prominent fugitive slipped out of Havana aboard a passenger steamer. In January 1898, Spanish authorities in Havana ordered the arrest of Richard Arnauto, a newspaper editor accused of setting off a spasm of rioting in the Cuban capital. His newspaper, *El Reconcentrado*, had criticized the policies of pro-Weyler elements in the Spanish military. In what was almost a reprise of the Cisneros escape, Arnauto went into hiding in Havana for several days, then donned a disguise and boarded a Ward Line steamer to New York.

He traveled under an assumed name, "Nestor Primelles Varona." See "Bold Editor Who Braved a Mob," *New York Journal* (January 29, 1898): 4; "Cuban Editor in New York," *Fourth Estate* (February 10, 1898): 2, and "Escaped Blanco's Edict," *New York Times* (January 28, 1898): 4. In an inevitable allusion to the Cisneros case, the *Journal* said Arnauto's leaving in disguise was "the fashionable way of getting out of Cuba now." See "Bold Editor Who Braved a Mob," *New York Journal* (January 29, 1898).

97. Duque, *Historia de Regla*, 173, 176.

98. "Miss Cisneros Will Wed After the War," *New York Journal* (May 21, 1898): 8.

99. "Miss Cisneros Will Wed," *New York Journal* (May 21, 1898).

100. "Miss Cisneros Will Wed," *New York Journal* (May 21, 1898).

101. "Miss Cisneros Will Wed," *New York Journal* (May 21, 1898). See also, "Lee Awaiting Orders," *Washington Post* (April 19, 1898): 3.

102. Lee received a hero's welcome upon his return to the United States in 1898, shortly before the Spanish-American War. See "Lee the Hero of the Hour," *New York Times* (April 13, 1898): 1. The *Times* said in a dispatch from Washington: "The ovation that has followed Consul General Fitzhugh Lee since he set foot on American soil on his return from Havana culminated … in what was in many ways the most remarkable demonstration the city has ever seen." See also, "A Nation's Hero," *Washington Evening Times* (April 6, 1898): 4.

103. See Mrs. John A. (Mary) Logan, letter to Henry S. Volkmer (May 27, 1898); John A. Logan family papers, Library of Congress, Manuscript Division, Washington, DC. Carbonell closely guarded Cisneros' privacy after their marriage in 1898. They lived for a time in Jacksonville, FL, while Carbonell served on the staff of Fitzhugh Lee, who commanded the U.S. Army's Seventh Corps during the Spanish-American War. In what probably was an allusion to Carbonell's protectiveness, a newspaper in Jacksonville complained: "Evangelina Cisneros does not seem to have valued the freedom … that was given her by yellow journalism. She is under bonds again." Untitled editorial comment, *Florida Times-Union and Citizen* (June 20, 1898): 4.

104. The collection at the University of Virginia is comprised of photocopies of Lee's correspondence, manuscripts, and other materials. The photocopies were made from originals owned by Fitzhugh Lee's great-grandson, Fitzhugh Lee Opie. The collection was opened to scholars in 2001, a little more than a year after Opie's death.

105. Curiously, Cisneros's account contains almost no details about her stay at Carbonell's house. See Cisneros and Decker, *The Story of Evangelina Cisneros*, 206–7.

106. Lee, "Rescue of Miss Cisneros," Fitzhugh Lee Papers, University of Virginia.

107. Lee, "Rescue of Miss Cisneros," Fitzhugh Lee Papers, University of Virginia.

108. Lee, "Rescue of Miss Cisneros," Fitzhugh Lee Papers, University of Virginia.

109. Lee, "Rescue of Miss Cisneros," Fitzhugh Lee Papers, University of Virginia.

110. Lee, "Rescue of Miss Cisneros," Fitzhugh Lee Papers, University of Virginia.

111. Lee, "Rescue of Miss Cisneros," Fitzhugh Lee Papers, University of Virginia. Timetables published in a leading Havana newspaper of the time show that the *Seneca* was two days behind schedule. The steamer was to arrive in Havana on October 7, 1897. See "Puerto de la Habana, Saldrain," *La Union Constitucional* (October 8, 1897): 1.

112. The description of Stevens appeared in "Seneca's Captain Knew Naught of the Cuban," *New York Journal* (October 14, 1897): 3.

113. Lee, "Rescue of Miss Cisneros," Fitzhugh Lee Papers, University of Virginia.

114. Lee, "Rescue of Miss Cisneros," Fitzhugh Lee Papers, University of Virginia.

115. Duque, *Historia de Regla*, 177.

116. Lee, "Rescue of Miss Cisneros," Fitzhugh Lee Papers, University of Virginia.

117. Lee, "Rescue of Miss Cisneros," Fitzhugh Lee Papers, University of Virginia.

118. Lee's correspondence shows, for example, that he was invited to a dinner party that Carbonell gave in early July 1897. "I backed out," Lee wrote in a letter to his wife, adding that their son, Fitzhugh Lee Jr., attended. See Lee to his wife (July 3, 1897), Fitzhugh Lee Papers, University of Virginia.

119. Lee to Lamont (December 3, 1898), Lamont Papers, Container 83, Library of Congress, Manuscript Division, Washington, DC.

120. Lee to his wife (November 23, 1897), Fitzhugh Lee papers, University of Virginia. Lee wrote that the manservant had been "recommended by Carbonell and others as thoroughly honest."

121. Lee to his wife (November 23, 1897), Fitzhugh Lee papers, University of Virginia.

122. Fitzhugh Lee, *Annual Report of Brig. General Fitzhugh Lee, Commanding the Department of the Province of Havana and Pinar del Rio* (Quemados, Cuba: 1899), 1.

123. Lee to Lamont (November 29, 1898), Lamont Papers, Library of Congress.

124. Lee to Lamont (December 3, 1898), Lamont Papers, Library of Congress.

125. Carlos F. Carbonell to Lee (November 30, 1898), Lamont Papers, Container 83, Library of Congress, Manuscript Division, Washington, DC.

126. Carbonell to Lee (November 30, 1898), Lamont Papers, Library of Congress.

127. Carbonell's name also surfaced during the U.S. Naval Court of Inquiry into the destruction in February 1898 of the U.S.S. *Maine*. In testimony before the Court of Inquiry, a U.S. consular clerk named Henry Drain said Carbonell had passed along an anonymous letter describing a purported plot to blow up the warship. Drain testified that Lee had instructed him "to consult with Mr. Carbonell, who would probably know more about it than anybody else." Drain further testified that he regarded Carbonell as reliable, "from having known him several years." The letter, which was included as an appendix to the Court of Inquiry's record, was never substantiated. See *Record of the Proceedings of a Court of Inquiry Upon the Destruction of the United States Battleship Maine in Havana Harbor February 15, 1898* (Washington, DC: U.S. Navy, 1898), 101.

128. Sherman's papers at the Library of Congress contain no reference to the Cisneros jailbreak. Day's papers at the Library of Congress contain nothing more than passing reference to the episode. The State Department was an unsettled place during the summer and autumn of 1897, given Sherman's mental and physical infirmities, which were increasingly noticeable. How long Sherman would remain secretary of state had become a topic of considerable newspaper commentary and speculation. See, for example, H. Gibson Gardner, "Too Old to Do His Work Well," *Chicago Journal* (October 22, 1897), scrapbook clipping, volume 614, John Sherman papers, Library of Congress, Manuscript Division, Washington, DC. See also, "John Sherman as Secretary of State," *Literary Digest*, 15, 17 (August 21, 1897): 486–87.

129. Cora Older, *William Randolph Hearst, American* (Freeport, NY: Books for Libraries Press, 1972, reprint of 1936 ed.), 172. Older's account erroneously stated that William B. MacDonald, another accomplice of Decker, was an aide to Fitzhugh Lee. MacDonald in fact was an official of a shipping company and was based in Cuba.

130. Older, *William Randolph Hearst*, 175. Older also erred in writing (180) that Cisneros lived in the United States "a little more than a year when she married" Carbonell, at Lee's home in Virginia. She married Carbonell in Baltimore, less than eight months after her arrival in the United States. See among other accounts, "Miss Cisneros Weds," *Washington Post* (June 10, 1898): 7; "Cuba's Heroine Now a Bride," *Richmond Times* (June 10, 1898): 6, and "Miss Cisneros Now A Bride," *New York World* (June 10, 1898): 12.

131. It is unclear why Lee did not publish the manuscript. Perhaps it was because the manuscript contained a measure of anonymity. One of the conspirators, for example, is described only by his initials, F.D.B.—which almost certainly is a reference to Francisco De Besche. Another reason is that the account of the escape would not have fit well with the contents of the book's final version, which included accounts of the Spanish-American War and the subsequent peace treaty negotiations in Paris. The book also had a co-author, Joseph Wheeler. See Lee and Wheeler, *Cuba's Struggle Against Spain With the Causes of American Intervention and A Full Account of the Spanish-American War, Including Final Peace Negotiations* (New York: American Historical Press, 1899).

132. Lee to Rockhill (July 4, 1896), Havana Consular Dispatches, Record Group 59, National Archives and Records Administration, College Park, MD. Lee also stated, "The information I am going to get is worth much more than [$]1200 to the Government."

133. Lee to Rockhill (July 4, 1896), Havana consular dispatches, National Archives, College Park.

134. Lee to William R. Day (June 5, 1897), Havana consular dispatches, National Archives, College Park.

135. Lee to Day (June 5, 1897), Havana consular dispatches, National Archives, College Park. Lee's spy network was mentioned by Gerald G. Eggert in a journal article about Lee's assignment to Cuba. See Eggert, "Our Man in Havana: Fitzhugh Lee," *Hispanic American Historical Review* 47, 4 (1967): 478. The article does not explore Lee's connection to the Cisneros case, however.

136. See "Extract from Letter of Gen. Lee to Judge Day, December 22, 1897," William R. Day Papers, Container 35, Library of Congress, Manuscript Division. See also, Lee to Day (March 30, 1898), Havana consular dispatches, National Archives, College Park.

137. Lee's intelligence-gathering was not without its failings. For example, in August 1896 he informed the State Department that Weyler was soon to be recalled to Spain. Lee cited sources "'near the Throne'" for that report, which was erroneous. Weyler remained in Cuba until the end of October 1897. See Lee to Rockhill (August 26, 1896), Reel 22, Richard Olney papers, Library of Congress, Manuscript Division, Washington, DC Lee wrote: "Accustomed to getting information in various ways, I have succeeded in getting some of the machinery necessary to do it here. This morning I heard that Weyler's departure from the island had been ordered and that it might take place as early as the 30th instant. ... This comes from persons 'near the Throne.'"

138. Lee to Valeriano Weyler y Nicolau (August 18, 1897), Fitzhugh Lee papers, University of Virginia.

139. Weyler to Lee (August 28, 1897), translation to English, Fitzhugh Lee papers, University of Virginia.

140. See Cisneros and Decker, *The Story of Evangelina Cisneros*, 69.

141. See Lee to Day (November 15, 1897), Havana consular dispatches, National Archives, College Park. In the letter, Lee formally notified Day that he had resumed his post in Havana on November 15, 1897.

142. See "General Lee Robbed on a Car," *Richmond Dispatch* (October 17, 1897): 13, and "General Lee Gets His Purse," *Richmond Dispatch* (October 19, 1897): 7. The letter's contents are not known. See also, "Consul-General Lee Robbed," *New York World* (October 18, 1897): 1.

143. "Gen. Lee May Not Return to Cuba," *New York Sun* (September 7, 1897): 2. The *Sun*'s report said: "In fact, it was arranged some time ago that ex-Congressman Frank Aldrich of Chicago would be appointed Consul-General at Havana when Gen. Lee came to this country." See also, "Gen. Lee Sails For Home," *New York Times* (September 5, 1897): 8.

144. Hearst's *Journal* had urged the McKinley administration to keep Lee in Havana. See "Let General Lee Be Retained," *New York Journal* (March 6, 1897): 6. The *Journal*'s editorial stated: "General Lee, more than any other appointee of the [Cleveland] Administration has typified the true American spirit."

145. "Hitt for Minister to Spain," *New York Times* (June 5, 1897): 1. The *Times* report said: "It is understood that ex-Representative Aldrich is to be appointed Consul General at Havana, and that his appointment will be made in the near future."

146. See "Gen. Lee in Washington," *New York Times* (October 11, 1897): 1. See also, "Consul-General Lee," *Richmond Dispatch* (November 6, 1897): 5. The *Dispatch* reported: "It is understood that [Lee] is to remain in Cuba until the island is 'pacified,' or, in other words, until the 'cruel war is over,' whenever that may be, and General Lee's return to this country will thus depend entirely upon circumstances." Lee at the time was contemplating a run for a U.S. Senate seat from Virginia in 1899. See "Lee to be a Candidate," *Washington Post* (October 16, 1897): 3.

147. James Franklin Aldrich to Charles G. Dawes (October 11, 1897), Day papers, Container 5, Library of Congress. Aldrich wrote in the letter: "I was wholly unprepared … for the recent report that General Lee had been asked to return to Havana in an official capacity, and am quite sure that he had no expectation of it himself." Privately, Lee was irritated that the McKinley administration contemplated replacing him in Havana, writing in a letter to his wife: "Don't know why [they] should send a *green man* here in a crisis!!!" Lee to his wife (July 17, 1897), Fitzhugh Lee papers, University of Virginia.

148. Thirty-five years afterward, Aldrich wrote that Lee had "strutted around Havana with a 'chip on his shoulder,' inflaming public sentiment until in exasperation certain hot-blooded [Spanish] royalists were led in their indiscretion to blow the Maine," the U.S. battleship destroyed in Havana harbor in February 1898. The cause of the *Maine*'s sinking has

never been ascertained. See J. Franklin Aldrich, "The War With Spain—Why?" unpublished essay (July 1932); J. Franklin Aldrich papers, Chicago Historical Society, Chicago, IL.

149. See "Banquet to Decker," *Richmond Dispatch* (October 26, 1897): 6. The article said Decker was "personally and favorably known" to Lee.

150. Cisneros and Decker, *The Story of Evangelina Cisneros*, 67.

151. Lee, "Rescue of Miss Cisneros," Fitzhugh Lee papers, University of Virginia. Lee's account, in this respect, is at odds with the more common version that Hearst sent Decker to Cuba with orders to free Cisneros. See Cisneros and Decker, *The Story of Evangelina Cisneros*, 61–62, 64. Lee's manuscript contains several spelling lapses and mistakenly says Decker arrived in Havana in September 1897. Such lapses are perhaps explained by the manuscript's being a draft.

152. Lee, "Rescue of Miss Cisneros," Fitzhugh Lee papers, University of Virginia.

153. Lee, "Rescue of Miss Cisneros," Fitzhugh Lee papers, University of Virginia.

154. Lee, "Rescue of Miss Cisneros," Fitzhugh Lee papers, University of Virginia.

155. Rockhill to Lee (March 17, 1897), Fitzhugh Lee papers, University of Virginia. In a handwritten postscript to his letter, Rockhill wrote: "Please let me know about Rockwell at your very earliest convenience. I am reliably informed he is drinking as hard as ever."

156. Lee to Rockhill (March 20, 1897), Havana consular dispatches, National Archives, College Park.

157. Lee to Rockhill (March 20, 1897), Havana consular dispatches, National Archives, College Park. Lee also wrote: "I must add[,] in justice to Mr. Rockwell, that he is gentlemanly, of good manners and generally conscientious in the discharge of his duties. I regret that his unfortunate propensity [to drink heavily] should stand in the way of his efficiency as a consular officer but hope that my action suspending him from his desk and your letter requesting his record here, will have effect and serve as a warning that hereafter any further transgression will not be overlooked." Rockwell did not keep his pledge of sobriety. Lee, in a letter home in the summer of 1897, noted: "Rockwell drunk again—poor fellow." Lee to his wife (August 7, 1897), Fitzhugh Lee papers, University of Virginia. Rockwell's fondness for the cup was no secret. The New York City gossip sheet, *Town Topics*, suggested in an item in December 1897 "that while under the influence of the cup," Rockwell "may have unwittingly" been married. See Untitled note, *Town Topics* (December 30, 1897): 9. Rockwell's assignment to Havana was his first diplomatic posting. He began his assignment there in May 1896, shortly before Lee arrived to take up the consul-general's position. See "Consular

Clerk at Havana," *Washington Post* (May 17, 1896): 10. The *Post*'s article described Rockwell as "a highly cultivated and elegant gentleman."

158. Lee to Day (June 5, 1897), Havana consular dispatches, National Archives, College Park.
159. Donnell Rockwell to Lee (July 29, 1897), Havana consular dispatches, National Archives, College Park. Musgrave in his book also described the suffering in Artemisa. See Musgrave, *Under Three Flags in Cuba*, 121.
160. Rockwell to Lee (July 29, 1897).
161. Lee to Day (July 30, 1897), Havana consular dispatches, National Archives, College Park.
162. "Hunting for the Girl's Rescuers," *New York Journal* (October 14, 1897): 2.
163. Joseph Springer, telegram to U.S. State Department (October 12, 1897), Havana consular dispatches, National Archives, College Park. There are no records that indicate how the State Department may have reacted to the interrogation of Rockwell.
164. Lee to his wife (November 23, 1897), Fitzhugh Lee papers, University of Virginia.
165. Lee to U.S. Secretary of State Richard Olney (July 22, 1896), Havana consular dispatches, National Archives, College Park.
166. Cited in "Campos Wants Weyler Removed," *New York Herald* (June 6, 1897): sec. 1, p. 9.
167. "The Cause of Cuba," *Washington Evening Star* (May 17, 1897): 1. See also, "Gunboats for Cuba," *Washington Post* (May 17, 1897): 1.
168. See "A Fighting Consul was Barker, of Sagua," *New York Journal* (April 11, 1898): 5.
169. Walter B. Barker to Day (September 30, 1897), Record Group 59, Sagua la Grande Consular Dispatches, National Archives, College Park.
170. Barker to Day (October 1, 1897), Sagua la Grande consular dispatches, National Archives, College Park.
171. Barker to Day (October 1, 1897), Sagua la Grande consular dispatches, National Archives, College Park. Barker's consular correspondence also shows that he cited ill health in justifying his two-week delay in replying to a letter from Lee. See Barker to Lee (August 4, 1896), Sagua la Grande consular dispatches, National Archives, College Park.
172. Springer appended a note of approval to Barker's letter to Day of October 1, 1897.
173. Cited in Barker to Day (October 8, 1897), Sagua la Grande consular dispatches, National Archives, College Park.
174. See "Shipping News," *New York Tribune* (October 12, 1897): 14.
175. "Passengers Love the Brave Little Refugee," *New York Journal* (October 14, 1897): 3.
176. "Miss Cisneros on Free Soil," *New York World* (October 14, 1897): 14.

177. Lee to Day (August 12, 1897), Havana consular dispatches, National Archives, College Park.
178. Barker's sudden departure meant that no fewer than three U.S. consuls assigned to Cuba were in the United States on leave in October 1897. In addition to Lee and Barker, the U.S. consul at Santiago de Cuba, Pulaski F. Hyatt, was on home leave. See Hyatt to Day (September 20, 1897), Santiago de Cuba consular dispatches, Record Group 59, National Archives, College Park.
179. See Lee to Rockhill (September 12, 1896), Reel 22, Olney papers, Library of Congress, Manuscript Division.
180. "Samuel S. Tolon Released," *New York Tribune* (September 27, 1896): 1.
181. Ramon Williams to Barker (May 24, 1896), Havana consular dispatches, National Archives, College Park.
182. Williams to Rockhill (May 27, 1896), Havana consular dispatches, National Archives, College Park.
183. Weyler to Lee (July 7, 1896), translation to English, Havana consular dispatches, National Archives, College Park.
184. Cited in Lee to Rockhill (March 26, 1897), Havana consular dispatches, National Archives, College Park.
185. Weyler to Lee (July 7, 1896), translation to English, Havana consular dispatches, National Archives, College Park.
186. Cited in Offner, *An Unwanted War*, 255 (n. 37). Offner, citing a report that Dupuy de Lôme sent to Madrid in October 1897, stated that the Spanish minister "considered the American consuls in Matanzas, Sagua la Grande, and Santiago de Cuba to be active agents of the insurgents."
187. Barker to Rockhill (July 26, 1897), Sagua la Grande consular dispatches, National Archives, College Park.
188. Barker to Rockhill (May 4, 1896), Sagua la Grande consular dispatches, National Archives, College Park.
189. Barker to Rockhill (July 26, 1897), Sagua la Grande consular dispatches, National Archives, College Park.
190. Barker to Rockhill (September 19, 1896), Sagua la Grande consular dispatches, National Archives, College Park.
191. Barker to Sylvester Scovel (February 27, 1897); Scovel papers, Missouri Historical Society Archives, St. Louis, MO.
192. Barker to Scovel (August 3, 1898); Sylvester Scovel papers, Missouri Historical Society Archives, St. Louis.
193. See "Karl Decker Toasted: A Guest of His Newspaper Friends at the Raleigh," *Washington Post* (October 27, 1897): 4. The guest list published in the *Post* also included the name "Donald Rockwell," presumably "Donnell" Rockwell, the U.S. consular clerk who was often misidentified as "Donald." The *Richmond Dispatch* reported that Fitzhugh Lee had been "specially invited by wire. In reply to the telegram, which was pressingly worded, General Lee said: 'Impossible. Am forced to decline

on account of other important engagements.' The [organizing] committee regret[s] very much that General Lee could not attend the banquet, as his presence would greatly enhance the compliment to their guest of honor." See "Banquet to Decker," *Richmond Dispatch* (October 26, 1897).

194. See, for example, Roggenkamp, "The Evangelina Cisneros Romance," 25–37, and Carol Wilcox, "Squeezing the 'Exotic Bug': The Madrid Press Criticizes Hearst's Coverage of the Cuban Revolutionary," paper presented to the annual convention of the Association for Education in Journalism and Mass Communication, San Antonio, TX, August 2005. Most recent accounts of the Cisneros case have appeared in biographies of William Randolph Hearst or Joseph Pulitzer. See, for example, Nasaw, *The Chief*, 128–129; and Denis Brian, *Pulitzer: A Life* (New York: John Wiley & Sons, 2001), 221–222.

195. Cisneros and Decker, *The Story of Evangelina Cisneros*, 87. A moonlit night may have been a particularly propitious occasion to have carried out the jailbreak. According to the *New York Herald*, many Cubans were wary of the moonlight and took pains to avoid it. "There is no kind of lunacy that is not attributed, directly or indirectly, to the effects of moonlight," the *Herald* said. "Mothers teach their children to avoid its rays as they would the smallpox.... 'Keep out of the moonlight,' is a Cuban mother's first maxim." See "Life in Havana," *New York Herald* (January 3, 1897): sec. 4, p. 1. However, Decker and his accomplices regarded the moon as nothing but a complicating factor. See Cisneros and Decker, *The Story of Evangelina Cisneros*, 93.

196. Cisneros and Decker, *The Story of Evangelina Cisneros*, 94.

197. Cisneros and Decker, *The Story of Evangelina Cisneros*, 204.

198. See "Havana: Altitude and azimuth of the Moon, Oct. 6, 1897," and "Havana: Altitude and azimuth of the Moon, Oct. 7, 1897," Astronomical Applications Department, U.S. Naval Observatory, Washington, DC; http://mach.usno.navy.mil/cgi-bin/aa_altazw (accessed August 14, 2002).

199. Geoff Chester, the U.S. Naval Observatory's public affairs officer, said that after allowing for adjustments in time and location, the moon "would have indeed been quite bright [over Havana] during the late evening/early morning hours" on October 7, 1897, provided that the sky was not obscured by clouds. See Chester, email correspondence with the author, August 19, 2002.

200. See W. F. R. Phillips, *Climate of Cuba* (Washington, DC: U.S. Weather Bureau, 1898), 11.

201. Karl Decker, "Spaniards Routed Near Havana," *New York Journal* (October 2, 1897).

202. The rainfall report for October 7, 1897 was included with meteorological data published by the Havana newspaper *El Pais* on October 8, 1897.

Unaccountably, however, the newspaper did not, in its edition of October 7, 1897, include meteorological data for the day before.

203. See "Service Meterologico de Marina, *La Union Constitucional* (October 7, 1897): 2, and "El Tiempo," *La Union Constitucional* (October 7, 1897): 3. The latter report included data from the Real Colegio de Belén.

204. "Service Meterologico de Marina, *La Union Constitucional,* (October 8, 1897): 2, and "El Tiempo," *La Union Constitucional* (October 8, 1897): 3.

205. "Original Monthly Record of Observations at Key West, Fla., for the Month of October, 1897," U.S. Department of Agriculture, Weather Bureau (1897): 3. The weather bureau's guidance to its observers was that a reading of "clear" should be recorded "when the sky is three-tenths or less covered with clouds." See "Original Monthly Record of Observations at Key West, Fla., for the Month of October, 1897: Instructions: Weather," 4.

206. "Original Monthly Record of Observations at Key West, Fla., for the Month of October, 1897," 5.

207. [Julio] Jover, "Servicio Meterologico du 'El Pais,'" *El Pais* (October 8, 1897): 2. The report noted "extraordinarily high" barometric readings had been recorded in New York City early in October 1897.

208. See "Spain's Ministry Falls," *New York Sun* (September 30, 1897): 1. The *Sun's* dispatch from Madrid reported speculation that Weyler's recall was likely to follow the change in government.

209. For an insightful discussion about the political turmoil in Madrid in late summer and early autumn 1897, see Offner, *An Unwanted War,* 65–67.

210. The policy, one historian has written, may have done "more to bring on the Spanish-American War than anything else the Spanish could have done." See Ivan Musicant, *Empire by Default: The Spanish-American War and the Dawn of the American Century* (New York: Henry Holt and Company, 1998), 69.

211. The *New York Sun* was routinely caustic in commenting about Weyler. "He has made for himself a record of incompetency, savagery, and shame," the *Sun* said in an editorial after Weyler's recall was announced. "Back to Spain let the malefactor go! Away from Cuba, the men and women of which he has massacred! ... For untold ages the name Weyler will be a name of horror in Cuba and in the records of modern war." See "The Disgraceful End of a Dishonorable Career," *New York Sun* (October 13, 1897): 6. The *New York Times* also deplored Weyler's conduct in Cuba, writing: "Of Spanish barbarity and inhumanity Weyler is perhaps the most conspicuous exemplar. His administration in Cuba was as contemptible as it was cruel." See "The Spanish Jingoes," *New York Times* (March 4, 1898): 6.

212. See, for example, "Spain and the Butcher," *New York Journal* (October 8, 1897): 8.

213. See Offner, *An Unwanted War*, 66.
214. "Adroit Move by Weyler," *Chicago Tribune* (October 8, 1897): 3.
215. Cisneros and Decker, *The Story of Evangelina Cisneros*, 86–87.
216. See Offner, *An Unwanted War*, 68.
217. "Havana Terror Stricken," *New York Sun* (October 7, 1897): 1. See also, "Weyler Awaits Orders," *New York Herald* (October 7, 1897): 9, and "Big Demonstration in Havana in Favor of Weyler," *New York World* (October 7, 1897): 7.
218. "Havana Terror Stricken," *New York Sun*. No such attacks were reported, however.
219. "Hurrahing for Weyler," *New York Sun* (October 8, 1897): 1.
220. "Gen. Weyler Recalled," *New York Sun* (October 10, 1897): 1. See also, "Weyler Will Be Recalled To-Day," *New York Journal* (October 9, 1897): 1, and "Weyler's Recall At Hand," *New York Times* (October 9, 1897): 1.
221. For an account of Weyler's departure, see Joseph A. Springer to Day (November 4, 1897), Havana Consular Dispatches, U.S. National Archives, College Park. Springer, the U.S. vice consul-general in Havana, reported to Day, an assistant secretary of state, that Weyler "held onto command as long as possible."
222. Cisneros and Decker, *The Story of Evangelina Cisneros*, 105.
223. Cisneros and Decker, *The Story of Evangelina Cisneros*, 108.
224. Cisneros and Decker, *The Story of Evangelina Cisneros*, 108.
225. Cisneros and Decker, *The Story of Evangelina Cisneros*, 108.
226. Decker gave a similar version in remarks to reporters upon his return to New York in mid-October 1897. "To reach the steamer to New York," he was quoted by the *Washington Post* as saying, "she was obliged to walk down Obispo street, the principal thoroughfare of Havana, at a time when the street was crowded, and yet take her time and smoke a cigar. If she had skulked about the back streets she would immediately have been suspected. It was over a mile from the house [where she was hidden] to the pier." See "Decker's Close Call," *Washington Post* (October 15, 1897): 1.
227. Lee, "Rescue of Miss Cisneros," 14.
228. Lee, "Rescue of Miss Cisneros," 14.
229. Cisneros and Decker, *The Story of Evangelina Cisneros*, 82.
230. Cisneros and Decker, *The Story of Evangelina Cisneros*, 200.
231. Cisneros and Decker, *The Story of Evangelina Cisneros*, 199.
232. Cisneros and Decker, *The Story of Evangelina Cisneros*, 100.
233. Abbot, *Watching the World Go By*, 215.
234. See "Vengeful Spaniards of Havana," *San Francisco Examiner* (December 20, 1897): 1. Hearst owned the *Examiner*, which frequently published material from the *New York Journal*.
235. "Tries to Bribe Her Father," *Chicago Tribune* (October 17, 1897): 2. The *Tribune* article was reprinted from the *New York Journal*.

236. See Musgrave, "Tried to Wreck Our Consulate in Havana," *New York Journal* (25 November 1897); "Spanish Bombs for Journal Men," *New York Journal* (December 18, 1897); 5, and "Bomb Found in Our Consulate," *New York Herald* (December 16, 1897): 9.

237. See "American Consul Guarded by Spain," *Philadelphia Inquirer* (November 26, 1897): 1, and "Another Fake Bomb in Havana," *New York World* (December 16, 1897): 7.

238. See "Spanish Bombs for Journal Men," *New York Journal* (December 18, 1897).

239. See "Assassination Failing, Eviction of Its News Bureau in Havana Is Resorted To," *New York Journal* (December 20, 1897): 1.

240. "Spain Makes War on the Journal by Seizing the Yacht Buccaneer," *New York Journal* (February 11, 1898): 1.

241. "The Spanish-Journal War," *New York Journal* (February 12, 1898): 2.

242. See "Karl Decker Again in Cuba," *Washington Post* (February 10, 1898): 1.

243. José Congosto to Lee (February 7, 1898); Havana consular dispatches, National Archives, College Park. The episode came a day after the *Journal* disclosed the contents of a private letter in which Spain's chief diplomat in the United States, Enrique Dupuy de Lôme, wrote disparagingly of President McKinley. Among other characterizations, Dupuy de Lôme called McKinley a "low politician" who catered "to the rabble." See "The Worst Insult to the United States In Its History," *New York Journal* (February 9, 1898): 1. Dupuy de Lôme's indiscretion cost him his posting in Washington—and the *Journal* reveled in the diplomat's humiliation. See "Journal's Letter Frees Country from De Lome," *New York Journal* (February 11, 1898): 1.

244. Lee to Congosto (9 February 1898); Havana consular dispatches, National Archives, College Park.

245. Lee to Day (March 1, 1898); Havana consular dispatches, National Archives, College Park.

246. Abbot, *Watching the World Go By*, 216.

247. Roggenkamp, "The Evangelina Cisneros Romance," 25.

248. Milton, *The Yellow Kids*, 205.

249. Brian, *Pulitzer*, 222.

250. See Sylvester Scovel, letter to his parents (6 October 6, 1897); Scovel papers, Missouri Historical Society Archives, St. Louis. Scovel's letter is dated: "New York–Oct 6th/97." In the letter, Scovel says, "I am in New York. ..."

251. Almost from the day Cisneros escaped the Casa de Recogidas, bizarre theories have grown up around the case. The most far-fetched of these theories was a report from Key West that said Cisneros escaped during a bungled attempt by Weyler's henchmen to smuggle her out of prison and send her to the Ceuta penal colony off the north coast of Africa.

"Through treachery at the palace," the report said, "Weyler's plans were overheard and the Cubans struck a bold blow. While she was getting into a carriage, Weyler's agents were overpowered by five or ten young Cubans and Senorita Cisneros taken away from them. Two of the [Cuban] secret agents were badly knifed and another was killed. The maid escaped and it is reported that she is now speeding toward the Southern sea coast as offering the best chances for her escape. Weyler, it is reported, is furious over the bad ending of his plans." See "Weyler's Scheme," *Philadelphia Item* (October 9, 1897): 6. The *New York Tribune* reported, erroneously, that Cisneros had really slipped into New York City on another passenger steamer, three days before the *Seneca* arrived. See "Safe Out of Spanish Hands," *New York Tribune* (October 14, 1897): 5.

252. See Nicholas Fraser, "Media: Playing Fast and Luce With the Facts," London *Guardian* (October 9, 1989).
253. William Tucker, "Call It A Democracy and the Hell With It," *The American Spectator* online (http://www.spectator.com/util/print.asp?art_id=6416), April 12, 2004 (accessed July 31, 2005).
254. See Offner, *An Unwanted War*, 226–27.
255. Offner, *An Unwanted War*, 69.
256. See Charles Campbell, *The Transformation of American Foreign Relations 1865–1900* (New York: Harper and Row, 1976), 257.
257. See W. Joseph Campbell, *Yellow Journalism: Puncturing the Myths, Defining the Legacies* (Westport, CT: Praeger Publishers, 2001), 109.
258. See Campbell, *Yellow Journalism*, 107–8.
259. "Strictly Personal," *Fourth Estate* (November 4, 1897): 5. The trade journal also stated: "Mr. Hearst is known to be generous with men who do well in his employ, and could have chosen no one more deserving of a liberal reward."
260. See, for example, "A War Trip in Cuba," *Washington Post* (September 26, 1898): 8; Karl Decker's Bravery," *Washington Post* (October 4, 1899): 10, and "Must Intervene in Mexico," *Washington Post* (September 6, 1913): 4.
261. "Karl Decker Returns to Cuba," *Washington Post* (February 5, 1899): 9.
262. See, among other reports, Karl Decker, "Looters Slain in Havana as Storm Rages," *New York Journal-American* (October 3, 1933): 4; Karl Decker, "Racial Strife Grows in Cuba," *New York Journal-American* (October 3, 1933): 2, and Karl Decker, "Havana Like an Armed Camp With 20 Factions Itching to Kill," *New York Journal-American* (October 23, 1933): 6.
263. See "Funeral Service Held Today for Karl Decker," *New York Journal-American* (December 5, 1941); "Karl Decker Dies; Correspondent, 73," *New York Times* (December 5, 1941): 24, and "Karl Decker Dies; Was Hearst Writer," *Editor & Publisher* (December 13, 1941): 66.
264. See "Funeral Service Held Today for Karl Decker," *New York Journal-American* (December 5, 1941).

265. See "Love Scorns Law: Evangelina Cisneros and Carlos Carbonel [*sic*] Consummate a Romance," *Washington Evening Star* (June 9, 1898): 1–2; "Cuba's Heroine Now a Bride," *Richmond Times* (June 10, 1898): 6, and "A Romantic Courtship," *Florida Times-Union and Citizen* (June 13, 1898): 6. Carbonell wore his officer's uniform; Cisneros was dressed in "a pale tan silk mohair traveling gown." See "Miss Cisneros Weds," *Washington Post* (June 10, 1898): 7.

266. See "Miss Cisneros Weds," *Washington Post* (June 10, 1898), and "Miss Cisernos Married," *New York Sun* (June 10, 1898): 7.

267. "Miss Cisneros Is A Happy Mother," *New York Journal* (May 24, 1899): 3.

268. Francisca Fuensalida, "Update," email correspondence with author, August 28, 2001. Under an agreement with the author, Fuensalida researched Spanish-language sources about the Cisneros case, in Madrid and elsewhere, in 2001.

269. See "Wed at Journey's End," *Washington Post* (October 4, 1900): 7.

270. See "Donnell Rockwell, of N.Y. American," *New York American* (March 23, 1915): 10.

271. "How Capt. Barker was Killed," *Washington Post* (September 16, 1905): 4.

272. See "Gen. Fitzhugh Lee Dies from Stroke of Apoplexy," *New York American* (April 29, 1905): 1.

273. See "Rests in Hollywood: Fifty Thousand People Pay Tribute to Gen. Lee," *Washington Post* (May 5, 1905): 4.

274. See "Stream of Callers at the Hospital," *Richmond Times Dispatch* (April 30, 1905): 3.

275. Cited in Edmond D. Coblentz, ed., *William Randolph Hearst: A Portrait in His Own Words* (New York. Simon and Schuster, 1952), 58.

276. "Harry I. Skilton," *New York Times* (August 27, 1897): 23.

277. These newspapers include the *New York Sun, New York World-Telegram, New York Herald-Tribune*, and Albany [NY] *Knickerbocker News*. Skilton was born in Albany in 1864.

278. "Harry I. Skilton Dies," *Havana* [Cuba] *Post* (August 26, 1947): 1. The *Havana Post*'s obituary stated: "In October 1897 he helped Karl Decker leave Havana after the latter had aided the escape from a Spanish prison of the Cuban patriot Evangelina Cisneros."

279. See Cisneros and Decker, *The Story of Evangelina Cisneros*, 117.

280. See "Affidavit" dated 4 September 1897; Box 93, folder 1, Frank A. Skilton papers, Carl A. Kroch Library, Cornell University, Ithaca, NY. See also, Julius A. Skilton, letter to Frank Skilton (September 21, 1897); Frank A. Skilton papers, Cornell University. In addition, Harry Skilton's correspondence indicates that he returned to New York from Cuba on November 1 or 2, 1897. See Box 66, Julius A. Skilton papers, Cornell University.

Chapter 5

1. Cited in Orville Schell, "Books of the Times: Hearst, Man and Mogul: Going Beyond the Myths," *New York Times* (June 28, 2000): E11.
2. For a recent discussion about diminished *joie de vivre* in American newsrooms, see Douglas McCollam, "The Crowded Theater: It's Time for American Journalism to Rise Out of Its Defensive Crouch," *Columbia Journalism Review* (July/August 2005): 24.
3. See W. Joseph Campbell, *Yellow Journalism: Puncturing the Myths, Defining the Legacies* (Westport, CT: Praeger Publishers, 2001), 175.
4. For a recent appearance of the Hearstian vow, see William Prochnau, "The Military and the Media," in Geneva Overholser and Kathleen Hall Jamieson, eds., *The Press* (New York: Oxford University Press, 2005): 313.
5. See, for example, Robert Taft, *Photography and the American Scene: A Social History, 1839–1889* (New York: Dover Publications, 1964), 446, and R. Smith Schuneman, "Art or Photography: A Question for Newspaper Editors of the 1890s," *Journalism Quarterly* 42, 1 (Winter 1965): 51.
6. Eric Newton, "Why 'Yes, Virginia,' Lives On," Freedom Forum online (http://www.freedomforum.org/templates/document.asp?documentID= 6220), posted December 16, 1997.
7. Geo Beach, "Shop Talk At Thirty: 'Yes Virginia,' 100 Years Later, Provides Enduring Reminder of Print's Power," *Editor & Publisher* (December 20, 1997): 34.
8. Beach, "Shop Talk At Thirty: 'Yes Virginia,' 100 Years Later," *Editor & Publisher*.
9. Rick Horowitz, "Yes, Virginia, Faith Overcame Skepticism 100 Years Ago," *St. Louis Post-Dispatch* (September 21, 1997): 3B.
10. See "Santa Survives Protest," *New York Times* (December 23, 1951): 24.
11. See Andrew Herrmann, "It's A Wonderful Lie," *Chicago Sun-Times* (December 9, 1997): 37.
12. See, for example, "Editorial: Can You Hear Me Now?" *Editor & Publisher* (October 20, 2005): 5. The *Editor & Publisher* commentary said "so many newspaper investigative projects these days" generate no more reaction than "some excuses and some feeble reassurances" from among local, state, or federal authorities.
13. "The Journal's Settled Policy," *New York Journal* (December 3, 1897): 6.
14. For a discussion of the parallels between "civic" journalism and Hearst's "journalism of action," see Campbell, *Yellow Journalism*, 180–83. See also, Thomas C. Leonard, "Making Readers into Citizens—The Old-Fashioned Way," in Theodore L. Glasser, ed., *The Idea of Public Journalism* (New York: Guilford Press, 1999), 85–90.
15. Chris Peck, "Civic Journalism: The Savior of Newspapers in the 21st Century?" address at national convention of the Association for Education in Journalism and Mass Communication, New Orleans, LA (August 6, 1999): 17.

16. Arthur Charity, *Doing Public Journalism* (New York: Guilford Press, 1995), 147.
17. "The Journalism of Action," *New York Journal* (October 5, 1897): 6.
18. "The Journalism of Action," *New York Journal* (October 5, 1897).
19. Cited in Rachel Smolkin, "Howell Much Is Too Much?" *American Journalism Review* (March 2003): 34.
20. Smolkin, "Howell Much Is Too Much?" *American Journalism Review* (March 2003).
21. Daniel Okrent, "Is The New York Times a Liberal Paper?" *New York Times* (July 25, 2004): sect. 4, p. 1.
22. Okrent, "Is The New York Times a Liberal Paper?" *New York Times* (July 25, 2004). Okrent also wrote: "But for those who also believe the news pages cannot retain their credibility unless all aspects of an issue are subject to robust examination, it's disappointing to see The Times present the social and cultural aspects of same-sex marriage in a tone that approaches cheerleading."
23. "Keller Says 'N.Y. Times' Must Look Beyond Its Urban, Liberal Base," *Editor & Publisher,* available online at http://www.editorandpublisher.com/eandp/news/article_display.jsp?vnu_content_id=1000968615, posted June 26, 2005 (accessed July 3, 2005).
24. Dan Barry and others, "Correcting the Record: Times Reporter Who Resigned Leaves Long Trail of Deception," *New York Times* (May 11, 2003): 1.
25. The phrase appeared in "Spanish Alliances," *New York Times* (March 1, 1898): 6.
26. Howell Raines, "My Times," *Atlantic Monthly* (May 2004): 49.
27. "The Journalism of Action," *New York Journal* (October 5, 1897).
28. See "New York Times Bans Guns for Correspondents," *Wall Street Journal* (January 30, 2004): B3. A controversy arose in 2003 when Dexter Filkins, a *New York Times* war correspondent in Iraq, was found to have carried a firearm—raising fears that such a practice could make journalists targets in war zones.
29. Bob Steele, "When Opposition Becomes Participation," Poynteronline, (http://www.poynter.org), posted February 21, 2003 (accessed August 1, 2005).
30. See Howard Kurtz, "Media Notes: At Last, Reporters' Feelings Rise to the Surface," *Washington Post* (September 5, 2005): C1. Kurtz, a prominent media critic, wrote (C7): "Maybe, just maybe, journalism needs to bring more passion to the table."

SELECTED BIBLIOGRAPHY

BOOKS

Abbot, Willis J. *Watching the World Go By*. Boston: Little, Brown, 1933.

Adams-Ray, Edward tr., *Andrée's Story: The Complete Record of His Polar Flight, 1897*. New York: Viking Press, 1930

Adney, Tappan. *The Klondike Stampede*. Vancouver: UBC Press, 1994. Reprint of 1899 edition.

American Journalism From the Practical Side. New York: Holmes Publishing Co., 1897.

Bailey, Thomas A. *A Diplomatic History of the American People*, 8th ed. New York: Appleton-Century-Crofts, 1969.

Barth, Gunther. *City People: The Rise of Modern City Culture in Nineteenth-Century America*. New York: Oxford University Press, 1980.

Berger, Meyer. *The Story of the New York Times*. New York: Simon and Schuster, 1951.

Berkove, Lawrence I., ed. *Skepticism and Dissent: Selected Journalism by Ambrose Bierce*. Ann Arbor: UMI Research Press, 1986.

Berryman, John. *Stephen Crane*. New York: William Sloane Associates, 1950.

Berton, Pierre. *The Klondike Fever: The Life and Death of the Last Great Gold Rush*. New York: Knopf, 1958.

Bleyer, Willard Grosvenor. *Main Currents in the History of American Journalism*. Boston: Houghton Mifflin Co., 1927.

Boorstin, Daniel J. *The Image: A Guide to Pseudo-Events in America*. New York: Harper and Row Publishers, 1961.

Brands, H. W. *The Reckless Decade: America in the 1890s.* New York: St. Martin's Press, 1995.

Briggs, Asa, and Daniel Snowman, eds. *Fins de Siècle: How Centuries End, 1400–2000.* New Haven, CT: Yale University Press, 1996.

Brown, Charles H. *The Correspondents' War: Journalists in the Spanish-American War.* New York: Scribner's, 1967.

Brown, Henry Collins. *In the Nineties.* Hastings-on-Hudson, NY: Valentine's Manual, 1928.

Calhoun, Charles W., ed. *The Gilded Age: Essays on the Origins of Modern America.* Wilmington, DE: Scholarly Resources, 1996.

Campbell, Charles. *The Transformation of American Foreign Relations 1865–1900.* New York: Harper and Row, 1976.

Campbell, W. Joseph. *The Spanish-American War: American Wars and the Media in Primary Documents.* Westport, CT: Greenwood, 2005.

_____. *Yellow Journalism: Puncturing the Myths, Defining the Legacies.* Westport, CT: Praeger, 2001.

Carlebach, Michael L. *American Photojournalism Comes of Age.* Washington, DC: Smithsonian Institutions Press, 1997.

Carlson, Oliver. *Brisbane: A Candid Biography.* New York: Stackpole Sons, 1937.

Charity, Arthur. *Doing Public Journalism.* New York: Guilford Press, 1995.

Churchill, Allen. *Park Row.* New York: Rinehart and Co., 1958.

Coblentz, Edmond D., ed. *William Randolph Hearst: A Portrait in His Own Words.* New York: Simon and Schuster, 1952.

Cohen, Stanley, and Jock Young, eds. *The Manufacture of News.* London: Constable, 1973.

Coleman, Harry J. *Give Us A Little Smile, Baby.* New York: E.P Dutton & Co., 1943.

Collier, Price. *America and the Americans: From a French Point of View,* 3rd ed. New York: Charles Scribner's Sons, 1897.

Creelman, James. *On the Great Highway: The Wanderings and Adventures of a Special Correspondent.* Boston: Lothrop Publishing, 1901.

Crouch, Thomas. *A Yankee Guerrillero: Frederick Funston and the Cuban Insurrection, 1896–1897*; Memphis, TN: Memphis State University Press, 1975.

Davis, Richard Harding. *Cuba In War Time.* New York: R. H. Russell, 1897.

_____. *Notes of a War Correspondent.* New York: Scribner's Sons, 1910.

Diner, Steven J. *A Very Different Age: Americans of the Progressive Era.* New York: Hill and Wang, 1998.

Douglas, Susan J. *Inventing American Broadcasting, 1899–1922.* Baltimore: Johns Hopkins University Press, 1987.

Duque, Francisco M. *Historia de Regla: Description Politica, Economica y Social, Desde su Fundacion Hasta el Dia.* Havana: Rambla, Bouza y Ca., 1925.

Epstein, Edward J. *Between Fact and Fiction: The Problem of Journalism.* New York: Vintage, 1975.

Faue, Elizabeth. *Writing the Wrongs: Eva Valesh and the Rise of Labor Journalism.* Ithaca, NY: Cornell University Press, 2002.

Fedler, Fred. *Lessons from the Past: Journalists' Lives and Work, 1850–1950.* Prospect Heights, IL: Waveland Press, 2000.

Fitzpatrick, Ellen F., ed. *Muckraking: Three Landmark Articles.* Boston: Bedford Books, 1994.

Galassi, Peter, and Susan Kismaric, eds. *Pictures of the Times: A Century of Photography from the New York Times.* New York: Museum of Modern Art, 1996.

Ginger, Ray. *Age of Excess: The United States From 1877 to 1914.* New York: Macmillan, 1965.

Goldstein, Tom, ed. *Killing the Messenger: 100 Years of Media Criticism.* New York: Columbia University Press, 1989.

Gould, Lewis L. *The Spanish-American War and President McKinley.* Lawrence: University of Kansas Press, 1980.

Halstead, Murat. *The Story of Cuba: Her Struggles for Liberty, the Cause, Crisis and Destiny of the Pearl of the Antilles*, 5th ed. Chicago: Henry Publishing Co., 1897.

Hapgood, Hutchins. *Types From City Streets.* New York: Garrett Press, 1970.

_____. *A Victorian in the Modern World.* Seattle: University of Washington Press, 1972.

Harstock, John C. *A History of American Literary Journalism: The Emergence of a Modern Narrative Form.* Amherst: University of Massachusetts Press, 2000.

Haverstock, Nathan A. *Fifty Years at the Front: The Life of War Correspondent Frederick Palmer.* Washington, DC: Brassey's, 1996.

Hearst, William Randolph Jr. with Jack Casserly. *The Hearsts: Father and Son.* Niwot, CO: Roberts Rinehart Publishers, 1991.

Hemstreet, Charles. *Reporting for the Newspapers.* New York: A. Wessels Co., 1901.

Hilderbrand, Robert C. *Power and the People: Executive Management of Public Opinion in Foreign Affairs, 1897–1921.* Chapel Hill: University of North Carolina Press, 1981.

Jackson, Holbrook. *The Eighteen Nineties: A Review of Art and Ideas at the Close of the Nineteenth Century.* St. Clair Shores, MI: Scholarly Press, 1972. Reprint of 1922 edition.

Johnson, Gerald W. *An Honorable Titan: A Biographical Study of Adolph S. Ochs.* Westport, CT: Greenwood, 1970.

Johnson, Julie. *A Wild Discouraging Mess: The History of the White Pass Unit of the Klondike Gold Rush National Historical Park.* Anchorage, AK: U.S. Department of the Interior, 2003.

Joshi, S.T., and David E. Schultz, eds. *Ambrose Bierce: A Sole Survivor; Bits of Autobiography*. Knoxville: University of Tennessee Press, 1998.

Kaplan, Justin. *Lincoln Steffens: A Biography*. New York: Simon and Schuster, 1974.

Kelly, Florence Finch. *Flowing Stream: The Story of Fifty-Six Years in American Newspaper Life*. New York: E. P. Dutton & Co., 1939.

Kluger, Richard. *The Paper: The Life and Death of the* New York Herald Tribune. New York: Knopf, 1986.

Kobre, Sidney. *The Yellow Press and Gilded Age Journalism*. Tallahassee: Florida State University Press, 1964.

Lawrence, Bobby. *Tennessee Centennial: Nashville 1897*. Charleston, SC: Arcadia Publishing, 1998.

Lee, Fitzhugh, and Joseph Wheeler. *Cuba's Struggle Against Spain With the Causes of American Intervention and A Full Account of the Spanish-American War, Including Final Peace Negotiations*. New York: American Historical Press, 1899.

Leech, Margaret. *In the Days of McKinley*. New York: Harper and Brothers, 1959.

Leguineche, Manuel. *"Yo pondré la guerra": Cuba 1898: la primera guerra que se inventó la prensa*. Madrid: El País/Aguilar, 1998.

Linderman, Gerald F. *The Mirror of War: American Society and the Spanish-American War*. Ann Arbor: University of Michigan Press, 1974.

London, Jack. *The God of His Fathers and Other Stories*. Freeport, NY: Books for Libraries Press, 1969. Reprint of 1901 edition.

Lowell, Percival. *Mars and Its Canals*. New York: Macmillan, 1907.

Lubow, Arthur. *The Reporter Who Would Be King: A Biography of Richard Harding Davis*. New York: Scribner's, 1992.

Lundberg, Ferdinand. *Imperial Hearst: A Social Biography*. New York: Equinox Cooperative Press, 1936.

Marzolf, Marion Tuttle. *Civilizing Voices: American Press Criticism 1880–1950*. New York: Longman, 1991.

McCabe, Lida Rose. *The Beginnings of Halftone: From the Note Books of Stephen H. Horgan, "Dean of American Photoengravers."* Chicago: Inland Printer, 1924.

McDougall, A. Kent, ed. *The Press: A Critical Look From the Inside*. Princeton, NJ: Dow Jones Books, 1972.

Meyer, Philip. *The Vanishing Newspaper: Saving Journalism in the Information Age*. Columbia: University of Missouri Press, 2004.

Michelson, Charles. *The Ghost Talks*. New York: G. P. Putnam's Sons, 1944.

Milton, Joyce. *The Yellow Kids: Foreign Correspondents in the Heyday of Yellow Journalism*. New York: Harper and Row, 1989.

Mindich, David T. Z. *Just the Facts: How 'Objectivity' Came to Define American Journalism*. New York: New York University Press, 1998.

Mitchell, Edward P. *Memoirs of an Editor: Fifty Years of American Journalism*. New York: Scribner's, 1924.

Mnookin, Seth. *Hard News: The Scandals at* The New York Times *and Their Meaning for American Media*. New York: Random House, 2004.

Muirhead, James Fullarton. *The Land of Contrasts: A Briton's View of his American Kin*. Boston: Lamson, Wolffe and Co., 1898.

Musgrave, George Clarke. *Under Three Flags in Cuba*. Boston: Little, Brown and Co., 1899.

Musicant, Ivan. *Empire by Default: The Spanish-American War and the Dawn of the American Century*. New York: Henry Holt and Co., 1998.

Musser, Charles. *The Emergence of Cinema: The American Screen to 1907*. New York: Scribner's, 1990.

Nasaw, David. *The Chief: The Life of William Randolph Hearst*. Boston: Houghton Mifflin Co., 2000.

Newhall, Beaumont. *The History of Photography From 1839 to the Present*. New York: Museum of Modern Art, 1994.

North, Michael. *Reading 1922: A Return to the Scene of the Modern*. New York: Oxford University Press, 1999.

Offner, John L. *An Unwanted War: The Diplomacy of the United States and Spain Over Cuba, 1895–1898*. Chapel Hill: University of North Carolina Press, 1992.

Older, Cora. *William Randolph Hearst, American*. Freeport, NY: Books for Libraries Press, 1972. Reprint of 1936 edition.

Paine, Ralph D. *Roads of Adventure*. Boston: Houghton Mifflin, 1922.

Painter, Nell Irvin. *Standing at Armageddon: The United States, 1877–1919*. New York: W. W. Norton and Co., 1987.

Palmer, Frederick. *In the Klondyke: Including an Account of a Winter's Journey to Dawson*. New York: Scribner's Son, 1899.

Pérez, Louis A. Jr. *Cuba Between Empires, 1878–1902*. Pittsburgh, PA: University of Pittsburgh Press, 1983.

Perrin, Tom. *Football: A College History*. Jefferson, NC: McFarland & Co., 1987.

Phillips, W. F. R. *Climate of Cuba*. Washington, DC: U.S. Weather Bureau, 1898.

Procter, Ben. *William Randolph Hearst: The Early Years, 1863–1910*. New York: Oxford University Press, 1998.

Rea, George Bronson. *Facts and Fakes about Cuba*. New York: Munro's Sons, 1897.

Robertson, Michael. *Stephen Crane, Journalism, and the Making of Modern American Literature*. New York: Columbia University Press, 1997.

Rubens, Horatio S. *Liberty: The Story of Cuba*. New York: AMS Press, 1970.

Rutland, Robert. A. *The Newsmongers: Journalism in the Life of the Nation 1690–1972*. New York: Dial Press, 1973.

Salisbury, Harrison E. *Without Fear or Favor: The New York Times and Its Times*. New York: Times Books, 1980.

Schudson, Michael. *Discovering the News: A Social History of American Newspapers*. New York: Basic Books, 1978.

Schwarzlose, Richard Allen. *The American Wire Services: A Study of Their Development as a Social Institution*. New York: Arno Press, 1979.

Seigel, Kalman, ed. *Talking Back to The New York Times: Letters to the Editor, 1851–1971*. New York: Quadrangle Books, 1972.

Seitz, Don C. *Joseph Pulitzer: His Life and Letters*. New York: Simon and Schuster, 1924.

Shepard, Richard F. *The Paper's Papers: A Reporter's Journey Through the Archives of the New York Times*. New York: Times Books, 1996.

Sinclair, Upton. *The Brass Check: A Study of American Journalism*. Self-published, 1920.

Slayden, Ellen Maury. *Washington Wife: Journal of Ellen Maury Slayden from 1897–1919*. New York: Harper & Row, 1963.

Smith, Susan Harris, and Melanie Dawson, eds., *The American 1890s: A Cultural Reader*. Durham, NC: Duke University Press, 2000.

Stallman, R. W., and E. R. Hagemann, eds. *The War Dispatches of Stephen Crane*. New York: New York University Press, 1964.

Starr, Paul. *The Creation of the Media: Political Origins of Modern Communications*. New York: Basic Books, 2004.

Stead, W. T. *Satan's Invisible World Displayed, or Despairing Democracy*. New York: R.F. Fenno & Co., 1897.

Steele, Janet. *The Sun Shines for All: Journalism and Ideology in the Life of Charles A. Dana*. Syracuse, NY: Syracuse University Press, 1993.

Steffens, Lincoln. *The Autobiography of Lincoln Steffens*. New York: Harcourt, Brace and Co., 1931.

Stephens, Mitchell. *A History of News*. Fort Worth, TX. Harcourt Brace, 1997.

Stevens, John D. *Sensationalism and the New York Press*. New York: Columbia University Press, 1991.

Swanberg, W. A. *Citizen Hearst: A Biography of William Randolph Hearst*. New York: Scribner's, 1961.

———. *Pulitzer*. New York: Scribner's, 1967.

Sweeney, Michael S. *From the Front: The Story of War*. Washington, DC: National Geographic, 2003.

Taft, Robert. *Photography and the American Scene: A Social History, 1839–1889*. New York: Dover Publications, 1964.

Talese, Gay. *The Kingdom and the Power: The Study of the Men Who Influence the Institution That Influences the World*. Cleveland, OH: New American Library, 1969.

Tebbel, John. *The Life and Good Times of William Randolph Hearst*. New York: E. P. Dutton and Company, 1952.

Tifft, Susan E., and Alex S. Jones. *The Trust: The Private and Powerful Family Behind the New York Times*. Boston: Little, Brown, 1999.

Tolnay, Stewart E., and E. M. Beck, *A Festival of Violence: An Analysis of Southern Lynchings, 1882–1930*. Urbana: University of Illinois Press, 1995.

Traill, Henry D. *The New Fiction and Other Essays on Literary Subjects*. Port Washington, NY: Kennikat Press, 1970. Reprint of 1897 edition.

Trask, David F. *The War with Spain in 1898*. New York: Macmillan, 1981.

Traxel, David. *1898: The Birth of the American Century*. New York: Vintage Books, 1998.

Turner, Hy B. *When Giants Ruled: The Story of Park Row, New York's Great Newspaper Street*. New York: Fordham University Press, 1999.

Waldrep, Christopher. *The Many Faces of Judge Lynch: Extralegal Violence and Punishment in America*. New York: Palgrave Macmillan, 2002.

Weiner, Joel H., ed. *Papers for the Millions: The New Journalism in Britain, 1850s to 1914*. New York: Greenwood Press, 1988.

Welch, Richard E. *Response to Imperialism: The United States and the Philippine-American War, 1899–1902*. Chapel Hill: University of North Carolina Press, 1979.

Wendt, Lloyd. *Chicago Tribune: The Rise of a Great American Newspaper*. Chicago: Rand McNally & Co., 1979.

Wilkerson, Marcus M. *Public Opinion and the Spanish-American War: A Study in War Propaganda*. Baton Rouge: Louisiana State University Press, 1932.

Winkler, John K. *W. R. Hearst: An American Phenomenon*. New York: Simon and Schuster, 1928.

_____. *William Randolph Hearst: A New Appraisal*. New York: Hastings House, 1955.

Wisan, Joseph E. *The Cuban Crisis as Reflected in the New York Press (1895–1898)*. New York: Octagon Books, 1965. Reprint of 1934 edition.

Ziff, Larzer. *The American 1890s: Life and Times of a Lost Generation*. Lincoln: University of Nebraska Press, 1966.

ARTICLES AND BOOK CHAPTERS

Adams, Edward F. "Newspaper Work: Limitations of Truth-Telling." *Arena* 20, 3 (September 1898): 604–14.

Allen, Thomas B., ed. "A Special Report: What Really Sank the *Maine*?" *Naval History* (March-April 1998): 30–39.

Banks, Elizabeth L. "American 'Yellow Journalism.'" *Nineteenth Century* 44 (August 1898): 328–340.

Barnhurst Kevin G., and John C. Nerone. "Design Trends in U.S. Front Pages, 1885–1985." *Journalism Quarterly* 68, 4 (Winter 1991): 796–804.

Blanchard, Margaret A. "The Ossification of Journalism History: A Challenge for the Twenty-first Century." *Journalism History* 25, 3 (Autumn 1999): 107–12.

Brisbane, Arthur. "The American Newspaper: Yellow Journalism." *Bookman* 19 (June 1904): 400–404.

Brooks, Sydney. "The Significance of Mr. Hearst." *Fortnightly Review* 88 (December 1907).

Campbell, W. Joseph. "1897: American Journalism's Exceptional Year." *Journalism History* 30, 1 (Winter 2004): 190–200.

_____. "Not a Hoax: New Evidence in the *New York Journal*'s Rescue of Evangelina Cisneros." *American Journalism* 19, 4 (Fall 2002): 67–94.

_____. "'One of the Fine Figures in American Journalism': A Closer Look at Josephus Daniels of the *Raleigh News & Observer*." *American Journalism* 16, 4 (Fall 1999): 37–56.

Carey, James W. "The Problem of Journalism History." *Journalism History* 1, 1 (Spring 1974): 3–5, 27.

Chenery, William L. "Unafraid and Free," in Harold L. Ickes, ed. *Freedom of the Press Today: A Clinical Examination by 28 Specialists*. New York: Vanguard Press, 1941.

Cody, Sherwin. "America To-day—Some Signs of the Times." *Self Culture* 6, 1 (April 1897): 14–16.

Commander, Lydia Kingsmill. "The Significance of Yellow Journalism." *Arena* 34 (August 1905): 150–55.

Connery, T.B. "Great Business Operations—The Collection of News." *Cosmopolitan* 23, 21 (1897): 21–32.

Curtis, David A. "Yellow Journalism." *The Journalist* (23 April 1898): 19.

Davis, Hartley. "The Journalism of New York." *Munsey's Magazine* 24, 2 (November 1900): 217–33.

Davis, Richard Harding. "The Battle of San Juan." *Scribner's Magazine* 24, 4 (October 1898): 387–403.

Dawley, Thomas R. Jr. "Some Truths About Cuba." *Self Culture* 6 (November 1897): 97–107.

"Defining Moments in Journalism." *Media Studies Journal* 11, 2 (Spring 1997): xv–xvi.

Eggert, Gerald G. "Our Man in Havana: Fitzhugh Lee." *Hispanic American Historical Review* 47, 4 (November 1967): 463–85.

Ferré, John P. "The Dubious Heritage of Media Ethics: Cause-and-Effect Criticism in the 1890s." *American Journalism* 5, 4 (1988): 191–203.

Garnsey, John Henderson. "The Demand for Sensational Journals." *Arena* (November 1897): 681–86.

Harmon, Richard. "Progress and Flight: An Interpretation of the American Cycle Craze of the 1890s." *Journal of Social History* 5, 2 (Winter 1971–72): 235–57.

Holmes, John H. "The New Journalism and the Old." *Munsey's Magazine* (April 1897): 76–79.

Hudson, Robert V. "Will Irwin's Pioneering Criticism of the Press." *Journalism Quarterly* 47, 2 (Summer 1970): 263–71.

Hughes, David Y. "*The War of the Worlds* in the Yellow Press." *Journalism Quarterly* 43, 4 (Winter 1966): 639–46.

Irwin, Will. "The New York Sun." *American Magazine* 67 (January 1909): 301-10.

Johnston, Alva. "Twilight of the Ink-Stained Gods." *Vanity Fair* (February 1932): 36, 70.

Kimball, Arthur Reed. "Newspaper Work as a Career." *The Writer* 10, 4 (April 1897): 45–48.

Langley, S.P. "The 'Flying-Machine.'" *McClure's Magazine* 9, 2 (June 1897): 647–60.

Lee, Fitzhugh. "Cuba Under Spanish Rule." *McClure's Magazine* 11, 2 (June 1898): 99–114.

Lemons, J. Stanley. "The Cuban Crisis of 1895–1898: Newspapers and Nativism." *Missouri Historical Review* 60, 1 (October 1965): 63–74.

Leonard, Thomas C. "Making Readers into Citizens—The Old-Fashioned Way," in Theodore L. Glasser, ed., *The Idea of Public Journalism*. New York: Guilford Press, 1999: 85–90.

Leupp, Francis E. "The Waning Power of the Press." *Atlantic Monthly* (February 1910): 145–56.

McCollam, Douglas. "The Crowded Theater: It's Time for American Journalism to Rise Out of Its Defensive Crouch." *Columbia Journalism Review* (July/August 2005): 24–27.

Montgomery-McGovern, J. B. "An Important Phase of Gutter Journalism: Faking." *Arena* 19, 99 (February 1898): 240–53.

"Moral Menace of Yellow Journalism." *Current Literature* 44, 4 (April 1908): 414–15.

Nerone, John. "The Mythology of the Penny Press." *Critical Studies in Mass Communication* 4 (1987): 376–404.

North, Michael. "Virtual Histories: The Year as Literary Period." *Modern Language Quarterly* 62, 4 (2001): 407–24.

Ogan, Christine, and others, "The Changing Front Page of the New York Times, 1900–1970." *Journalism Quarterly* 52, 2 (Summer 1975): 340–344.

Park, Robert E. "The Yellow Press." *Sociology and Social Research* 12 (1927–1928): 3–11.

Pauly, John J. "Rupert Murdoch and the Demonology of Professional Journalism," in James W. Carey, ed. *Media, Myths, and Narratives: Television and the Press*. Newbury Park, CA: Sage Publications, 1988.

Peck, Harry Thurston. "A Great National Newspaper." *Cosmopolitan* (December 1897): 209–20.

Phillips, Evelyn March. "The New Journalism." *New Review* 13 (August 1895): 182–89.

Pinkerton, W. Stewart, Jr. "'New Journalism': Believe It or Not," in A. Kent McDougall, ed. *The Press: A Critical Look From the Inside*. Princeton, NJ: Dow Jones Books, 1972.

Ponder, Stephen. "The President Makes News: William McKinley and the First Presidential Press Corps, 1897–1901." *Presidential Studies Quarterly* 24, 4 (Fall 1994): 823–36.

Raines, Howell. "My Times." *Atlantic Monthly* (May 2004): 49–81.

Roggenkamp, Karen. "The Evangelina Cisneros Romance, Medievalist Fiction, and the Journalism that Acts," *Journal of American & Comparative Cultures* 23, 2 (Summer 2000): 25–37.

Rossiter, William S. "Printing and Publishing," in *Census Reports: Twelfth Census of the United States, Taken in the Year 1900*, vol. 9. Washington: United States Census Office, 1902.

Schudson, Michael. "Toward a Troubleshooting Manual for Journalism History." *Journalism and Mass Communication Quarterly* 74, 3 (Autumn 1997): 463–76.

Schuneman, R. Smith. "Art or Photography: A Question for Newspaper Editors of the 1890s." *Journalism Quarterly* (Winter 1965): 43–52.

"Shades of Yellow Journalism," *Outlook* 65 (August 25, 1900): 947.

Shaw, Donald Lewis, and Sylvia L. Zack. "Rethinking Journalism History: How Some Recent Studies Support One Approach." *Journalism History* 14, 4 (Winter 1987): 111–17.

_____. "The Diffusion of the Urban Daily, 1850–1900." *Journalism History* 28, 2 (Summer 2002): 73–84.

Smythe, Ted C. "The Reporter, 1880–1900." *Journalism History* 7, 1 (Spring 1980): 1–10.

Steffens, Lincoln. "The Business of a Newspaper." *Scribner's Magazine* 22, 4 (October 1897): 447–67.

_____. "Hearst, The Man of Mystery." *American Magazine* 63, 1 (November 1906): 3–22.

Stevens, John D. "Sensationalism in Perspective." *Journalism History* 12, 3–4 (Autumn-Winter 1985): 78–79.

Stevenson, Robert L. "Readability of Conservative and Sensational Papers since 1872." *Journalism Quarterly* 41 (Spring 1964): 201–06.

Stone, Melville E. "Newspapers in the United States: Their Functions, Interior Economy, and Management." *Self Culture* 5, 3 (June 1897): 300–09.

Taylor, Hannis. "A Review of the Cuban Question in its Economic, Political, and Diplomatic Aspects." *North American Review* (November 1897): 610–35.

Trevor, John. "The Tendency of New Journalism." *The Journalist* (12 June 1897): 58–59.

Welter, Mark M. "The 1895–98 Cuban Crisis in Minnesota Newspapers: Testing the 'Yellow Journalism' Theory." *Journalism Quarterly* 47 (Winter 1970): 719–24.

Wiggins, Gene. "Journey to Cuba: The Yellow Crisis," in Lloyd Chiasson Jr., ed., *The Press in Times of Crisis*. Westport, CT: Greenwood, 1995: 103–17.

Wilcox, Delos F. "The American Newspaper: A Study in Social Psychology." *Annals of the American Academy of Political and Social Science* 16 (July 1900): 56–92.

Wright, John Livingston. "Newspaper Work: Reporters and Oversupply." *Arena* 20, 3 (September 1898): 614–22.

INDEX